THE
NEGRO IN MISSISSIPPI

hARPER 🔥 tORChBOOKS

*A reference-list of Harper Torchbooks, classified
by subjects, is printed at the end of this volume.*

THE
NEGRO IN MISSISSIPPI
1865-1890

By

VERNON LANE WHARTON

HARPER TORCHBOOKS ♥ The Academy Library

Harper & Row, Publishers

New York, Evanston, and London

THE NEGRO IN MISSISSIPPI, 1865-1890

Printed in the United States of America.

This book was first published in 1947 by The University of North Carolina Press as a volume in *The James Sprunt Studies in History and Political Science*. It is here reprinted by arrangement.

First HARPER TORCHBOOK edition published 1965 by Harper & Row, Publishers, Incorporated 49 East 33rd Street New York, New York 10016

PREFACE

Mississippi entered the Union in 1817, with a population of about 40,000 whites and 30,000 Negroes. The number of the whites increased with amazing rapidity, but that of their slaves grew even more rapidly. In 1860, the Negroes made up fifty-five per cent of the total population of 791,000.

The place of the Negro in the ante-bellum life of the state has received fairly adequate study, both in general and special works,[1] and there seems to be no evidence of a decline in interest in the treatment of all the ramifications of the institution of slavery. These studies picture a relatively stable social order, with the place of the Negro definitely established, and regulated by a legal code that had grown with the institution.

The Civil War brought a violent and comparatively sudden destruction to this old social order. But new social systems do not come into being in a moment or in a year. They cannot be created merely by the passage of a law or the changing of a name. The legal abolition of the system of slavery, on which, to a large extent, the old order was built, did not immediately bring into existence the system which now prevails. It brought instead a period of instability and uncertainty in which new problems had to be faced by both races. These problems are not yet solved. A *modus vivendi* had to be found, and one was found in Mississippi in the period between 1865 and 1890.

No serious student of the problem can believe that the method worked out in this period, even with the modifications that have gradually developed, offers the final answer to the question of the relations of the races. In fact, there is abundant evidence that it is even now breaking down, and that the rate of the breakdown is increasing. These evidences of weak-

---

[1] These include Charles S. Sydnor, *Slavery in Mississippi;* articles by the same author entitled "Life Span of Mississippi Slaves," *American Historical Review,* Vol. XXXV (1930), and "The Free Negro in Mississippi before the Civil War," *American Historical Review,* Vol. XXXII (1927) ; Percy L. Rainwater, *Mississippi—Storm Center of Secession;* Dunbar Rowland, *History of Mississippi;* Susan Dabney Smedes, *Memorials of a Southern Planter;* J. F. H. Claiborne, *Mississippi as a Province, Territory and State;* John Fletcher, *Studies in Slavery;* Alfred Holt Stone, "Early Slave Laws of Mississippi," *Publications of the Mississippi Historical Society* (hereafter cited as *P.M.H.S.*), Vol. II; W. W. Magruder, "Legal Status of the Slaves in Mississippi before the War," *P.M.H.S.,* Vol. IV; James Hall, "A Brief History of the Mississippi Territory," *P.M.H.S.,* Vol. IX; Dunbar Rowland, "Plantation Life in Mississippi before the War," *P.M.H.S.,* Vol. III; Henry Hughes, *Treatise on Sociology;* and Ruth B. Hawes, "Slavery in Mississippi," *Sewanee Review,* Vol. XXI (1913).

ness, however, serve to make the system even more important as an object of study.

Just as many vestigial remains of slavery are apparent in the present system, so may we expect many of the aspects of the present order to carry over into any system that may evolve out of it. There is reason to believe that these coming changes in race relations in the South will, to an extent at least, be intentional changes guided by the more intelligent and far-sighted leaders of both races. If this be true, it is essential that more knowledge be gained of the forces that have been at work, and of actual results of measures that have been tried in the past. This study, inspired and directed by Professor Fletcher M. Green of the University of North Carolina, and sponsored by the Institute for Research in Social Science, is an effort to contribute to that knowledge.

V. L. W.

CONTENTS

CHAPTER I

SLAVERY AND THE NEGRO TO 1865

THE SLAVERY BACKGROUND

The territory which makes up the state of Mississippi was known to Europeans for centuries before any large number of them chose to make it their home. The tattered army of De Soto cut its way through the northern portion of the region in 1540, but the survivors of that unhappy band certainly could tell no stories that would make the land attractive to settlers. One hundred forty-two years later, in 1682, La Salle, standing in the dismal marshes near one of the mouths of the Mississippi, claimed the entire valley for France. It was not until the spring of 1699, however, that the brothers Lemoyne succeeded in establishing a small settlement near the present town of Ocean Springs, on the eastern shore of the Bay of Biloxi.

The story of the efforts of the French to develop the region is one of disappointment, mismanagement, Indian massacres, and finally of almost complete failure. The enumeration of the colony of Louisiana for 1744 shows only eight white males and fifteen Negroes in the present city of Natchez, and ten white males with sixty Negroes at Pascagoula. It is safe to say that when the territory became a part of British West Florida in 1763, there were, besides the very troublesome Indians, not five hundred persons, white and black combined, in the entire region.

The establishment of English control was marked by vigorous efforts to secure settlers. The governor was instructed to make land grants to officers and soldiers who had served against the French. These grants varied in size from one hundred to five thousand acres, with exceptional awards running as high as twenty-five thousand acres. As a result, extensive settlement began in the vicinity of Walnut Hills (now Vicksburg), Bayou Pierre (now Claiborne County), and Natchez.

The development of the revolutionary spirit on the Atlantic seaboard sent a large number of intelligent and substantial Tories into the West Florida region, where they quickly took the best of the land that remained unsettled. There can be no doubt that this element had much to do with the expansion of the plantation system in the region, and with the establishment of the distinctly conservative and aristocratic tone which came to typify the section adjoining Natchez.

The period before 1817 saw an ever-increasing flow of immigrants to this southern section of the territory, made up largely of substantial but restless and adventurous spirits from the seaboard states and Kentucky and Tennessee. Mingled with them was an element composed of the backwash which moved slowly along through the region of the pine barrens, drifting from the poor land of South Carolina, Georgia, and the region above Mobile to take up a wretched existence in the pine land of the southern and eastern portions of what was soon to become the state of Mississippi.

At the time of the admission of this territory into the Union in 1817, only its southern quarter and a narrow strip up the Mississippi to the Yazoo were open to legal settlement. The rest of the state was held by the Chickasaw and Choctaw nations. By a series of arrangements concluded in 1835, the claims of the Indians were extinguished, and the land was thrown open to rapid settlement. In general, newcomers who possessed capital quickly located and took possession of the better dark-soil lands for the establishment of plantations, leaving the cheaper uplands for those of lesser means.

It has already been implied that the French introduced slavery into this region early in the eighteenth century. The settlers of the period of English control, both the soldiers who received land grants and the Tory refugees, were eager purchasers of slaves to add to the number which the latter group brought with them. When the government of the United States established the Mississippi Territory in 1798, the region around Natchez, which held the bulk of the population, contained about five thousand whites and thirty-five hundred slaves.[1]

As Charles S. Sydnor has pointed out,[2] there was never any considerable opposition to the continuance of the institution of slavery in either the territory or the state. Furthermore, Mississippi received slavery as a fully matured system and made no contribution of any importance to its theory or practice. The same is true of her reception of the plantation system, which, with its staple crop economy, was immediately established wherever the soil was suitable.

With the exception of the interior of the Delta region, which remained largely isolated and unsettled until after the Civil War, Mississippi by 1840 had generally attained the form which she was to hold until the upheaval of the sixties. The Cane Hills or Natchez region, the Loess-Alluvial counties which follow the eastern border of the Delta, the Northeast Prairie, and, to a lesser extent, the Brown Loam counties which run north and south through the center of the state, had come under the plantation system with all that it implied. The Northeast Highlands, the Shortleaf Pine region in the east-central portion of the state, and the

[1] Charles S. Sydnor, *Slavery in Mississippi*, p. vii.
[2] *Ibid.*, pp. vii-viii.

Longleaf Pine section of the southeast contained a population made up largely of subsistence farmers who held few or no slaves, and who were already beginning their long political quarrel with the people of the dark-soil regions. Scattered through the pine lands, especially in the distinctive Gulf Coast fringe, were poverty-stricken unfortunates who eked out an existence from the sandy soil or from the forests, and who sometimes sold a little truck or seafood to New Orleans.

The Negro population, of course, was concentrated in the sections where the plantation was the predominant agricultural unit. There the Negro went, willy-nilly, under the pressure of slavery, and there, to a large extent, he remains to this day. This is the equivalent of saying that the best agricultural land of the state has always been cultivated by Negro labor. The general feeling in the state was that this labor was absolutely essential to the maintenance of the plantation economy, and that the Negro would work only as a slave. Furthermore, it was generally said, and just as generally believed, that the Negro would be entirely incapable of caring for himself in a system of free competition.

It is apparent, however, that slavery was for the Negro an effective civilizing influence. With or without conscious effort on his part, he absorbed the basic materials of western culture. It is true that his education was weak in many essentials, but there is no other example in history in which so large a mass of people were brought so far out of barbarism in so short a time. In order to get a proper view of the Negro as a free man, it is necessary to study briefly his preparation as a slave.

The great mass of Negroes who faced freedom at the end of the war had received thorough training in the fundamentals of the best agricultural methods known to the land and the time. In general they had worked for the more able and successful agriculturists, for the incapable planter lost his slaves to one who could use them more profitably. However little they might understand the underlying theories of preparation of the land and cultivation of the crop, they knew the actual practice of the culture of cotton and corn as well as H. W. Vick or Joseph Shields. This was no small endowment.

In addition to work in the field, the Negro performed the necessary mechanical work on practically all of the plantations. On a large estate, there was generally much specialization of labor, with skilled slaves devoting their time exclusively to carpentry, iron-working, weaving, or the manufacture of shoes, shingles, or bricks. In spite of the opposition of white artisans, many of these skilled workers were hired to contractors or put to work on small jobs in neighboring towns.

There were large numbers of slaves who lived permanently in the towns. In the plantation sections, they seem to have made up about one-third of the urban population. They served in a wide variety of occupations. In addition to the house servants, there were mechanics, draymen, hostlers, common laborers, and washwomen. Some served as apprentices or helpers to white mechanics and builders, or worked in small factories catering to the local market. Near Greenville, Negroes made up the entire staff of a cotton mill.[3]

These skilled Negro artisans, with a practical monopoly of their trades in many neighborhoods, and with experience in dealing with the whites who hired them, found little difficulty in making the transition to freedom.

In general the slaves who were house servants may be regarded as an especially favored lot. Originally chosen for their superior intelligence and attractive appearance, they had the greatest opportunities for self-improvement, and often succeeded in handing their status down to their sons and daughters. Large planters often took great pride in their house servants and made an effort to have them appear to best advantage. Many were taught to read and write by indulgent masters or mistresses. Others took advantage of their position to acquire such knowledge and to pass it on to their children without the aid or consent of the master. The value of their training is shown by the eagerness with which they were sought by those desiring house servants, and by inns and other such establishments, after the war.

The free Negroes of Mississippi were never very numerous, since manumission came into general disfavor before the state was well developed. They reached their greatest number about 1840, when the census listed 1,336, and they declined steadily, numbering only 775 in 1860. Of this latter group, a majority were in the southwestern counties, with 255 in Adams alone.

Whether in large numbers or small, however, they were everywhere objects of popular displeasure, and after 1831 were burdened with many oppressive state and local laws and regulations. There were numerous efforts to persuade them to go into other states or to emigrate to Africa. The single purpose of the short-lived Mississippi Colonizing Society was to secure the emigration of these free Negroes.[4] After the first emancipation act of 1822, a special act of the legislature was required for the emancipation of any slave. After 1842, the freeing of slaves by will was absolutely forbidden.

In spite of this general evidence of disapproval, however, a number of free Negroes seem to have fared very well. Fully three-fourths of them lived in town, where odd jobs were plentiful. Free Negro washwomen were in demand all over the South. Some of the free artisans built up reputations that were known throughout several counties. Others, often aided by bequests or gifts from former owners, established small shops or

[3] Charles H. Wesley, *Negro Labor in the United States*, p. 17.
[4] C. S. Sydnor, *op. cit.*, p. 204.

offered drays or carriages for hire. As early as 1830, seventeen free Negroes in Mississippi were listed as slaveholders.

As has been indicated, this free-Negro element was too small to have much significance in the make-up of the population. For such Negroes, the transition to freedom was devoid of any major problems, but their small number prevented them from furnishing the leadership which the mass of emancipated Negroes needed.

In 1860, the last of the normal years of slavery, the Negroes of Mississippi numbered 437,303, as compared with 353,901 whites. An insignificant group of 773 Negroes, of whom 601 were mulattoes, was managing more or less successfully to live outside the slave system. Of the 436,631 slaves, the great majority lived in the plantation counties, in some of which they outnumbered the whites more than ten to one. They were owned by 30,943 slaveholders, who possessed an average of 14.1 slaves each, but of whom only about 6,000 owned more than the average number.[5] The great mass of those who were of working age were field hands, and knew little more than the simple skills which were needed in their daily tasks. Relatively small numbers had received special training as artisans or house servants. Even smaller numbers had received the cultural veneer and comparative sophistication that came with town life.

Most of them were fairly well fed, housed, and clothed, and few were overworked. The best effort to estimate their span of life indicates that the expectancy of a slave at the age of twenty was only one and one-half years lower than that of a white of similar age.[6] As slaves they received generally good care and as slaves they were happy. If as men they thought of freedom, it was only as an imaginary condition to be whispered about in dark cabins or to be hinted at in the figurative language of the spirituals.

In Clinton, however, there was a slave blacksmith who within eight years would be helping to frame a constitution for his state. In Raymond, little Billy Johnson, a bootblack, hurried in and out of the boarding house of his owner with no thought of the problems that within ten years would face him in the state legislature. Near Holly Springs there was a slender young mulatto who in 1872 would give the order for the election of another Negro to the Senate of the United States. Just across the river from Vicksburg there was a little Negro of thirteen who before he was forty would be speaker of the Mississippi House of Representatives, three times member of the United States Congress, and temporary chairman of the Republican National Convention. Freedom, with its opportunities and its responsibilities, was at hand.

[5] U. S. *Census,* 1860, *Agriculture,* p. 232; see also C. S. Sydnor, *op. cit.,* pp. 192-193.
[6] C. S. Sydnor, "The Life Span of Mississippi Slaves," *American Historical Review,* XXXV (1930), 573.

The Negro During the War

In spite of the opposition of a majority of her larger slaveholders, Mississippi in 1861 entered a war to defend the "peculiar institution." Votes for secession in counties dominated by small farmers overcame the natural conservatism of the leaders of the black belt and threw the state into the struggle that was to bring the end of slavery.[7]

From the beginning, it was apparent that the Negro would play an important, if generally passive, part, in this struggle. Efforts to gain a heavy increase in the taxation of slaves as property failed to receive the approval of the secession convention.[8] This fact, in combination with the regulation which exempted the manager of twenty or more slaves from military service, helped to arouse among the poor whites bitter hatred for the plantation owners and their Negroes.

The use of the Negro as an active factor in the prosecution of the war was a matter of controversy. From the initiation of the conflict, many slaves were with the armies as body servants, cooks, and teamsters, and in 1862 the Confederate Government began its efforts to impress them for work on the fortifications. These efforts met with little success. Planters charged that their slaves were so badly used while in the service of the army that they either ran away or were returned to their owners in such a condition as to be useless.[9] The high death rate of the impressed Negroes gave weight to these charges.[10] It was also declared by owners in the interior that slaves returning from the fortifications brought back dangerous ideas and information and created dissatisfaction and unrest.[11] In spite of this opposition, matters had become so critical by January, 1863, that the legislature empowered the governor to impress all able-bodied slaves who might be needed by the military engineers or by the commanders of state or Confederate military forces.[12] It appears, however, that the lawmakers soon regretted this action. In a subsequent resolution they called on the governor to protect the planters from the illegal impressment of slaves, and especially to prevent the wholesale seizure of Negroes in the border counties. They felt that the continuation of this policy would cause the slaves to desert almost as a body to the enemy.[13]

After the fall of Vicksburg, some opinion developed in the state in favor of using the Negroes as a fighting force with the army. The editor of the *Mississippian*, which led this school of thought, declared that if the

[7] J. S. McNeily, "War and Reconstruction in Mississippi," *Publications of the Mississippi Historical Society, Centenary Series* (hereafter cited as *P.M.H.S.C.S.*), II, 282.
[8] John K. Bettersworth, *Confederate Mississippi*, p. 12.
[9] *Ibid.*, pp. 169-170.
[10] Loose sheet in Vol. XII, E. J. Capell Papers, Louisiana State University.
[11] Bell Irvin Wiley, *Southern Negroes*, p. 17.
[12] J. S. McNeily, "War and Reconstruction in Mississippi," *P.M.H.S.C.S.*, II, 285.
[13] *Ibid.*, II, 285.

slaves were not used by the South, they would be employed against her by the enemy. Pointing to the apparently successful use by the North of Negroes as soldiers, this paper suggested that the Confederacy adopt the same policy and promise freedom to all who would enlist. It admitted that this would revolutionize the entire Southern system, but insisted that the loss of the Negro for the salvation of liberty was better than the loss of both. It also suggested that the step would place the South in a better light before the world.[14]

In general, however, opinion in the state was against this plan of action. Similar opposition throughout the South prevented the Confederacy from taking any definite steps in this direction until the desperate days of February and March, 1865. Efforts to apply the conscription law passed by the Confederate Congress in the latter month found few of the Negroes willing to serve. The rumor that they were to be called into the army caused fourteen of them to leave Pleasant Hill Plantation in one week.[15] According to their master, they were "off to the Yankees." A planter in Jefferson County warned Governor Charles Clark that the Negroes were "stampeding" to avoid conscription.[16] Of doubtful value, even if it had been tried earlier in the war, this effort in the spring of 1865 was a futile gesture. By that time most of the Negroes were acquainted with the fundamental issues of the war, and felt that their interests lay with the advancing Federal armies.

If slave labor failed as a source of fighting men for the South, it also showed a lack of adaptability to the new conditions imposed by the war. The chief function of the Negro was to produce cotton, and cotton that could not be sold was piled in every gin yard. Everywhere the faith of the South in her staple began to waver. The Woodville *Republican* spoke of "King Cotton! discrowned king! with his Privy Council of Avarice, Arrogance, Presumption, Prodigality and Dependence. If cotton has not been a curse to us for years past history is a tissue of nonsense."[17]

It almost immediately became apparent that slavery without its staple was an organ without a function, and an inconvenient one at that. Planters who leased the services of slave mechanics from their idle plantations brought unemployment and misery to white laborers and helped to increase their bitter feeling against the Negroes.[18] Everywhere the realization came that in a subsistence system the slave was practically a dependent member of the family, with a mouth to be fed and a body to be clothed. Planters ordered their slaves to develop gardens, and some bought wool cards and fish lines "for feeding and clothing the negroes when it comes

[14] J. K. Bettersworth, *op. cit.*, p. 170.
[15] E. J. Capell, "Diary," March 11 and March 19, 1865, E. J. Capell Papers.
[16] B. I. Wiley, *op. cit.*, p. 158.
[17] J. K. Bettersworth, *op. cit.*, p. 152.
[18] Charles H. Wesley, *Negro Labor in the United States*, p. 96.

to the worst."[19]   E. J. Capell kept men and women busy making shoes, weaving cloth, and repairing the rapidly deteriorating agricultural implements.[20]   Finding themselves unable to keep their Negroes, some owners turned them over to more fortunate friends, allowed them to go out to sell their produce and services on their own initiative, or even turned them out to forage off the countryside.[21]   After the war, J. F. H. Claiborne was to write, "The negro had become an elephant on our hands. . . . He was now a non-producing consumer. He was up in arms against us or a plunderer on his own account."[22]

There is, of course, a great deal of exasperation and resultant exaggeration in such an attitude. On efficiently run plantations with good locations Negro labor was still producing commodities that found a ready market in the towns, and even on plantations which had been shifted to a subsistence basis, the Negro supplied the labor for the production of most of the necessities. But he was no longer a reliable source of cash income for his owner, and in periods of great scarcity of supplies he undoubtedly appeared to his harassed master or mistress to be more of a burden than an aid.

This breakdown of an economy based on cash crops was almost immediately reflected in the value of slaves. Such data as can be obtained from the infrequent sales of the period show a steady decline in the prices of slaves as compared with those of other "commodities." The same is true of the wages of slaves who were hired.[23]

The question of the behavior of the Negroes during the war offers a peculiar problem. Southerners writing in later periods have generally described it as exemplary. The comment of Susan Dabney Smedes, daughter of one of the largest planters of central Mississippi, is typical of this group:

The plantation life went on as usual. The servants went about their duties, we thought, more conscientiously than before. . . . They sewed on the soldiers' clothes and knit socks for the army, and packed the boxes with as much alacrity as the white people did. They were our greatest comfort during the war.[24]

Thomas Dabney went so far as to declare that no one had ever heard or would ever hear of a single case of rudeness from a Negro to his mistress or her children during the war.[25]

Recent studies have tended to discredit such sweeping assertions. In the words of B. I. Wiley, "The tenor of statements made during the war

[19] J. K. Bettersworth, op. cit., p. 166.
[20] E. J. Capell, "Diary," January and February, 1864, E. J. Capell Papers.
[21] J. K. Bettersworth, op. cit., p. 166.
[22] Ibid., p. 159.
[23] Ibid., pp. 167-168.
[24] Susan Dabney Smedes, Memorials of a Southern Planter, pp. 196-197.
[25] Ibid., p. 313.

is generally in marked contrast to those made afterwards."[26] His investigation leads him to the conclusion that insubordination was common in the invaded areas, and that it appeared at times in the interior. "Insolence" toward the whites was a common type of misconduct, and assaults upon women were not unheard of.[27]

Even more serious was the fear aroused by rumors of approaching insurrections. Reports of plots and uprisings were numerous during the early part of the war,[28] and were especially prevalent in the river counties. Evidence of plans for a Fourth of July uprising was discovered at Fayette in 1861. In September there was a report that a rebellion of the entire region was scheduled to begin with the burning of Natchez. So great was the excitement that masters dared not let their slaves venture off their plantations. In July, 1862, the provost marshal of Natchez reported that forty Negroes had been hanged and about as many more imprisoned there during the past year.[29] During that same month two minor outbreaks occurred in the state.[30] News of the Emancipation Proclamation served further to arouse the fear of the whites. Many expected an insurrection at the beginning of 1863, and one serious uprising did occur at that time. This took place in Lafayette County, where the Negroes drove off their overseers, and divided among themselves the mules and other property of their masters.[31]

Altogether, it may be said that this new material simply reveals the Negro as a human being, rather than as an unreal, flawless creature who delighted in humility and in the opportunity of rendering constant service and unquestioning obedience. The fact remains, however, that when all reports of crime and misbehavior have been considered, and when rumors of insurrections have been properly discounted to allow for the excitement of the time, the great mass of the Negroes remained amazingly docile and "faithful" throughout the war. This docility reflected not only the absence of positive grievances on the part of the Negro, but also servility and lack of initiative developed through generations of dependence and discipline in slavery. This same servility was later to play an important part in the relative ease with which the whites overthrew the reconstruction governments.

Early in the war the state legislature thought it necessary to tighten up the laws for the regulation of slave conduct during the emergency. Severe penalties were prescribed for tampering with slaves. Owners were required to quarter their Negroes not more than a mile from those who

[26] B. I. Wiley, *op. cit.*, p. 63.
[27] *Ibid.*, pp. 72 and 81.
[28] J. K. Bettersworth, *op. cit.*, pp. 161-162; B. I. Wiley, *op. cit.*, p. 82.
[29] J. K. Bettersworth, *op. cit.*, pp. 162-163.
[30] B. I. Wiley, *op. cit.*, p. 82.
[31] J. K. Bettersworth, *op. cit.*, pp. 163-164.

had them in charge, and were strictly forbidden to allow their slaves to go at large and trade as free men.[32] Free Negroes were more than ever objects of suspicion. The legislature in 1861 authorized the board of police of Pike County to issue licenses to those free Negroes who had their permission to remain in the county. The sheriff was to sell into slavery any free person of color who was found without a license after the first of the following March.[33]

In the meantime, in many neighborhoods, the old men and boys formed themselves into "home guards" to supply patrol units and to keep the slaves under observation and control.[34] For the frontier sections, patrol groups or "mounted police" were supplied by the military authorities.[35]

In spite of these efforts, actual discipline became more and more slack as the war progressed. A citizen of Bolivar County complained to the governor in June, 1863, that "the county is left almost alone and the negroes are going where they please."[36] In December of the preceding year, a free Negro seems to have had no difficulty in making a round trip from Hinds County to Georgia.[37] From Port Gibson came a report that the Negroes there were under no restraint at night.[38] The *Mississippian* in April, 1863, declared that the streets of Jackson were full of impudent, well-dressed Negroes, who filled the air with cigar smoke and profanity.[39] In February, 1864, a resident of Port Gibson asserted that soldiers sent there to maintain order were rather adding to the confusion. He declared that there was "no discipline or order among them. The cavalry have been . . . a riding through the county afrolicing and stealing. The civil laws have been trampled under foot."[40]

In the meantime, the advance of the Federal troops and their sweeping raids across the state were adding to the difficulty of the situation. The planters who still hoped to save something from the general ruin usually attempted to remove their slaves before the arrival of the enemy. Abandoning their crops, many in the river counties carried their Negroes westward into Louisiana or Texas.[41] Others tried the simpler if less effective expedient of hiding their slaves in the swamps when there seemed to be danger of a raid.[42] Perhaps a majority of those who were endeavoring to retain their slaves moved to eastern Mississippi or into Alabama and

[32] *Ibid.*, p. 161.
[33] J. W. Garner, *Reconstruction in Mississippi*, note, p. 28.
[34] J. K. Bettersworth, *op. cit.*, p. 162; B. I. Wiley, *op. cit.*, p. 37.
[35] B. I. Wiley, *op. cit.*, p. 37.
[36] *Ibid.*, p. 38.
[37] Franklin L. Riley, ed., "Diary of a Mississippi Planter," *P.M.H.S.*, X, 481.
[38] B. I. Wiley, *op. cit.*, p. 38.
[39] J. K. Bettersworth, *op. cit.*, p. 164, from *Mississippian*, April 15, 1863.
[40] B. I. Wiley, *op. cit.*, p. 38.
[41] J. H. Browne, *Four Years in Secessia*, p. 224; T. W. Knox, *Camp-Fire and Cotton-Field*, p. 326; J. K. Bettersworth, *op. cit.*, p. 173.
[42] S. D. Smedes, *op. cit.*, p. 203; J. H. Browne, *op. cit.*, p. 224.

Georgia.[43] The planters found these migrations both expensive and in-effectual. Thomas Dabney, after carrying a very large group of Negroes to Macon, Georgia, heard of the approach of Sherman and freighted them back to Mississippi at a cost of several thousand dollars.[44] Some com-pleted the migration to Texas just in time to have their slaves taken from them.[45] However burdensome these journeys may have been to the plant-ers, some of the older Negroes now remember them as having supplied the most interesting experiences their lives have known.[46]

This policy of removing the slaves from the path of the enemy had the official endorsement of the Confederate Government. In fact, after the Federal forces began to use the Negroes as soldiers, President Davis ordered their removal from the counties near the Northern lines. The effect of this order was disastrous. As soon as the Confederate officers began to seize Negroes for removal, they began to move almost as a mass to the Union camps. For this reason the governor and the legislature demanded that attempts to carry out the program be abandoned.[47]

It is interesting to speculate as to the probable thoughts and attitudes of the Negroes themselves during this period of disorder and uncertainty. B. I. Wiley takes the view that "The majority of the Negroes in the Con-federacy . . . were neither loyal nor disloyal in a positive way. They simply waited to see what would happen."[48] This is undoubtedly true as applied to the "majority."

On the other hand, there is evidence that many of the Negroes had yearned for freedom for years, and expected it to come. One observer wrote:

Their ideas of government, and of personal and property rights, were all drawn from the Bible. That was their sole authority, and they had that down fine. . . . Deliverance from slavery was not a suprise to them; they had been hoping and praying for it for years with perfect faith that their prayers would be answered. It seemed that they had always expected it to come from some out-side source, and had never entertained a thought of taking a part themselves in their deliverance.[49]

Veiled allusions to this longing for and expectation of freedom are seen by B. I. Wiley in the spirituals.[50] One of the most popular of the songs used by the slaves carried the words:

[43] Robert Bowman, "Reconstruction in Yazoo County," *P.M.H.S.*, VII, 115; Rob-ert Bowman, "Yazoo County in the Civil War," *P.M.H.S.*, VII, 67; J. K. Betters-worth, *op. cit.*, p. 173; S. D. Smedes, *op. cit.*, pp. 213-214.
[44] S. D. Smedes, *op. cit.*, pp. 220-221.
[45] J. T. Trowbridge, *The South*, p. 390.
[46] Statement of former slaves of Thomas Dabney, Dry Grove, Mississippi, January 20, 1939.
[47] J. W. Garner, *op. cit.*, p. 27.
[48] B. I. Wiley, *op. cit.*, p. 83.
[49] Melvin Grigsby, *The Smoked Yank*, p. 160.
[50] B. I. Wiley, *op. cit.*, p. 19.

> But some ob dese days my time will come,
> I'll year dat bugle, I'll year dat drum,
> I'll see dem armies, marchin' along,
> I'll lif my head an' jine der song.[51]

Some knowledge of anti-slavery agitation had been held for years by Negroes in all sections.[52]

News of the progress of the war and of the issues involved seems to have penetrated quickly even into the remote interior. With the increasing scarcity of provisions in 1862 and 1863, a great many of the body servants of Confederate soldiers were sent back to their homes. They were fertile sources of information. The same is true of Negroes who returned from work on the fortifications or in the supply services of the army. Any choice bit of information was rapidly passed from group to group by the amazingly efficient "grapevine telegraph." Slaves who went for the mail sometimes read the papers or picked up information from conversations at the post office.[53] Literate house servants had access to papers and letters, and others could often listen to conversations of the master's family. Now and then contacts were made with fleeing Unionists, Federal scouts, or Northern soldiers who had escaped from prison camps.[54]

Aroused by this accurate and inaccurate information, and constantly stirred by rumors, some Negroes gathered for midnight meetings where they whispered prayers for freedom and for the success of the Union armies.[55] Years later Booker T. Washington remembered the cautious discussions that he had heard as a child.[56] Freedom to these Negroes was at most a vague idea, but for the sake of it they were ready at the first opportunity to move in massed hundreds from their old homes toward the Federal camps.

In spite of this general desire for freedom, enormous numbers of the Negroes continued to act with and for their owners as opposed to their deliverers. Slaves sometimes informed the master of plans of others to escape from the plantation. Southern papers told of cases in which stragglers from the Union army were taken by slaves and turned over to their owners.[57] Stories of faithful Negroes who hid the family silver and held the horses in the swamp during raids have become a part of the folklore of the South.

On the other hand, the invading forces seem to have expected and generally to have received aid from slaves. Even on the model plantation of Thomas Dabney a raiding troop found a Negro who would drink Dab-

---

[51] John H. Aughey, *Tupelo*, p. 244.
[52] Robert R. Moton, *What the Negro Thinks*, p. 10.
[53] B. I. Wiley, *op. cit.*, pp. 17-18.
[54] J. H. Aughey, *op. cit.*, pp. 200, 293-294; M. Grigsby, *op. cit.*, p. 169.
[55] B. I. Wiley, *op. cit.*, p. 20.
[56] Booker T. Washington, *Up from Slavery*, pp. 7-8.
[57] B. I. Wiley, *op. cit.*, p. 70.

ney's wine with them and act as a sentry to prevent the family from leaving the house.[58] Other raiding groups received information from the Negroes as to the position of their Confederate opponents.[59] A Union soldier who escaped from Andersonville was aided time and again by Negroes on his furtive journey to the North. He seems never to have hesitated to call on them and tell them freely who he was. Only once was he refused aid, and that was by a woman who declared that she held such hate for all whites that she would do nothing even for a Yankee. In the words of the fugitive, "She was the only one of the race I ever applied to in vain for assistance."[60] Negroes also furnished aid to Southern Unionists who were attempting to reach the Federal lines.[61]

Altogether, it may be concluded that while personal ties of affection often caused the slaves to do all in their power to protect the immediate family of their master from the effects of raids, their sympathies under other circumstances were usually with the invading groups, and their services generally were at the command of those invaders.

In the face of the breakdown of the system of slavery, there developed in the South an increasing interest in its modification. Within the Confederate cabinet itself, Judah P. Benjamin was the leader of a scheme looking toward the linking of general emancipation with the introduction of the Negro into the Southern armies. It was felt that this move would increase the chances for European recognition, and would at the same time cause the abolitionist forces in the North to lose much of their interest in the war.[62] Reverend James A. Lyon, chairman of a committee of the General Assembly of the Presbyterian Church in Mississippi, declared that the matter could now be approached without embarrassment, as attacks by Northern fanatics need no longer be considered.[63] This same minister seems to have drawn up a bill for the correction of some of the abuses of the system and to have received for it the approval of the governor. The project won a favorable report from the Judiciary Committee of the state senate in the spring of 1865, but a declaration that the time was inopportune caused its consideration to be postponed.[64]

During the same session of the legislature, J. L. Alcorn, a prominent political figure and a large slaveholder, warned that body that the face of the entire civilized world was set against the South on the question of slavery, and suggested that a joint declaration be made by the Confederate

[58] S. D. Smedes, op. cit., p. 209.
[59] Edward Bacon, Among the Cotton Thieves, p. 69.
[60] M. Grigsby, op. cit., pp. 168-169.
[61] J. H. Aughey, op. cit., pp. 200, 246, 293-294.
[62] B. I. Wiley, op. cit., p. 154.
[63] J. K. Bettersworth, op. cit., pp. 304-305.
[64] B. I. Wiley, op. cit., p. 170.

Congress and the state legislatures that it was the intention of the Confederacy to free its slaves at the end of twenty years.[65]

There probably were many reasons for the growth of this emancipation sentiment in the state and throughout the South during the closing months of the war. Part of it must be attributed to the declining morale which was destroying the internal strength of the Confederacy. Some saw it as the only possible way to obtain the Negro troops who might yet preserve for the South her independence at the cost of her "peculiar institution." Others would offer it as a last desperate bid for European aid. But it is also evident that this development marked the breaking through of the crumbling walls of Southern self-assurance by a force that must have been growing in the South for decades. It cannot be imagined that this section alone was not affected by the revulsion against slavery that swept through the world in the hundred years prior to the Civil War. A large part of the task of the Southern defenders of slavery in the antebellum period had been to convince themselves. In her hour of adversity, the South turned too late toward the solution of the problem through modification and gradual emancipation. It seems possible that, under the influence of the humanitarian movement of the first half of the nineteenth century, she would have turned to that solution long before if slavery had not become the center of the angry strife of the sections.

It is useless to speculate on the "ifs" of history. But in this case one cannot escape the feeling that the greater part of the ills that have cursed the South in the relations of her races could have been avoided if this humanitarian feeling had been allowed to develop in its proper time. In 1865 it was too late. The forces of the enemy were hammering at the gates. Emancipation by violence was soon to make the Negro free. At the same time its methods would take from his side the very men who could best have guided his steps in the new paths. Freed by forces despised by his masters, and used as a pawn in political war, the freedman was the symbol of the South's defeat, and the scapegoat of the Lost Cause.

[65] Franklin A. Montgomery, *Reminiscences of a Mississippian in War and Peace*, p. 228.

CHAPTER II

FROM BONDAGE TO FREEDOM

THE FEDERAL ARMY AND THE NEGRO

With the beginning of the war, the problem of the Negro became a very real one for the Federal government. The time for debating in the abstract the virtues or evils of slavery had passed. Instead, there were questions that demanded immediate and concrete answers. In those slave states which remained in the Union, there were many Negroes who took advantage of the confused period of military preparation to desert their masters. From the Confederate sections of those same states others escaped at the first opportunity and clustered around the camps of the Federal forces. Immediately the question arose as to the application of the fugitive slave law to these refugees. If the law was to be enforced against them, must the military authorities act as a police force in its application? Negroes were being used in various capacities by the Confederate armies. What was to be the status of such slaves if they escaped to the Federal lines or if they were taken by the advancing forces of the Union? Very soon there were to be inside the Union lines tens of thousands of slaves who had had no connection with military activities. Were they, to the disadvantage of the North, to be returned to their masters as private property, or were they to be regarded as prisoners of war? Could they be seized by the Federal commanders and used as labor battalions? If so, why should they not also be used as soldiers?

These practical questions had to be answered by a congress and a president elected on a platform that pledged protection to slavery in those states where it existed by law. These men faced the fact of the Supreme Court decision which declared slaves to be personal property, and the respect of most of them for property rights was very high. Any radical move on their part might throw three or four more states into the Confederacy, and lose for the war the already doubtful support of the Northern Democrats. Lincoln, like other tens of thousands of the members of his party, shuddered at the thought of the introduction of millions of free Negroes into the economic, social, and political life of the nation. In speech after speech he had made it clear that he had absolutely no desire for such a development. These facts account to a large extent for the fumbling manner in which the administration handled the problem of the Negro in the early period of the war.

The first question to be met was that of slaves who had been used by the military arm of the Confederacy. Certainly these men could not be returned to do further damage to the Union cause. Late in May, 1861, General Butler declared such Negroes contraband of war,[1] a declaration which, strangely enough, could be based only on the assumption that slaves were property. It was not until August that Congress gave approval to this action in a law that was signed by a reluctant president.[2] This Confiscation Act left still undecided the status of slaves who had not been used for military purposes, and General Butler was unable to get a satisfactory answer to this phase of the question. The Secretary of War would only say that all existing rights must be respected in all the states, and that in cases of slaves from loyal states the fugitive slave law must be applied by the military authorities.[3]

When it became apparent that in the anarchic conditions of the border states the slaves were literally freeing themselves, and that in face of the issues of the war slavery within the Union was a paradox, the president turned to the idea of voluntary emancipation with compensation for the owners. Coupled with this plan in the mind of the president and his advisers was that of the colonization of the emancipated group. A number of projects with this end in view were attempted. It quickly became apparent, however, that mass deportation was impracticable, and that the free Negroes and those who were becoming free were determined not to leave the United States. The thorough discipline of slavery had made the culture of the Negroes that of the nation in which they lived, and for them Africa, Central America, and Haiti held no attractions. By July 2, 1864, all plans for colonization by action of the government were abandoned.[4]

In the meantime, the handling of the problem by the generals of the Union armies showed no uniformity. In the absence of any clear policy formulated by the War Department, each commander to a large extent followed his own inclinations. It appears that in the early part of the war the most common practice was that of aiding the slaveholders to maintain possession of their "property." Some officers forbade slaves to enter their lines, and either drove out those who defied the order or allowed their masters to come into the camps and reclaim them.[5] In November, 1861, General Henry W. Halleck embodied these principles in an order that was to apply to the entire Department of the West. This command, which caused much dissension, was never fully enforced by Halleck's subordinates.[6]

[1] Paul Skeels Peirce, *The Freedmen's Bureau*, p. 5.
[2] Bell Irvin Wiley, *Southern Negroes*, pp. 177, 193.
[3] *Ibid.*, p. 193; P. S. Peirce, *op. cit.*, p. 6.
[4] P. S. Peirce, *op. cit.*, p. 11; Walter L. Fleming, "Deportation and Colonization: An Attempted Solution of the Race Problem," *Studies in Southern History and Politics*, p. 26; B. I. Wiley, *op. cit.*, pp. 194-195.
[5] P. S. Peirce, *op. cit.*, pp. 3-4; B. I. Wiley, *op. cit.*, p. 181.
[6] B. I. Wiley, *op. cit.*, p. 182.

During the first half of 1862, Congress continued to wrestle with the problem, and gradually approached a policy more in accord with the realities of the situation. In March of that year, a law was approved which forbade the use of military forces in returning slaves to those who claimed to be their owners.[7] The second Confiscation Act, adopted in July, declared that all slaves coming within the Federal lines after serving a disloyal owner were captives of war and forever free from any claim the owner might present. No officer was to surrender any Negroes to such claimants.[8] Since it was practically impossible to distinguish between loyal and disloyal slaveholders, and since military officials were forbidden to pass on the validity of claims, this law began to operate almost as a blanket statute of emancipation in those sections of the Confederacy which were coming under Federal control.

The Emancipation Proclamation completed the recognition of the fact that slavery could not be maintained in regions where military activities were being prosecuted. It gave a tremendous stimulation to the movement of Negroes from Confederate to Federal territory, and greatly clarified their status after their arrival within the lines.[9]

In the meantime, it had become apparent that however long Congress might debate the question, and whatever the final decision in reference to the fugitive Negroes might be, some method of controlling them and caring for them had to be adopted. As early as July, 1861, General Butler had put them to work on fortifications in the vicinity of Fortress Monroe.[10] When, early in 1862, Edward L. Pierce put the Negroes under his charge to growing a crop of cotton in the Sea Island district, the broad outlines of a method of maintaining the refugees were beginning to take shape.[11]

Not the least of the complicating factors to be overcome in this groping for a satisfactory Federal policy was that of the prejudice of many Northern soldiers and officers against the Negroes who were looking to them as deliverers. John Eaton declared that this prejudice against their color was often more bitter than that which they left behind.[12] Most of the soldiers seemed to be opposed to aiding the Negroes in any manner, and those who did undertake to help the fugitives were forsaken by their friends.[13] At least half of the members of some of the companies operating in the Department of the West were Democrats. The great mass of them felt that they had enlisted to fight for the integrity of the Union and the honor of its flag, and that their use in freeing Negroes and in caring for them in the camps was a violation of the terms under which they had entered the service.[14] In reply to questions as to the handling of the

[7] John Eaton, *Grant, Lincoln, and the Freedmen*, p. 50.
[8] B. I. Wiley, *op. cit.*, p. 10.   [9] P. S. Peirce, *op. cit.*, p. 10.
[10] B. I. Wiley, *op. cit.*, p. 176.   [11] *Ibid.*, p. 178.
[12] J. Eaton, *op. cit.*, p. 2.   [13] *Ibid.*, p. 22.
[14] Theodore G. Carter, "The Tupelo Campaign," *P.M.H.S.*, X, 112-113.

Negroes, one chaplain in the Department of the West wrote, "Their treatment has by no means been complimentary to the officials and subordinates. . . ."[15] A colleague answered, "Generally bad—very *bad*. Maj. Gen. Curtis, Gen. Washburn, Gen. A. P. Hovey, and some others, have dealt justly and humanely with them, but many officers and their subordinates have been hard, unjust, and cruel to them. And by the ordinary privates of the army they are treated as savages and brutes. . . ."[16]

It is true that some of the soldiers and officers of the Union armies had willingly aided the slaves to escape and maintain themselves even before such aid was legal,[17] but such men were generally unsuitable for handling the problem because they were temperamentally unfitted to give justice to the Negroes' masters.[18] Exactly the same dilemma was later to be met in the choice of the personnel of the Freedmen's Bureau, and its solution was never found.

The examples already cited of the use of Negroes on fortifications and cotton plantations came from the Federal army on the Atlantic coast. Practically all of the slaves in that region had belonged to masters who had fled or who were known to be disloyal. The situation in the West was much more complicated, for here were many loyal owners in loyal states. In addition, many planters in territory taken from the Confederates hastened to take the oath of allegiance, and demanded protection for their slave property.[19] Communications were so badly maintained that Western commanders could not be guided by the experiences of their colleagues in the East.[20]

Whatever the legal technicalities might be, hundreds of the Negroes rushed to the camps of the Union armies and hailed the soldiers as their deliverers.[21] As one recent Negro author has said:

The moment the Union army moved into slave territory, the Negro joined it. Despite all argument and calculation and in the face of refusals and commands, wherever the Union armies marched, appeared the fugitive slaves. It made no difference what the obstacles were, or the attitudes of the commanders. It was "like thrusting a walking stick into an ant hill," says one writer. And yet the army chiefs tried to regard it as an exceptional and temporary matter, a thing which they could control, when as a matter of fact it was the meat and kernel of the war.[22]

With the gradual development of a Federal policy which denied rights of ownership to disloyal slaveholders, and later with the application of the Emancipation Proclamation, the flow of Negroes into territory held by the Union armies was greatly accelerated. To this mass were added the

[15] Emancipation League, *Facts Concerning the Freedmen*, p. 7.
[16] *Ibid.*, p. 9.
[17] Melvin Grigsby, *The Smoked Yank*, p. 301.
[18] J. Eaton, *op. cit.*, p. 32.   [19] B. I. Wiley, *op. cit.*, p. 181.
[20] J. Eaton, *op. cit.*, p. 13.   [21] B. I. Wiley, *op. cit.*, p. 181.
[22] W. E. Burghardt DuBois, *Black Reconstruction*, p. 62.

thousands brought back from Federal raiding expeditions. In June, 1863, General Frank Blair returned to Grant's lines from a raid to Mechanicsburg accompanied by a body of former slaves equal in number to his entire command.[23] In January of the following year, Sherman returned from his Meridian expedition with 8,000 Negroes.[24] As a result of the raid into the Red River region, 2,500 were added to the number of those being cared for at Vicksburg.[25] After January of 1864, the state of Mississippi was almost entirely without defense against Federal troopers who rode through its territory at their own pleasure.[26] During one such raid on Jackson in July, 1864, Negro cavalrymen busied themselves in persuading those of their own race in the city to return with them to the Union army. It was said that they succeeded in carrying off about nine-tenths of Jackson's Negro population.[27]

After its fall in July, 1863, Vicksburg was the greatest rallying point for the Negro refugees of Mississippi. A representative of the United States Christian Commission wrote that the city was looked upon by the slaves as the very gate of heaven and that they came trooping to it as pigeons to their roost at night. Natchez, further down the river, served as a similar point of attraction for slaves of the Cane Hills region, and also for large numbers who were escaping from the interior of Louisiana.[28]

It is impossible to make any accurate estimate of the total number of the Negroes of Mississippi who were freed before the end of the war. The Philadelphia *North American,* however, estimated that as early as August 1, 1863, as many as 155,140 Negroes of the state had shaken off the bonds of slavery.[29] Although this figure seems to be far too large, it is probable that by spring of 1865, almost two years later, at least a third, and possibly more than half, of the Negroes of Mississippi had gained experience in the joys and sorrows of freedom.

The first great rush of slaves from Mississippi was encountered by Grant and his army near Grand Junction, Tennessee, in the fall of 1862. John Eaton, a witness, has given a vivid description of the arrival of these Negroes:

With the advance of the forty-five thousand or more in Grant's command, the cotton plantations were abandoned by their owners, and the Negroes, thrown thus upon their own resources, flocked in vast numbers—an army in themselves —to the camps of the Yankees. . . . Imagine, if you will, a slave population, springing from antecedent bondage, forsaking its local traditions and all the

[23] Clement A. Evans, *Confederate Military History,* VII, 152.
[24] Stephen D. Lee, "Sherman's Meridian Expedition," *P.M.H.S.,* IV, 47; J. Eaton, *op. cit.,* p. 135, gives the number of these refugees as 5,000.
[25] J. Eaton, *op. cit.,* p. 135.
[26] J. S. McNeily, "War and Reconstruction in Mississippi," *P.M.H.S.C.S.,* II, 203.
[27] Mobile *Evening News,* July 15, 1864.
[28] B. I. Wiley, *op. cit.,* p. 10; T. W. Knox, *Camp-Fire and Cotton-Field,* p. 376.
[29] James W. Garner, *Reconstruction in Mississippi,* p. 256.

associations and attractions of the old plantation life, coming garbed in rags or in silks, with feet shod or bleeding, individually or in families and larger groups—an army of slaves and fugitives, pushing its way irresistably toward an army of fighting men, perpetually on the defensive and perpetually ready to attack. The arrival among us of these hordes was like the oncoming of cities. There was no plan in this exodus, no Moses to lead it. . . . But their interests were identical, they felt, with the objects of our armies: a blind terror stung them, an equally blind hope allured them, and to us they came. There were men, women, and children in every stage of disease or decrepitude, often nearly naked, with flesh torn by the terrible experiences of their escapes. Sometimes they were intelligent and eager to help themselves; often they were bewildered or stupid or possessed by the wildest notions of what liberty might mean—expecting to exchange labor, and obedience to the will of another, for idleness and freedom from restraint. Such ignorance and perverted notions produced a veritable moral chaos. Cringing deceit, theft, licentiousness—all the vices which slavery inevitably fosters—were the hideous companions of nakedness, famine, and disease. A few had profited by the misfortunes of the master and were jubilant in their unwonted ease and luxury, but these stood in lurid contrast to the grimmer aspects of the tragedy—the women in travail, the helplessness of childhood and old age, the horrors of sickness and of frequent death. Small wonder that men paused in bewilderment and panic, foreseeing the demoralization and infection of the Union soldiers and the downfall of the Union cause.[30]

Although the war had been going on for a year and a half, this "oncoming of cities" was a shock to General Grant and his officers. It was their first encounter with conditions in the real black belt. Until this time, the commander had been able to handle the problem by allowing each of his division officers to do as he thought best, under general instructions to treat the Negroes kindly. Under this decentralized system, small squads of the blacks had been used in building fortifications and handling supplies, and for general labor around the camps. Their personal welfare had been the charge of the benevolent societies, with the cooperation of the commanding general.[31]

With the arrival of the fugitive slaves in groups of hundreds, some planned and unified system of care and control had to be devised. To exercise general authority over this system, Grant chose one of the most able of his chaplains, John Eaton. On November 15, 1862, the commander issued to Eaton Special Order No. 15, instructing him to take charge of the "contrabands" coming into the camp, organize them into companies, see that they were properly cared for, and "set them to work picking, ginning and baling all cotton now out and ungathered in the field."[32] During the next few days, further details of the plan were outlined in other orders from the general. That of November 14, author-

[30] J. Eaton, *op. cit.*, pp. 1-3.
[31] T. W. Knox, *op. cit.*, p. 225; P. S. Peirce, *op. cit.*, p. 9.
[32] J. Eaton, *op. cit.*, pp. 4-5; Carter G. Woodson, *A Century of Negro Migration*, pp. 109-110.

ized Eaton to set up a special camp for the Negroes, to call on a regiment to guard the camp, and to use the doctors of the regiment for necessary medical services. In addition this order gave the chaplain power to draw supplies from the military stores, and under it he drew hundreds of thousands of dollars worth of condemned tents, and clothing and rations for his charges.[33] A few days after the establishment of the camp at Grand Junction, a similar one was set up at Corinth, Mississippi.[34]

The Negroes under Eaton's command were soon busy in the abandoned fields, where the cotton was open and demanding attention. As was to be expected, immediate difficulties were encountered. Division and brigade officers were slow to comply with Grant's order, and the Commissary Department was reluctant to fill Eaton's requisitions, which certainly were of doubtful legality.[35] Residents of the vicinity were scornful of the experiment, and endeavored to insure its failure by stealing stock and disabling equipment. Guerilla bands attacked the Negroes in the fields, and desisted only after some of the raiders were killed.[36] In spite of all this, however, the experiment was judged to be a success, and most of the cotton in the vicinity of Grand Junction and LaGrange was ginned and sold for the credit of the government.[37]

Although the Emancipation Proclamation was not to take effect until the following January, the idea that the Negro was a free agent penetrated all the territory around Grant's army. In theory the commander was still supposed to make an effort to distinguish between the slaves of loyal and disloyal owners, but this was a practical impossibility. In fact, all owners who remained in the region and wished to continue the operation of their plantations soon found that in order to prevent their slaves from running off to the army, or to regain them after they had taken leave, it was necessary to make them paid laborers. In realistic fashion, Eaton and his aides adopted the installation of this system of wage labor as a policy, and saw it established rather generally throughout the north-central portion of Mississippi before the end of 1862.[38]

In December, Eaton's experiment suffered a rude interruption with the successful Confederate raid on Grant's base of supplies at Holly Springs, and the resultant abandonment of the campaign from that area. The Negroes of the camps were determined not to be left behind when the troops retired, and Eaton was able to obtain a number of freight and passenger cars for their removal to Memphis. In their fright the Negroes swarmed into every available space in the cars, and many clung to the

[33] J. Eaton, *op. cit.*, pp. 20-21.
[34] *Ibid.*, p. 31.
[35] T. W. Knox, *op. cit.*, p. 227; J. Eaton, *op. cit.*, p. 21.
[36] T. W. Knox, *op. cit.*, p. 227.
[37] *Ibid.*, p. 228.
[38] J. Eaton, *op. cit.*, p. 24.

roofs. In spite of the slow and cautious movements of the trains, the suffering in the chill of winter was indescribable. This misery continued through a bitterly cold night at Memphis, during which the refugees huddled around fires on the streets. As soon as possible, large numbers were transferred to a camp which was constructed below the city.[39]

In addition to the gathering of fugitive Negroes into camps and their use in the cotton fields, the military officials continued to use them as labor battalions for the army. In the Commissary Department, on railroads and steamboats, and especially in the construction of fortifications, the armies found the former slaves extremely useful. Late in 1863, no less than three thousand of them were being employed in the building of Federal breastworks around Natchez.[40] Although it was soon decided that these workers were to receive a small payment for their labor, much lower than that for whites, the government was slow in delivering the money to them. In January, 1863, chaplains in the Department of the West reported that the government was $20,000 behind in the wages of the Negroes, and that many of them had worked for several months with no pay at all. In some cases, after the arrival of the money, the generals ordered the wages retained for a decision as to whether it should be paid to the Negroes or to their former masters.[41]

Early in 1863 the President and his Secretary of War abandoned much of their earlier caution, and decided on the enlistment of large numbers of the freedmen as soldiers. This decision grew out of the realities of the situation. It was made logical by the Emancipation Proclamation, and almost essential by the stubborn resistance of the South and by the bitter opposition to general conscription in the North. Steps in this direction had already been taken in South Carolina, Rhode Island, and the Department of the Gulf when Adjutant-General Lorenzo Thomas in March, 1863, arrived in the Department of the West with orders for a general mobilization of the Negroes for labor and for military service. He was to find suitable officers who were willing to take command of these forces, and "to organize such troops for military service to the utmost extent to which they can be obtained in accordance to the rules and regulations of the service."[42]

In spite of the growing popularity of the Emancipation Proclamation, this absorption of the freedmen into the fighting forces of the Union met opposition from within the ranks. Eaton, who had long been disturbed by the friction "engendered . . . by any forced relationship between the Negro and the Union soldier," immediately recommended the estab-

[39] *Ibid.*, p. 30.
[40] Howill Hinds to Jefferson Davis, Home Hill, Mississippi, October 11, 1863, quoted in J. Dunbar Rowland, *Jefferson Davis*, VI, 59.
[41] Emancipation League, *op. cit.*, pp. 7-9.
[42] J. Eaton, *op. cit.*, pp. 52-54; P. S. Peirce, *op. cit.*, p. 14.

lishment of separate regiments for the freedmen, although he insisted upon the necessity of their having white officers.[43] These officers, when obtained, faced the scorn of their white colleagues.[44] General Halleck, who had steadily opposed the increasing emphasis placed on the Negro in the conduct of the war, told Sherman that Thomas' order was ridiculous, but must be accepted. He admitted the apparent impossibility of filling the Federal ranks through conscription.[45] The enlistment of Negroes also aroused strong opposition among the civilians in the North. By December of 1863, however, President Lincoln was able to declare that this opposition had subsided and that "the crisis which threatened to divide the friends of the Union" had passed.[46]

Large numbers of the Negro refugees who entered the army did so because of a sincere desire to carry on the campaign that seemed to them to be one for the liberation of their race; equally large numbers felt the attraction of the uniform and military display; white officers used pressure to enlist many others. They found the refugees especially susceptible to persuasion just after their arrival within the lines. Eaton's comment on this matter is revealing: "Having frequently observed the readiness with which the able-bodied enlisted before their minds had been corrupted or made restless by life in private service . . . my officers promptly directed the Negro's attention to the duty of enlisting. . . ."[47] Those who resisted this early pressure often succumbed to the lure of recruiting officers swarming in from the North to offer bounties for recruits to be credited on the draft quotas of their states.[48]

Of the 186,017 Negroes reported as regularly enlisted in the Federal armies, 134,111 were from the slave states, and 17,800 from Mississippi.[49] Thus, in a very real sense, in labor battalions and in the ranks of the army, the Negroes of the state participated in the struggle for their freedom, and, to this extent, the common statement that they waited idly for it to be thrust upon them is untrue.

The induction of the Negro into the military arm fulfilled only a part of General Thomas' instructions. It was also his duty to work out a plan of labor for the freedmen which would work to the advantage of the government and would, to as large extent as possible, relieve it of the support of the refugees. He therefore immediately initiated a study of the problem which was rapidly outgrowing the simple system that Eaton had set up.

After the abandonment of the Grand Junction region, most of the

[43] J. Eaton, op. cit., p. 67.
[44] B. I. Wiley, op. cit., p. 311.
[45] J. S. McNeily, "War and Reconstruction in Mississippi," P.M.H.S.C.S., II, 175.
[46] James D. Richardson, Messages and Papers of the Presidents, VI, 189.
[47] J. Eaton, op. cit., p. 135.
[48] J. S. McNeily, "War and Reconstruction in Mississippi," P.M.H.S.C.S., II, 174.
[49] Ibid., II, 174; B. I. Wiley, op. cit., p. 311; W. E. B. DuBois, op. cit., p. 112.

Negroes whom Eaton had at work were occupied in supplying the necessary wood for their own camps and those of the army, and for boats on the various rivers. During the winter of 1862-1863 conditions in the camps were undoubtedly very bad, in spite of the fact that Eaton's recently organized staff did the best they could under the circumstances, and in spite of the receipt of large amounts of money and clothing and of a number of workers from the benevolent societies of the North.[50]

With the coming of spring, the superintendent made efforts to put the freedmen to work in abandoned fields which were close enough to the camps to allow reasonable protection against guerillas. This effort met with many delays and difficulties, since it was essentially experimental, and since most of the necessary agricultural equipment had to be obtained through the benevolence of private individuals and of societies.[51] Strangely enough, the Negroes themselves furnished some of the stock and implements which were used. Many of them came into the lines riding on horses and mules, or in carts which carried varying amounts of property they had picked up before leaving the plantations. The general practice was for the picket officers to take all stock from the refugees as they entered the camps. Eaton endeavored so far as possible to obtain for the Negroes payment for these animals of which they had "spoiled the Egyptians." One group received $2,408 in payment for such property. Other fugitives succeeded in selling their stock before they arrived at the camps.[52]

It was the immediate decision of General Thomas that this system of camps could not properly meet the problem of handling the tens of thousands of Negroes who came into the Union lines. It is interesting to speculate on the possibilities which might have developed if Thomas had favored the continuation and expansion of Eaton's method. It seems that this must have resulted in the setting up of a tremendous governmental agency for the production, processing, and sale of cotton; or in the establishment of enormous communal or semi-communal enterprises under the sponsorship and control of the government. There can be no doubt, however, that the decision of General Thomas reflected the attitude of a large majority of the American people, and that the development of either of the alternatives inherent in Eaton's experiment would have aroused overwhelming disapproval. The Adjutant-General probably gave neither of these possibilities any consideration. At any rate, it was his immediate decision to deliver the freedmen into the hands of private enterprisers.

The plan drawn up by General Thomas offered an excellent bargain to the lessees of the abandoned plantations. For the lands which were

[50] J. Eaton, *op. cit.*, pp. 36, 58.   [51] *Ibid.*, p. 59.
[52] *Ibid.*, p. 135; T. W. Knox, *op. cit.*, p. 376.

assigned to them they were to pay only a tax of two dollars for each bale of cotton produced. They were allowed to use the equipment found on the plantations, and so far as possible were supplied with horses and mules from the confiscated stock. They were to feed the freedmen and pay an extremely low wage ranging from $2.50 to $5.00 per month according to sex and age. The cost of clothing and other supplies, except food and shelter, was to be deducted from the wages of the workers. Deductions were also allowed for days missed from work because of sickness or for any other cause, even though it be the fault of the lessee. The plantations were to receive protection from the army.[53]

General Thomas' system has been the subject of much adverse criticism, and most of it seems to have been deserved. The lessees were generally men of low character who came largely from the group of "sharks" who followed the army. One investigator, after careful study, declared: "The desire of gain alone prompts them, and they care little whether they make it out of the blood of those they employ or from the soil."[54] One of the lessees wrote later that the majority of the speculators had as little regard for the rights of the Negroes as the most brutal slaveholder had ever shown.[55] In spite of the late start of operations, hasty plowing and overplanting, the devastating sweep of the army worm, and guerilla raids that brought fear, abduction, and death to many of the Negroes, the favorable contracts and the high price of cotton allowed most of the planters to make a profit, and brought large fortunes to some.[56]

To most of the Negroes, however, the scheme brought cruel disappointment, and to many abject misery. Even if they happened to work for one of the few honest and humane lessees, they found little or nothing left of their small wages after deductions had been made for lost time, clothing, medical service, and supplies needed to piece out the meager rations. Although clothing was supposed to be furnished at cost, most of the lessees seem to have doubled and redoubled the price to their workers. There was a uniform deduction for medical care, though the service itself was almost never supplied.[57] These deductions, honest and dishonest, seem in most cases to have absorbed the wages entirely. Some lessees openly boasted of having swindled their Negroes out of all of their money by taking advantage of their ignorance.[58] Living quarters were often poor, and the workers suffered terribly from overcrowding and disease.[59]

[53] *Appleton's Cyclopedia*, 1863, pp. 428-429; P. S. Peirce, *op. cit.*, p. 14; B. I. Wiley, *op. cit.*, pp. 185-186, 231; T. W. Knox, *op. cit.*, p. 311; J. Eaton, *op. cit.*, pp. 59-60.
[54] James E. Yeatman, *Report*, p. 8.
[55] T. W. Knox, *op. cit.*, p. 316.
[56] *Ibid.*, p. 317; P. S. Peirce, *op. cit.*, p. 15; J. W. Garner, *op. cit.*, p. 251.
[57] J. E. Yeatman, *op. cit.*, p. 8.
[58] T. W. Knox, *op. cit.*, p. 316.
[59] P. S. Peirce, *op. cit.*, p. 15.

Some employers furnished no rations other than a small amount of meat, and forced their freedmen to search for corn on distant plantations which had been abandoned. They also made charges for flour or other food furnished, and issued no molasses, rice, beans, or hominy.[60]

It is small wonder that many of the Negroes, finding themselves absolutely penniless after a season of hard work on overplanted fields, with poor and insufficient food, and crowded, unsanitary quarters, became the victims of absolute despair. James Yeatman, after an investigation for the Western Sanitary Commission, reported:

The poor negroes are everywhere greatly depressed at their condition. They all testify that if they were only paid their little wages as they earn them, so that they could purchase clothing, and were furnished with provisions promised they could stand it; but to work and get poorly paid, poorly fed, and not doctored when sick, is more than they can endure. Among the thousands whom I questioned none showed the least unwillingness to work. If they could only be paid fair wages they would be contented and happy. They do not realize that they are free men. They say that they are told they are, but then they are taken and hired out to men who treat them, so far as providing for them is concerned, far worse than their "secesh" masters did. . . .[61]

Not all the Negroes who were engaged in agriculture in 1863 were employed by the lessees. Many of them arranged in one fashion or another to cultivate small lots of land on their own account. Most of them seem to have enjoyed fair success.[62] General Thomas mentioned in his report for October fifteen Negro lessees. They had succeeded in producing crops ranging from four to one hundred fifty bales of cotton.[63] It is apparent, however, that the lack of money and credit for the acquisition of land, supplies and equipment, and the natural shortage of initiative in a population just emerging from slavery made it impossible for most of the Negroes to undertake such activities.

Many of the freedmen continued in 1863 to work at the wood yards that had been established during the preceding winter. These yards were generally set up on islands or at protected points along the river. From them the army and the Commissary Department drew many thousands of cords of wood, either without any payment or at a price far below that of the commercial yards. In the government yards in the Vicksburg district alone more than a thousand Negroes were employed, and in spite of the low prices paid for the wood, the receipts from this district added over $125,000 to the Freedmen's Fund. The Negro men attended to the chopping of the wood, while the women and children loaded, unloaded, and corded it. The chief difficulty seems to have been that of finding capable

[60] J. E. Yeatman, op. cit., p. 7.
[61] Ibid., pp. 7-8.
[62] T. W. Knox, op. cit., p. 320.
[63] J. E. Yeatman, op. cit., p. 10.

managers who were willing to give humane treatment to the Negroes.[64]

In addition to the government yards, there also sprang up a large number of small private establishments which offered employment to the freedmen. In these yards, as on the leased plantations, the workers often suffered wrongs from dishonest and irresponsible employers.[65]

In spite of this rapid reabsorption of the refugee Negroes into agriculture and other pursuits, and their enlistment in the army, the camp system which Eaton had set up could not be abandoned, and indeed had to be expanded. These camps served as temporary gathering places for masses of Negroes brought in by Federal raiding parties, and for those who came in of their own accord. There they were kept until arrangements had been made for their employment or their transfer to an "infirmary farm." In addition, the camps had a large permanent population, made up of woodchoppers, laborers for the army, women, children, and the aged.

By the fall of 1863 it seems that the largest of these camps was that at Natchez, where Yeatman found a population of 2,100 remaining from the more than 4,000 who had been there earlier. It appears that almost criminal mismanagement marked the handling of these camps, which was at best a difficult task. The cabins at Natchez were described as poorly constructed, badly lighted and ventilated, overcrowded, and infested with disease. The death rate was exceedingly high. Some of the Negroes were reported to have returned to their masters to escape the suffering.[66]

For the wives of the Negro soldiers, other women and children, and the old and infirm, a dozen or more "infirmary farms" were established. On these places rations and other supplies were furnished by the government, and all inmates who were able to work were put to chopping wood, clearing land, farming, or some form of lighter labor.[67]

This entire system of control, and especially the application of the Thomas plan to the leased plantations, came in for a great deal of harsh criticism. Perhaps the most effective of these attacks was that made late in 1863 by James Yeatman of the Western Sanitary Commission. His criticisms and suggestions for change played perfectly into the hands of the Treasury Department. This branch of the government had long been demanding control of the entire system of leased plantations, under the plea that it would be a source of revenue to the government. The outcome was that in the winter of 1863-1864 the Treasury took over the leasing system, and immediately began to put into operation the reforms which Yeatman demanded.[68]

In general, this plan struck heavily at the profits and excesses of the

[64] *Ibid.*, p. 6; J. Eaton, *op. cit.*, pp. 135, 137-139.
[65] J. Eaton, *op. cit.*, p. 138.
[66] J. E. Yeatman, *op. cit.*, p. 13; C. H. Wesley, *op. cit.*, p. 89.
[67] J. E. Yeatman, *op. cit.*, p. 6.
[68] P. S. Peirce, *op. cit.*, pp. 23-24.

speculators, and pointed toward a great improvement in the condition of the freedmen. To reduce the evils of absentee landlordship, it limited each leaseholder to one plantation, and gave preference to those seeking small tracts. It called for a very large increase in the wages of the laborers, on a complicated scale ranging from ten to twenty-five dollars per month and based on differences of age, sex, and ability. These wages were to stand as a first lien against the crop, and were to be provided for in definite contracts supervised by the superintendents of the Home Farms and subject to their intervention. Half of the wage was to be paid each month in money, clothing, or provisions, and the remaining half was to be turned over to the worker on the sale of the crop. All lessees were required to supply good quarters and garden spots to their workers, and to keep on hand suitable clothing and good food to be sold to them at cost, plus a handling charge of fifteen per cent. On all plantations where Negroes were employed, a tax of one cent a pound on cotton and a proportional amount on other products was to be paid into a fund for the support of indigent freedmen. A similar tax, varying according to the value of the property, was to be levied on the leased plantations in lieu of rent.[69]

Trouble developed immediately. Although practically all of the speculating planters hastened to make contracts under the new system, they resented the increase in wages and the prospect of supervision in the interest of the Negroes. Their partisans, General Thomas and his staff, and most of the military officials, seem to have done everything in their power to prevent the system from succeeding. Thomas himself appealed directly to the President and received from him a blanket delegation of authority which stripped the Treasury officials of most of their power.[70]

The struggle which followed between the Treasury and War departments is one of the darkest blots on the record of the government's treatment of the freedmen, whose suffering went largely unheeded while treasury agents, military officials, politicians, and their satellites fought for power and political and financial advantage. Eaton, who worked for the interests of the War Department, although he disliked Thomas and many of his methods, was sternly critical of the system which W. P. Mellen, agent of the Treasury, attempted to set up. He insisted that in the face of the uncertainties surrounding the plantation system, the schedule of wages was entirely too high. Leasing agents abandoned all caution and encouraged the occupation of lands that could not be protected. He also charged that there was an alarming increase in the number of speculators whose only interest was exploitation, and that there was even more corruption than there had been under military control.[71]   On the other

[69] J. Eaton, op. cit., p. 145; P. S. Peirce, op. cit., p. 23.
[70] J. Eaton, op. cit., p. 153; J. S. McNeily, "War and Reconstruction in Mississippi," P.M.H.S.C.S., II, 185.
[71] J. Eaton, op. cit., pp. 147, 154.

hand, some less biased than Eaton have held that the Mellen-Yeatman system brought real improvement.[72]

As a matter of fact, the new plan was not allowed to operate without broad modifications. General Thomas emerged from a conference with Mellen in March with an order for a sweeping reduction of wages. Freedmen who had contracted a month or two before for as much as $25.00 per month now found themselves reduced to a schedule which called for only $3.50 to $10.00 per month plus rations and clothing. Evidence that this constituted a real reduction is to be seen in the fact that only six planters failed to take advantage of it. The schedule provided that the clothing allowance might be commuted into $3.00 per month in additional wages, an option which most of the planters exercised. Under this arrangement adult men and women received $13.00 and $10.00 per month respectively. Then almost immediately there was authorized another breach of the freedmen's contracts which abolished the allowance for clothing. Only ten planters failed to take advantage of this second reduction.[73]

Troubles continued to develop. Eaton's Department of Freedmen, as a military arm, had cared for the helpless and dependent Negroes through the use of army supplies and of revenue gained from the abandoned plantations, wood yards, and infirmary farms. This group now took the attitude that as the Treasury had absorbed most of the revenue, and had sent the able-bodied freedmen off to the plantations, it must also assume the care of the destitute. While Eaton and his subordinates sulked, and the Treasury agents refused to shoulder the responsibility, contacts with benevolent organizations were lost, the infirmary farms deteriorated, and new refugees were left to suffer without attention. It took a direct order from General Brayman to set Eaton's Department of Freedmen to work again. In the meantime, its superintendent was in Washington on a lobbying expedition in which he succeeded in blocking a renewed effort of the Treasury to gain complete control.[74]

The quarrel between the military authorities and the Treasury agents was reflected in other ways. The army was unable to exercise authority over affairs controlled by the Treasury, and the Treasury was unable to gain enforcement of its own regulations in a region which was under martial law. As has been said, the area of the leased plantations was now much larger than in 1863, and the army was either unable or unwilling to give it military protection.[75] As a result, sweeping guerilla raids threw the entire region into chaos. Stock was stolen, houses were burned, and Negroes were abducted, driven off, or murdered, as were the lessees. Threats of military vengeance or of indemnities to be levied on the native

[72] P. S. Peirce, op. cit., p. 24.
[73] J. Eaton, op. cit., pp. 153, 167-170.
[74] Ibid., pp. 161-163, 167-170.
[75] Ibid., p. 147.

population were absolutely ineffective. Practically all the plantations in the vicinity of Natchez, Vicksburg, and Milliken's Bend were given up, while the Negroes who were not carried off by the raiders fled to the army camps for protection. An agent of Eaton's who visited ninety-five of the safest plantations found that from them the guerillas had carried off 966 Negroes and 2,314 horses and mules.[76]

In July and August there came a new disaster. Army worms covered the fields and left them looking as though they had been swept by fire. Planters who had expected to harvest a thousand bales of cotton found themselves reduced to ten or a hundred. The Vicksburg *Herald* declared that many of the fields in that vicinity would not yield five bales to a hundred acres.[77]

In spite of the financial failure of most of the planters and the general wretchedness of the Negroes, not all of the developments of 1864 were bad. The possibility of producing cotton with free labor was fully established, and practically all of the lessees who could make the necessary arrangements rushed into preparations for the following year.[78] In spite of the determined opposition of the planters, a number of Negroes had leased land on their own account, and those who managed to survive the guerillas and to save something from the worms were successful enough to demonstrate the possibilities of Negro enterprise.[79] By a system of certificates and shipment permits, the authorities managed to assure the full payment of wages to the Negroes by planters who were not bankrupt.[80] Of the 11,363 old and indigent Negroes on the Home Farms, practically all had worked well, and only 985 had received rations from the government. Those who were far enough up the river to have escaped the worst ravages of the army worm managed to repay the department for all of its outlays, and to have something left for themselves. According to the superintendent, all of these infirmary farms would have shown profits but for devastation by the caterpillars.[81]

Before leaving this consideration of the introduction of the Negro to the system of free labor in agriculture, it is necessary to give some attention to a peculiar and interesting experiment which had been going on just below Vicksburg since the middle of 1863. Before the fall of the city in July of that year, Grant called the superintendent of the Freedmen's De-

[76] T. W. Knox, *op. cit.*, pp. 448-449; J. Eaton, *op. cit.*, pp. 157-158; J. S. McNeily, "War and Reconstruction in Mississippi," *P.M.H.S.C.S.*, II, 182-183.
[77] T. W. Knox, *op. cit.*, pp. 320, 449; J. Eaton, *op. cit.*, p. 140; Vicksburg *Herald*, August 20, 1864; J. S. McNeily, "War and Reconstruction in Mississippi," *P.M.H.S.C.S.*, II, 189.
[78] T. W. Knox, *op. cit.*, p. 450; J. S. McNeily, "War and Reconstruction in Mississippi," *P.M.H.S.C.S.*, II, 189.
[79] T. W. Knox, *op. cit.*, p. 320; J. Eaton, *op. cit.*, p. 157.
[80] J. S. McNeily, "War and Reconstruction in Mississippi," *P.M.H.S.C.S.*, II, 187.
[81] J. Eaton, *op. cit.*, p. 140.

partment to him and told him that he had been making plans for some of the Negroes of the vicinity. In one of the numerous elbows of the river, about twenty-five miles below Vicksburg, lay a large and fertile peninsula which was known as Palmyra or Davis Bend. This pear-shaped body of land was about twelve miles long and twenty-eight miles in circumference, and held within its limits six plantations, including the great "Briarfield" and "Hurricane" places of Joe Davis and his brother, the President of the Confederacy. It was Grant's plan to make of the peninsula "a Negro paradise."[82]

Rapid progress was made on the project, in spite of a guerilla raid which succeeded in killing or wounding a number of the Negroes and driving the rest into the woods. Almost complete protection against other similar attacks was provided by stationing at the peninsula a small body of soldiers and a gun boat, and by cutting a canal across the narrow neck which connected the area with the mainland. By December, 1863, over 600 freedmen had been assembled at the Bend and preparations were under way for producing crops in the following year.[83]

In 1864, the project suffered heavily from the struggle of the Treasury and military authorities discussed above. This conflict resulted in late planting, and in the admission of three or four white lessees, who took up a large portion of the land.[84] In spite of these difficulties, however, some seventy-five of the freedmen succeeded in setting themselves up on their own account, cultivating parcels of from five or ten to one hundred acres. Rations, teams, and equipment, supplied to them by the Freedmen's Department, were charged to their accounts, and these charges were to be deducted from the proceeds of their crops. By mid-summer, the prospects of most of them looked very bright.[85]

Then came the army worm, and at the Bend, on account of the late planting, its attack was especially devastating. Five-sixths of the crop was lost. In general, however, the Negroes fared better than the white lessees, since they had not overplanted their small allotments. Some of them sold their crops to speculators for very large prices before the arrival of the worms.[86] These independent cultivators, a chosen group, seem to have been able to repay the government for all advances, and some of them showed profits of from five hundred to a thousand dollars.[87]

The real significance of the experiment was not to become apparent

[82] *Ibid.*, p. 85; J. T. Trowbridge, *The South,* p. 383; W. W. Brown, *The Negro in the American Rebellion,* pp. 298-299.

[83] J. E. Yeatman, *op. cit.,* p. 13; W. W. Brown, *op. cit.,* pp. 298-299; J. T. Trowbridge, *op. cit.,* p. 383.

[84] J. S. McNeily, "War and Reconstruction in Mississippi," *P.M.H.S.C.S.,* II, 184, 189; J. Eaton, *op. cit.,* p. 165.

[85] W. W. Brown, *op. cit.,* p. 299; J. Eaton, *op. cit.,* p. 163; J. S. McNeily, "War and Reconstruction in Mississippi," *P.M.H.S.C.S.,* II, 184.

[86] *Ibid.,* II, 189; J. Eaton, *op. cit.,* p. 163.

[87] Whitelaw Reid, *After the War,* pp. 285-286.

until 1865. In the fall of the preceding year, General N. J. T. Dana issued an order extending the supervision of the Freedmen's Department over the entire peninsula, and expelling all white speculators.[88]

The officers in charge immediately adopted the policy of allowing the Negroes to exercise a great deal of self-control, in spite of the objections of neighboring planters. They divided the colony into three judicial districts, and appointed a sheriff and a judge for each. In the courts of these districts, judge, jury, counsel, and all the officers were Negroes, and no whites interfered during the progress of the trials. When brought in for trial, the offending freedman was allowed to decide whether he wished to stand judgment before a jury, or have his case tried by the judge alone. When the decision had been reached and the penalty prescribed, a statement of the case and of the action recommended was submitted to the superintendent of the plantations. The offender generally accepted the sentence cheerfully; and in cases where the superintendent found it necessary to intervene it was generally because he found the punishment too severe. The usual sentence consisted of a fine and a term of forced labor on the Home Farm. Petty thievery and idleness were the most common offenses, but officers declared that theft of exposed property was remarkably rare.[89] In the words of the Superintendent of Freedmen, "The community distinctly demonstrated the capacity of the Negro to take care of himself and exercise under honest and competent direction the functions of self-government."[90]

In the economic sphere the freedmen were also allowed to exercise a great deal of freedom and initiative. About 500 acres on the place of Jefferson Davis were set aside as a Home Farm, and on them were established orphaned children, the aged and infirm, the incompetent and thriftless, and transients.[91] About 5,000 acres of the remaining land were parceled out to 181 voluntary companies and partnerships comprised of 1,300 adults and 450 children. These people were then left to manage their own affairs, and not even officers of the newly established Freedmen's Bureau were allowed to intervene in their economic or domestic activities. They raised their own crops, made their own sales, and pocketed their profits. White officers took an active part only in seeing that just settlements were made with whites who had furnished the freedmen with stock and supplies.[92]

The results were remarkable. In spite of the inferior quality and char-

        [88] J. Eaton, op. cit., p. 165; J. S. McNeily, "War and Reconstruction in Mississippi," P.M.H.S.C.S., II, 184.
        [89] J. Eaton, op. cit., pp. 165-166; T. W. Knox, op. cit., p. 353; J. T. Trowbridge, op. cit., p. 383.
        [90] J. Eaton, op. cit., p. 166.
        [91] J. T. Trowbridge, op. cit., p. 383; Senate Executive Documents, no. 27, 39th Congress, 1st session, p. 38.
        [92] Senate Executive Documents, no. 27, 39th Congress, 1st Session, p. 38.

acter of the workers on the Home Farm, and of damage from heavy rains in June, that branch of the project came through the year with a surplus of $25,929.80, which was turned over to the receiving and disbursing officer of the Bureau. As presented by Sub-Commissioner Samuel Thomas, the statement of the achievements of the individual enterprisers is even more impressive :[93]

Receipts:

12,000 bushels of corn, worth at least............		$ 12,000
Vegetables, potatoes, melons, &c, sold............		38,500
1,736 bales of cotton..........................		347,200
Total amount of receipts......................		397,700
Paid for expenses............................	160,000	
Paid to white partners for stock, supplies, &c.....	60,000	
Paid . . . Freedmen's Bureau for rations drawn..	18,500	
Total disbursements..........................		238,500
Balance in hands of colonists..................		$159,200

According to a contemporary investigator, fifty of the Negro planters in the colony accumulated $5,000 each in 1863 and 1864, and a hundred others had gained from $1,000 to $4,000. They were looking for opportunities to invest their money.[94] It should be noticed that no rent is included in the charges to the freedmen in the above statement, but their profits, in a year of bad weather and insect pests, would still have been respectable after the deduction of appropriate rentals.

The significance of this one-year experiment lies in what it shows might have developed from Eaton's early system of camps if the "radicals" in Congress had allowed their radicalism to extend into the field of economics instead of confining it to that of politics. A wiser and more benevolent government might well have seen in Davis Bend the suggestion of a long-time program for making the Negro a self-reliant, prosperous, and enterprising element of the population. It would have cost a great deal of money for the purchase of lands, or would have involved an attack on the sacredness of property rights in their confiscation, but it would certainly have greatly altered the future of the South, and it might have made of her a much happier and more prosperous section.

But Davis Bend was doomed at the end of its first year. Four of the plantations were immediately returned to owners who had received presidential pardons.[95] Joe Davis, pardoned later, received rent for the other two places for the year 1866, and had full possession restored to him in January, 1867.[96]

[93] *Ibid.*, p. 38.   [94] J. T. Trowbridge, *op. cit.*, p. 384.
[95] *Senate Executive Documents*, no. 27, 39th Congress, 1st session, p. 39.
[96] *Senate Executive Documents*, no. 6, 39th Congress, 2d session, p. 99.

The future history of these Davis plantations is of some interest. Before their actual restoration, the owner leased them for a term of years to the remarkable Negro Benjamin T. Montgomery, who had been his slave and his plantation manager before the war.[97] Montgomery handled the plantations very successfully, and later bought them from Davis.[98] In 1873 he paid taxes amounting to $2,447.09.[99] According to a leading white landowner, he gained the reputation of being the best planter in the county and perhaps in the state. His cotton took all the prizes at the Cincinnati Exposition.[100] After his death in 1878, his son, I. T. Montgomery, continued the enterprise until 1883, when he abandoned it in the face of recurring floods. In 1887, the younger Montgomery established a new town in Bolivar County, and carried there a majority of the people who had lived at Davis Bend. Thus the idea of an all-Negro town, often discussed by Ben Montgomery with Jefferson Davis, reached its fulfillment many years later. The progressive and prosperous town of Mound Bayou, owned and admirably managed by a population made up entirely of Negroes, is the legitimate offspring of Davis Bend.[101]

It has already been pointed out that the great mass of the Negro fugitives from the black belt of the state rushed toward the army camps at Natchez and Vicksburg. With the refugees arriving at times by thousands in one day, conditions in those towns, especially in 1863, were indescribably bad. John Eaton described the new arrivals as "crowded together, sickly, disheartened, dying on the streets, not a family of them all either well-sheltered, clad, or fed; no physicians, no medicines, no hospitals; many of the persons who had been charged with feeding them either sick or dead."[102] Bewildered and frightened, and spoiled by idleness and association with the army, few of them were willing to work any longer at one time than was necessary to gain immediate necessities. Housekeepers often had a new cook for each meal in the day. On the other hand, those who employed the Negroes often tried to avoid paying them, and less scrupulous whites swarmed about to cheat them of such money and property as they had.[103]

As rapidly as possible, the refugees were transferred from the towns to the camps, infirmary farms, or leased plantations. Those who insisted on remaining were granted the necessary military passes and permits only after their trustworthiness had been established to the satisfaction of the Superintendents of Freedmen. By this method the Negro population of

[97] Hinds County *Gazette,* November 23, 1866.
[98] *Ibid.,* June 13, 1877; Edward King, *The Great South,* p. 290.
[99] Hinds County *Gazette,* January 24, 1874.
[100] S. D. Smedes, *Memorials of a Southern Planter,* pp. 313-314.
[101] Maurice Elizabeth Jackson, "Mound Bayou—A Study in Social Development," unpublished master's thesis, University of Alabama, 1937, pp. 27-28.
[102] J. Eaton, *op. cit.,* p. 105.
[103] *Ibid.,* pp. 105, 135.

the towns was brought under control, and vagrancy and petty crimes were materially reduced. By the spring of 1865, Dr. Joseph Warren was able to write that many of the urban Negroes had shown a remarkable capacity for business, and were well able to take care of themselves without any form of guardianship. In both Vicksburg and Natchez, he declared, blacksmith shops, shoe shops, and other enterprises conducted by freedmen were "too numerous to mention."[104]

In addition to supervising the economic activities of the Negroes, the Department of Freedmen under Eaton attempted to meet a number of other needs. Not a cent of government money was ever used in those activities, which were financed through the Freedmen's Fund. This fund, as has already been indicated, was derived from a tax on the wages of the able-bodied refugees, and from profits derived from the labor of those in the camps, wood yards, and infirmary farms. It was sufficient to provide for a number of hospitals, orphanages and schools, and for agricultural implements, clothing, and household utensils for the various camps.[105]

Health conditions among the refugees were of course very bad, and satisfactory arrangements for caring for them were never made. By the use of its fund, the Department of Freedmen managed to offer a small amount of hospital service, and to maintain physicians on some of the infirmary farms. As has already been pointed out, the death rate in the large camps was extremely high, and it was even higher on some of the leased plantations. Many of the plantations offered no medical service whatsoever, and Chaplain Fiske reported to Eaton that on some of them over half of the workers had died. Smallpox prevailed throughout the area.[106]

The high mortality rate left many orphans, most of whom were cared for on the Home Farm. The plans of the Department to provide for a large and well-equipped asylum required the cooperation of the benevolent societies because of the shortage of funds. The jealousy which these societies held for each other prevented this necessary cooperation, and obliged the superintendents to work instead with several small and insufficient asylums established by the various societies individually.[107]

Superintendent Eaton and his aides also concerned themselves with the morals and the family life of their charges. In the confusion of the time, including the separation of families and the crowded and almost unregulated life of the early camps, licentiousness naturally ran riot. The superintendent, with some justice, attributed much of this to the effects of the system of slavery. The family, never a legal unit under that system, had faced few social or economic responsibilities. Records of the

[104] Ibid., pp. 137, 210.
[105] Ibid., pp. 127-128.
[106] Ibid., pp. 128, 160; J. E. Yeatman, op. cit., p. 7.
[107] J. Eaton, op. cit., pp. 201-202.

Vicksburg post showed that one-sixth of the more than three thousand Negroes married there during eight months in 1864 had been forcibly separated from earlier husbands or wives by the direct operations of slavery.[108]

From the beginning, the Freedmen's Department attempted to maintain the marriage relation, and even went to the extent of ejecting from the camps some of those who refused to comply with the ruling. In March, 1864, its efforts were aided by a special order from General Lorenzo Thomas that authorized any ordained minister accredited by Eaton to perform marriage ceremonies for the freedmen. Records kept by the superintendents show that at the Vicksburg post alone fifteen hundred marriages of this type were solemnized within the first eight months after the issuance of the order. All observers testify to the natural eagerness and enthusiasm with which the freedmen assumed this new evidence of freedom and elevation. Chaplain Warren of Vicksburg believed that practically all the marriages in his department were successful, but the superintendent was not so optimistic. He saw evidence of a natural reaction among the Negroes as the novelty of the ceremony and the relation disappeared.[109] The culture pattern formed in generations of slavery could not be changed merely by the posting of an order from the Adjutant-General.

Such moral advancement as was achieved by painful effort and supervision in the camps and towns was absent on most of the plantations. Few of the lessees made an effort even to provide for marriages, and the small number who wished to better living conditions among their workers had no authority to carry out their desires.[110]

The enthusiastic participation of the freedmen in marriage ceremonies was not the only activity which marked their recognition of their new status. Most of them immediately tried to assume a new dignity. This was marked by the deep seriousness with which they went about the choice of family names, which appendages they held to be badges of freedom.[111] The words of Dr. Warren carry to the reader some of the pathos of the situation:

They become ambitious in speech; and their high-sounding phrases are in strange contrast with their rustic and imperfect dialect. Their courtliness and gravity of manner are oddly mixed up with childishness. The spectacle they present excites fear and hope, laughter and tears in succession. On the whole, hope predominates. They will make mistakes; and they will learn caution and shrewdness by them. . . . We can see the wants, desires, and hopes of civilized life struggling within them. In some these feelings are well formed; in others dim and uncertain.[112]

[108] *Ibid.*, pp. 211-212.
[109] *Ibid.*, p. 212.
[110] *Ibid.*, p. 160.
[111] W. Reid, *op. cit.*, p. 532.
[112] J. Eaton, *op. cit.*, p. 215.

This new sense of self-respect and a yearning to better their condition caused the Negroes to grasp eagerly the few available opportunities for education. It is true that in this eagerness and in their lack of background they exhibited little sense of discrimination. A book was a book, and it was felt that one who learned to read had guaranteed his freedom.[113] It is possible that the prohibition of their learning to read and write in the old slave codes had something to do with the development of this attitude.

From the first, army chaplains and workers in the Department of Freedmen encouraged the Negro in his desire for education, but the lack of funds and equipment prevented them from giving much more than simple encouragement. The actual task of setting up schools fell to the various benevolent societies of the North. Workers for the American Missionary Association and the Feedmen's Aid Commission were the first in the field, arriving in some numbers soon after the surrender of Vicksburg and the occupation of Natchez. It is regrettable to learn that these workers, although in general sincerely devoted to their task, often allowed a desire to secure the best places for themselves and their organizations to hinder their work. In September, 1863, Eaton gained authority to furnish the teachers with rations, quarters, and transportation, but still lacked the power to settle their disputes, assign them to specific locations, or to secure any kind of uniformity in books or methods. Under these conditions, schools were quickly established in and near the towns and camps, but their functioning left much to be desired. Almost no satisfactory buildings were available, and school equipment was almost totally lacking. On the plantations conditions were even worse than in the towns and camps, and the desire of the superintendents that the laborers receive some form of instruction received practically no attention from the planters.[114]

Some order and improvement were brought to the situation in September, 1864, when the Superintendent of Freedmen gained authority to take almost complete control of the schools established by the societies. He quickly established a discipline that was almost military in its character, but which was probably necessary in such disorganized territory. Among other reforms, he regularized the system of tuition fees which most of the teachers were collecting, and which some had used to defraud their pupils. Eaton was unable to abolish the fee system entirely, but set up a uniform schedule of charges which ranged from twenty-five cents to $1.25 per month. Pupils from families which were absolutely destitute received a free ticket. These charges made the schools almost entirely self-supporting, and the Superintendent believed their effect upon the Negroes was good.[115]

Under the new regulations the schools developed rapidly, and by the

[113] *Ibid.*, p. 208.
[114] *Ibid.*, pp. 160, 192-194; Joseph Warren, *Extracts from the Reports of the Superintendents of the Freedmen*, p. 43.
[115] J. Eaton, *op. cit.*, pp. 196-197.

spring of 1865 there were in the vicinity of Vicksburg and Natchez alone no less than thirty institutions, with sixty teachers and 4,393 pupils. Dr. Joseph Warren, appointed General Superintendent of Education for the Department in February, 1865, declared that the progress made by the Negroes was gratifying and astonishing. "Their unsettled condition, want of clothing, lack of parental discipline, . . . the temptations of new-found freedom, and the contemptuous opposition of all lovers of the old regime," he said, "are difficulties that would be seriously in the way of educating any class of people. Only an enthusiastic desire for improvement could lead any people to put forth the efforts which the freed people are making to procure instruction."[116] It should be noted, however, that the number of Negroes enrolled in these schools, plus those soldiers who were receiving instruction from white and Negro colleagues in the army, made up a very small portion of the freed population. The problem of the education of the Negroes was as yet relatively untouched.

Before the end of the war, approximately half of the Negroes of Mississippi had found their way into freedom. Its discovery had brought to them many stern lessons. The very first order of the commanding general in establishing a department to control them directed that they be "set to work." Crowded into filthy camps, put to hard labor on the fortifications, used by overbearing officers as servants without pay, pushed forward as cannon fodder in the army, defrauded of their small wages on the leased plantations, and abducted or murdered by guerillas, they died by thousands in this period of transition. But they carried themselves with a new pride; to a certain extent they were able to say "Yes" or "No" to men about them; and to an even more limited extent they held the greatest of freedom's blessings, the ability to come and go as they chose. They looked toward the future with a faith that would not be denied; they sought education, and believed that through it all doors would be opened to them. Almost as a unit they preferred their new liberty, with its privations, uncertainty, and suffering, to the sluggish security of slavery. "Discouraged, panic-stricken, suspicious they were; but ready to exchange their hard-won and unhappy freedom for the sometimes easier conditions of slavery, they were not."[117]

In the deep interior sections of the state thousands of their race plodded on in the old way, and even close to or within the Federal lines many thousands of others continued to work for their old masters. It seems that by the spring of 1865 most of those in contact with the outer world had made with their owners some arrangement which gave them wages or an interest in the crop—they were no longer slaves. Even those in the deep interior enjoyed a relaxed discipline and felt the stirrings of great things going on outside their narrow world. To almost none of them did the end of the war in April come as a very great shock; the events of the conflict had

[116] *Ibid.*, p. 209.   [117] *Ibid.*, p. 207.

brought many adjustments. They were ready to join their brothers who had already entered the long, long struggle to find the meanings and the limits of this new freedom.

ADJUSTMENT TO FREEDOM WITH THE COMING OF PEACE

Many writers have found melodrama in the coming of freedom to the slaves at the close of the war. A Negro historian has written, "Like men coming from long confinement in a dark dungeon, the first rays of freedom blinded their expectant eyes. They were almost delirious with joy. . . ."[118] From the other point of view, and with less excuse, a fanciful writer declared in the Aberdeen *Sunny South:* "Freedom came to them rather like a tempest than a sunshower—rather like a curse than a blessing. The shackles fell off at the margin of the grave. . . ."[119]

Such descriptions of the experiences of the Negroes at the close of the conflict must be dismissed as largely imaginary. It has already been shown that approximately half of the slaves in Mississippi had known a form of freedom within the Federal lines or through arrangements with their owners for months or for years before April, 1865. Of this group, a few found a new joy in returning to homes from which they had fled or in welcoming relatives who had continued in bondage. To all the rest, May was just such a month as March and April had been, save that their crops were a little further advanced, and their cabins were a little less cold at night. To those who had remained in bondage, mostly in the deep interior counties, freedom came in a slow and capricious fashion. Some of them heard of it from the lips of kind masters, who coupled their news with a promise of some form of compensation. In such cases, most of the Negroes worked on just as before.[120] Some of them obtained from masters returning from the army a ratification of their freedom and an acceptance of arrangements the workers had already made for sharing in the proceeds of the crop.[121] In the interior of some of the more isolated counties, news of the turn of events was as far as possible kept from the Negroes, and they were confined to their former owner's plantation by the use of patrols made up of young men or returned soldiers.[122] In July, the Freedmen's Bureau was still issuing circulars to be read to the Negroes as notice of their freedom, and attempting to get these circulars into the hands of Negro preachers.[123] Such notices were still being run in the newspapers in August.[124] The Natchez *Courier* in May and again late in July warned planters that emancipation

[118] George W. Williams, *History of the Negro Race in America,* p. 378.
[119] Aberdeen *Sunny South,* January 18, 1866.
[120] Susan Dabney Smedes, *Memorials of a Southern Planter,* p. 228.
[121] F. A. Montgomery, *Reminiscences of a Mississippian in Peace and War,* p. 260..
[122] *Senate Executive Documents,* no. 2, 39th Congress, 1st session, pp. 15, 19; A. T. Morgan, *Yazoo,* p. 51.
[123] J. W. Garner, *Reconstruction in Mississippi,* p. 256.
[124] Jesse Thomas Wallace, *A History of the Negroes in Mississippi,* note, p. 18.

was real and that they must no longer try to make their workers believe that it did not apply to them.[125] With the news of freedom and its actuality coming to the Negroes of the state in so many ways and times in various localities, the transition from slavery was gradual and almost entirely unspectacular.

The efforts of many planters to keep their former slaves from receiving information, and to prevent them from leaving their plantations reflected a widespread feeling that the Emancipation Proclamation did not have the weight of law and could not be enforced. Governor Charles Clark, in the proclamation that marked his abortive effort to reestablish the state government early in May, declared: "Masters are still responsible as heretofore for the protection and conduct of their slaves, and they should be kept at home as heretofore."[126] The editor of a Natchez paper regretted the existence of a "very general belief" among the former slave owners of the state that slavery still had a legal existence, and that emancipation, if it came at all, would be gradual and directed by state legislation. This group planned to carry the question to the Supreme Court if necessary.[127] Both of the newspapers in Jackson carried in July editorials which held that Lincoln's proclamation was unconstitutional, and that the only question was whether the state should adopt a system of gradual emancipation.[128] Some planters who made contracts with their freedmen did so with the avowed purpose of keeping them on the place so that they might more easily take advantage of court decisions which would declare the illegality of presidential emancipation.[129] Although this attitude was prevalent enough during the summer to cause some trouble, it was almost entirely, if reluctantly, abandoned by the end of August. At that time the only remaining hope was for compensation.[130]

With the acceptance of the fact that slavery could no longer be maintained, there came to many of the planters, and to an even larger percentage of the newspaper men and politicians, the conviction that the Negro could no longer be depended upon as a laborer. Carl Schurz reported that nineteen in every twenty of the Southern men with whom he talked insisted that the freedmen could not be made to work without physical compulsion.[131] Newspapers carried letters and editorials which declared that the Negro could not be adapted to the free labor system, and that the South must look elsewhere for her workers.[132] Travelers heard the same

[125] Natchez *Tri-Weekly Courier*, May 27, July 11, 22, 1865.
[126] *Ibid.*, May 23, 1865; *Appleton's Cyclopedia*, 1865, p. 578.
[127] Natchez *Tri-Weekly Courier*, May 23, July 11, 1865.
[128] *Senate Executive Documents*, no. 2, 39th Congress, 1st session, p. 75.
[129] *Ibid.*, p. 18.
[130] Mississippi Constitutional Convention of 1865, *Journal*, p. 6 and *passim*.
[131] *Senate Executive Documents*, no. 2, 39th Congress, 1st session, p. 16.
[132] Meridian *Clarion*, November 19, 26, 30, 1865; Natchez *Tri-Weekly Democrat*, December 28, 1865; Hinds County *Gazette*, October 7, 1865; Friar's Point *Coahomian*, December 28, 1865; Jackson *Mississippian*, November 11, 1865.

opinion expressed on boats and trains and in hotels.[133]   To Edward King
a planter sadly remarked, "Not much like the old times, when they were
all working quiet-like in the fields. . . . Now it's all frolic.   I reckon
they'll starve.   What kin they do alone, Sir?"[134]

For many years this had been the heart of the Southern argument for
the preservation of the "peculiar institution."   The Negro, member of an
inferior race, unmoved by the ambition and aspiration which motivated
the whites, would not labor without compulsion, and his emancipation
could result only in the ruin of the economic system of the region.   Furthermore, the Negro was incapable of living without a master, and the race
must soon become extinct.   To many this attitude had become something
of a religious faith.   They would continue to cherish any bit of evidence
to uphold it long after it had become apparent that the Negroes were a
permanent element in the population, and that they supplied relatively
satisfactory labor at a cost so low that there was no possibility of replacing
them.[135]   It was the endowment of this attitude with the sanctity of a creed
that caused men who discussed other questions calmly and sensibly to fly
into violent anger the moment their stand on the Negro problem was
questioned.[136]

Out of this belief, and out of later social and political complications,
grew the demand that the freedmen be expelled from the country.   Although the Federal government had already found this idea impractical,
it was injected into the congressional campaign in Mississippi in the fall
of 1865.[137]   In the same year, Mississippians told Whitelaw Reid, "Now
that you've got them ruined, take the cursed scoundrels out of the country."[138]   Another native who was migrating to Texas said to Edward
King, "I hain't nothin' agin a free nigger, but I don't want him to say
a word to me. . . .   We ain't made to live together under this new style
of things.   Free niggers and me couldn't agree."[139]   The idea would not
die.   In 1873, the Vicksburg *Herald* urged that the United States seize a
large portion of Mexico, turn it over to the Negroes, and tell them to go
to it.[140]   Fourteen years later a leading citizen of Vicksburg asked that
the Blair Education Bill be defeated and that the money be used to buy

[133] Whitelaw Reid, *After the War*, pp. 397, 417; Edward King, *The Great South*,
p. 291.
[134] E. King, *op. cit.*, p. 291.
[135] Vicksburg *Daily Times*, March 5, 1869; Hinds County *Gazette*, January 3,
1872, September 8, 1880; Jackson *Clarion*, February 17, 1881; *Senate Reports*, no.
527, 44th Congress, 1st session, p. 1064; * * * to S. C. Davis, October 2, 1872,
Stephen Duncan Papers, Louisiana State University.
[136] *Senate Executive Documents*, no. 2, 39th Congress, 1st session, p. 17; A. T.
Morgan, *Yazoo*, p. 91.
[137] *Senate Executive Documents*, no. 2, 39th Congress, 1st session, p. 65, from the
Vicksburg *Journal*.
[138] W. Reid, *op. cit.*, p. 417.
[139] E. King, *op. cit.*, p. 291.
[140] Vicksburg *Herald*, May 8, 1873.

Cuba and other Caribbean islands and to transport the Negroes to them.[141] The idea was to be agitated again in Congress in 1889, and to be advocated later by many writers who sought an "easy" solution to the race problem.

In spite of much apparent public favor, the idea of colonization never gained any real strength. Most of its strongest supporters were members of the poor white group, who were largely without influence. Storekeepers and landowners knew what its effect would be upon the value of their property, and, in the words of W. L. Fleming, "Every white man would be glad to have the entire race deported—except his own laborers."[142]

The attitude of bitter hopelessness certainly was not held by all of the population, and among the planters it was voiced only by a dissatisfied, articulate minority. Most of the Northern planters, who held a large part of the rich acreage along the river and in the Yazoo section, had already worked with free Negro labor for a year or two, and were enthusiastic over their prospects.[143] The same is true of those native planters in the river section who were able to get enough capital to operate. Even in the interior, large landowners who had accepted the situation saw things going smoothly.[144] Travelers found the planters in the region along the Mississippi much more hopeful than those in Georgia and Alabama. "Few apprehensions were expressed as to the labor question, and the only want concerning which much was said was the want of capital."[145] The reason for this difference in attitude is clear. Operators throughout western and northern Mississippi had had from one to two years to see the free Negro at work, and in general were in a better position to obtain money to finance their enterprises. Those in the interior had neither of these advantages. These men, busy supervising their plantations in the summer of 1865, ran no newspapers, made no political speeches, and did not linger to carry on pessimistic tirades on the streets, at bars, and in hotel lobbies. They were planting cotton.

In the meantime, the general attitude of the Negroes was that of meekness and submissiveness which had been bred into them during generations of servitude. There seems to be no record of any single case in the state in which freedmen resorted to violence to avenge wrongs suffered under slavery.[146] In July, 1865, the editor of the Natchez *Courier* saw in the Negro a habit of absolute dependence, and an entire absence of self-reliance.[147] As late as the end of 1867, General Alvin C. Gillem, com-

[141] H. S. Fulkerson, *The Negro,* pp. 106, 118.
[142] Walter L. Fleming, "Deportation and Colonization: An Attempted Solution of the Race Problem," *Studies in Southern History and Politics,* p. 30.
[143] W. Reid, *op. cit.,* pp. 291, 571.
[144] F. A. Montgomery, *op. cit.,* p. 260; S. D. Smedes, *Memorials of a Southern Planter,* p. 228; E. J. Capell, "Diary," 1865, E. J. Capell Papers.
[145] W. Reid, *op. cit.,* p. 415.
[146] *Senate Executive Documents,* no. 2, 39th Congress, 1st session, p. 27.
[147] Natchez *Tri-Weekly Courier,* July 1, 1865.

mander in Mississippi, was to report, "One of the greatest difficulties to be overcome . . . will be the freedmen's natural feeling of timidity and fear when brought into a controversy with white men."[148] Whitelaw Reid was seriously disappointed by answers given by Negro children to a teacher who asked what they would do if anybody tried to take away their freedom: "It was fine to watch the play of surprise and apprehension across their animated faces. 'We'd fight,' exclaimed a sturdy fellow, twelve or fourteen years old. 'We wouldn't let them,' said many more. 'The soldiers would stop it,' murmured the most. That, alas! seemed still the main hope of these submissive, long-enslaved people. They had not reached —not even the oldest of them—the conception of organized effort to protect themselves. 'The soldiers would stop it.' That was all."[149]

Although the great mass of the freedmen remained at work there was enough moving about in the summer and fall of 1865 to give the impression that a large part of the population was on the march. Some of these migrants were returning to homes from which they had fled, or seeking friends and relatives who had gone on before them. Others were moving to plantations which had long borne a good reputation among the Negroes.[150]

The greater part of this early movement, however, was toward the towns. In the days of bondage, slaves had longed to see the reported glories of nearby villages,[151] and many of them now gratified their curiosity, if only for a few days. Some, finding that in the interior they received little protection from beatings and abuse, sought that protection in the towns.[152] Others had been driven from their homes by planters who were unable to finance a crop and who found the idle freedmen an impossible burden.[153] Large numbers made visits to the military posts and camps to learn from Federal officers just what their rights were to be under the new order of things; others wandered off because of restlessness, a wish to avoid work, or a mere desire to "test" their freedom.[154] A large part of those who moved into the towns were spurred by economic motives. Wages offered there greatly exceeded those paid on the plantations,[155] and this fact proved to be especially attractive to those freedmen who had been artisans or house servants during slavery.[156]

The condition of some of these wanderers was very bad. Lieutenant Colonel Brinkerhoff, from a post on the main route between Jackson and

[148] *House Executive Documents,* no. 1, 40th Congress, 2d session, p. 680.
[149] W. Reid, *op. cit.,* p. 258.
[150] S. D. Smedes, *op. cit.,* p. 228.
[151] William Howard Russell, *My Diary, North and South,* p. 146.
[152] Report of Captain J. H. Weber, Vicksburg, September 28, 1865, *Senate Executive Documents,* no. 2, 39th Congress, 1st session, p. 78.
[153] *Senate Executive Documents,* no. 2, 39th Congress, 1st session, p. 16.
[154] *Ibid.,* pp. 15, 29.
[155] J. Eaton, *Grant, Lincoln, and the Freedmen,* p. 220.
[156] *Ibid.,* p. 105.

Vicksburg, reported in July: "As a rule they are hungry, naked, foot-sore, and heartless, aliens in their native land, homeless, and friendless. They are wandering up and down the country, rapidly becoming vagabonds and thieves from both necessity and inclination." Many of them were subsisting on berries, and begging without result for food, drink, and employment.[157]

It must be pointed out again that those who moved into the towns or wandered about the countryside made up only a small part of the Negro population. This was especially true in Mississippi, where so large a part of the adjustment had taken place before the end of the war, and where there were so very few towns in which the freedmen might gather. With the exception of Natchez, Vicksburg, Columbus, Jackson, and Holly Springs, which in 1860 ranged in population from 2,987 to 6,612, the towns were mere villages.[158] The arrival of from fifty to a thousand Negroes in every black-belt town with a population of more than one hundred would have been enough to give the impression that the freedmen were moving en masse. But such a movement would have involved only the tiniest fraction of the half million Negroes in the state; and, as a matter of fact, the problem had been met and solved in many of the black-belt towns a year or two earlier under Federal occupation. Colonel Brinkerhoff, who at first glance thought that the Negroes moving into the towns were a part of a mass migration, was correct when, after further study, he concluded that "those who have done so compose comparatively a very small part of the whole, and are almost entirely composed of those belonging to plantations adjoining the towns."[159]

Altogether then, the transition to freedom came very gradually to most of the Negroes of Mississippi who had remained in slavery until the end of the war. Most of them remained on their old places, and retained the habit of obedience to their white employers.[160] Those who desired to move about and seek a better location generally restrained that desire until the end of 1865.[161]

DESTITUTION

Extensive devastation during the war, the shattering of an economic system based on slave labor, and a succession of poor crops brought poverty and suffering to many of the people of Mississippi, both white and black. The situation naturally brought misery to a larger percentage of the latter group, a race almost entirely without property.

Contemporary reports are filled with stories of general destitution

---

[157] Senate Executive Documents, no. 2, 39th Congress, 1st session, pp. 75-76.
[158] E. King, op. cit., p. 313; U. S. Census, 1860, Population, p. 271.
[159] Senate Executive Documents, no. 2, 39th Congress, 1st session, p. 76.
[160] F. A. Montgomery, op. cit., p. 264.
[161] Ibid., p. 264; Senate Executive Documents, no. 2, 39th Congress, 1st session, p. 101.

among the freedmen. The wretched living conditions of those Negroes who had recently come into the towns naturally received most of the attention. At Meridian, a new railroad town in the eastern part of the state, freedmen had crowded into some forty huts recently left by Negro soldiers. In April the squatters were ruthlessly driven out and the huts burned, on the ground that conditions in the encampment favored the spread of smallpox.[162] Others in Meridian were packed into miserable log huts near the mule yard. The *Clarion,* reporting three deaths there within two weeks, urged that if the Negroes desired to live they must go back to the farms and seek employment from white families.[163] In Vicksburg, to which the movement of the freedmen had been heaviest, they were living in cabins built of such scraps as they could find, or in the burrows in the hillsides which whites had used during Federal bombardments. According to the *Herald,* "In the catfish season these voters fatten and do well, and in the winter they draw rations from the Government and chickens from the neighboring roosts. In all seasons they are happy and contented; and an inspection of their places of abode will show more filth and less meat than any other habitations in Vicksburg."[164] At Jackson, the *Clarion* declared that filth and destitution abounded in the cabins of the freedmen to an extent that justified alarm. The Bureau had been called upon to take action, but had denied responsibility.[165]

In the fall of 1866, these wretched habitations were swept by an epidemic of cholera, which was especially fatal in Vicksburg and Natchez. In the former town there were in the two-weeks period ending September 10, 1866, one hundred eighty-four interments, of which one hundred and nine resulted from cholera. Of the dead, one hundred thirty-one were Negroes.[166] The Hinds County *Gazette* had information that a thousand Negroes had died of cholera in the immediate vicinity of Vicksburg.[167] A few months later the Jackson *Clarion* reported that in the misery of the winter season Negro funerals had become very common events.[168]

All of this seemed to give support to that section of the creed which held that the Negro race in a state of freedom must perish. In August, 1865, the Meridian *Clarion* reported that the opinion that the race was doomed was rapidly gaining ground. In an editorial in which a feeling of satisfaction could not be concealed, it declared: "A hundred years is a long time to one man; but to a nation or a race, it is but a limited period. Well, in that time the negro will be dead. Slavery is abolished now, but in a hun-

[162] Meridian *Clarion,* April 25, 1866.
[163] *Ibid.,* August 16, 1865.
[164] Vicksburg *Herald,* November 29, 1867.
[165] Natchez *Daily Courier,* September 29, 1867, quoting the Jackson *Clarion.*
[166] Natchez *Daily Courier,* September 7, 15, 18, 19, 1866; Vicksburg *Times,* September 4, 11, 1866; Jackson *Clarion,* September 5, 13, 1866.
[167] Hinds County *Gazette,* October 5, 1866.
[168] Jackson *Clarion,* December 25, 1866.

dred years the negro himself will be abolished. Nothing but the fiat of the Almighty can stay the hand of his fate. . . . Perhaps it is set down in the councils of the eternal, and the abolitionists are but the instruments to carry out his purposes. If so, the play must be played out."[169]   Dr. C. K. Marshall, the wealthiest and one of the most learned preachers of the state, agreed with this conclusion in November in a message that received wide attention.[170] During the same month a correspondent informed President Johnson that most of the freedmen and half of their women and children had left the state or were dead.[171] Early in the following year, Provisional Governor William Sharkey, one of the most intelligent of the native leaders, told the Committee on Reconstruction that half of the Negroes had perished since the close of the war, and that the rest must soon follow them.[172] The editor of the Natchez *Democrat* spoke with equal assurance: "The child is already born who will behold the last negro in the State of Mississippi. With no one to provide for the aged and the young, the sick and the helpless incompetent to provide for themselves, and brought unprepared into competition with the superior intelligence, tact, and muscle of free white labor, they must surely and speedily perish."[173]

These prophesies seemed to be substantiated by the state census of 1866, an unreliable piece of work that has been taken seriously by some excellent historians, and has been used to show the demoralization and resultant mortality among the freedmen.[174] This census showed for the period between 1860 and 1866 a decline in the Negro population of the state of more than 56,000, or more than twelve per cent of its total.[175] For some counties the loss was as much as twenty-eight per cent.[176] The inaccuracy of these figures was indicated by the Federal census of 1870, which reported an actual increase of more than 7,000 in the state's Negro population during the decade. It later became apparent that this figure itself was the result of a tremendous undercount, and probably needed to be increased by between fifty and seventy-five thousand.[177] This was revealed when the greatly improved Federal census of 1880 found the Negro population to be 650,291, as compared with 437,404 in 1860, and 444,201 in 1870.[178]

[169] Meridian *Clarion,* August 17, 1865.

[170] *Ibid.,* November 30, 1865, quoting the Jackson *Daily News.*

[171] Ross Henderson Moore, "Social and Economic Conditions in Mississippi during Reconstruction," p. 32, unpublished doctoral dissertation, Duke University, 1938. From Johnson MS, October 2, 1865.

[172] J. W. Garner, *Reconstruction in Mississippi,* p. 124.

[173] Natchez *Tri-Weekly Democrat,* January 6, 1866.

[174] J. W. Garner, *op. cit.,* p. 124; J. S. McNeily, "War and Reconstruction in Mississippi," *P.M.H.S.C.S.,* II, 266.

[175] J. W. Garner, *op. cit.,* p. 124.

[176] Natchez *Daily Courier,* September 25, 1866.

[177] U. S. *Census,* 1890, *Population,* part i, pp. xi, xii, xvi; Bureau of the Census, *Negro Population,* 1790-1915, p. 26.

[178] *Ibid.,* p. 44.

The belief in the relatively rapid extinction of the Negro was clung to by some for a number of years. The Hinds County *Gazette* reiterated it in 1868, 1871, and 1875.[179] A paper in the eastern part of the state was still holding it as "an article of faith" in 1870, and regarded the scorn of the *Mississippi Pilot* as something like a crime.[180] The conviction of the eminent Dr. C. K. Marshall was just as strong in 1880 as it had been in 1865. In widely discussed pamphlets and news articles, he declared: "In all probability New Year's Day, on the morning of the 1st of January, 1920, the colored population in the South will scarcely be counted. . . . A few old people will linger as the Cherokees do on their reservation in North Carolina, and a small number here and there who may still earn precarious bread as they pass away."[181] But this "easy" solution of the race problem was not to be. Although the Negro death rate remained very high, and in the towns was almost twice that of the whites,[182] the race was to hold its majority in the state for many years to come.

The care of the destitute Negroes and of the white refugees was taken over in the spring of 1865 by the new Bureau of Refugees, Freedmen and Abandoned Lands. Although the system of furnishing food to the destitute freedmen was attacked as an encouragement to idleness,[183] it actually had little real significance. Of the more than 400,000 Negroes in the state, only 3,262 received rations in August of 1865, and only 2,855 in September. These numbers were reduced in November to 1,787, and in December to 570. Most of those being fed were either orphan children, or old and infirm. The group also included government employees.[184] During the first nine months of 1866, a total of 155,889 rations was issued to the freedmen.[185] This, on the regular basis of one ration per day,[186] means that an average of 566 persons were receiving such relief. After the first of October of this year, rations were supplied only to Negroes in asylums and hospitals, who made up between 250 and 300 of the 566 mentioned above.[187]

The exceedingly short crop of 1867 brought stark misery to the poor

[179] Hinds County *Gazette*, February 7, 1868, January 18, 1871, May 19, 1875.

[180] Mississippi *Weekly Pilot*, June 4, 1870.

[181] C. K. Marshall, *The Exodus*, p. 4.

[182] Lee Richardson and Thomas D. Goodman, *In and About Vicksburg*, p. 116.

[183] Vicksburg *Herald*, November 29, 1867; J. W. Garner, *op. cit.*, p. 261.

[184] *House Executive Documents*, no. 11, 39th Congress, 1st session, p. 30; *Senate Executive Documents*, no. 27, 39th Congress, 1st session, p. 41.

[185] Report of Assistant Commissioner Thomas J. Wood to General O. O. Howard, *Senate Executive Documents*, no. 6, 39th Congress, 2d session, p. 96.

[186] Meridian *Clarion*, July 30, August 10, 1865. The average cost of these daily rations ranged from sixteen to twenty cents each. *House Executive Documents*, no. 1, 40th Congress, 3d session, p. 531.

[187] *Senate Executive Documents*, no. 6, 39th Congress, 2d session, pp. 94-96; P. S. Peirce, *The Freedmen's Bureau*, pp. 95-96. Some of those in the state who had opposed the issuance of rations now changed their tactics, and declared that the native whites would not accept the burden of caring for indigent Negroes. Hinds County *Gazette*, September 7, 1866.

of the state during the succeeding winter and the growing season of 1868. A writer in the New Orleans *Times* of November 15, 1867, declared that not one Negro in fifty in the hill counties of Mississippi had breadstuffs to last to Christmas, and that practically none had any meat at all. The sick were without medicine or medical care, and all were in rags. They were unable to give any further support to their schools, and their future was dark indeed. Conditions were just as bad in the overflow districts.[188]

Recognizing the desperate situation that had developed in the South, Congress in March of 1868 authorized the Bureau to supply to "any and all classes of destitute or helpless persons" enough food to prevent starvation.[189] This authorization, however, had no effect in Mississippi, where General Gillem, a stern and conservative commander, held that the issuance of relief rations would encourage "extravagance in the planters and idleness and independence on the part of the laborers."[190] As a result of this attitude, he issued during the entire miserable year from September, 1867 to September, 1868 only 59,332 rations to whites and 101,484 to Negroes.[191] This means that an average of only 278 Negroes received such relief; they were those who were confined in institutions under the care of the Bureau. During the last nine months of the period of destitution, 108 rations were issued to freedmen outside institutions;[192] in other words, one Negro received a sixteen-cent ration every two and one-half days.

Many of the planters felt that the widespread destitution among the Negroes would have some good effects. A writer from Grenada in November informed the New Orleans *Crescent* that "Negro labor will be at a discount in this section about Christmas. . . ."[193] One of the three reports on which General Gillem based his refusal to supply rations stated that all the Negroes in the river counties could obtain employment for the following year if they would accept wages amounting to one-third of those they had been receiving.[194] Inspector N. R. Williams reported that there was a combination of a great many planters to hold off in hiring laborers for the next year, with the idea that the government would compel them to work for food and clothing alone.[195] Not all of the planters held this attitude, however. Many of them joined in the appeals for aid which were sent to the commander.[196]

[188] New Orleans *Times,* November 15, 1867.
[189] P. S. Peirce, *op. cit.,* p. 97.
[190] *House Executive Documents,* no. 1, 40th Congress, 3d session, p. 524.
[191] *Ibid.,* p. 1027.   [192] *Ibid.,* p. 531.
[193] New Orleans *Crescent,* November 10, 1867.
[194] Mississippi Constitutional Convention of 1868, *Journal,* p. 226; J. S. McNeily, "From Organization to Overthrow of Mississippi's Provisional Government," *P.M.H.S.C.S.,* I, 363.
[195] Mississippi Constitutional Convention of 1868, *Journal,* p. 225; J. S. McNeily, "From Organization to Overthrow of Mississippi's Provisional Government," *P.M.H.S.C.S.,* I, 362.
[196] *House Executive Documents,* no. 1, 40th Congress, 3d session, p. 524.

In the meantime, efforts were being made to persuade state and county authorities to furnish some aid to Negro paupers. Even before General O. O. Howard's request of August, 1866, a few of the counties were giving such aid,[197] and others undertook it before it was demanded by General E. O. C. Ord in September, 1867.[198] The general custom was to supply money to some white person who would agree to care for the Negro indigent.[199] This method of care was never really adequate, however, for either race. As late as 1883, Hinds County, which contained the capital city of the state and a population of more than 65,000, was giving poor relief to only four whites and seven Negroes.[200]

[197] P. S. Peirce, *op. cit.*, p. 95; Friar's Point *Coahomian*, June 1, 1866.
[198] Hinds County *Gazette*, November 1, 1867.
[199] *Ibid.*, November 1, 1867; Ruth Watkins, "Reconstruction in Marshall County," *P.M.H.S.*, XII, 181.
[200] Hinds County *Gazette*, August 18, 1883.

CHAPTER III

ADJUSTMENTS IN AGRICULTURE

THE NEGRO AND THE LAND

As in all lands and all times when a servile agricultural class is freed, the question of endowing the freedmen with land arose in the South. The idea that a victorious North would confiscate and distribute the plantations had been expressed in the Southern press as early as the summer of 1863,[1] and warnings that this would be done were issued in the addresses of the Confederate Congress.[2] The Confiscation Act of March, 1863, which authorized the Secretary of the Treasury to seize abandoned lands in the Confederacy, seemed to substantiate this belief.

As a result of this law, the Freedmen's Bureau held in Mississippi, in 1865, about 80,000 acres of farm land and 142 town lots.[3] It is apparent that such small holdings offered no possibility for supplying farms to more than 400,000 landless Negroes. Even these small holdings, however, were soon lost. In June, 1865, in spite of the opposition of the Bureau, President Johnson ordered that all property be restored to its owners on the presentation of a pardon from him, or of a copy of the amnesty oath properly signed and authenticated. Before the end of 1865 the Bureau had restored all but 35,000 acres of the land it held in Mississippi, and by November, 1867, it no longer held any at all.[4]

The Negroes, many of whom had already shown ample ability to succeed as independent farmers,[5] turned almost instinctively to the idea that they would receive a part of the land that they had cultivated for so many generations.[6] Early in 1863, a small detachment of soldiers carried the message of freedom to the slaves on a large plantation near Jackson. In the words of James S. Allen, "The Federals went on their way but the Negroes measured off the land with a plowline, making a fair apportionment among themselves, and also divided the cotton and farm imple-

[1] James S. Allen, *Reconstruction*, p. 43, from the Clarke County (Ala.), *Journal*, quoting the Jackson *Mississippian;* J. S. Allen, *op. cit.*, p. 138.
[2] J. S. Allen, *op. cit.*, p. 33.
[3] *Senate Executive Documents*, no. 27, 39th Congress, 1st session, p. 41.
[4] *Ibid.*, p. 41; James W. Garner, *Reconstruction in Mississippi*, p. 258; Paul Skeels Peirce, *The Freedmen's Bureau*, pp. 130-131.
[5] John Eaton, *Grant, Lincoln, and the Freedmen*, pp. 157, 163, 209; Thomas W. Knox, *Camp-Fire and Cotton-Field*, p. 320; John T. Trowbridge, *The South*, p. 384; *Senate Executive Documents*, no. 27, 39th Congress, 1st session, p. 38.
[6] *Ibid.*, p. 31.

ments."[7] Their very lives were entwined with the land and its cultivation; they lived in a society where respectability was based on ownership of the soil; and to them to be free was to farm their own ground. The common stories of their persistent faith in the coming of "forty acres and a mule," and of their buying little sticks to mark their future holdings, carry more of pathos than of humor.

The origin of this legend of forty acres and a mule cannot be established. Many of the slaves must have heard during the war the declarations of their masters that the downfall of the Confederacy would mean the confiscation and distribution of their lands. The action of Sherman in making such a distribution on the Sea Islands probably helped to spread the belief. Negro troops played a part in its growth,[8] and General Grant charged that it was fostered by some agents of the Bureau.[9] The idea grew in spite of the strenuous opposition of higher officers of the Bureau, rather than on account of anything they said.[10] So strong an appeal did it have for the freedmen that any attention to it, even an absolute denial, helped to speed its growth.

At any rate, there was by the fall of 1865 a general belief among the Negroes throughout the state that they were to receive land from the government as a Christmas present.[11] At the same time, there developed on the part of the whites the idea that the freedmen, disappointed in their hopes, would rise in insurrection and slay them "from the cradle to the grave."[12] Governor Benjamin Humphreys quickly obtained the passage of an act greatly increasing the militia, and set to work disarming the Negroes. This work was accomplished in a fashion so effective and brutal as to alarm even those who had requested it.[13]

The disappointment of 1865 did not prevent the freedmen from becoming hopeful again as the Christmas of 1866 approached,[14] and they became even more confident late in 1867. Many expected the lands to be distributed after the adjournment of the Constitutional Convention which assembled in January, 1868.[15] In each case the Negroes peacefully accepted their disappointment, but continued to cling to their hope.

[7] J. S. Allen, op. cit., p. 43.
[8] Ibid., p. 55.
[9] Senate Executive Documents, no. 2, 39th Congress, 1st session, p. 107.
[10] J. S. McNeily, "War and Reconstruction in Mississippi," P.M.H.S.C.S., II, 326; Natchez Daily Courier, October 5, 1865; Natchez Tri-Weekly Democrat, November 25, 1865.
[11] Meridian Clarion, August 8, 1865, quoting the LaGrange Reporter; Natchez Daily Courier, October 5, 1865, quoting the Quitman Advertiser; Natchez Tri-Weekly Democrat, November 25, 1865.
[12] Jackson Clarion, December 20, 1865; Natchez Tri-Weekly Democrat, November 25, 1865; A. T. Morgan, Yazoo, pp. 54-67.
[13] J. W. Garner, op. cit., p. 104; Jackson Clarion, December 23, 1865.
[14] J. W. Garner, op. cit., pp. 108-109.
[15] J. S. McNeily, "From Organization to Overthrow of Mississippi's Provisional Government," P.M.H.S.C.S., I, 336, 362.

In March of 1867 Thaddeus Stevens, one of the few Republican leaders who carried radicalism beyond the realm of politics, offered to Congress a bill which provided for the assignment of forty acres of land and $50.00 to each freedman who was the head of a family. These assignments were to be obtained by the confiscation of the estates of all those in the South who held more than two hundred acres. Stevens' effort went far beyond the limits to which his colleagues were willing to go, and was doomed from the beginning. Capital was just as sacred to the Northern industrialists whom the "Radicals" represented as it was to the largest Southern planter. In the words of W. E. B. DuBois, "They did not want to set an example of confiscation before a nation victimized by monopoly. . . ."[16] The tremendous experiment of setting up almost an entire race as small farmers was not to be.

Some believed that a simple and almost immediate solution of the Negro problem might be found in opening to the freedmen the public lands which were still unclaimed in the South.[17] As a matter of fact, the act of June 21, 1866, did throw open the public lands of Mississippi to settlement by blacks and whites alike.[18] As there were more than 3,000,000 acres of such land in Mississippi, this act would seem to open some hope to the landless masses. General Thomas J. Wood was still interested in its possibilities late in 1866, although at that time he had been unable to secure maps which would show where the land was located.[19] Actually, nothing was ever accomplished. Land alone would not solve the problem of a race that was practically penniless, unable to obtain the credit necessary for the purchase of stock and equipment, and incapable of living through the first year without some assistance. To add to the difficulty in Mississippi, the public land was practically all located in the sandy shortleaf pine region, and it was not suitable for agricultural purposes. Eight years later, it was still practically untouched, and the state was trying without success to attract settlers to sections that it owned by offering them at five cents per acre.[20] This avenue toward independence was therefore closed to the Negroes.

Many of the Negroes who saw the hopelessness of waiting for distribution of land wished to purchase small tracts in the cotton belt. These met stern opposition from their white neighbors, and the white landowner who would make such arrangements brought on himself the enmity of his fellows.[21] In its first session after the end of the war, the state legis-

[16] W. E. Burghardt DuBois, *Black Reconstruction*, p. 368.
[17] J. K. H. W., "Reconstruction," *Social Science Review*, October, 1866.
[18] *House Reports*, no. 30, 40th Congress, 2d session, p. 16.
[19] *Senate Executive Documents*, no. 6, 39th Congress, 2d session, p. 96.
[20] Richard Griggs, *Guide to Mississippi*, p. 34 and *Appendix*, p. 1.
[21] Whitelaw Reid, *After the War*, p. 564; Hinds County *Gazette*, November 25, 1865.

lature wrote into law the prohibition of the sale of farm land to Negroes.[22] Although the law itself was not allowed to go into effect, it reflected the attitude of a large portion of those who had land for sale.

This attitude gradually became less and less effective. Some leaders of public opinion became convinced that it would be for the good of the state if the large plantations were broken up and the land sold to small farmers.[23]   In 1871, a convention of planters, who found that they were making little money under share-cropping arrangements, favored the sale of small parcels of land "upon the most favorable terms to the colored people that they may soon become better citizens. . . ."[24]   The editor of the Hinds County *Gazette* was angered in 1874 by the charge of a Negro paper that Southern sentiment would not allow the sale of the land to the freedmen.   He declared that in his county the Negro could buy just as many tracts of land as he could pay for at the prevailing low prices.   He later stated that only a small cash payment was needed, and that the balance might be paid over a long period.[25]

In the meantime, however, Negro enterprise in agriculture had been discouraged by the disastrous crop failures of 1866 and 1867.   In these catastrophes most of the Negroes who had set themselves up as independent operators, or who were well on the way toward that status, lost everything that they had accumulated.   Failure was also very common among the whites, but with the Negroes, who generally were operating on a very small margin, and who found credit hard to obtain, it was almost universal.[26]   The effects of such disastrous years on the small farmer explain to a large extent the hopeless attitude, and the refusal to make an effort at self-improvement, that so often characterized the tenant farmers, both white and black.   Certainly the losses of 1867 caused many a Negro to return to the status of laborer or tenant, and to make no further effort toward advancement.

Only a small portion of the Negro agricultural workers of the state ever found the way to ownership of their farm lands.   E. W. Hilgard learned from a questionnaire circulated among planters in various parts of the state in 1880 that in seventeen counties not one Negro in a hundred owned the land on which he worked.   The proportion in twelve counties was less than one in twenty, and in a number of others was less than one in fifty.[27]   Of the 87,819 Negro farm homes in Mississippi in 1890, only 10,032 or 11.4% were owned by their occupants.   About 1,500 others held

[22] Mississippi *Session Laws*, regular session, 1865, p. 82.
[23] Vicksburg *Daily Times*, November 29, 1868.
[24] Hinds County *Gazette*, February 8, 1871.
[25] *Ibid.*, May 13, August 26, 1874.
[26] U. S. Commissioner of Agriculture, *Report*, 1867, pp. 420-422.
[27] E. W. Hilgard, "Cotton Production in the State of Mississippi," U. S. *Census*, 1880, V, 154.

an equity in their places.[28]   The years from 1890 to 1910 saw a slow increase in these figures and percentages,[29] but between 1910 and 1930 there was an actual decline.[30]   The great mass of the Negroes became completely entangled in the system of share-cropping that slowly absorbed more and more of their white colleagues.

CROPPERS, WAGE-HANDS, AND RENTERS

It has been seen that the great majority of the Negroes remained on the land, and that of these very few managed to advance to the status of independent farmers.   The rest continued to grow cotton for the landlords under a multitude of local systems that tended to fall into one of three forms.   Under one of these, the Negro rented the land he worked for a definite amount in money, a certain number of bales of cotton, or a share of the crop; under the second he worked a portion of the land under the direction of the owner and received for his labor a certain fraction of the crop; under the third he received cash wages by the day, week, or month. Various combinations and modifications of these systems allowed a multitude of variations in individual arrangements.   The controversy as to their relative desirability for the landlord and the worker continued throughout the period of this study, as it does today.

The natural tendency of the Northern speculators who took over plantations in 1863 and 1864 was to follow the system of wage labor which they had known at home, and which was contemplated in the general orders concerning the leasing of the abandoned lands.   From the beginning, however, a certain share of the crop could be substituted for money payments by the agreement of the planter and his freedmen.[31]   As has been shown, some of the Negroes within the Confederate lines made such arrangements even before their freedom was completely assured.   Most of those cases in which the freedmen rented land from a private owner came after the close of the war.

In 1863, T. W. Knox found a group of planters in Vicksburg who held three plantations, and were trying a different system of compensation on each.   On the first they furnished the Negroes with food and clothing, and divided with them the year's income.   On the second they paid wages of ten dollars a month, furnished rations free, and retained half of the money due the freedmen until the end of the year.   On the third they paid daily wages of one dollar, and allowed the Negroes to buy food and rations as they saw fit.   According to Knox, both the planters and the laborers found the third system much more satisfactory than the other two.[32]   In considering this opinion allowance must be made for an evi-

[28] U. S. Bureau of the Census, *Negro Population, 1790-1915*, p. 470.
[29] *Ibid.*, p. 468.
[30] T. J. Woofter, Jr., *Landlord and Tenant on the Cotton Plantation*, p. 24.
[31] Bell Irvin Wiley, *Southern Negroes*, pp. 199, 231.
[32] T. W. Knox, *op. cit.*, p. 354.

dent tendency on the part of Northern men to prefer the system of simple cash wage payments with which they were familiar.

Experimentation and differences of opinion on the part of the land owners continued. A planter near Natchez told James T. Trowbridge in 1866 that on twenty plantations near him, ten different styles of contracts were being used.[33] In the first month of the following year, the Jackson *Clarion* reported that most planters seemed to be disappointed in the wage system, and favored giving the laborer compensation in the form of a part of the crop.[34] Here again, however, the Southern planters' general lack of cash and of familiarity with the wage system may have been the deciding factor, rather than any advantage inherent in the system itself. Four years later, a planters' convention in Jackson took the opposite view. They held farming on shares to be false in theory and ruinous in practice, and recommended a system of wages based on contracts stipulating the hours and type of work, and payable partly in supplies and the rest at the end of the season.[35]

The question was still unsettled in the seventies and eighties. A report from the Delta region in 1879 stated that the large planters simply offered the Negro the choice of rent, share-crop, or wage arrangements.[36] A similar report was made in 1882.[37] A survey of the entire state in 1880 brought dozens of conflicting opinions.[38] Five years later the Hinds County *Gazette* declared that most planters had tried all the methods under discussion, and that there was still no general agreement.[39]

Whatever the feelings of the planters might be, there can be little doubt that most of the Negroes, next to owning the land themselves, preferred to rent. This gave them a maximum of freedom for themselves and in the supervision of the land. Then too, it offered the possibility, in a good season, of large profits. In bad seasons, the freedmen, having little or no property on which the landlord might levy, could often escape part of their loss by simply moving away. Whitelaw Reid found some of them in 1866 determined to wheedle from the planter permission to handle half an acre or so for themselves.[40] Later, some Negroes tried to bring pressure through organization to raise their status to that of renters rather than of laborers or croppers. The Loyal Leagues of Hinds County considered having the freedmen pledge themselves not to work as laborers in

[33] J. T. Trowbridge, *op. cit.*, p. 391.
[34] Jackson *Clarion*, January 1, 1867.
[35] Hinds County *Gazette*, December 21, 1870, January 8, 1871.
[36] "Statement of the Planters of Washington County," May 28, 1879, *Appleton's Cyclopedia*, 1879, p. 634.
[37] Mississippi Board of Immigration and Agriculture, *Hand-Book of the State of Mississippi*, 1882, p. 29.
[38] E. W. Hilgard, *op. cit.*, V, 154.
[39] Hinds County *Gazette*, February 21, 1885.
[40] W. Reid, *op. cit.*, p. 550.

1870, and not to pay over $1.50 per acre as rent.[41] Negroes in Holmes County in an open meeting adopted such a resolution.[42] These methods, however, accomplished nothing. Democratic papers answered with absolute defiance, and even the chief Republican organ warned the Negroes that the idea was insane.[43]

In spite of the liberal statements and policies of planters in the labor-hungry Delta, the whites in most of the state were strongly opposed to the desire of the Negro to set himself up as a semi-independent tenant. This opposition grew out of the same economic and racial attitudes that were expressed in the early efforts to prevent him from purchasing farm land,[44] and the law that forbade such purchase also denied the right of the Negro to rent.[45] Citizens of Hinds County met in November, 1865, to pledge themselves not to rent land to the freedmen, or to accept them as croppers unless they came absolutely under the control of the landlord, and were fed by him. These citizens would regard anyone who did not follow their policy as "an enemy to the interests of the country."[46] This attitude on the part of the whites and the Negroes' inability to obtain cash or credit for supplies prevented any large number of the latter from gaining the status of renters.

In those cases where the Negro did succeed in making an arrangement to rent, he paid either a definite amount in money, a certain number of pounds of cotton, or a certain portion of the crop.[47] In 1880, four hundred pounds of lint cotton paid for the use of from ten to fifteen acres of land, and of the accompanying house and implements.[48] The highest rate in 1882 seems to have been about eighty pounds of lint per acre.[49]

Important differences must be pointed out between the situation in which the Negro paid a share of the crop as rent and that in which he *received* a share as a wage for his labor. Under the former system he generally had more control over the planting, harvesting, and sale of the crop. Another difference was of especial importance to the planter. When the Negro was a share-renter, the cotton belonged to him, and the rent claim was, during a large portion of the period of this study, a simple debt that took its place with other debts, such as those made at the country store. Thus the landowner might at the end of the season lose most of his rent, although his tenant had made a good crop. These factors increased the difficulties of the Negroes who desired to become renters.

[41] Hinds County *Gazette,* September 15, 1869.
[42] Mississippi *Weekly Pilot,* November 26, 1870.
[43] *Loc. cit.;* Hinds County *Gazette,* September 15, 1869.
[44] W. Reid, *op. cit.,* p. 564.
[45] Mississippi *Session Laws,* regular session, 1865, p. 82.
[46] Hinds County *Gazette,* November 25, 1865.
[47] U. S. Commissioner of Agriculture, *Report,* 1867, p. 417; *Appleton's Cyclopedia,* 1879, p. 634.
[48] E. W. Hilgard, *op. cit.,* V, 154.
[49] Mississippi Board of Immigration and Agriculture, *op. cit.,* 1882, p. 29.

The system of cash wages, favored by Northern planters but disliked by Southerners, seems to have met the early favor of the Negro, and to have spread widely over the state in 1866.[50] The general practice of the planters was to retain half the wages until the end of the season.[51] Some planters used a system of vari-colored tickets to allow the Negroes to retain a count of their earnings. These tickets in some cases might be traded in at their full value at the plantation store. Those not used in this manner might be turned in for the fifty per cent cash payment and due bills for the remainder.[52] Most planters, "little at home in the management of free labor," were reported to feel that the system encouraged mass idleness, which was contagious in the gangs of workers that the method involved. Laborers also tended to neglect the crops and, in the crucial picking season, to abandon them for better offers.[53]

For the year 1865, officials of the Freedmen's Bureau suggested to the planters a basic wage of $15 per month for full hands. The employer should also supply quarters, medical service, and rations, including flour, sugar, and molasses. The laborer was to be free on Saturday afternoons.[54] The planters, considering this schedule too generous, generally offered instead a total wage of $150, payable at the end of the year, rations of two hundred pounds of pork and fifty-two pecks of meal, and quarters.[55] For 1866, an actual contract for a first-class hand stipulated a wage of $15 per month, less deductions for time lost for any reason, and for medical care. One half of the amount due to the Negro was to be paid at the end of each three months, and the remainder at the end of the year. The employer agreed to furnish quarters, a garden spot, cloth for two suits, one pair of shoes, and simple rations of four pounds of pork and one peck of meal per week.[56] A contract between the same employer and a Negro woman was phrased in similar terms, with the exception of the fact that the monetary compensation was only $10 per month.[57] For an inferior male worker, the wage was also $10 per month, and there was no allowance for clothing. As an interesting example of comparative values, he was to receive $5 per month for the use of his horse.[58]

[50] *Senate Executive Documents,* no. 2, 39th Congress, 1st session, p. 29; U. S. Commissioner of Agriculture, *Report,* 1867, p. 416.
[51] W. Reid, *op. cit.,* pp. 526, 530-531; Jackson *Clarion,* February 16, 1866; Lemuel P. Conner, "Account Book," pp. 122, 127, Lemuel P. Conner Papers, Louisiana State University.
[52] W. Reid, *op. cit.,* p. 431; Jackson *Clarion,* February 16, 1866.
[53] U. S. Commissioner of Agriculture, *Report,* 1867, p. 416.
[54] J. T. Trowbridge, *op. cit.,* p. 366.
[55] *Loc. cit.*
[56] Contract between Jonathan Rucker and John Nelson, freedman, dated March 1, 1866, William N. Whitehurst Papers, Mississippi State Archives.
[57] Contract between Jonathan Rucker and Sarah Nelson, freedwoman, dated March 1, 1866, William N. Whitehurst Papers.
[58] Contract between Jonathan Rucker and Wash Turner, freedman, dated January 1, 1866, William N. Whitehurst Papers.

From 1869 to 1875, on the large plantation of Lemuel P. Conner, hands of various types received quarters, simple rations, and cash incomes that ranged from $70 to $300 for the year. Half of their money was retained until the end of the season.[59] The trend of the average wage during these years was upward. By 1880, however, the declining price of cotton, and, perhaps, the Negro's loss of political influence, had brought a noticeable decline in the laborers' income.[60] From 1880 to 1890, the schedule remained almost unchanged, with a range from $8 to $15 per month, depending on the quality of the worker and the location of the plantation.[61]

For workers by the day, the rate in the poorer counties was thirty cents for women and forty cents for men. In each case meals were furnished. In counties with richer land, men received fifty cents per day with meals, or seventy-five cents per day without meals.[62] During the rush of the cotton-picking season, these wages were slightly higher. In the red hills, where picking from a scanty crop was slow work, the Negroes generally insisted on being paid by the day. In the Delta, where yields were heavy, they preferred payment according to the amount picked. This payment ranged from seventy-five cents to one dollar per hundred pounds.[63]

The contracts made under the system of wage labor generally specified in detail all of the relations between the employer and the employee. That between Jonathan Rucker of Adams County and John Nelson and his wife Sarah is typical of those of the early part of the period. It provided that John and his wife were to perform all kinds of useful plantation labor for the year 1866, "and at all times to be respectful and obedient toward their employer, and toward his agent or manager on the plantation, and to all the rules needful for the good order of the plantation." Rucker was to supply them with good and comfortable quarters and a garden spot, in which they were to grow no cotton. He was also to supply cloth for one suit of summer clothing and one for winter for each of them. Each was to have a pair of shoes. John was to receive fifteen dollars per month and Sarah ten, "one half of the wages respectively [sic] to be paid them every three months, dating from their time of serv-

[59] Lemuel P. Conner, "Account Book," pp. 114-115, 120-121, 122-127, 130-131, 140-141, Lemuel P. Conner Papers.

[60] E. W. Hilgard, op. cit., V, 154.

[61] Senate Reports, no. 693, 46th Congress, 2d session, II, 518; E. W. Hilgard, op. cit., V, 154; Mississippi Board of Immigration and Agriculture, op. cit., 1882, p. 29; Mississippi Commissioner of Immigration and Agriculture, Report, 1884-1885, p. 8; Patrick Murphy, "Journal," vol. 5, account of John Warren, and "Diary," vol. 16, February 4, 1885 and June 19, 1885, Patrick Murphy Papers, Louisiana State University.

[62] E. W. Hilgard, op. cit., V, 154; P. Murphy to P. Kelledy, January 30, 1882, Patrick Murphy Papers; Hattie Magee, "Reconstruction in Lawrence and Jeff Davis Counties," P.M.H.S., XI, 196.

[63] Vicksburg Daily Times, September 26, 1869; Hinds County Gazette, October 13, 27, 1880; E. W. Hilgard, op. cit., V, 155.

ice, and the residue to be paid them at the close of the year." An account was to be kept of the time lost from work, and wages and rations for such time deducted from the amount due them. They must not steal. For every breach of this rule they were liable for damages and a fine of five dollars. Rucker might fire them at any time, with forfeiture of all wages due, for disobedience or idleness. He was to give them care and attention in case of sickness, but would deduct from their pay any expense involved in the calling of a physician.[64]

A contract made in the same county in 1885 reads as follows:

This agreement made and entered into by and between Patrick Murphy and John Warren both of Adams County Mississippi

John Warren agrees to work ten (10) months of 26 working days to a month he to do all kinds of work such as plowing hoeing chopping work &c such as is done about farming and about a house he is to work honestly the hours usually worked by such help P. Murphy to pay him 4 dollars cash per month as above and 4 dollars more the first of January 1886 to give him a room & a little spot for a garden rent free, while working for P. Murphy also for *each week* he *works* to give him 5 lbs of Pork one Peck of corn meal ½ lb of coffee and one lb of sugar the said John Warren to conduct himself honestly for if he quits before January 1886 or is detected in any stealing he is to forfit [sic] all of any wages due him as I want it plainley [sic] understood that there is to be *no stealing* or taking anything without permission John is to work the usual hours worked on a farm and to always rub, curry and feed the mules &c chop and saw wood clean up about yard stables &c to work at any and all work he may be put at P. Murphy to pay him as as above as long as he suits and dose [sic] his work.

                                              his
                              Signed   John X Warren
                                             mark
                                       Patrick Murphy

Signed this fourth day of Feb. 1885.[65]

The relations of Murphy and Warren under this contract offer an example of the possibilities for trouble that lay in the system. In the employer's "Journal" there is an account headed "John Warren (Nig)," followed by the penciled notation, "a thief." Murphy took the regulations as to the hours to be worked very seriously, watching Warren closely and deducting for all time missed. Because of bad weather, the Negro gained credit for only two and one-fourth days during the first week; Murphy figured this total to be worth seventy cents under the contract. In the first nineteen weeks, Warren was able to gain credit for only $29.76, and in the meantime took up in extra rations $31.20. His relations with Murphy became progressively worse. When Murphy heard that during his absence in town Warren was idle, he estimated the amount of time

[64] Contract of Jonathan Rucker with John and Sarah Nelson, March 1, 1866, William N. Whitehurst Papers.
[65] Patrick Murphy Papers.

lost and charged it to the Negro. Then on May 6 John's financial standing suffered a major catastrophe. Murphy's journal carries the laconic passage, "found a Peach tree Broke down either John or his wife done it I charged him as I told him I would long ago if he broke one of them $2.50." This amounted to more than John's wage for eight ten-hour days. The entries for the next thirty-five days complete the story:

May 16 I gave full of jug of sugar 3 times which I found was 1½ lbs over the 1 lb I was to give : 10 cts per lb   .45

June 13 John loafing his time while I was off in Port Gibson leaving the mule & plow in the field he up at House yet I give him credit for 5½ days   1.63

June 21 Settled up in full drove him off as he was Robbing me and others I paid his lawyer 10 dollars in full altho I need pay Nothing by our agreement as he was seen stealing

Actually, John had no ten dollars due. From Pat's diary it is evident that in his disgust he had beaten the Negro with a hoe, and as a result had had to face him in court. The ten dollars was a settlement.[66] It is probable that John's lawyer was the only man of the three who could look upon the season's work with any degree of satisfaction.

Under the conditions existing in the post-war South, such difficulties as those of Pat Murphy and John Warren were implicit in the effort to shift from slavery to free labor and wages. The low, retained wages, the tendency of the Negro to loaf in the absence of supervision, the suspicious efforts of the employer to watch his every move, the complicated attempt to translate the annual contract into terms of days and hours, the application of fines and penalties, the dependence of the worker upon the employer for food and lodging, the contract requiring the Negro to continue at work under unpleasant conditions or to forfeit any wages due him, and the reluctance of his employer to fire him in spite of the mutual unpleasantness—all of these things indicate the difficulties involved in adapting a system of wage labor to cotton culture. It is fortunate that long before the date of John Warren's contract a system more satisfactory to employer and laborer alike had been adopted generally over the state.

As has been shown, the system that came to be known as "sharecropping" was used to some extent in 1863 and 1864 under Federal control. It was, of course, no new thing, but was a method of landlord-tenant relationship used in almost every land and age since the ancient Sumerian and Egyptian empires. It seems to develop naturally wherever certain predisposing conditions exist. These conditions include such factors as the existence of a large class of landless workers, a shortage of money or ready credit, and general dependence upon a cash crop which requires a long growing season. All of these factors existed in Mississippi in the

⁶⁶ Patrick Murphy, "Journal," vol. 5; "Diary," vol. 16, June 19, 1885.

period following the war. With agricultural credit costing from twenty
to thirty per cent interest,[67] planters were reluctant to make any payment
for wages until the crop was sold. The Negroes, generally unable to rent
land or to furnish themselves in those cases where they might have rented,
came to prefer share-cropping rather than closely supervised labor for
wages. To this extent, the system was a compromise, and one which
grew out of the facts of the situation.

The disastrous short crop of 1867, following that of 1866, seems to
have been the deciding factor that made share-cropping by far the most
prevalent system in Mississippi. Many planters who had wage agreements
with their laborers simply turned over to them the entire crop. Others
sacrificed not only the crop, but also their mules and implements.[68] Such
men were determined never again to come to the end of a season with
large claims for cash wages. Of course the Negroes who in 1867 had
worked on a share-crop basis were terribly disappointed with the results,
but they were faced with no more misery than many of those who had
worked for wages and had failed to receive them.[69] In any case, however,
the Negroes at the end of this year were in no condition to bargain. From
the Federal Commander at Vicksburg came a refusal of rations, and an
order that they accept work at any terms that might be offered or be arrested for vagrancy.[70] The terms offered by the impoverished planters
generally constituted a form of cropping on shares.

So widespread was the adoption of this system in 1868 that some
writers have held that it was a new idea.[71] As a matter of fact, it was
probably more widely used than any other method in the preceding year.[72]
The disaster of 1867 merely completed the work of the short crop of 1866
in spreading the system in those counties where it had not yet become
prevalent.

The general form was subject to many local variations. In those sections of the state which were made up of rich land, the planter generally
paid the laborer one-fourth of the crop with rations, or one-third without.
This was true in the vicinity of Greenville, with the additional stipulation
that the cropper might also supply half of the feed for the stock and
receive half of the product. The same was true of the Yazoo section. In

[67] Hinds County *Gazette,* November 1, 1867; Robert Somers, *The Southern States,* p. 243.
[68] General Alvin C. Gillem, "Report," December 10, 1867, *Appleton's Cyclopedia,* 1867, p. 518.
[69] U. S. Commissioner of Agriculture, *Report,* 1867, p. 416; Hinds County *Gazette,* December 6, 1867.
[70] J. S. McNeily, "From Organization to Overthrow of Mississippi's Provisional Government," *P.M.H.S.C.S.,* I, 338.
[71] Jesse Thomas Wallace, *History of the Negroes of Mississippi,* p. 43.
[72] U. S. Commissioner of Agriculture, *Report,* 1867, p. 417; General Alvin C. Gillem, "Report," *House Executive Documents,* no. 1, 40th Congress, 2d session, p. 681.

less productive regions, the rates offered the laborer were somewhat higher. In the neighborhood of Louisville, the Negro who supplied only his labor received three-tenths of the crop; in Amite County, labor and rations were equivalent to the farm and stock; in Tippah County, the Negro who supplied labor, rations, and feed divided the crop evenly with the landlord who furnished the farm, tools, and stock.[73]   In general, the system that became most popular was that under which the Negro supplied his labor and rations, and sometimes half of the feed, and in return received half of the crop.[74]

An English writer who traveled in the state in 1875 was scornful of share-cropping as a system, and felt that it gave far too much advantage to the laborer. He learned, however, that the planters were generally satisfied with it, and defended it stoutly.[75]   Charles Nordhoff, in the same year, considered the method "admirable in every respect." He believed that it tended to make the laborer independent and self-reliant, and that the division with the planter was generally equitable.[76]   From scattering reports obtained from most of the cotton counties in 1880, E. W. Hilgard drew the conclusion that the system was unpopular with the planters in only ten. The general complaint was that in the face of a bad crop the laborer was likely to become dissatisfied and hire out as a picker. In answer to the question as to which system was better for the Negro, planters in nineteen of the counties declared in favor of share-cropping. They felt that it gave him an interest in the crop, improved his habits, and employed his entire family. In the other cotton counties, the wage system was thought to be better for the worker, since it allowed more control by the planter. Because of this, the Negro worked better, made more cotton, spent less, and had a surplus in cash at the end of the year.[77]

However the planters might feel, it is evident that among the Negroes, as they lost their lingering hopes of becoming independent farmers or renters, the cropping system rapidly gained favor. There is no evidence to indicate that any large number of the freedmen would work for wages after 1867 if they could obtain a cropping arrangement. So general was this attitude that the *Clarion* in 1879 incorrectly stated that the share system was adopted "solely to please the whims of the negro who would not be hired because he did not like the restraints of employment. . . ."[78] In the same year the state Board of Immigration announced that the method had gained the favor of the laborers,[79] and in 1880 a survey of the

[73] U. S. Commissioner of Agriculture, *Report,* 1867, p. 417.
[74] "Report of the Planters of Washington County," *Appleton's Cyclopedia,* 1879, p. 634.
[75] R. Somers, *op. cit.,* pp. 128-129, 280-281.
[76] C. Nordhoff, *op. cit.,* pp. 21, 34.   [77] E. W. Hilgard, *op. cit.,* V, 154.
[78] Jackson *Weekly Clarion,* April 16, 1879.
[79] Mississippi Board of Immigration and Agriculture, *The State of Mississippi,* p. 18.

entire state showed that the preference was general.[80]   Again in 1885 the state Commissioner of Immigration and Agriculture reported that it was a rule for the Negroes to seek an arrangement for a share of the crop, because they felt that under it they had more freedom than they could obtain while working for wages.[81]   During a mass movement of Negroes to the Delta in 1886, some of those remaining in the hills took advantage of the anxiety of their landlords to hold a meeting and demand the extension of the share system.[82]   By 1890, working for wages in agriculture had almost entirely lost favor with the Negroes, and it was difficult to hire them on any other basis than that of a share of the crop.[83]

Another major advance gained by the Negro between 1865 and 1890 was a natural outgrowth of the spread of the share system.   This was the break-up of the old slave quarters, and the establishment of the workers in small, scattered cabins, each generally located on that portion of land cultivated by its occupant.   This "segregation of quarters," highly favored by the Negroes, also gained the support of the landlords.   Having lost much of their power over the behavior of their employees, they found that the scattering of the cabins greatly reduced the vice and misconduct practiced by the freedmen when closely crowded together.[84]

Under whatever system the Negro might work, even under those in which he was supposed to furnish rations for himself and feed for the stock, his penniless condition practically always made it necessary for the planter to furnish him, and to charge the supplies, deducting their cost from the worker's share at the end of the season.[85]   In the disorganized condition that followed the war, the old lines of credit between the large planter and the New Orleans factor largely broke down, and a multitude of small stores, whose proprietors acted as middlemen between the growers and the market, sprang up all over the state.   This development was even more conspicuous in Mississippi than in other parts of the cotton region.[86] These small merchants, often operating on credit themselves, wrote enormous mark-ups onto the prices of the goods they sold to planters or Negroes for payment at the end of the season.   The mark-up in the Summit region in 1871 was 100 per cent, raising the price of meal to seventy-five cents per bushel, of fat meat to twenty-six cents per pound, and of molasses to one dollar per gallon.[87]   In 1875, the mark-up on such goods near Jackson was somewhat lower, running around fifty per cent.   In cases

[80] E. W. Hilgard, op. cit., V, 154.
[81] Mississippi Commissioner of Immigration and Agriculture, Report, 1884-1885, p. 8.
[82] Appleton's Cyclopedia, 1886, p. 572.
[83] Goodspeed Publishing Company, Biographical and Historical Memoirs of Mississippi, II, 116.
[84] Edward King, The Great South, p. 273.
[85] Loc. cit.; U. S. Commissioner of Agriculture, Report, 1867, p. 417.
[86] R. Somers, op. cit., pp. 198, 241.
[87] Ibid., p. 241.

where the planter bought the supplies on his own credit and passed them on to the Negroes, the price generally underwent another increase.[88]

Some planters whose workers furnished their own rations and supplies ran on the plantations stores that sold all or part of the goods needed. In such cases, they usually insisted that the Negroes make all of their purchases at the plantation store, or at least all those for which they did not pay cash. They felt that an offer of credit to their workers from an outside party was a blow both at their profits and at their system of control.[89]

It soon became apparent that for the Negro, unused to the possession of money or credit, the store exercised an irresistable charm. Especially attractive were canned goods, such as sardines and mackerel, and candy, rings, and pins.[90] Unscrupulous planters, merchants, and wood-yard operators quickly learned to take unfair advantage of this weakness, which was even more apparent among the women and girls than among the men.[91] The Negro was even easier game for the transient peddler, with his flashy trinkets of brass and glass, and his gaudy calicoes and muslins.[92] Venders of such attractive articles as medical books hovered about the Negro churches.[93]

It has already been shown that in many of the contracts, both for wages and for a crop arrangement, the planter agreed to supply rations as a part of the compensation of the worker. In cases where this agreement was made, the rations for each week generally consisted of from three to five pounds of pork and a peck of corn meal. In many cases either a pound of sugar or a quart of molasses was also furnished, and in a few a little coffee was added.[94] Any additional food used by the Negro was charged to his account.

In some of the contracts, the planter also agreed to furnish his workers with clothing. This supply, either in cloth or in finished form, generally amounted to two simple outfits, one for summer and one for winter. One or two pairs of shoes, or a pair of boots, were also supplied.[95]

The usual arrangement, however, was to allow the laborer to buy his own clothing, generally in the form of cloth to be made into shirts, pants, and dresses. The most popular goods for this purpose were grey, blue,

---

[88] C. Nordhoff, op. cit., p. 84.

[89] Hinds County Gazette, November 25, 1865; * * * to W. H. Noble, Natchez, March 3, 1879, Leslie Farr Papers, Louisiana State University; W. Reid, op. cit., pp. 526, 530; J. T. Trowbridge, op. cit., p. 366.

[90] R. Somers, op. cit., p. 146; W. Reid, op. cit., pp. 294, 528-529.

[91] Ibid., pp. 293-294, 532; J. T. Trowbridge, op. cit., p. 366.

[92] W. H. Hardy, "Recollections of Reconstruction in East and Southeast Mississippi," P.M.H.S., VII, 129; W. Reid, op. cit., pp. 565-566.

[93] Vicksburg Daily Herald, October 9, 1872, quoting the Charleston (Miss.) News.

[94] U. S. Commissioner of Agriculture, Report, 1867, p. 416; contracts dated January 1, 1866 and March 1, 1866, William N. Whitehurst Papers; contracts dated February 4, 1885, Patrick Murphy Papers; R. Somers, op. cit., p. 241.

[95] U. S. Commissioner of Agriculture, Report, 1867, p. 416; contracts dated March 1, 1866, William N. Whitehurst Papers.

red, and black jeans, plaid linseys, and osnaburgs, a cloth used for rough clothing and cotton sacks. In 1866 the prices on such materials at one of the large plantations of Stephen Duncan ran as follows:

> Grey jeans, 80c per yard
> Blue jeans, 80c
> Black jeans, 80c
> Red jeans, 50c
> Sheeting, 30c
> Shirting, 50c
> Osnaburgs, 40c
> Plaid linseys, 60c

These high prices were probably typical. Shoes for men, women, and children sold at the uniform price of $2.25. Individual Negroes on the Duncan place spent for clothing during the year total amounts ranging from $4.05 to $15.70. The most extravagant family, one of six adult members, spent a total of $66.25 for such supplies.[96]

[96] Stephen Duncan, "Cash and Account Book," 1866, Stephen Duncan Papers, Louisiana State University.

CHAPTER IV

THE FREEDMEN'S BUREAU

The difficulties involved in the transfer of millions of workers from a state of slavery into that of free labor became apparent to the Federal Congress in 1864. It was evident that the situation could not be handled by the Freedmen's Department, with its doubtful status and vaguely defined powers. Yet it was not until March, 1865, that the bill setting up the Bureau of Refugees, Freedmen, and Abandoned Lands could be passed. Petty political bickering and the eternal jealousies of the various governmental departments had so delayed the setting up of the Bureau that it could have little effect on the planting arrangements or the handling of the freedmen during the crucial spring and summer of 1865.[1]

On the advice of Colonel John Eaton, his able colleague, Samuel Thomas, was left as Assistant Commissioner in charge of the operations of the Bureau in Mississippi, and finally on May 30 the order definitely setting up the organization in the state was issued by General Howard. The same order directed that from its headquarters in Vicksburg the Bureau was to exert every effort to render the freedmen self-supporting and to discontinue the relief establishments as soon as possible. In all places where there was an interruption of civil law, officers of the Bureau were to adjudicate all difficulties arising between Negroes, or between Negroes and whites or Indians, with the exception of those involving men in military service. In accordance with an earlier announcement of policy by General Howard, Negroes were to be free to choose their own employers, and were to be paid for their labor. The agreements arrived at by employer and employee were to be witnessed by members of the staff, and were to be enforced on both parties. The old system of overseers was prohibited. Family rights were to be regarded, and if local statutes made no provision for marriages of the freedmen Colonel Thomas was to appoint an officer to keep records of such marriages as were performed by an ordained minister. Plans for education were to be made later in the summer.[2]

Under these orders, the offices of the Bureau issued on June 2, 1865, a series of regulations covering labor of the freedmen. The very first of

[1] John Eaton, *Grant, Lincoln, and the Freedmen*, pp. 225-228; Paul Skeels Peirce, *The Freedmen's Bureau, passim*.
[2] Bureau of Refugees, Freedmen, and Abandoned Lands, "Circular no. 5," quoted in the Friar's Point *Coahomian*, September 29, 1865. See also J. Eaton, *op. cit.*, p. 238.

this series declared that the Negroes must work. Those who would not accept jobs and abide by their contracts would be put at forced labor on the home farms without compensation. For those who would contract, a suggested wage schedule was presented, but compliance with it was not required. It was announced that there was to be freedom of contract, but in fact this freedom was limited by a number of stipulations. In all cases, food, clothing, houses, and medical attendance must be furnished in addition to the money or share of the crop allowed the laborer. Deductions might be made from wages for time lost because of illness, and for idleness both wages and rations were to be forfeited by the Negro. Such idling freedmen, having been reported to the nearest assistant superintendent, would be put at forced labor on the home farm or on public works, as would those who failed to secure some form of employment without delay. All wages would be forfeited if the Negro abandoned his contract. He was to work from daylight until dark during the summer, and nine hours a day in the winter, with Saturday afternoon and Sunday off except in times of necessity. Garden spots were to be furnished to the workers in proportion to the size of their families, and their wages were to be protected by a lien on the crops of the land they cultivated.[3]

The tone of these orders certainly shows no indication of any intention to pamper the freedmen. As a matter of fact, however, they received almost no application. Issued late in the growing season, they were to be applied by an organization that as yet had only a skeleton staff in three scattered offices. When the acting assistant commissioner at Meridian began setting up his office in June he found as his portion of the state, in the words of a pessimistic cavalry officer, "an area of about 10,000 square miles of territory, every square mile of which is in a state of fermentation and becoming every day more and more surcharged with gathering disgust and more dangerous passions. The whites hear nothing of his announcements, much less the blacks. He is the party by whom all contracts are to be registered; to him all complaints of the negroes are to be submitted, and by him all discipline is to be enforced. He is 160 miles away, and needs to exercise a positive jurisdiction over every plantation every day; to be, in fact, universal overseer."[4] Although this statement is an exaggeration, it is true that regulation of the free labor system by the Bureau was almost entirely ineffective during the growing season of 1865. This time was taken up in organization, and in an effort to distribute representatives in the interior counties. Most of the Negroes on the interior plantations went on working under such arrangements as they had been able to make with their masters earlier in the season. Thomas and his subordinates confined themselves almost entirely to proclamations that in general

[3] Meridian *Clarion*, June 21, 1865.
[4] Report of Colonel Forbes, 7th Illinois Cavalry, quoted in J. S. McNeily, "War and Reconstruction in Mississippi," *P.M.H.S.C.S.*, II, 244.

terms urged the Negroes to patience and industry and insisted that their brutal treatment by some of the whites must cease.[5]

Before its work of organization was completed, the Bureau found the system it proposed radically altered by the advance of events. In November of 1865, the state legislature passed a law providing that

. . . all contracts for labor made with freedmen, free negroes, and mulattoes, for a period longer than one month, shall be in writing, and in duplicate, attested and read to such freedman, free negro, or mulatto by a beat, city or county officer, and two disinterested white persons of the county in which the labor is to be performed, of which each party shall have one; and such contracts shall be taken and held as entire contracts, and if the laborer shall quit the service of the employer, without good cause, he shall forfeit his wages for that year up to the time of quitting.[6]

General Howard immediately declared these regulations acceptable and included them in his instructions to agents of the Bureau in the state. Because of this unusual development, the Bureau in Mississippi never exercised much authority over the contractual relations of the freedmen and the planters. The regulations of June, 1865, had obtained no general application, and from the offices of Colonel Thomas and his staff there came no further orders in this sphere.[7] Having lost much of their power to the civil authorities, agents of the Bureau acted henceforth merely as watchers to see that the contracts, as signed, were carried out by both parties.

A similar development occurred in the field of relations of freedmen with the civil courts. In his order of August 4, 1865, in which he announced the establishment of the Bureau in the state, General Henry W. Slocum declared that until the state laws were so amended as to allow Negro testimony, cases involving freedmen would be tried before subordinates of Colonel Thomas, the Assistant Commissioner. At the same time, however, he stated that this order was intended to give the freedmen no special privileges, and that officers were not to interfere in any way in their trials in courts which granted to them the rights usual to prisoners.[8] In the following month, Colonel Thomas amplified the offer to turn the Negro over to the civil courts,[9] and a few days later Provisional Governor William Sharkey accepted the offer in a proclamation in which he declared that Negro testimony could no longer be legally refused in cases where

[5] Circular no. 7, Vicksburg, July 29, 1865, quoted in Meridian *Clarion*, August 15, 1865; Circular no. 9, Vicksburg, August 4, 1865, quoted in Meridian *Clarion*, August 23, 1865.

[6] Mississippi *Session Laws*, regular session, 1865, p. 83.

[7] *Senate Executive Documents*, no. 27, 39th Congress, 1st session, p. 173; P. S. Peirce, *op. cit.*, p. 141.

[8] General Orders no. 10, Vicksburg, August 4, 1865, quoted in Meridian *Clarion*, August 9, 1865.

[9] Friar's Point *Coahomian*, September 29, 1865.

their interests were involved.[10]   Accordingly, Colonel Thomas announced on October 31, 1865, that there were no longer any Bureau courts in the state.[11]   Thus the very few instances in which Thomas' organization removed cases involving Negroes from the civil courts occurred in the summer of 1865.[12]   After October of that year, Bureau officials simply acted as observers to see that the rights of the freedmen were protected and that they were able to obtain counsel.

In spite of the fact that the Bureau in Mississippi gave up the control of contracts and closed its courts before it was even fully organized, the presence of its agents was enough to arouse strong opposition on the part of the whites.   Until the latter part of 1868, when the organization practically ceased to operate in Mississippi, the agents continued to hear complaints from the Negroes, to give them advice, to protect them from real or imaginary abuses, and to aid them in carrying their cases into the civil courts.   There can be no doubt that many of the charges brought to these agents by the Negroes were frivolous and that honest employers suffered inconvenience on this account.[13]   Charges to this effect, however, are general, and it is difficult to find any specific examples.

It is not difficult at all to find specific charges of dishonesty and inefficiency directed against minor officers of the agency.   Some developed the unpleasant habit of blackmailing employers into paying them a fee for each freedman employed.[14]   In return for a small bribe, Captain Sturgis, representative of the Bureau in Marshall County, freed a man who had whipped a Negro and advised him that the next time the freedman was impudent he should not only whip him but "wear him out."[15]   The agent in a county near Jackson went even further and whipped Negroes for their employers.[16]   This toleration of whipping was not an uncommon trait among the provost marshals.[17]   The whites in Lafayette County were almost invariably able to control their sub-commissioner,[18] and the same was true of those in Adams.[19]   The agent at Jackson, Lieutenant H. Smith, was described as a "popinjay," who, in order to gain the favor of the young ladies of the place, soundly berated the freedmen and paid little

[10] Meridian *Clarion*, October 1, 1865; *Appleton's Cyclopedia*, 1865, p. 584.
[11] General Orders no. 13, Vicksburg, October 21, 1865, quoted in Meridian *Clarion*, November 5, 1865.
[12] James W. Garner, *Reconstruction in Mississippi*, pp. 263-265.
[13] J. S. McNeily, "War and Reconstruction in Mississippi," *P.M.H.S.C.S.*, II, 328, 341; Steedman and Fullerton, "Report," *House Executive Documents*, no. 120, 39th Congress, 1st session.
[14] Meridian *Clarion*, November 8, 1865.
[15] Ruth Watkins, "Reconstruction in Newton County," *P.M.H.S.*, XII, 176.
[16] Whitelaw Reid, *After the War*, p. 419.
[17] Bell Irvin Wiley, *Southern Negroes*, p. 245; J. S. McNeily, "War and Reconstruction in Mississippi," *P.M.H.S.C.S.*, II, 328.
[18] Julia Kendel, "Reconstruction in Lafayette County," *P.M.H.S.*, XIII, 239.
[19] W. Reid, *op. cit.*, p. 515.

attention to their needs.[20] It was, of course, a natural tendency for many of the sub-commissioners to make an effort to gain the favor of the whites in the communities in which they had to live. Neither men of this type, nor those who, like Sturgis, were subject to bribery, offered much aid to the freedmen.

In general, the men who served as assistant commissioners in charge of the Bureau in Mississippi were personally pleasant to the native whites. The people had no complaints to offer in regard to Colonel Thomas,[21] and were enthusiastic over his successor, General Thomas J. Wood.[22] General Alvin C. Gillem, who followed General Wood, was as popular with the whites[23] as he was unpopular with the Negroes. One of the Negro leaders went so far as to say that his people would have preferred to have no Bureau at all rather than that administered by Gillem.[24]

In the face of the popularity of the assistant commissioners, the early abandonment of any attempt to dictate contracts or to maintain courts, and the fact that the dishonesty of subcommissioners was more often disadvantageous to the Negro than to the planter, it is difficult to explain the hatred for the Bureau expressed by so many of the whites. Yet there can be no doubt that much of the hatred was real.[25] For months a newspaper at Panola County carried at its masthead the lines:

> "Breathes there a man with soul so dead,
> Who never to himself hath said,
> G—d d—n the Freedmen's Bureau."[26]

Some have attributed much of the Bureau's unpopularity to its feeding the Negroes and thus encouraging idleness, but this activity never involved more than a minute portion of the freedmen, and was entirely insignificant after the summer of 1865.[27] There can be no doubt, however, that the charge was made at the time, and even more often in later years. J. W. Garner felt that the chief objection of the white Mississippian to the organization was that it established "a sort of espionage" over his conduct.[28] Perhaps closer to the truth is the conclusion of a more recent student of

[20] Jackson *Clarion*, March 25, 1866, quoting the Cincinnati *Commercial*.
[21] *Ibid.*, March 3, 1866, quoting the Vicksburg *Herald*.
[22] *Ibid.*, February 11, 1866; J. W. Garner, *op. cit.*, pp. 107, 267; J. S. McNeily, "From Organization to Overthrow of Mississippi's Provisional Government," *P.M.H.S.C.S.*, I, 267.
[23] *Loc. cit.*; J. S. McNeily, "War and Reconstruction in Mississippi," *P.M.H.S.C.S.*, II, 356; J. W. Garner, *op. cit.*, pp. 181, 228.
[24] Hinds County *Gazette*, January 27, 1869; *House Miscellaneous Documents*, no. 53, 40th Congress, 3d session, p. 141.
[25] Natchez *Tri-Weekly Democrat*, December 5, 1865.
[26] John W. Kyle, "Reconstruction in Panola County," *P.M.H.S.*, XIII, 49.
[27] *House Executive Documents*, no. 11, 39th Congress, 1st session, p. 30; *Senate Executive Documents*, no. 27, 39th Congress, 1st session, p. 41; *ibid.*, no. 6, 39th Congress, 2d session, p. 96.
[28] J. W. Garner, *op. cit.*, p. 267.

the reconstruction of the state: "Much of the criticism leveled at the Bureau was doubtless justified, but the fact remains that had it not been for this agency the Negro would have been at the mercy of his employers. Some of the agents were visionaries, a few were dishonest, but the real foundation of the Southerners' hatred was obviously the fact that white planters did not want any interference from anyone in handling their laborers. The planters were opposed to any organization of the Negroes, nor did they want the black man's interest looked after by the Bureau. . . ."[29] To the whites of the state, the very presence of the Bureau, like that of the Negro troops, was a constant reminder of their defeat. Its activities in behalf of the Negroes ran counter to the fundamentals of their social and economic codes. Most of them never had any direct contact with it at all, but those of their fellows who did found them ready and eager to join in its condemnation.

[29] Ross H. Moore, "Social and Economic Conditions in Mississippi during Reconstruction," p. 54, unpublished doctoral dissertation, Duke University, 1938.

CHAPTER V

THE BLACK CODE

For most of the interior plantations of Mississippi, the end of the war in the spring of 1865 came too late for any large-scale ventures in cotton planting. The loss of a cotton market for four years had naturally reduced most of them to a subsistence basis. Owners returning from the armies, largely stripped of capital, short on equipment, and confused by the whole situation, usually tried merely to continue subsistence operations for the rest of the season.[1]

The river districts, where planting under Federal control had been going on for the past two seasons, presented a different picture. In that section, the Northern speculators and those of the natives who were able to secure capital were planting heavily, while the eager bidding of dozens of new arrivals ran the cost of land up to unusual figures.[2]

As was to be expected in the midst of general confusion and uncertainty, there was in the interior much idleness on the part of both races. Colonel Charles H. Gilchrist estimated that not more than one-tenth of the whites and one-fourth of the blacks in Holmes County had any employment or business of any kind,[3] while Carl Schurz was inclined to believe that idleness was a general Southern characteristic.[4] Native whites, of course, tended to place all of their emphasis on the existence of Negroes who were not at work. Some observers were inclined toward an opposite prejudice, as that expressed by Colonel Samuel Thomas when he reported: "It is nonsense to talk so much about getting the negroes to work. . . . Who are the workmen in these fields? Who are hauling the cotton to market, driving hacks and drays in the cities, repairing streets and railroads, cutting timber, and in every place raising the hum of industry? The freedmen, not the rebel soldiery. . . . There are today as many houseless, homeless, wandering, idle white men here as there are negroes in the same condition, yet no arrangements are made for their working."[5] Thomas and his colleagues could not understand the great concern of the whites over the question as to whether the Negro would work. They were inclined to the view that if the whites had work to be done they could very well do it for themselves, or hire some of the idle of their own race.

[1] Canton *Tri-Weekly Citizen*, June 11, 1865, quoting the Jackson *Mississippian*.
[2] A. T. Morgan, *Yazoo*, p. 19; Whitelaw Reid, *After the War*, pp. 291, 414.
[3] *Senate Executive Documents*, no. 2, 39th Congress, 1st session, p. 65.
[4] *Ibid.*, p. 27.
[5] *Ibid.*, p. 82.

In this attitude they overlooked the fact that all of the businessmen and planters of the state felt that everything depended on the large-scale production of cotton, and that for such production they believed disciplined Negro labor to be essential. Also overlooked was the fact that any large group of idle freedmen would immediately constitute a serious social problem, and threaten the maintenance of order and the protection of property.

In those fields where crops had been undertaken, specific reports show that the Negroes were doing very well,[6] in spite of sweeping charges of politicians and some newspaper editors to the contrary. Almost the entire Delta region reported good crops and satisfaction with free labor.[7] For the interior of the state, of course, no conclusions could be drawn until the end of the growing season of the following year.

Among those freedmen at work a few definite changes could be noticed. There was a general tendency for them to refuse to fill the old sixteen-hour, "daylight to dark" schedule of the summer months.[8] Many of the laborers felt that in their new status as freedmen their employers should address them in a more respectful manner than custom dictated. In this matter they gained little success.[9] They had much more luck in obtaining Saturday afternoon for a trip to town.[10] This has since become an almost universal custom.

The approach of the end of the season of 1865 found both Negroes and planters in the interior still bewildered and uncertain as to what they should expect.[11] There had been enough examples of breach of contract by laborers, and of non-payment of the freedmen by poverty-stricken planters, to create mutual distrust.[12] Furthermore, it had become more and more apparent as the season progressed that thousands of the Negroes who had remained with their former masters in 1865 intended to look for new places for the next year.[13]

The evidence that many of the Negroes were dissatisfied and intended to look about for better opportunities brought increased demands for action

[6] *Ibid.*, p. 101; Franklin A. Montgomery, *Reminiscences of a Mississippian in Peace and War*, p. 264; Susan Dabney Smedes, *Memorials of a Southern Planter*, p. 228; James T. Trowbridge, *The South*, p. 366; Pleasant Hill Plantation Records, 1865, E. J. Capell Papers, Louisiana State University.

[7] Meridian *Clarion*, August 9, 1865.

[8] J. T. Trowbridge, *op. cit.*, p. 366.

[9] Report of Colonel Charles H. Gilchrist, September 17, 1865, *Senate Executive Documents*, no. 2, 39th Congress, 1st session, p. 69.

[10] Pleasant Hill Plantation Records, November 4, 1865, E. J. Capell Papers; Hinds County *Gazette*, January 3, 1872.

[11] *Ibid.*, October 7, 1865.

[12] *Senate Executive Documents*, no. 2, 39th Congress, 1st session, p. 30; *ibid.*, no. 27, 39th Congress, 1st session, pp. 83-84; J. T. Trowbridge, *op. cit.*, p. 330; Jackson *Clarion*, August 25, 1866.

[13] *Senate Executive Documents*, no. 2, 39th Congress, 1st session, pp. 30, 101; F. A. Montgomery, *op. cit.*, p. 264.

by the state legislature. Large groups of the whites who had been thoroughly subdued at the end of the war had regained courage in the face of the mild policies of presidential reconstruction. It seemed that there were to be almost no reprisals. It was more and more apparent that Andrew Johnson was a friend, and William Sharkey, his provisional governor for the state, had been a leading citizen and slaveholder before the war. The legislature which assembled in November was quite a different body from the conservative, conciliatory group that had made up the constitutional convention early in the summer. Men and newspapers now spoke out boldly, and demanded from their representatives legislation that would definitely fix the place of the Negro in the new scheme of things.

Before the end of the summer, Carl Schurz, studying conditions in the state, was convinced that a movement toward this end was under way. As he saw it, the whole matter was based on the arguments that had been used for the defense of slavery.

It is that the negro exists for the special object of raising cotton, rice and sugar *for the whites,* and that it is illegitimate for him to indulge, like other people, in the pursuit of his own happiness in his own way. Although it is admitted that he has ceased to be the property of a master, it is not admitted that he has a right to become his own master. . . .

It is, indeed, not probable that a general attempt will be made to restore slavery in its old form . . . but there are systems intermediate between slavery as it formerly existed in the south, and free labor as it exists in the north, but more nearly related to the former than to the latter, *the introduction of which will be attempted.* . . .[14]

There was much truth in Schurz' interpretation of the basic attitude involved. His error lay, of course, in regarding that attitude as something peculiar to the South. Men guided by a similar feeling had helped to drive him from his own Germany, and solid citizens in the North were soon to exhibit it in dealing with "radicals" who appeared among their own laborers.

At any rate, the demand for regulation of Negro labor spread rapidly over the state as the legislature began to assemble. The *Coahomian* declared that it was "simply ridiculous" to believe that the Negro would be influenced by the self-interest which caused the white man to labor, and called on the people to make their views known to their representatives.[15] A month later, the editor of this paper concluded that the problem fell under three main heads. Some way must be found to overcome the disorganized state of labor which made it hazardous to undertake a cotton crop ; something must be done to check the ruinous competition for workers which had driven their wages up to the "fabulous prices" of fifteen, twenty, or twenty-five dollars a month ; Negroes working at odd jobs about the

[14] *Senate Executive Documents,* no. 2, 39th Congress, 1st session, pp. 21, 32.
[15] Friar's Point *Coahomian,* September 29, 1865.

towns must be driven back into the country.[16]   The *Clarion* represented
a more conservative element of the press, which called only for a law,
applying to whites and blacks alike, to impose a heavy penalty on breach
of contracts.[17]   The Columbus *Sentinel* simply stated that it was the duty
of the legislature to "systematize" the labor of the country, and that no
man who failed in this duty should expect ever again to be honored by
the citizens of the state.[18]

Upon the assembling of the legislature in mid-October, Governor Benjamin Humphreys called to its attention the problems it must face.   Several hundred thousand Negroes, he said, had been turned loose upon society,
and the state must assume guardianship over them.   They must be allowed
to rise as high in the scale of civilization as they could, but the social and
political superiority of the white race must be maintained.   The purity
and progress of both races required that caste be preserved and intermarriage forbidden.   Then, turning to the economic side of the problem, the
Governor declared: "To work is the law of God. . . .   The cultivation of
the great staples of the South require continuous labor from January to
January.   The planter cannot venture upon their cultivation unless the
laborer is compelled to comply with his contract . . . and if he attempts
to escape he should be returned to his employer. . . .   By such a system
of labor, the welfare and happiness of the African may be secured . . .
and our homes again become the abode of plenty."[19]

A few days later, the special committee set up by the constitutional
convention to recommend changes in the laws submitted its report.   The
language of this report was tangled and vague, but its meaning was
obvious :

While some of the proposed legislation may seem rigid and stringent to the
sickly modern humanitarians, they can never disturb, retard or embarrass the
good and true, useful and faithful of either race, but only the better and absolutely necessary to secure their repose, usefulness and happiness, while the
wayward and vicious, idle and dishonest, the lawless and reckless, the wicked
and improvident, the vagabond and meddler must be smarted, governed, re-
formed and guided by higher instincts, minds and morals higher and holier than
theirs, and by laws stronger and more potent than those of mere public opinion
and sentiment, and if they rudely thrust their hands and feet in the flames of
the law, it will be a wilful and deliberate act of self punishment and trouble
that can excite no sympathy from the good and pure in heart, of any clime or
age, that should induce them to unloose the workers of evil and the instruments
of fearful destruction.[20]

[16] *Ibid.,* November 3, 1865.
[17] Jackson *Clarion,* November 26, 1865.
[18] Jackson *Daily Mississippian,* November 7, 1865, quoting the Columbus *Sentinel.*
[19] Meridian *Clarion,* October 19, 1865; see also J. S. McNeily, "From Organization to Overthrow of Mississippi's Provisional Government," *P.M.H.S.C.S.,* I, 15-16.
[20] Meridian *Clarion,* October 20, 1865.

What the committee meant was that it proposed laws which would protect the Negroes, but which at the same time would stimulate them to
"labor and honest rectitude." The legislature referred the ponderous sentences of the report to the proper committees, and then waited anxiously
for the "nigger question" to come to the floor.[21] On November 20, the
Governor, feeling that there had been too much delay, again prodded the
legislature with a message. "Under the pressure of Federal bayonets,"
he said, "urged on by the misdirected sympathies of the world . . . the
people of Mississippi have abolished the institution of slavery. . . . The
Negro is free, whether we like it or not; we must realize that fact now
and forever. To be free, however, does not make him a citizen, or entitle
him to political or social equality with the white race. But the Constitution and justice do entitle him to protection in his person and property. . . ." He then presented a program, the application of which he
believed would bring about the withdrawal of Federal troops. Negro
testimony should be admitted to the courts; the freedmen should at once
be encouraged to go to work, and the idler should be dealt with; and a
militia should be provided to protect the whites against insurrections.[22]
The legislature immediately went to work on the matter, and within a very
few days presented a series of laws that went beyond the desires of the
Governor and many of their constituents.

The first of the laws that came to be known as the "Black Code" received the approval of the Governor on November 22. It was largely a
routine law providing for the binding out of minor children as apprentices, but it applied only to the children of Negroes, and contained several
clauses which invited hostile criticism. Among these was one which apparently allowed the court to bind out, without consent, the children of
parents who were unable or unwilling to provide for them. A second
provision which attracted much attention stated that the former owner
of the minor being bound should have the preference if he were a suitable
person for the purpose. The third set up severe penalties for anyone who
should entice any Negro apprentice away from his master.[23] Altogether,
this law was not far in spirit from the usual apprentice laws of the time,
and most of the criticism it excited seems to be unjustified. It was a
tactical blunder, however, and an entirely unnecessary one, for the legislature to set up a separate law for Negro children when that providing for
whites was entirely adequate. Furthermore, it cannot be denied that
county courts, by arbitrary decisions as to the ability of freedmen to
provide for their children, might easily have delivered most of the Negro
minors into the hands of their former masters. Here, as in most laws,

---

[21] *Ibid.*, November 11, 1865.
[22] *Ibid.*, November 21, 1865; Hinds County *Gazette*, November 25, 1865.
[23] Mississippi *Session Laws*, regular session, 1865, pp. 86-90.

the important question was that of the spirit in which it would be administered.

The second of the series, an act to amend the vagrant laws of the state, received the approval of the Governor two days later. The first section of this act applied to both races, defined in detail the classes to be held as vagrants, and limited the penalty to be applied. The second section set up vagrancy regulations that applied only to Negroes, and attacked the problem of social relationships. It declared

. . . all freedmen, free negroes and mulattoes in this State, over the age of eighteen years, found on the second Monday in January, 1866, or thereafter, with no lawful employment or business, or found unlawfully assembling themselves together, either in the day or night time, and all white persons assembling themselves with freedmen, free negroes or mulattoes, or usually associating with freedmen, free negroes or mulattoes, on terms of equality, or living in adultery or fornication with a freed woman, free negro or mulatto, shall be deemed vagrants, and on conviction thereof shall be fined a sum not exceeding, in the case of a freedman, free negro or mulatto, fifty dollars, and a white man two hundred dollars, and imprisonment at the discretion of the court, the free negro not exceeding ten days, and the white man not exceeding six months.

Section three provided machinery for the enforcement of the law, and section four listed additional groups who were to be considered vagrants. Section five also made a distinction between the whites and the blacks:

. . . All fines and forfeitures collected under the provisions of this act shall be paid into the county treasury for general county purposes, and in case of any freedman, free negro or mulatto shall [sic] fail for five days after the imposition of any fine or forfeiture upon him or her for violation of any of the provisions of this act to pay the same, that it shall be, and is hereby, made the duty of the sheriff of the proper county to hire out said freedman, free negro or mulatto, to any person who will, for the shortest period of service, pay said fine and forfeiture and all costs: *Provided,* a preference shall be given to the employer, if there be one, in which case the employer shall be entitled to deduct and retain the amount so paid from the wages of such freedman, free negro or mulatto, then due or to become due; and in case said freedman, free negro or mulatto cannot hire out, he or she may be dealt with as a pauper.

Section six declared it to be the duty of the Negroes to support their own indigents, and directed the county boards to levy a capitation tax, not to exceed one dollar annually, "on each and every freedman, free negro, or mulatto, between the ages of eighteen and sixty years. . . ." This tax was to be paid into a fund to be used for the maintenance of Negro paupers. The next section made the failure to pay this tax *prima facie* evidence of vagrancy, and ordered the hiring out of the delinquent as in other vagrancy cases. Finally, the act provided that anyone convicted under its provisions after trial by the local authorities might, upon posting a bond of from twenty-five to one hundred fifty dollars, appeal to the county court. The decision of this court was to be final.[24]

[24] *Ibid.,* pp. 90-93.

This legislation immediately drew the fire of those who opposed the code. Its protagonists defended it on the ground of necessity, declaring that it was enacted by men who understood the Negro, and that its provisions were essential if the freedmen were to be put to work and the economic system of the state restored. If this were not done, ruin must come to blacks and whites alike. Even on this basis, however, it is difficult to justify some of the provisions. The freedmen were to be allowed only a very short time after the publication of the act in which they might find work, and a literal application of the phrase "or thereafter" would have prevented them from ever again quitting one job in order to seek another. Even if the need of such a strenuous act was accepted, reasons why it should not also apply to unemployed whites could hardly be found. The racial distinction made in section five, providing for the hiring out of the Negro who was unable to pay fine and costs, and preventing him from gaining the relief usually provided paupers, was also subject to attack. The imposition of a special levy on the freedmen for the care of their poor was based, of course, on the fallacious reasoning that because few of them paid any direct tax, they were not contributing to the support of the state. Even the acceptance of this reasoning would not justify the exemption of non-tax-paying whites from the levy. The stringent provision which made failure or inability to pay this tax immediate evidence of vagrancy, and subjected the delinquent to hiring out by public outcry, seems to have been something new in American legislation. Finally, the requirement of a relatively large bond for appeal from conviction under the act practically put the Negro at the mercy of the local magistrate.

In another act approved on the same day as that on vagrancy, the Negro was specifically barred from the general privilege of being released from custody after proof of inability to pay fines and costs. Unlike the whites, who might secure such release by due process under chapter sixty-one of the *Revised Code,* the freedman who was unable to pay a fine imposed under any law of the state was condemned to be hired out to the bidder who would pay his fine and costs for the shortest term of service.[25]

On November 25, the Governor placed his approval on the most comprehensive act of the series. This lengthy piece of legislation, in twelve sections, covered a variety of matters, and bore the title, "An Act to confer Civil Rights on Freedmen, and for other purposes." The first four sections bestowed upon the Negroes certain important privileges under the law. They might sue and be sued in the courts of the state, and might acquire, hold, and dispose of personal property in the same manner as the whites. They were to be allowed to intermarry with each other, and separate records were to be kept of their marriages. In civil cases where they or members of their race were party or parties, they were to be held as competent witnesses. The same was to be true in criminal cases where

[25] *Ibid.,* p. 71.

the crime was charged to have been committed by a white against one of their race.[26]

These same sections, however, established definite limits for the new privileges. The most important of these was couched in the terms, *"Provided,* That the provisions of this section shall not be so construed as to allow any freedman, free negro or mulatto to rent or lease any lands or tenements except in incorporated cities or towns, in which places the corporate authorities shall control the same."[27] This proviso has been defended on the ground that lands leased or purchased by freedmen would have constituted rallying places for the idle and disorderly of the race.[28] Actually, it is probably the hardest of the whole group to justify. It stood as a direct discouragement to the most industrious and ambitious of the Negroes, and as an almost insurmountable obstacle to those who hoped to rise from the status of common laborers.

The section which declared legally married those Negroes who had been living together as husband and wife also set the penalty for intermarriage of whites and blacks. This was to consist of a sentence to the state penitentiary for life. For the purpose of the act, anyone having one-eighth or more of Negro blood was deemed to belong to that race. Finally, in the section on Negro testimony, evidence by the *affidavit* of a freedman was banned.[29]

The granting of civil rights ceased with section five, and a series of economic limitations followed. After the second Monday in January, 1866, all Negroes must have homes and occupations, and written evidence to that effect. This evidence was to be in the form of a written contract if the term of service was for more than one month. If the freedman was engaged in irregular or job work, he must carry a license issued by local or county authorities. These licenses might be revoked for cause at any time.[30]

Section six established the form and procedure for labor contracts for terms longer than one month.[31] The next three sections set up stringent regulations to provide for the observance of contracts by the freedmen. Every civil officer must, and any person might, arrest and carry back to his employer any freedman who quit his service before the expiration of his term. The person making the arrest was to receive five dollars, plus ten cents for each mile of travel involved. The necessary amount was to be deducted from the wages of the laborer. After his return, the freedman might appeal to local or county authorities if he cared to do so. Warrants

[26] *Ibid.,* pp. 82-83.
[27] *Ibid.,* p. 82.
[28] J. S. McNeily, "From Organization to Overthrow of Mississippi's Provisional Government," *P.M.H.S.C.S.,* I, 37.
[29] Mississippi *Session Laws,* regular session, 1865, pp. 82-83.
[30] *Ibid.,* p. 83.
[31] *Ibid.,* p. 83.

for the arrest of Negroes breaking their contracts might be issued by any justice of the peace or member of the county board, and must be executed by any officer to whom they were presented in any county of the state. Any person enticing or causing any freedman to break his contract, or knowingly employing him, or giving or selling him food or clothing after such breach of contract, was made subject to a fine of twenty-five to two hundred dollars and costs, or imprisonment for two months in the county jail. If the enticement was for employment outside the state, the law provided a fine of fifty to five hundred dollars and costs, or six months in the county jail.[32]

Section ten modified the provision against Negro affidavits to the extent of allowing the freedmen to issue such documents when they were necessary to institute criminal proceedings against whites. The closing paragraph of the act provided that "the penal laws of this State, in all cases not otherwise specially provided for, shall apply and extend to all freedmen, free negroes and mulattoes."[33]

To the portion of this act which allowed Negroes to bring criminal charges against whites through affidavits, a supplement was added a few days later. This provided that if it became apparent to the court or jury that the Negro had falsely or maliciously caused the arrest of the white person, the court was to render a judgment against the freedman for all costs of the case, a fine not to exceed fifty dollars, and a term up to twenty days in the county jail. Failure to pay fine or costs was to result in the usual hiring out at public outcry.[34]

The legislature practically concluded its work on the subject of the freedmen in a comprehensive act which received approval November 29. This provided that no Negro, save those in the service of the United States government, or licensed to do so by his county board, should keep or carry firearms of any kind, or any ammunition, dirk, or bowie knife. The penalty was set at a fine of ten dollars and costs, and the forfeit of the weapon to the informer. The same act established penalties to apply to any white who sold, lent, or gave weapons or intoxicants to freedmen. Section two, an effort to cover all subjects not yet touched, provided,

That any freedman, free negro, or mulatto, committing riots, routes, affrays, trespasses, malicious mischief, cruel treatment to animals, seditious speeches, insulting gestures, language or acts, or assaults on any person, disturbance of the peace, exercising the function of a minister of the Gospel, without a license from some regularly organized church, vending spirituous or intoxicating liquors, or committing any other misdemeanor, the punishment of which is not specifically provided for by law, shall, upon conviction thereof, in the county court, be fined, not less than ten dollars, and not more than one hundred dollars, and may be imprisoned, at the discretion of the court, not exceeding thirty days.

[32] Ibid., pp. 83-85.   [33] Ibid., p. 86.
[34] Ibid., p. 194.

Finally, feeling that even this blanket coverage was not enough, the legislators took a step which practically amounted to the re-enactment of the restrictions of the old slave code, with the exception of changes in the mode of trial and punishment.

Be it further enacted, That all the penal and criminal laws now in force in this State, defining offences and describing the mode of punishment of crimes and misdemeanors committed by slaves, free negroes or mulattoes, be and the same are hereby re-enacted, and declared to be in full force and effect, against freedmen, free negroes and mulattoes, except so far as the mode and manner of trial and punishment have been changed by law.[35]

The virtues and faults of these laws, and the effects of their partial application, have been the subject of much controversy. Robert Bowman, a native of Yazoo County, declared: "The negroes under this regime were contented and industrious and most of them became diligent and faithful laborers. There was but little discord between the white men and the negroes, or between capital and labor."[36] Another observer took a different view: "In the county Yazoo, under these provisions, men and women were cheated, swindled, robbed, whipped, hunted with bloodhounds, shot, killed; nay, more, men were robbed of their wives, their children, their sweethearts; father, brothers, sons, saw their mothers, wives, sisters, seduced, betrayed, raped, and if Yazoo *law* afforded them any promise of redress, Yazoo *practice* gave them no remedy whatever."[37]

Even among the native whites, there was much disagreement. The editor of the Natchez *Courier* felt that the legislature had realized and accepted the situation, remembering that it was a white man's state it was legislating for.[38] His fellow townsman of the *Democrat*, feeling that the right to own or rent land might have been granted, would not go quite so far. He felt, however, that, so far as the law was concerned, the Negro had little cause for complaint. In the realm of personal relations there was much room for improvement, especially in view of the fact that the whites were watching a race in the process of rapid extinction.[39] On the other hand, many of the papers which had asked for some regulation of the freedmen by the legislature were shocked by its response. The conservative *Clarion*, whose correspondent as early as November 11 had described the body as "composed of a motley crew," felt that the laws were unwise and unfortunate.[40] The editor of the Columbus *Sentinel* bemoaned the fact that the legislature had been controlled by "a hard and shallow-headed majority, that were far more anxious to make capital at home than to propitiate the powers at Washington. They were as complete a set

[35] *Ibid.*, pp. 165-166.
[36] Robert Bowman, "Reconstruction in Yazoo County," *P.M.H.S.*, VII, 119.
[37] A. T. Morgan, *op. cit.*, p. 270.
[38] Natchez *Daily Courier*, December 14, 1865.
[39] Natchez *Tri-Weekly Democrat*, January 6, 1866.
[40] Jackson *Clarion*, November 11, 1865, January 7, 1866.

of political Goths as were ever turned loose to work destruction upon a State. . . ."[41] The Vicksburg *Herald* said that the legislature had failed in its duty.[42] Even the *Coahomian,* most active of the proponents of labor legislation, shifted its front after consideration of the enactments. In its issue of December 8, it offered praise. The laws were stringent, perhaps, but necessary. A week later, the editor stated that if the Negro proved his right to a relaxation of the code the legislature could allow it. By February, however, the legislators were a group of Falstaffs, who in their obstinacy had betrayed the efforts of state leaders to regain a place in the Union. They were "a set of men who seem bent on following the dictates of every blind prejudice, let the consequences be ever so ruinous to the State and the people."[43]

Altogether, the conclusion may be drawn that the Black Code was not approved by the best thought of the state.[44] The legislature, unlike the conservative majority of the convention of 1865, represented and expressed instead the feelings of the small farmers and the poor whites of the hills,[45] a group now thoroughly aroused and beginning the advance that was to give them control of the state after 1890. Substantial men of affairs, anxious to regain the good graces of the Federal government and to restore the state to its place in the Union, generally regarded these laws as largely unnecessary and extremely unfortunate. They and those newspapers under their influence did not hesitate to make their attitude clear. Although the *Clarion* was by act of the legislature the official journal of the state, it openly declared that the representatives had endeavored to restore the Negro to slavery, and that in doing so they had "attended to the prejudices of a certain class as opposed to the sentiment of the sober, sensible men of the State."[46]

The prohibition of the ownership or leasing of land by the freedmen drew immediate fire from Washington. In answer to the protest of Colonel Thomas, General Howard on November 30 sent instructions that no attention was to be paid to this section.[47] Some of the local courts added to the strength of this order by declaring that this section, like much of the rest of the hastily drawn legislation, was directly in conflict with the constitution of the state.[48] On January 30, 1866, the laws received an-

[41] Hinds County *Gazette,* December 23, 1865, quoting the Columbus *Sentinel.*
[42] Vicksburg *Herald,* December 4, 1865.
[43] Friar's Point *Coahomian,* December 1, 8, 1865, February 23, 1866.
[44] Jackson *Clarion,* December 6, 1865; Frank Johnston, "Suffrage and Reconstruction in Mississippi," *P.M.H.S.,* VI, 171; *Senate Miscellaneous Documents,* no. 45, 44th Congress, 2d session, p. 636; *Senate Reports,* no. 527, 44th Congress, 1st session, pp. 933, 936.
[45] Report of Benjamin C. Truman, *Senate Executive Documents,* no. 43, 39th Congress, 1st session, p. 8.
[46] Jackson *Clarion,* December 6, 1865.
[47] *Ibid.,* December 6, 9, 1865; Vicksburg *Herald,* December 1, 5, 1865.
[48] J. W. Garner, *op. cit.,* p. 116; Meridian *Clarion,* November 21, 1865.

other heavy blow when General Wood announced that he would apply strictly an order of the War Department which forbade the prosecution of Negroes charged with offences for which whites were not prosecuted or punished in the same manner or degree.[49]

It would seem that General Wood's order wiped out at a single stroke almost all of the legislation applying only to the freedmen. As a matter of fact, however, the disorganized condition of the state, the reluctance of the Bureau and the military officers to interfere with the civil authorities, the inefficiency of local officials of the Bureau and the army, and the practical inability of the Negro to appeal from local decisions allowed some of the laws to be applied in a number of localities.

Whatever the effect of Wood's order might be, the Negroes were still subject to those stringent sections of the vagrancy law which in theory applied to whites and blacks alike, no matter how seldom they might be applied to the former race. The mayor of Aberdeen applied the law to "hundreds" of idle freedmen, giving them a certain number of hours to select an employer for the year, or to have him choose one for them.[50] He made others sweep and scrub the sidewalks of the town. The mayor of Brandon was equally active.[51] In Natchez, the *Courier* as late as September, 1866, was demanding that something be done about the vagrants, quoting as the law to be used that section which applied only to Negroes.[52] In Vicksburg as late as March, 1868, more than sixty Negroes were arbitrarily arrested and thrown into jail on the charge of vagrancy, although only two of them were really vagrants, and although a warrant was required for the arrest of whites on this charge.[53]

In Jackson and in Hinds County the act that required freedmen without a yearly contract to secure licenses was rigidly enforced. Mayor Barrows at Jackson charged a dollar for such licenses, and the mayor at Raymond demanded a fee of five dollars. Of those living outside the towns, the county board required ten dollars as a license fee. This system was also being followed in other parts of the state.[54]

The special law for apprenticing Negro minors was also applied in some places. The probate court at Calhoun City apprenticed two hundred and twenty at one term.[55] In two cases the parents were able to carry an appeal to higher courts in 1866 and regained their children.[56] In 1868 such cases were still arising, but representatives of the Bureau were gen-

[49] General Orders, no. 5, Vicksburg, January 30, 1865, quoted in Jackson *Clarion*, February 14, 1866.
[50] Jackson *Clarion*, April 13, 1866, quoting the Aberdeen *Sunny South*.
[51] Natchez *Tri-Weekly Democrat*, August 7, 1866.
[52] Natchez *Daily Courier*, September 6, 1866.
[53] Vicksburg *Republican*, March 3, 1868.
[54] Jackson *Clarion*, March 6, 1866.
[55] Jackson *Clarion and Standard*, June 10, 1866.
[56] Natchez *Daily Courier*, March 20, 1866; Vicksburg *Herald*, March 14, 1866.

erally able to right the wrongs by aiding the Negroes in appeals to the courts.[57]

General Thomas J. Wood's order also failed to prevent enforcement of the law covering desertion by Negro apprentices or by those under contract. The Panola *Star* in May, 1866, carried an advertisement requesting the arrest of such a freedman; the advertisement included one of the little pictures so common in the days of runaway slaves. The editor of the *Clarion* was moved to say, "It is positively refreshing to look at it."[58] In November of the same year, a Negro in Natchez served a term imposed by the county court for feeding an apprentice who had run away from "a most estimable lady."[59]

General Wood reported to his superior in the fall of 1866 that these state laws were still giving a great deal of trouble, and that he was finding it impossible to gain thorough enforcement of the Civil Rights Bill.[60] In fact, a number of the local courts had already declared that bill unconstitutional.[61]

In spite of these troubles, the opposition of leading citizens to the provisions of the code was having effect. The *Clarion* pointed out the change in public opinion, declared that most of the laws were already dead letter, and asked their immediate repeal.[62] At the opening of the special session of the legislature in October, 1866, the Governor joined in this appeal. The Negroes, he declared, had shown a confiding and friendly disposition toward the whites, and a desire to engage in the pursuits of honest labor. Justice and honor now demanded the removal of those laws which discriminated against them.[63]

That section of the vagrancy act which placed a capitation tax on "every freedman, free negro, or mulatto, between the ages of eighteen and sixty years," was the first of the undesirable laws to be considered by the legislature. This law had excited much opposition because sheriffs, taking it literally, had pressed collection of the tax against Negro women and minors. An act of February 13 repealed this tax so far as it applied to minors and *freedwomen*.[64] In the poorly printed volume of the laws of this session, the latter word was written "freedmen." Overlooking the errata slip placed in the front of some of the volumes, the state auditor in July, 1867,

[57] *House Executive Documents*, no. 1, 40th Congress, 1st session, p. 1048.
[58] Jackson *Clarion*, May 9, 1866.
[59] Natchez *Daily Courier*, November 21, 1866.
[60] *Senate Executive Documents*, no. 6, 39th Congress, 2d session, p. 96.
[61] *Ibid.*, p. 2.
[62] Jackson *Clarion*, May 9, 1866.
[63] Message of Governor B. G. Humphreys, October 16, 1866, quoted in J. S. McNeily, "From Organization to Overthrow of Mississippi's Provisional Government," *P.M.H.S.C.S.*, I, 233.
[64] Mississippi *Session Laws*, special session, 1866-1867, p. 227 and errata slip, front of volume.

declared that the law had been repealed *in toto*, and ordered the sheriffs to cease making collections under it.[65]

On February 21, the Governor gave his approval to an act repealing the special law on Negro apprentices and applying to Negro orphans the same laws which covered those of white parents.[66] At the same time, he signed a general law which extended to the freedmen the right to hold real property and removed restrictions on their testimony in the courts. Finally, the fourth section of this act repealed all laws imposing discriminating punishment on the Negroes and declared that they should be subject to "the same courts and same proceedings as are the whites, and upon conviction, shall be subject to the same pains, penalties, forfeitures, and punishments."[67]

Liberally applied, this final section, like General Wood's order a year earlier, would practically have wiped out all of the laws tinged with racial discrimination. Actually, however, the situation of the Negro under the law was surrounded by capriciousness and uncertainty until after the installation of the Reconstruction government of 1870. This government quickly repealed all sections of the vagrancy act applying especially to Negroes, and replaced the entire law with one greatly simplified and clarified.[68] This act was followed by a general law on apprentices which made no distinction between the races and required the consent of the parents.[69] In June of 1870, the Reconstruction legislature swept the slate clean by repealing all of the slave code of 1857, and all of the chapters four and five of the Laws of 1865. This act closed with the declaration that it was its intention to remove from the records of the state all laws which in any manner or degree discriminated between citizens of the state on the basis of race.[70]

So passed the Black Code of 1865. It had ample precedent, if not justification, in methods applied to subjected races in almost all lands and all times, from the laws of ancient empires to those of England in Jamaica. In some of its particulars, it copied earlier laws of the Northern states and orders of the Freedmen's Bureau. Suggested by planters who felt unable to control labor that was completely free, it was carried to an extreme in Mississippi by pressure from less affluent portions of the white population. An entirely natural, and almost entirely unnecessary product of its time and of the forces at work, it complicated rather than simplified the relations of the races, and served as one of the strongest factors in driving the Negroes into the arms of the Republican party.[71]

[65] Jackson *Weekly Clarion*, July 4, 1867.
[66] Mississippi *Session Laws*, special session, 1866-1867, pp. 443-4.
[67] *Ibid.*, pp. 232-233.
[68] Mississippi *Session Laws*, regular session, 1870, p. 95; Mississippi *Revised Code*, 1871, section 2836.
[69] Mississippi *Session Laws*, regular session, 1870, pp. 374-377.
[70] *Ibid.*, p. 73.
[71] *Senate Miscellaneous Documents*, no. 45, 44th Congress, 2d session, p. 636; *Senate Reports*, no. 527, 44th Congress, 1st session, pp. 933, 936.

The death of the code did not end the efforts of the planter group to find some means of organized control of free labor. In 1865, landowners in the Natchez region held several meetings to work out rules and regulations to apply generally to workers on their plantations.[72] Similar meetings were held at various times in other parts of the state.[73] In some places these meetings resulted in the formation of more or less permanent bodies which set up regulations and attempted to bring about their general application. The committee in Jefferson County issued printed circulars for the information of the laboring population. These outlined the rules which were to be put into effect "for governing contracts, regulating labor, insuring order, and affording protection to the property of all classes and colors." To provide for the enforcement of the regulations, the announcement closed with the declaration that, "Laborers and lessees in this county, when they leave a place in debt to the employer or lessor, must, before they can find employment with others, be able to show a certificate of some satisfactory settlement, by note or otherwise, of said debt, with said employer or lessor."[74] In the face of the traditional inability of agricultural groups to cooperate effectively, and of the mobility of the propertyless laborers, it appears that such efforts as these were generally unsuccessful.[75]

The landowners naturally turned once more toward the state government to secure some legal backing in their efforts toward control. A colleague of the great planter Stephen Duncan felt in 1872 that, by a rigid enforcement of acts on theft and vagrancy, the state could quickly make from nine-tenths to ninety-nine-hundredths of the Negroes public slaves, and then lease them out to those who desired their services. He had little doubt that the hand of God would in some fashion bring this about, since He had ordained the proper relationship of the races.[76] The Reconstruction legislature, however, resolutely refused to pass such helpful laws.[77] Complaints continued that inconsiderate landowners enticed Negroes away by offering higher wages, and that dissatisfied laborers deserted their contracts in large numbers.[78] In 1879, a large planter in Hinds County cried out, "I have a good hand; my neighbor offers him a higher price, and also tells him I will cheat him out of his wages. I have had this done by the richest men in the neighborhood. Is there any Law to protect me?" The

[72] Pleasant Hill Plantation Records, June 24, 1865 and December 29, 1865, E. J. Capell Papers.
[73] Jackson Clarion, November 24, 1866, October 12, 1867; Vicksburg Times, January 8, 1868; Vicksburg Herald, December 13, 1865, December 15, 1868; Natchez Democrat, December 21, 1865; John W. Kyle, "Reconstruction in Panola County," P.M.H.S., XIII, 84.
[74] Hinds County Gazette, January 3, 1877; Fayette Standard, January 5, 1877.
[75] Ross H. Moore, "Social and Economic Conditions in Mississippi during Reconstruction," p. 60; Forest Register, August 27, 1870.
[76] * * * to S. C. Davis [?], Natchez, October 2, 1872, Stephen Duncan Papers.
[77] Mississippi Senate Journal, 1874, pp. 457, 566.
[78] Hinds County Gazette, February 8, 1871, May 7, 1878.

Gazette agreed with him that the situation was "simply scandalous."[79]   A letter to Patrick Murphy in 1882 carried a plaintive note : "What can I do. Nothing, Nothing, perfect Nothing Niggers need a master, yes they need one bad. and so does some white people, But master is played out, so is all Honour and all Honesty."[80]

The influence of labor-hungry Delta planters, who were able to offer better terms than those of the hills, probably prevented action by the legislature until 1884.   In that year a stringent act was finally passed.   It provided that any person who decoyed, enticed, or persuaded any apprentice, child, or servant to leave the service of his parent, guardian, or employer was to be fined from ten to fifty dollars.   Enticement of a laborer bound by a contract carried a heavier penalty as a misdemeanor. Any tenant or employee breaking his contract without just cause forfeited all wages or crops due or belonging to him, and became subject to a lien held by his former employer on all his wages or crops until the expiration of the term of the contract.   The act further provided that any employer who broke a contract without cause was liable to the laborer for reasonable damages.[81]

Even this law was not strong enough to satisfy some, and local justices of the peace near Vicksburg hit upon the scheme of placing heavy penalties on laborers who broke contracts by applying to them the law on receiving money or goods under false pretenses.   The editor of the Raymond *Gazette* became enthusiastic over this scheme, because it allowed the imposition of a jail sentence.   He urged its use throughout the state,[82] and applied it himself in his capacity as a local magistrate.   The Negro in this case appealed the decision, but the result is not reported.[83]   It is probable that most of those so sentenced were unable to post bond or make other arrangements to carry their cases beyond the court of the local justice.

In some cases, the appeal to law was considered too feeble an effort in dealing with those who enticed Negro laborers.   A group of planters who went from Dry Grove into Simpson County to obtain workers was fired on by infuriated whites and driven out of the county.   One man, shot at eight times, escaped with his life only by swimming the river.   According to the editor of the *Gazette,* "That neighborhood will now be safe from raids in search of hands."[84]   In Lowndes County, a Negro agent who was enrolling laborers to go with him to Arkansas was found hanging to the limb of a tree.[85]   A planter in the lower section of Hinds County accused

[79] *Ibid.,* April 2, 1879.
[80] P. Kelledy t₋ P. Murphy, Port Gibson, February 7, 1882, Patrick Murphy Papers.
[81] *Appleton's Cyclopedia,* 1884, p. 528.
[82] Raymond *Gazette,* March 26, 1887.
[83] *Ibid.,* April 16, 1887.
[84] *Ibid.,* February 5, 1887.
[85] Jackson *Clarion-Ledger,* February 28, 1889.

a neighbor of enticing one of his tenants and gave him a bad beating. He later assembled friends and repeated the attack at night. He riddled the cabins with bullets, carried two of the Negroes out and beat them, and then ordered the owner of the place to leave the county.[86]

It is evident that as late as 1890 the employer group had not succeeded in solving the problem of maintaining rigid control over their laborers. The legislature tried once more to prepare an effective law against enticement.[87] So delicate did the planters feel their position to be that in the same year they persuaded the Governor not to accept government rations and aid for Negroes driven out of the Delta by a terrible overflow of the Mississippi River.[88] The editor of the leading paper of the state felt that the Governor's action might "seem pretty rough to the darkies," but sensible men would not criticise him for it. Control of labor must not be endangered.[89] This struggle for mastership was to go on for many years, but could never be entirely successful. So long as the great mass of the Negroes were practically without worldly goods, nothing could keep them from moving off in the middle of the night, carrying a small bundle of personal effects, to seek a better opportunity or a more liberal employer. Fines and terms in the county jail held few terrors for such a group. Through their very poverty and degradation they gradually obtained a certain modicum of freedom of action.

[86] Raymond *Gazette*, March 8, 1890.
[87] Mississippi *Session Laws*, 1890, p. 69.
[88] Raymond *Gazette*, May 10, 1890.
[89] Jackson *Clarion-Ledger*, May 22, 1890.

CHAPTER VI

EFFORTS TO DISPLACE THE NEGRO LABORER

For a large portion of the white population of Mississippi, the break-down of the Black Code only strengthened an already firm conviction that new laborers in large numbers must be brought in to replace the Negroes. Outside of slavery, it was said, the freedmen would not work. Without the control and guidance of a master, they must quickly perish. Some new source of labor must be discovered for the cultivation of the staples of the South.

Within a few months after the close of the war, the idea of replacing free Negroes with Chinese coolies gained great popularity. Throughout the state there were rumors of the amazingly low wages that satisfied the Chinese, of the simplicity of their food and clothing, and of their freedom from the evil habit of impudence. Common gossip had it that they would work for four dollars a month, live on next to nothing, and clothe themselves.[1] So convincing were these rumors that a commercial agency offered to obtain and deliver coolies for a fee of fifty dollars a head, and to place them on plantations under five or seven-year contracts at from five to seven dollars a month.[2]

By 1867 some of the facts of the situation were available. Even to bring Chinese in from Cuba would involve a cost of a hundred dollars a head. Furthermore, they demanded twelve dollars for a twenty-six day month, plus rations more subsantial than those given the Negroes. Although they were used to the hoe and spade, they had no acquaintance with mules, plows, or the techniques of cotton culture. An additional discouragement was the fact that the Federal government was becoming obstinate about letting them into the country.[3]

Even these facts did not prevent the subject from being revived again and again during the period. On June 30, 1869, Vicksburg was aroused by the rumor that the steamer *Great Republic* would touch at the town the next day with 500 Chinese bound for southwest Louisiana. The *Times* saw this as the beginning of a tide that would swell until these hardy, industrious people could be numbered by the tens of thousands. There was room in the valley for 500,000 of them. The editor urged the whites to go down to see "the coming laborer," and the ungrateful Negroes to go and view the men who were destined to crowd them from the American

[1] Whitelaw Reid, *After the War*, pp. 397, 417.
[2] Meridian *Clarion*, October 21, 1865.
[3] Jackson *Weekly Clarion*, August 22, 1867.

farm.[4] As a matter of fact there was not a single coolie on the *Great Republic*.[5] This did not prevent a correspondent of the Vicksburg paper from declaring that the replacement of the Negroes by Chinese was inevitable unless the freedmen immediately saw the light. The whites should make it plain to them that if they did not join in the election of Southern men with Southern feelings to public offices, and if they did not do much better work in the fields, the coolies would be brought in to drive them to the wall and make their race forever extinct throughout the land.[6]

On the urgent suggestion of the *Times,* the Vicksburg Chamber of Commerce sent General W. R. Miles to San Francisco to investigate the possibilities of Chinese labor. Late in August the General returned to report that he had succeeded in making arrangements to bring from China some eight or ten thousand laborers for the next season. Then someone had received a letter from the Secretary of the Treasury which apparently forbade the importation of such workers under long-term contracts. This had so discouraged the shippers with whom Miles worked that they had decided to abandon the entire enterprise.[7]

In the following month, P. P. Koopmanschap and Company of San Francisco offered through the Mississippi press to supply laborers directly from China to work under a five-year contract at from eight to twelve dollars a month and found. The cost of their transportation, about $300 per head, was to be paid by the employer. Full security for payment of costs and wages must be deposited with New York bankers.[8] A week later, news came that Koopmanschap was traveling through the South to take orders. He had come to an understanding with Secretary Boutwell and planned to leave on November 4 for China. In the meantime, he had raised his estimate of wages to a schedule of from ten to fifteen dollars per month.[9]

So far as Mississippi is concerned, nothing seems to have come from the Koopmanschap enterprise. Even before the return of General Miles, many of the people of the state had lost interest, and still others had begun to oppose the idea.[10] Reasons for this are apparent. Most of the planters had already learned that the labor of free Negroes was much more satisfactory than the talk of bar-room and hotel lobby idlers, or the diatribes of some politicians and newspaper editors, would indicate. Then too, the wages asked for the Chinese were higher than those generally prevailing for the freedmen. Finally, the relatively enormous transportation costs

[4] Vicksburg *Daily Times,* June 30, July 1, 1869.
[5] *Ibid.,* "River News," July 1, 1869.
[6] *Ibid.,* July 3, 1869.
[7] *Ibid.,* July 1, August 26, 27, 1869; J. S. McNeily, "War and Reconstruction in Mississippi," *P.M.H.S.C.S.,* II, 380.
[8] Vicksburg *Daily Times,* September 26, 1869.
[9] Hinds County *Gazette,* October 6, 1869.
[10] Vicksburg *Daily Times,* August 27, 1869.

and the requirement of security for all payments made the scheme almost entirely unattractive.

During the decade of the seventies, however, the idea of importing coolies continued to receive some attention. A colleague of Stephen Duncan tried to interest some New Yorkers in the project in 1872,[11] and a few families in the Delta secured Chinese girls as house servants.[12] There was also some feeling that the mistreatment of the Chinese in California might drive them into the South, where they would be welcomed.[13]

The real revival of interest in the importation of labor from the Orient did not come until the Exodus of 1879 threatened to bring a scarcity of Negroes in the South. During the height of the anxiety over this situation the great Chinese "Six Companies" in San Francisco received letters almost daily from Mississippi planters who wished to arrange for the transportation of coolies.[14] Much additional interest was excited by a communication from a resident of California who had formerly been a planter in Hinds County. This man gave the Chinese laborers an enthusiastic recommendation, declaring that they would work for small wages, and that they also possessed the virtue of having no interest in religion, education, or politics. The New Orleans *Times* offered the further information that the Orientals could live on almost nothing, and that in the swamps and bayous they could find a perpetual feast.[15] Then the whole matter was exploded by a letter from the Chinese consul at San Francisco. He reported that there was absolutely no chance for the South to obtain Orientals from the west coast, because their wages in that region ran from two to four times those being received by the Negroes. The only hope, he thought, was for those interested to send an agent to Hong Kong, where they might enroll workers at from eight to ten dollars a month.[16]

This was the end of Mississippi's interest in Chinese labor. It soon became apparent that only the tiniest fraction of the Negroes were involved in the movement to Kansas, and with good Negro labor available at about ten dollars per month, nobody was going to spend three hundred dollars to bring from the Orient a man who had never seen a cotton plant. By 1882, the Mississippi delegation in Congress, with one exception, was voting fc ˉ Chinese exclusion.[17]

The idea of bringing in white labor from the North broke down even before Mississippi's planters had ceased to look toward China. For some months in 1865, influential papers in the North carried glowing descriptions of opportunities in the South and urged migration in that direction.[18]

[11] * * * to S. C. Davis [?], Natchez, October 2, 1872, Stephen Duncan Papers.
[12] Hinds County *Gazette,* October 10, 1877.
[13] *Ibid.,* March 10, 1879.   [14] *Ibid.,* April 16, 1879.
[15] *Ibid.,* May 21, 1879, quoting the New Orleans *Times.*
[16] Hinds County *Gazette,* June 4, 1879.
[17] Jackson *Weekly Clarion,* August 11, 1886.
[18] A. T. Morgan, *Yazoo,* p. 25.

Mississippians hoped that this movement would include men who could displace Negro artisans and mechanics.[19] As a matter of fact, however, most of those who came from the North looked only for plantations or business enterprises in which they could invest their capital. By 1867, even this movement had ceased, and many of the Northerners, ruined by crop failures and discouraged by social ostracism, had departed for their former homes.[20] Few Northern artisans chose to enter into competition with workers whose standard of living had been set under a regime of slavery. The challenge to the Negroes in this line of work, when it came, was to be borne by the native whites.

The idea of replacing the Negroes with cheap labor from Europe developed some strength even before the failure of the Black Code. Men of enterprise saw in it a possibility of profit through setting up importation agencies. The most active in Mississippi were those of W. Dix and Company at Natchez and W. Battaile at Mobile, Alabama.[21] Their advertising and the discussion of it among the whites seem to have brought anxiety to a few of the Negroes.[22] This anxiety, however, was entirely without cause. Casual examination of the advertising of these early agencies gives evidence that their directors set them up while completely ignorant of the problem which they were attacking. W. Dix, for example, offered to supply reliable laborers from Europe for a fee of $43.00 to cover costs of arrangement and transportation. The workers he imported were to receive from eight to fifteen dollars per month plus the usual quarters and simple rations of pork and meal that were supplied to the Negroes.[23] As late as 1869 a company under General A. M. West was offering to secure laborers from Sweden who were to serve for ten dollars per month.[24] There can be no wonder that these companies accomplished almost nothing.

Even in those few cases where companies or individuals managed to arrange for the importation of Europeans, the immigrants seldom completed the trip to Mississippi from the port of their arrival. "Corrupted by the influence of their fanatical countrymen of the North," they yielded to the lure of the higher wages of the East or of the cheap and open lands of the West.[25] Ideas of getting Slavs who would not be led astray by Northern Germans,[26] or of importing laborers directly through Southern ports, "untainted with the tenets of the Puritan,"[27] seem to have received practically no application.

[19] Hinds County *Gazette*, October 7, 1865.
[20] A. T. Morgan, *op. cit.*, p. 134.
[21] Meridian *Clarion*, October 21, 1865; Natchez *Weekly Democrat*, November 18, 1865, January 4, 1866.
[22] Jackson *Clarion*, December 22, 1865.
[23] Natchez *Weekly Democrat*, January 4, 1866.
[24] Hinds County *Gazette*, December 22, 1869.
[25] Jackson *Clarion*, February 24, 1866; Hinds County *Gazette*, March 16, 1866.
[26] Jackson *Clarion*, February 24, 1866.
[27] Hinds County *Gazette*, March 16, 23, 1866; Jackson *Clarion*, March 9, 1866.

In spite of the various obstacles, the state did succeed in attracting a few European laborers of various types. The region around Natchez received a small party of Germans and Norwegians in 1866.[28] A farmer near Aberdeen secured four Englishmen,[29] and one from Terry went to New York and brought back about thirty Swiss.[30] Another near Jackson found his four Swedes "good workers, polite, and easily managed."[31] The Panola Immigration Society succeeded in obtaining about thirty-five white laborers through an agent they sent to Chicago.[32] Small numbers of Swedes, Germans, Scotch or Italians came into Lafayette, Marshall, Monroe, De Soto, Yalobusha, Oktibbeha, Jefferson, Madison, and Lauderdale counties.[33]

Altogether, however, the matter was hopeless, and this should have been apparent from the beginning. The very first group of immigrant laborers of any importance, disgusted with the conditions of their work, the low wages, and the poor food, absolutely refused to carry out their contract. As a result, they were jailed on a charge of vagrancy, to be held until called for by their employer.[34] This incident, with desertions on a larger scale in Louisiana, attracted much attention in the press. Some few papers, like the *Clarion,* held that the immigrants were justified in their attitude.[35] The *Gazette* probably represented the feelings of the majority in declaring that all that was needed was a stringent law for the punishment of desertion.[36]

Discontent and almost immediate departure on the part of the white immigrants seem to have been the general result all over the state.[37] The slave quarters, long hours of work under a hot sun on a strange crop, rations of pork and meal, and low, retained wages quickly convinced these immigrants that the Negro supplied a kind of competition that they did not care to meet.

[28] Natchez *Tri-Weekly Democrat,* February 6, 1866.
[29] Hinds County *Gazette,* April 21, 1875, from the Aberdeen *Examiner.*
[30] Hinds County *Gazette,* December 8, 1869; *ibid.,* December 22, 1869, from the New York *Daily Star,* December 1, 1869.
[31] Hinds County *Gazette,* February 18, August 18, 1880.
[32] John W. Kyle, "Reconstruction in Panola County," *P.M.H.S.,* XIII, 85.
[33] Natchez *Weekly Democrat,* March 10, 1870; Julia Kendel, "Reconstruction in Lafayette County," *P.M.H.S.,* XIII, 254; Ruth Watkins, "Reconstruction in Marshall County," *P.M.H.S.,* XII, 203; E. F. Puckett, "Reconstruction in Monroe County," *P.M.H.S.,* XI, 140; Irby C. Nichols, "Reconstruction in De Soto County," *P.M.H.S.,* XI, 312; Hinds County *Gazette,* June 5, 1872; Jackson *Clarion,* September 4, 1869.
[34] Natchez *Tri-Weekly Democrat,* February 6, 1866; Jackson *Clarion,* March 9, 1866.
[35] Jackson *Clarion,* March 9, 1866.
[36] Hinds County *Gazette,* March 16, 1866.
[37] Ruth Watkins, *op. cit.,* p. 203; E. F. Puckett, *op. cit.,* p. 140; John W. Kyle, *op. cit.,* p. 85; Julia Kendel, *op. cit.,* p. 254; Edward King, *The Great South,* p. 792; George W. Cable, *The Southern Struggle for Pure Government,* p. 17; Vicksburg *Daily Times,* April 10, 1869; Hinds County *Gazette,* December 25, 1878; Jackson *Weekly Clarion,* February 17, 1881.

Stirred to envy by the sweep of immigrants to the West, the editor of the *Gazette* mourned:

Oh, how we need, here in Hinds county, some good honest old-fashioned laborers—men who would go out and come in with the sun, faithfully from Monday morning until Saturday night! Oh, how we need hundreds and thousands of men who would ignore politics and turn right into systematic labor. . . . Oh, that a few thousands might be turned hither.[38]

It was left to the Republican organ of the state to point out the fact that this very feeling that the laborers should have nothing to do with public affairs served as a potent force to turn immigration from the region.[39]

In spite of the general failure of almost every one of the projects, writers in the newspapers continued to be hopeful for several years. The arrival of a small group of Europeans in any part of the state attracted immediate attention and brought prophecies that the tide would now flow.[40] Individuals went off to Europe confidently offering to send back at low wages any number of workers that might be desired.[41] Public meetings were held, and immigration societies were formed in many of the counties.[42] Railroads offered special rates for immigrants in groups or four or more.[43] Some of the projects verged on the fantastic. One of these involved bringing over English female orphans to serve as house servants. It was said that a hundred thousand of these were available in the streets of the English cities.[44]

The county immigration societies achieved almost nothing at all, and were generally short-lived. Agents who went to Europe met with immediate disappointment. The experience of Major George Torrey of Fayette was typical. Leaving Mississippi in the fall of 1872, he announced through the newspapers that he would secure white laborers from England and Scotland at extremely low costs.[45] In December, he reported that the matter was much more difficult than he had expected to find it. He had sent out his circulars and was offering $150 a year for men and $100 for women. He had been able to interest only a few large families, and found none willing to enter a share-cropping arrangement.[46] Undaunted by this failure, he again took up the effort in 1874 as agent in England for the

[38] Hinds County *Gazette*, April 21, 1875.
[39] Mississippi *Weekly Pilot*, May 1, 1875.
[40] Jackson *Clarion*, September 4, 1869; Hinds County *Gazette*, February 23, 1870, June 5, July 10, 1872, June 4, 1879; Natchez *Weekly Democrat*, March 10, 1870.
[41] Hinds County *Gazette*, December 22, 1869, June 5, July 10, 24, 1872; Jackson *Clarion*, September 4, 1869.
[42] Natchez *Weekly Democrat*, March 10, 1870; Hinds County *Gazette*, March 23, 1866, June 5, 1872, April 29, 1874, July 27, 1881; Raymond *Gazette*, March 16, 1889; Irby C. Nichols, *op. cit.*, XI, 312.
[43] Hinds County *Gazette*, February 23, 1870.
[44] *Ibid.*, December 22, 1869.
[45] *Ibid.*, June 5, July 24, 1872.
[46] *Ibid.*, December 18, 1872.

Grangers of Mississippi. Carrying orders for a large number of laborers, he advertised in all parts of the United Kingdom. By January of the following year, he had to report that it was impossible to secure immigrants of a suitable character. He had been unable to fill his orders of the year before, and warned that it was useless to send him further requests for house-servants. Those in England demanded such wages as the South could not possibly pay.[47]

Greatest interest, however, centered in the possibilities of the state bureau of immigration. This department, although provided for by the Constitution of 1868, and demanded again and again in newspaper editorials, was not established until April, 1873. It was then put under the management of Richard Griggs, a Negro of Issaquena County. The *Gazette* declared that this was a death blow aimed at the state, cutting off the only hope to save it from ruin.[48] As a matter of fact, the bureau under Griggs did efficient work in bringing in Negro labor from the Southeast[49] but, however satisfactory this may have been to the planters of the Delta, it did not please the politicians and the editors. As a measure of economy and a blow at the Negro director, the Democratic legislature of 1876 reduced the salary of the office to $100 per year and allowed no appropriation for any other expenses.[50] Renewed hope in the possibilities of the agency led to the restoration of a respectable appropriation for a white incumbent in 1878.[51] Its complete failure to obtain any demonstrable results, plus the rise of a poor white class who were as much opposed to foreigners as they were to Negroes, led to the practical abolition of the bureau in 1886. The salary of the commissioner was reduced to ten dollars a year, the offices of the deputy commissioner and the assistant commissioner were abolished, unexpended funds were recaptured, and the distribution at the expense of the state of literature on hand was forbidden.[52] The whole troublesome business was omitted in the Constitution of 1890. Unsatisfactory as Negro labor might seem, Mississippi had discovered that it was definitely superior to any she might obtain in its place at similar cost. Appeals for the introduction of the more expensive and independent white labor as a patriotic duty seem to have had little effect.[53]

The failure of schemes for the introduction of white labor, and the desertion of the hills by the Negroes, shifted much of the interest of the latter part of the period to the possibility of selling small plots of land to

[47] *Ibid.*, February 10, 1875.
[48] *Ibid.*, April 30, 1873.
[49] Mississippi *Weekly Pilot*, January 16, 1875; Hinds County *Gazette*, May 20, 1881.
[50] Mississippi *Session Laws*, 1876, pp. 26-27.
[51] *Ibid.*, 1878, pp. 125-129.
[52] *Ibid.*, 1886, pp. 89-90.
[53] Hinds County *Gazette*, March 6, 1886, February 15, 1867, March 3, 1875, September 8, 1880.

white immigrants. Although there was some interest in this idea very soon after the war,[54] those who wished to preserve the plantation system offered strong opposition. With the mass movement of Negroes to the rich new fields of the Delta, and a similar movement of whites to places vacated by freedmen and to the towns, the problem became very serious. From the poor land of Winston County there came the cry: "There is not more than 15 or 20 per cent of our land in cultivation, and we would gladly welcome all industrious classes of WHITE PEOPLE. . . . I say white, because this is a white man's country; the people here are white, and though poor, quite proud—proud too, of the fact that they are all of the same color."[55] If not quite so proud, the planters in the central part of the state soon were equally anxious to find purchasers for land deserted by Negro emigrants, and they filled their newspapers with demands for action.[56] So strong was this need that politicians and editors even cried out against the treasured prerogatives of carrying pistols and exacting personal vengeance, declaring that these were the strongest forces which kept prospective purchasers of lands from the state.[57]

In answer to the cry for white buyers and tenants to fill the places left by migrating Negroes, many small white farmers came down from the hills. Forsaking their long struggle with the thin red soil, they quickly took portions of the deserted plantations.[58] In return for some slight betterment in their economic condition, they surrendered their treasured independence and became the first large portion of a white tenant population that has grown with constantly increasing rapidity. In smaller numbers, there also came groups from the Middle West. These people, better endowed with skills, health, and capital, set up on deserted cotton land the generally prosperous trucking section which now centers around Hazelhurst and Crystal Springs.[59]

The demand for the importation of white labor, then, grew out of a number of factors present at the end of the war. The belief that the Negro would not work in freedom, a conviction that the race was soon to die out, fear of Negro political domination, the actual decrease in the availability of Negro labor, the movement of the freedmen to the Delta, and a desire to prevent the economic improvement of the former slaves all played a part. Those interested in the movement overlooked a number of

[54] Jackson *Clarion*, November 30, 1865, March 9, 1866.
[55] Mississippi Board of Immigration and Agriculture, *The State of Mississippi*, p. 150.
[56] Hinds County *Gazette*, September 26, 1867, September 22, 1869, May 13, 1874, January 26, 1876, February 14, 1877, February 26, 1887; Jackson *Clarion*, April 7, 1881, and many other issues for this year.
[57] Mississippi *Weekly Pilot*, May 28, 1870; Raymond *Gazette*, May 19, 1888; Jackson *Clarion-Ledger*, June 7, 1888.
[58] Hinds County *Gazette*, February 17, 24, March 17, December 15, 29, 1875, February 6, 1878; Robert Somers, *The Southern States*, pp. 142-143.
[59] Hinds County *Gazette*, January 9, 1877.

factors which made it hopeless from the beginning. The South, a relatively poor region even before the war, emerged from that struggle economically disorganized and unable to compete with the industrial and agricultural expansion going on in the North and West.   Southern planters, accustomed to slave labor and caught almost entirely without capital, would not and could not offer to immigrants conditions of life and work which they were willing to accept.   It became apparent almost immediately that, in spite of his newly acquired ability to move about, the Negro remained a very cheap and relatively docile laborer.   Finally, after the freedmen were shorn of political power, the great mass of the native whites found that they liked Negroes much better than they did "foreigners."   This was still true in 1939.[60]

[60] Hortense Powdermaker, *After Freedom,* p. 383.

CHAPTER VII

NEGRO MIGRATION

The chief advantage that freedom brought to the Negro was the ability to move about, and thus to establish among the employer class a certain amount of competition for his labor. Overlooking the fairly constant movement from plantation to plantation in the immediate vicinity, there were in Mississippi during this period four types of migration which involved large numbers of the freedmen. These included a drift to the towns and villages, a large-scale influx from other states of the Southeast, a steady movement from the poorer cotton lands to the rich new sections of the Delta, and the short-lived "exodus" to Kansas.

It has already been seen that at the close of the war enough Negroes came into the small cities and towns of the state to give alarmists the impression that the greater portion of the population had deserted the fields. Within a few months many of these early adventurers or visitors returned to the countryside and agriculture, but some remained to form a steadily growing group of urban workers. From the scanty and faulty information furnished by the Census Bureau for 1860 and 1870 it is possible to gain some evidence of the volume of this movement.[1]

Towns with increasing Negro population	Negroes 1860	Negroes 1870
Vicksburg	1,433	6,805
Natchez	2,340	5,329
Jackson	1,084	1,964
Columbus	1,594	2,738
Macon	466	488
Rodney	168	256
Liberty	168	223
Monticello	102	105

Towns with decreasing Negro population	Negroes 1860	Negroes 1870
Holly Springs	1,075	923
Brookhaven	692	688
Brandon	347	323
Ripley	259	158
Carrollton	360	120
Fayette	111	73

The very large increase in the Negro population of Vicksburg and Natchez undoubtedly reflects the fact that these towns were Federal havens

[1] *Census* of 1860, p. 271; *Census* of 1870, I, 182-186.

of refuge for slaves before the end of the war. With the exception of Natchez, the larger towns in the group with increasing Negro population also showed a healthy growth in the number of whites. The towns with decreasing population were found in regions of declining agricultural importance. With the exception of Brookhaven, they suffered from a similar decrease in their white population.

This movement of Negroes to the towns in Mississippi involved, of course, only a very small portion of their number. The great mass of them remained, and still remain, rural workers in agriculture. The urban group, however, possessed an importance out of proportion to its size. Out of it were to emerge, in later years, the articulate racial leaders of the state.

During the years of slavery, masters and slave traders brought to the new lands of Mississippi tens of thousands of Negroes from the worn fields of the upper Southeast. This movement of the Negro population did not cease with the coming of freedom. By the fall of 1860 freedmen and their families were leaving Virginia for the Southeast in steadily increasing numbers. Late in October a train left Richmond carrying fifty for one Mississippi plantation.[2] In spite of some opposition from Virginia interests, enthusiastic reports from these emigrants stimulated the movement. In the fall of 1869, two railroads alone carried out of Virginia, in cars attached to mail trains, fifteen thousand Negroes. Among these emigrants, and also among those in 1870, there were large groups bound for Mississippi.[3] Although the movement gradually slowed down as the older states were relieved of their surplus and the needs of the Southwest were satisfied, labor agents were still actively at work in 1886. Jefferson Davis in that year arranged for an agent to send him by rail a number of hands from Charlotte, North Carolina.[4] Three years later the Raymond *Gazette* reported that Negroes in North Carolina were still sending representatives to find places for them in the Mississippi Delta.

Of far more importance than the movement from Virginia, North Carolina, and South Carolina to Mississippi was that from Georgia, Alabama, and Tennessee. In the fall of 1865, Whitelaw Reid found a Mississippian enrolling laborers near Eufaula, Alabama. Offering fifteen dollars a month, he quickly obtained sixty-five Negroes, to whom the wage seemed enormous. According to his story, he never had any difficulty in obtaining as many as he desired.[5] The high offer in this case indicates that the agent represented Delta planters. At the same time, however, some of the freedmen from Georgia and South Carolina were moving into

[2] A. A. Taylor, *The Negro in the Reconstruction of Virginia*, p. 91, quoting the Richmond (Va.) *Enquirer*, October 31, 1866.
[3] Hinds County *Gazette*, October 8, 1870, quoting the Richmond (Va.) *Whig*.
[4] Thomas F. Drayton to Jefferson Davis, Charlotte, N. C., March 5, 1886, Stanton Papers, Library of Congress.
[5] Whitelaw Reid, *After the War*, p. 563.

the poorer counties of Mississippi to replace others of their race who had gone on to richer soil.[6]

Stimulated to some extent by the Negroes' loss of political power in surrounding states,[7] the movement to Mississippi continued to grow, and reached its height in 1874, 1875, and 1876. From De Kalb, near the eastern border of the state, there came in January, 1874, the report that hundreds of Alabama Negroes were passing through on trains or in wagons. At the same time, a traveler reported that at Uniontown, Alabama, two hundred and fifty freedmen boarded his train for Mississippi. Practically every west-bound train of the Vicksburg and Meridian Railroad carried large crowds.[8] Later in the same month, a planter of Hinds County returned from Alabama with thirty hands, and declared that Negroes "by the hundreds and thousands" were leaving that state for Mississippi. Labor agents from Mississippi, Louisiana, Arkansas, and Texas were busily at work, and were obtaining as many of the freedmen as they wanted.[9] It seems that some of these agents deluded the Negroes with fantastic promises. At least this was the plaint of a resident of Huntsville, Alabama.[10]

Agents of the state Bureau of Immigration added their efforts to those of the private enterprisers to stimulate the westward flow of the freedmen in the winter of 1874 and 1875. The growing tenseness of the political situation now caused some editors, politicians, and small farmers to cry out against the system. The Hinds County *Gazette* based its opposition on the argument that such immigration meant more cotton and therefore lower prices.[11] The Columbus *Democrat* showed less self-restraint:

Considerable excitement prevails in Chickasaw county in regard to the coming into that county of considerable numbers of ragged, penniless, worthless-looking negroes from Alabama—specimens of the black *riff-raff* with which the negro Commissioner of Immigration is endeavoring to flood the State. The County Grange unanimously resolved *not to employ any of them,* and to discountenance any farmer who does. . . . Every one of Griggs' immigrants that secures employment crowds out a home negro—takes bread out of the mouth of his children. This is the regard the big-headed negro politicians have for their brothers. . . .[12]

The Forest *Register* was even more outspoken in opposition:

Every negro that comes into the State of Mississippi is a curse, every one that leaves a blessing. It is directly through their indolence and votes that we see our noble State falling into ruin, and yet men's cupidity, not their judg-

[6] J. W. Kyle, "Reconstruction in Panola County," *P.M.H.S.,* XIII, 85.
[7] A. T. Morgan, *Yazoo,* p. 445.
[8] Hinds County *Gazette,* January 7, 1874; *ibid.,* quoting the Selma (Ala.) *Times.*
[9] *Ibid.,* January 21, 1874; *ibid.,* quoting the Montgomery (Ala.) *Advertiser.*
[10] *Ibid.,* March 24, 1875.
[11] Mississippi *Weekly Pilot,* January 30, 1875, quoting the Hinds County *Gazette.*
[12] *Ibid.,* quoting the Columbus *Democrat.*

ment, prompts them to call for negro immigrants. Run the white line and save your State and estate![13]

In this matter, however, cupidity was due to carry the day. As the *Pilot* pointed out, Griggs' bureau was really doing a good job in obtaining laborers, but was unable to supply the full desires of the planters.[14] At that very time, many of the large enterprisers of the Delta section were making personal trips to Georgia and Alabama and bringing back Negroes by scores and hundreds.[15] In spite of the bold resolutions of the Chickasaw Grange, the immigrants there received immediate employment, to the disappointment of planters who wanted them in neighboring counties.[16]

The overthrow of the Reconstruction government of the state in 1875, and the practical abolition of the Bureau of Immigration by the Democrats, seem to have had little effect on the incoming tide of Negro workers.[17] As late as April, 1881, the *Clarion,* noticing the continuing flow, blamed it on the long-extinct radical Bureau. Disregarding the economic factors at work, the editor insisted that such immigration was not "self-starting."[18] Neither was it self-stopping. The Democratic Commissioner of Immigration and Agriculture estimated in 1881 that the influx in the past four years had amounted to between ten and eleven thousand.[19] Although its volume now steadily diminished, the movement continued throughout the period.

The major portion of the Negroes coming into Mississippi from the surrounding region went immediately to the rapidly expanding plantations of the river counties. In this movement they were joined by many others of their race who had been held as slaves in the badly worn or naturally less fertile lands in other parts of the state. As early as 1865, the Freedmen's Bureau officials had recognized the wisdom of this migration, and had aided it by furnishing free transportation for a time.[20] By the spring of 1866 the movement was well under way, and the Friar's Point *Coahomian* estimated that over a thousand laborers had been introduced into the counties of Coahoma, Tunica, and Bolivar alone.[21]

The Delta planters who sent agents into Alabama, Georgia, and Tennessee did not hesitate to use the same plan to take the laborers of their less fortunate brothers of the hills and prairies.[22] One of the most suc-

[13] *Ibid.,* quoting the Forest *Register.*
[14] Mississippi *Weekly Pilot,* January 16, 1875.
[15] *Senate Reports,* no. 527, 44th Congress, 1st session, p. 55.
[16] Mississippi *Weekly Pilot,* January 30, 1875, quoting the Okolona *Prairie News.*
[17] Hinds County *Gazette,* January 20, February 17, 1875, January 26, February 2, 1876; Jackson *Clarion,* January 28, 1876, February 10, 1881.
[18] Jackson *Clarion,* April 7, 1881.
[19] Mississippi Commissioner of Immigration and Agriculture, *Report,* 1880-1881, p. 9.
[20] *Senate Executive Documents,* no. 27, 39th Congress, 1st session, p. 37.
[21] Friar's Point *Coahomian,* March 21, 1866.
[22] Forrest Cooper, "Reconstruction in Scott County," *P.M.H.S.,* XIII, 179; Mississippi *Weekly Pilot,* September 18, 1875.

cessful of these agents was a Negro woman named Fannie Cromwell, who was described by the Columbus *Index* as "materially reducing the Negro population" in that part of the state. In one week in 1882 this woman secured over a hundred workers for the river lands from the immediate vicinity of Columbus.[23] In their work, these solicitors could not only point to the much greater prosperity of the freedmen in the Delta counties,[24] but after 1875 they could also play on the fact that the workers there received much better treatment, and retained many of the civil and political rights which Negroes had lost in the rest of the state.

The wholesale desertion of the poorer lands of Mississippi by the Negroes naturally brought to those sections falling values and economic distress. In general, poor whites tended to move into their places, to the satisfaction of Democratic politicians, if not to that of the landowners.[25] In some cases, however, the lands left by migrating freedmen were worked for a time by Negroes from even poorer land in neighboring sections. This was especially true in the vicinity of Hinds County, where the places of Negroes who moved into the Yazoo region were filled by others of their race from Pike, Amite, and Lincoln.[26] By the spring of 1878, however, even this central portion of the state was greatly alarmed over the migration, and the *Gazette* was declaring that unless something could be done the fields would soon be grown over with weeds and briars.[27] About the only satisfaction that could be gained was that of laughing at even less fortunate sections. In this spirit in 1880 the editor of the *Gazette* reported that five hundred Negroes had recently been taken from Oktibbeha County to stock one Delta plantation. "Oktibbeha doesn't like it, but we reckon she'll have to stand it, or secede."[28] The only solution that could be offered by the State Commissioner of Agriculture was the long-discredited one of sending immigration agents to New Orleans, New York, and Europe.[29] The census of 1880 showed for the river counties a population increase of thirty-five to forty-nine per cent over 1870.[30] The unreliability of the census of 1870, however, makes this estimate almost worthless.

In 1866 the movement to the river counties partook of the nature of an exodus. Early in January, an alarming report came from a correspondent in Greasyville, Hinds County, and in the following month one in Queen's Hill wrote: "We have the worst roads in the county, I bet, and

[23] Jackson *Weekly Clarion,* March 1, 1882, quoting the Columbus *Index.*
[24] E. W. Hilgard, "Cotton Production in the State of Mississippi," *Census of 1880,* V, 154.
[25] Robert Somers, *The Southern States,* pp. 142-143; Hinds County *Gazette,* February 6, 1878.
[26] Hinds County *Gazette,* February 20, 1878.
[27] *Ibid.,* February 27, 1878.
[28] *Ibid.,* February 11, 1880.
[29] Mississippi Commissioner of Immigration and Agriculture, *Report,* 1880-1881, p. 9.
[30] Jackson *Clarion-Ledger,* December 11, 1890.

the freest labor. Nearly all that can be moved have gone to the river counties."[31] The migration gradually increased in volume during the year, and by November the central section of the state was thoroughly aroused. The editor of one of the papers reported that the fact that the Negroes were leaving by hundreds could no longer be denied. He attributed most of this movement to the activity of agents of land companies which held property along the new Louisville, New Orleans & Texas Railroad.[32] A few weeks later the same editor tried once more the old trick of saying that the emigrants were returning in disgust, but at the same time he called a public meeting to discuss the problem.[33] In his next issue he announced that the situation was really dangerous, and cried out against the nefarious activities of paid agents who were enticing the laborers. Planters present at the meeting had authorized him to warn the agents that they must go; "that the honest people of Hinds county will not tolerate such practice a day longer. More than one gentleman of the number present promised to 'shoot on the spot' the first man found on his premises endeavoring to decoy away his labor; while others promised to resort to 'tar and feathers.'" The Negro was free, said the *Gazette,* but this did not mean that agents would be allowed to enter his premises for the purpose of enticing him away. "Right is right, and the white people propose to maintain it—paid agents to the contrary, notwithstanding."[34] At a similar meeting held in Edwards, resolutions were adopted which demanded that agents immediately leave the community. A committee of fifteen was also appointed. Its duty was "to wait on in a becoming manner all such agents who refuse or neglect to comply with our modest but earnest demands."[35]

An observer of this migration reported at the end of the year that, beginning in Hinds and Rankin counties, it had spread through a large portion of the state. Disregarding the charges against the railroad agents, he attributed it to the recently completed levee systems in the Yazoo section, the failure of crops in the hills, and the long-standing discontent of the mass of the Negro workers.[36] Once more the Negroes had interpreted freedom in terms of movement, and once more they had gained for themselves, both in the Delta and in the partly depopulated hills, some few small social, educational, and economic advantages.[37]

As to the effect of the influx of the Negroes upon the Delta itself, a white resident has written:

[31] Raymond *Gazette,* January 9, February 6, 1886.
[32] *Ibid.,* November 20, 1886.
[33] *Ibid.,* December 11, 1886.
[34] *Ibid.,* December 18, 1886.
[35] *Ibid.,* December 25, 1886.
[36] *Appleton's Cyclopedia,* 1886, pp. 571-572.
[37] *Ibid.,* p. 572.

Every step taken in the development of this section has been dependent upon, and marked by, an increased Negro population. The railroad rights of way through its forests have been cut out by the Negro, and every mile of track laid by his hands. These forest lands have been cultivated by him into fertile fields, and their subsequent cultivation has called for his constant service. The levees upon which the Delta depends for protection from floods have been erected mainly by the Negro, and the daily labor in field and town, in planting and building, in operating gins and compresses and oil mills, in moving trains, in handling the great staple of the country—all, in fact, that makes the life behind these earthen ramparts—is but the Negro's daily toil.[38]

More spectacular than either this migration of Negroes into the state or that from the hills to the Delta was the peculiar movement of 1879 which came to be known as the "Exodus." The motives which led so many of the Southern Negroes to leave their homes and rush toward Kansas in this year have been the subject of much controversy, and even of a Congressional investigation. The charges and counter-charges of Democratic and Republican politicians have surrounded the whole affair with mystery and suspicion. As a matter of fact, however, when this mass of verbiage has been cleared away, the causes of the movement from Mississippi are apparent and logical.

In the first place, the crop of 1878 in the central and southwestern portions of the state brought terrible disappointments. A combination of drought, low prices, and the worst scourge of yellow fever in the history of the region resulted in economic disaster and stark misery. As early as November 13, 1878, the Hinds County *Gazette* said, "It is estimated that from 2,000 to 4,000 of the colored laborers of this county will be homeless, breadless and in rags in January next." Few of these could hope to obtain any work at all between December 1 and March, and the editor feared that there might be food riots, such as had been seen in the North. It was his opinion that many of the Negroes would leave the section, and that the movement would be the usual one toward the river counties.[39] Further comments on the misery and dissatisfaction of the laborers came at frequent intervals.[40] The editor of the *Clarion* reported that the great mass of the freedmen were hopelessly burdened by debts and were haunted by the desire to escape from them.[41] Interviews with the more intelligent Negroes brought the almost universal complaint that they had done their best and had found it impossible to make a living, coming to the end of each year in debt. They felt that they were charged too much for the rent of land, too much for the hire of mules, and too much for everything they bought. Furthermore, no aid was given them when accidents and calamities, such as the current short crop, reduced them to misery and

[38] Alfred Holt Stone, *Studies in the American Race Problem*, p. 87.
[39] Hinds County *Gazette*, November 13, 1878.
[40] *Ibid.*, November 27, December 11, 25, 1878, January 1, 1879.
[41] Jackson *Weekly Clarion*, April 16, 1879.

starvation.[42] The editor of the *Gazette* refused to pass judgment on the justice of these complaints, but warned the planters that real dissatisfaction was involved, and that those who were interested in keeping their laborers should get to work at once to remove discontent by kindness.

At the same time other factors were at work. Through the river counties in 1878 went a Negro called Dr. Collins. With frenzied oratory, he told the laborers of a great mass migration that they were to make into the wonderful land of Liberia, where food grew on the trees and no one would have to work. They were to get ready at once, and soon a boat would come for them.[43] This news spread rapidly among the Negroes, and there was much talk of Moses and the land of Caanan.[44]

The freedmen were also troubled by the comparatively recent overthrow of the Republican state government, and by the gradual elimination of Republican control in the counties of the black belt. Then too, they lived in constant fear of the "race riots" which had cost the lives of scores of their comrades in the preceding years.

Into the midst of this situation, late in 1879, there came a new element. Labor agents from Texas, Arkansas, Louisiana, and the Delta were well known to the Negroes. They told the same old stories of work and wages, good wages, but wages still. There now came new agents, talking in the strange brogue of the Middle West. There were only a few of these men, but there were enough, for they not only talked of work and wages but they also spoke a magic word. This word was "land," rich, open land that was practically being given away to settlers. The agents also brought literature, heavily illustrated with brilliant chromos.[45] These mysterious circulars, the object of much complaint by the planters, seem to have been only the ordinary advertising that the land companies were scattering over the nation,[46] but to the Negroes in their excitement they were a special invitation to come to Kansas.[47] The old belief that some day the government would give land and homes to the freedmen had not been destroyed by the disappointments of 1865, 1866, and 1867. It had become a part of the creed of the race, and to some extent it survives today. The Negroes accepted without question the rumors about Kansas because those rumors declared true a belief that had become a matter of faith for many of them.

To the starving, unemployed freedmen of the brown loam counties, to those who had seen friends killed in "riots," and to those who resented the loss of civil rights, the stories of land in Kansas brought new hope. This

[42] Hinds County *Gazette,* February 19, 1879.
[43] *Senate Reports,* no. 693, 46th Congress, 2d session, part ii, pp. 520, 530.
[44] *Appleton's Cyclopedia,* 1879, p. 634, quoting a "Memorial of the Planters of Washington County."
[45] *Ibid.,* p. 634.
[46] Carter G. Woodson, *A Century of Negro Migration,* p. 130; Hinds County *Gazette,* July 2, 1879.
[47] *Senate Reports,* no. 693, 46th Congress, 2d session, part ii, p. 224.

hope blended easily into the excitement of the religious enthusiasts of the river counties to bring sweeping rumors of trains and boats that soon would arrive to give free transportation to the West.[48]

Negro political leaders at Washington quickly became interested in the migration, and called for a Colored Convention to meet at Nashville, Tennessee. This group, presided over by John R. Lynch, Negro congressman from Mississippi, quickly gave general approval to the Exodus, and asked Federal aid to the extent of $500,000.[49] This was not granted.

The opinion of whites within Mississippi was divided. The influential Reverend C. K. Marshall declared from his pulpit that the Negroes were being used by the enemies of the South, and that he would do everything possible to remove them to the bosoms of their guardians. The South, he said, could not stand erect until the last Negro was gone.[50] The Summit *Sentinel,* in a section of small farms, hoped that the freedmen would continue to go to Kansas until there was a white majority in every county of the state.[51] A writer who used the initials "J.M.D." represented the poor white farmers in a declaration that they could not compete with the Negroes in the production of cotton, and could have no hope until the freedmen were gone.[52] A new attitude was presented by the Mississippi Live Stock Breeders Association, which urged that the state give up Negroes and cotton and turn to horses, mules, cows, and sheep.[53] Even Senator L. Q. C. Lamar, who publicly opposed the Exodus for political purposes, privately believed it to be a good thing.[54] Finally, such conservative papers as the *Clarion* and the *Gazette,* bristling under Northern criticism, declared that the South would make no concessions to hold the Negroes, and their loss would be no serious matter.[55] In general, it may be said that the small white farmers and their representatives, a majority of the white population, probably wished to see the Negroes removed from the state as rapidly and as thoroughly as possible.

The attitude of the employer group was an entirely different matter. They prophesied general ruin for the state if the Exodus continued, and quickly turned to newspaper progapanda to try to dissuade the emigrants.[56] When propaganda failed, some did not hesitate to use violence. This in-

[48] *Ibid.,* p. 501; Hinds County *Gazette,* March 5, 1879; *Appleton's Cyclopedia,* 1879, p. 634.
[49] Jackson *Weekly Clarion,* February 19, May 14, 1879; Hinds County *Gazette,* May 14, 1879; *Appleton's Cyclopedia,* 1879, p. 357.
[50] Hinds County *Gazette,* February 25, 1880.
[51] *Ibid.,* January 15, 1879, quoting the Summit *Sentinel.*
[52] *Ibid.,* January 22, 1879.
[53] Mississippi Board of Immigration and Agriculture, *The State of Mississippi,* p. 100.
[54] W. A. Cate, *Lucius Quintus Cincinnatus Lamar,* pp. 374-375.
[55] Jackson *Weekly Clarion,* April 30, 1879; Hinds County *Gazette,* April 30, 1879.
[56] Hinds County *Gazette,* November 27, December 11, 25, 1878, January 5, February 5, 19, March 5, 26, April 2, 1879.

cluded the use of irregular courts,[57] the breaking up of crowds of Negroes waiting for boats,[58] the arrest of emigrants on charges of vagrancy and of obtaining goods under false pretences,[59] and the beating and kidnaping of Negro leaders.[60]   Others tried to find jobs for unemployed laborers in railroad construction.[61]

In April, 1879, leading white planters and businessmen joined Governor J. M. Stone in calling the Mississippi Valley Labor Convention to meet at Vicksburg early in the following month.   The freedmen were requested to send representatives.[62]   The assembled convention heard a report by W. L. Nugent, planter, capitalist, and Democratic political worker. Nugent attributed the Exodus to the low price of cotton and the partial failure of the crop, irrational systems of planting, the vicious results of the credit system and lien law, the feeling among the Negroes that their civil and political rights were endangered, and false rumors of advantages to be gained in Kansas.   The whites who were present then adopted unanimously a series of resolutions which declared the interests of planters and laborers to be identical, guaranteed to the freedman all rights promised to them by the Constitution, asked for the repeal of the lien laws, called on the Negroes to deny the false rumors in regard to Kansas, and recognized the right of laborers to emigrate after the fulfillment of their contracts.[63] The Negroes, who outnumbered the whites by six to one, sat through all this in stony and unhappy silence.   The empty guarantees of Nugent's resolutions, possibly prepared for Northern consumption, left them completely unmoved.   They had heard such political promises too often from Democratic leaders.   Finally there arose to speak an old man, H. S. Foote, who had been a Whig governor and senator before the war.   He declared that the Negroes had just cause to believe that their rights had been invaded in some sections, and called for "the appointment of local committees of men of known probity, impartiality and patriotism to watch with unceasing vigilance the rights to be protected."   Now, at last, the freedmen were aroused to enthusiastic approval.   The whites of the convention, however, immediately rejected Foote's substitute resolutions, and the *Clarion* accused him of displaying "the bloody shirt."[64]

In the meantime, Kansas had actually received a few thousand Mississippi Negroes, some of whom suffered from misery and betrayal both before and after their arrival.[65]   They made up between five and six thou-

[57] Jackson *Weekly Clarion,* April 23, 1870.
[58] *Ibid.,* May 14, 1879, quoting the Greenville (Miss.) *Times.*
[59] *Ibid.,* April 23, 1879; *Senate Reports,* no. 693, 46th Congress, 2d session, part ii, p. 501.
[60] *Senate Reports,* no. 693, 46th Congress, 2d session, part ii, p. 500.
[61] Hinds County *Gazette,* December 25, 1878, January 1, 1879.
[62] Jackson *Weekly Clarion,* April 23, 1879; Hinds County *Gazette,* April 30, 1879.
[63] Jackson *Weekly Clarion,* May 14, 1879; Hinds County *Gazette,* May 14, 1879.
[64] Jackson *Weekly Clarion,* May 14, 1879.
[65] Hinds County *Gazette,* January 28, 1880, quoting the St. Louis *Globe-Democrat.*

sand of the thirty thousand who arrived in Kansas during 1879. Few made the trip after that date, and many of them soon returned to their old places.[66]

As the Exodus drew to a close in the summer of 1879, Joseph M. Kern of Bolton, Mississippi, made a trip to Kansas to study the situation. Upon his return he made one of the very few reports that give evidence of intelligence and objectivity. He had learned that the Negroes from the various sections of Mississippi had left the state for different reasons. Those from the river counties had gone under the influence of a religious frenzy, obeying God's command to seek the "Promised Land." Those from the impoverished central section of the state had gone in an effort to better their lot. He felt that the people of Kansas had had nothing to do with the movement, and were in fact opposed to it. Land companies had sent out the usual advertising, but had clearly stated that money was necessary. The movement had been started by excitable Negroes in Mississippi and by letters from a few of their race in Kansas. Not more than five or six thousand of the freedmen of the state had emigrated, and most of those were in a miserable condition.[67]

Altogether, then, the Exodus involved only a tiny fraction of the Negro population of the state, and excited far more attention than it really deserved. In his address to the legislature in December, 1879, Governor Stone dismissed the Exodus in the following manner:

A partial failure of the cotton crop in portions of the State, and the unremunerative prices received for it, created a feeling of discontent among plantation laborers, which, together with other extraneous influences, caused some to abandon their crops in the spring to seek homes in the West. For a time the planting interest in the Mississippi Valley was seriously threatened; but the excitement soon subsided and the supply of labor continued about equal to the demand.[68]

The real Exodus of the Negroes of the state was not to come until the first quarter of the next century.

[66] *Ibid.*, July 2, 16, 1879; *Appleton's Cyclopedia*, 1880, p. 417.
[67] Hinds County *Gazette*, July 2, 1879.
[68] Mississippi *House Journal*, 1880, p. 13.

CHAPTER VIII

THE REVALUATION OF NEGRO LABOR

Late in the fall of 1865 preparations were begun for the cotton year of 1866, which for the interior of the state was the first full season under the system of free labor. It soon became apparent that there was going to be a period of great confusion. Thousands of Negroes who had remained quietly with their former masters during the abbreviated season of 1865 had determined to look for opportunities to better their condition at the end of the year.[1] This was to be their first real experience in bargaining for wages. Many had been defrauded of their earnings in 1865.[2] Others, who had used all their credit for supplies, believed that they had been tricked. Still others, who had cleared a little on their cotton, decided to use the first money that they had ever known for jaunts to neighboring towns, or for Christmas visits to relatives. Some undoubtedly believed that the new year would find them established on free land, while the more credulous were victims of rumors that signing a contract or remaining with their former owners would subject them once more to slavery.[3] For various reasons, then, a great number of the Negroes of Mississippi showed a determination to sign no full-year contract for 1866 until they had had time to investigate and consider the situation.

Many of the planters were little less confused than the freedmen. For the first time in their lives they found it necessary to deal and bargain with their laborers. Negroes who had worked for them for twenty years were simply walking off the place. How did one go about getting new workers under this abominable system? There was a strange and unhappy silence around the old slave-auction blocks.

Furthermore, the state law said that written contracts had to be made. Officials of the Freedmen's Bureau, who had turned the whole matter over to the civil magistrates, contented themselves with high-flown addresses and proclamations in which they urged the Negro to industry and piety, and threatened him with the state vagrancy law.[4] Efforts to draw up proper contracts and to persuade the Negroes to sign them must have

[1] *Senate Executive Documents*, no. 2, 39th Congress, 1st session, p. 30; Franklin A. Montgomery, *Reminiscences of a Mississippian in Peace and War*, p. 264.
[2] Jackson *Clarion*, December 21, 1865; James T. Trowbridge, *The South*, p. 330; *Senate Executive Documents*, no. 27, 39th Congress, 1st session, pp. 83-84.
[3] Hinds County, *Gazette*, December 16, 1865; Jackson *Clarion*, December 19, 1865.
[4] *Senate Executive Documents*, no. 27, 39th Congress, 1st session, pp. 34-35, 36-37; Jackson *Clarion*, November 12, 1865; John Eaton, *Grant, Lincoln, and the Freedmen*, pp. 242-244.

driven some of the more impatient planters frantic. The mayor of Kosci-usko drew up a contract form for the convenience of his bewildered clients. Its small type covered a full page of foolscap, and in it the word "afore-said" occurred one hundred and twenty-one times.[5]

To some of the planters, it seemed that more than half of the labor force had disappeared from the face of the earth. There can be no doubt that the expanding enterprise of 1866 did find a shortage of workers in some parts of the state. Many of the Negro men were still in the garrisons of the army, and thousands of the women now retired partially or entirely from field work to keep house for their families. Other thousands of freedmen found work in the towns, on levees and railroads, or on the farms of the men who in the old days had been unable to buy slaves. This scarcity of labor caused planters to cluster eagerly around the army camps when, in March of 1865, most of the Negro soldiers were mustered out of service. Many of them were thus able to fill out their labor rolls, through Federal officers who set themselves up as efficient, if at times thoroughly dishonest, labor agents.[6]

In the meantime, the entire labor situation cleared up with remarkable rapidity. There has been a great deal of speculation as to how well the Negroes worked during the early years of the Reconstruction period. Dozens of citations could be given to uphold any view that any writer might choose to take. In general, it may be said that Federal officials and Northern planters in Mississippi gave favorable reports. The testimony of the officials is of some value, since few of those who served in Mississippi in 1866 and 1867 possessed very tender feelings for the Negro. That of the Northern planters comes from men who were accustomed to handling free labor. Then too, most of them were operating in those river counties where the process of adjustment had been under way since 1863. It is just as generally true that the mass Southern sentiment, as reported by travelers and in the press of the state in 1865, was to the effect that the Negroes were not working and would not work as freedmen. These statements of 1865 were made before the new system had received a real test in the interior of the state, and were to a large extent merely expressions of the Southern credo. Throughout 1866 and 1867, and, to a much smaller extent, the rest of the period, editorials, political speeches, and individual letters of complaint may be found in which the general declaration was made that the free Negroes were almost worthless as laborers. The same statement was made much more often in later years by writers who were critical of the policy of Reconstruction, or who sought to justify the Black Codes.

When one turns away from editorial columns to the brief, specific news reports from individual counties, a different story is found. These items,

[5] E. C. Colemen, Jr., "Reconstruction in Attala County," *P.M.H.S.*, X, 151.
[6] Whitelaw Reid, *After the War*, pp. 559, 561-562.

so, easily overlooked, are almost unanimous in giving a favorable report.[7] As early as April, 1866, the editor of the Woodville *Republican* gave reluctant recognition to the weight of this evidence:

Our local exchanges from all parts of the state are replete with encouraging accounts of the weather, crops and operations of the freedmen. . . . The opinion, so generally entertained in the planting community, that free labor could never be made available in farm operations, has, if our exchanges be correct, been somewhat dissipated by the recent conduct of the freedmen. . . .[8]

Strangely enough, such papers and records of individual planters as are available for these early years are almost completely silent on the question of the quality of their laborers. The only exceptions are expressions of wrath or dismay registered each Christmas as contracts expired and the Negroes wandered about before signing new ones. E. J. Capell, for example, entered in his journal only routine comments on the progress of his crop in 1865 until three days before Christmas. From December 23 to January 4 everything was wrong. "Negroes doing nothing. . . . A miserable dull time & horrible state of things owing to the Negroes all being set free. . . . A perfect confusion all over the country. . . . Can hardly get a Negro to cut wood or feed the Horses. all going to and fro through the neighborhood. . . . all confusion &c here among the negroes. A horrible state of things and no dependence in any thing a Negro tells you." Then suddenly with January 4 the weather was clear again, the Negroes had signed, and Capell went back to routine comments on the progress of the work. Through the entire year of 1866 there was only one unfavorable notation in regard to the laborers; on March 20 they quit work to prepare for a funeral. Then came Christmas and gloom again. "A great confusion in the country among the whites and blacks as regards hiring for next year. . . . I am perfectly disgusted with free negroes. . . . The negroes roving all about over the country. . . . I never saw such a state of things. Not one on my place except old Love has as yet said they would stay with me." Finally, however, there came the notation, "I and Mr. Goodbee all day dividing the Negroes corn & contracted them for 1867." Routine work reports followed.[9]

Direct reports on labor from counties or sections are very rare in 1867, and practically non-existent after that time. The few that can be found

---

[7] Aberdeen *Sunny South,* January 18, 1866; Jackson *Clarion,* February 2, 3, 16, August 16, 1866; Jackson *Daily Mississippi Standard,* April 2, 1866; *ibid.,* April 10, 1866, quoting the Lexington *Advertiser;* Jackson *Clarion,* April 28, 1866, quoting the Canton *Citizen; ibid.,* May 3, 1866, quoting the Panola *Star;* Jackson *Clarion and Standard,* May 30, 1866; *ibid.,* June 5, 1866, quoting the Holly Springs *Reporter;* Natchez *Tri-Weekly Democrat,* June 28, 1866; Natchez *Daily Courier,* January 27, May 19, September 21, 1866; *DeBow's Review,* After the War Series, II, 211; John W. Kyle, "Reconstruction in Panola County," *P.M.H.S.,* XIII, 79.

[8] Woodville *Republican,* April 6, 1866.

[9] Pleasant Hill Plantation Records, "Journal," 1865, 1866, 1867, E. J. Capell Papers.

are almost entirely favorable. From this fact, from the large crop of 1868, and from General A. C. Gillem's report, J. W. Garner draws the conclusion that a satisfactory adjustment of the relations of the planters and their laborers had been gained by that year.[10] It should be noted, however, that the reports of General Gillem's predecessors for 1866 and 1867 are no less favorable than his own, and that the large increase in the crop of 1868 seems to have been due almost entirely to more suitable weather, and especially to a slackening in the attack of the army worms. Furthermore, the decline in interest in the quality of free labor, as reflected in newspaper editorials and public speeches, can be attributed very largely to the fact that by 1868 editors and politicians had become much more concerned with the Negro as a political factor than as a worker.

Altogether, it does not seem probable that there was any great change in the quality of Negro labor during and immediately after 1868. Garner is inclined to attribute much of the supposed improvement to the disastrous crop failure of 1867 and the resultant destitution among the freedmen. If this interpretation were correct, there should have been a reaction with the satisfactory crop of 1868 and the enormously profitable one of 1869. There is no evidence of such a reaction. There are other arguments against the improvement which is supposed to have come after 1867. This was the very year in which the Negroes first became active in political affairs, and began to attend numerous public meetings and those of the Loyal Leagues. Soon, their churches, schools, and clubs began to supply attractions which undoubtedly took some of their attention from their work. Then too, the Negroes by 1870 held the power to choose the officers of the state government and of those in the cotton counties, and this fact should have made them much more independent in their relations with their employers.

It would seem, then, that the chief factor in the decline of complaints against the system of free Negro labor after 1867 was a change in the attitude of the planters, and especially of the editors and public leaders. They had become reconciled to the fact that slavery was dead, and that codes to enforce peonage could not be applied. It had become apparent that the Negroes must be paid, and that their right to move about in search of better contracts could not be blocked. Furthermore, planters had learned that Negroes lost at Christmas could generally be replaced before the beginning of the planting season, that money could be made from the cultivation of cotton with their labor, and that more satisfactory workers could not be obtained. Most important of all was the shift in the interest of the newspapers to the Negro in politics.

Altogether, it seems probable that in 1866 there were indeed many idle and worthless Negroes. There were probably about as many in 1868, and in 1890. But in 1866, as in these other years, the great masses of Negroes,

[10] James W. Garner, *Reconstruction in Mississippi*, p. 183.

in the words of Governor Humphreys, "showed a desire to engage in the pursuits of honest labor."[11] They were not quite so amenable to discipline as formerly, they did not work quite so regularly or so many hours, and if greatly dissatisfied they walked off the place, but statements that they had been "rendered totally unfit for anything"[12] in the years immediately following the war cannot be maintained.

It has been shown that very soon after the war direct reports declared that the freedmen were working very well, "considering the fact that they were Negroes." It also soon became apparent to those who gave the matter an actual trial that the freedmen in agriculture furnished a more satisfactory type of labor than could be obtained from white workers, either natives or immigrants. A planter in Hinds County wrote in 1873 that he was tired of hearing railings against the Negro workers and wished to know whether the critics had ever tried white labor. Swedes and Englishmen would not work nearly so well at low costs as the freedmen, nor did they require so little attention and waiting on. His conclusion was that "This labor business is all bosh."[13] By 1875, witnesses declared that there was a universal preference for Negro workers, and that few would hesitate to reject whites when there was an opportunity to obtain them.[14] A planter worried by the Exodus in the winter of 1878 declared, "It is a well known fact that colored labor for many reasons is the only kind that our southern planters can control to any advantage whatever. . . ."[15] Finally, in 1886, the Raymond *Gazette* presented what it called "A Sensible Communication" from a landowner near Terry. This writer was aroused by declarations that the Negroes should be colonized. He too would like to obtain "good, intelligent, thrifty white labor" in their place, but after years of experience and swapping around he had failed to find any. He continued:

I do not say this to decry white labor, for I like it, when of the right kind, but if either must go, give me the nigger every time. The nigger will never "strike" as long as you give him plenty to eat and half clothe him: He will live on less and do more hard work, when properly managed, than any other class, or race of people. As Arp truthfully says "we can boss him" and that is what we southern folks like. . . . I have worked both kinds of labor, side by side, with varying results. The nigger will do the most work and do it according to personal instructions. . . . I record Experience against Theory.[16]

The reference to the fact that the Negroes would not "strike" reflected a powerful impression that had been made on the Southern planters by the growing labor troubles of the North. Sir George Campbell in 1878

[11] J. S. McNeily, "From Organization to Overthrow of Mississippi's Provisional Government," *P.M.H.S.C.S.*, I, 233.
[12] Natchez *Democrat*, December 28, 1867.
[13] Hinds County *Gazette*, April 9, 1873.
[14] *Senate Reports*, no. 527, 44th Congress, 1st session, p. 55.
[15] Hinds County *Gazette*, December 25, 1878.
[16] Raymond *Gazette*, May 8, 1886.

found that the freedmen had come to be cherished as a conservative labor element, and in the same year Governor J. M. Stone in his message to the legislature exhorted the people of Mississippi to be thankful that "amid our poverty and gloom, no riotous spirit of communism has raised its head in our midst; that the earnest conservatism which has ever characterized our people, has preserved us from the terrible scenes . . . which, during last summer, struck terror to the hearts of thinking men in other communities. . . ."[17] The Natchez *Democrat* warned the Negroes against "unscrupulous and bogus labor organizers," and urged that such men on their very first appearance should be arrested by the strong arm of the law. Real friends of the laboring classes would "guard with vigiligance against selfish and baneful attempts of agrarian emissaries to disturb the peaceful relations existing between employers and employees in our section of the country."[18]

It is apparent that long before 1890, the planters, much as they might complain of the faults of the Negroes, had come to prefer them to any other class of laborers they could obtain. They were ready to use almost any means to retain them, even to the extent of meeting land and labor agents with violence. According to the *Clarion*, "The negroes of the South are its wealth. . . . The South, without the negro, for a generation at least, would be a wilderness and a waste. . . ."[19] As a result of this growing preference for their labor, the docile and disfranchised Negroes everywhere made up the working force on the best lands of the state,[20] and continued to produce the greater part of its cotton.

Thus the great mass of the Negroes of Mississippi, in freedom as in slavery, found their lives largely concerned with a single staple. As freedmen, however, they were more personally concerned with the success or failure of the crop. No matter how many of them might move off to seek new contracts, their chances of betterment were small indeed in those seasons in which the planters themselves suffered heavy losses.

In general, conditions throughout the state early in 1866 justified the expectation of an excellent crop. By late summer, however, almost all hope had been lost. All over the state there had been extremely heavy rains, with alternating periods of intense drought.[21] Then, in August, there came one of the worst attacks from army worms the state had ever

[17] Inaugural Address of Governor J. M. Stone, January 10, 1878, Mississippi *Annual Reports*, 1877 [*sic*].
[18] Raymond *Gazette*, May 22, 1886, quoting the Natchez *Democrat*.
[19] Jackson *Weekly Clarion*, April 28, 1886.
[20] J. H. Jones, "Reconstruction in Wilkinson County," *P.M.H.S.*, VIII, 153; E. F. Puckett, "Reconstruction in Monroe County," *P.M.H.S.*, XI, 105.
[21] *Senate Executive Documents*, no. 6, 39th Congress, 2d session, p. 97; J. S. McNeily, "From Organization to Overthrow of Mississippi's Provisional Government," *P.M.H.S.C.S.*, I, 140, 220, 225; Jackson *Clarion and Standard*, June 10, 1866; Jackson *Clarion*, May 8, August 28, September 7, 13, 20, October 12, 1866; Natchez *Daily Courier*, May 19, September 21, October 2, 1866.

known.[22] The result was a small crop of only a little more than 300,000 bales. So high was the price, however, that the sale of the cotton brought at least as much money as had the 860,000 bales of 1860,[23] and those who had managed to save part of their crop entered 1867 with some capital and high hopes.

Again came disaster, this time much worse than in 1866. Unfavorable weather delayed planting and prevented early cultivation in much of the state, and in the Delta the worst overflow in twenty years caused a very late crop.[24] This gave a perfect setting for the arrival of the army worm, which came in such numbers as to make the invasion of the year before seem unimportant. As one writer had described them in an earlier year, they seemed to spring out of the ground and fall from the clouds, and the more they were tormented and destroyed, the more perceptible was their power. Across the state they moved, and in county after county the fields came to look as though they had been swept by fire.[25]

The disaster brought immediate misery to the Negroes, for many of the planters dismissed their workers as quickly as possible. In November, the *Gazette* gave a rather callous report of the situation:

Employers are dismissing their laborers as rapidly as possible, and no contracts are being made for next year. . . . It would be well, we think, for our citizens to encourage all freedmen, as they get out of employment, to go to Vicksburg. There is a free Government boarding house there, called the "Freedmen's Bureau," and hence starvation may be avoided. . . . Hinds county would be infinitely better off could we get rid of ten thousand of our negro population for the present winter. We could possibly provide for those remaining. Cannot we get rid of say ten thousand by setting on foot a tide of emigration to Vicksburg?[26]

In Vicksburg, however, General Gillem absolutely refused relief of any kind, and many of the Negroes, offering to work for food and clothing, or for food alone, entered 1868 without having received any of their wages for the past two years.[27]

The satisfactory cotton crop of 1868[28] was followed by one of 565,000

[22] Jackson *Clarion*, August 28, September 20, 1866; Fayette *Chronicle*, August 25, 1866; Natchez *Daily Courier*, August 21, 1866; Pleasant Hill Plantation Records, 1866, E. J. Capell Papers.
[23] Ross H. Moore, "Social and Economic Conditions in Mississippi during Reconstruction," unpublished doctoral dissertation, Duke University, 1938, p. 71.
[24] J. S. McNeily, "From Organization to Overthrow of Mississippi's Provisional Government," *P.M.H.S.C.S.*, I, 306.
[25] Natchez *Tri-Weekly Democrat*, July 30, August 3, 15, September 5, 19, September 27, 1867; J. D. Shields Papers, Louisiana State University, August 9, 12, 1867; A. T. Morgan, *Yazoo*, p. 220; *House Executive Documents*, no. 1, 40th Congress, 3d session, p. 524.
[26] Hinds County *Gazette*, November 29, 1867.
[27] *House Executive Documents*, no. 1, 40th Congress, 3d session, p. 524; J. S. McNeily, "From Organization to Overthrow of Mississippi's Provisional Government," *P.M.H.S.C.S.*, I, 338, 340; Hinds County *Gazette*, November 1, December 6, 1867.
[28] J. W. Garner, *op. cit.*, p. 182; Hinds County *Gazette*, January 27, February 10, 1869.

bales in 1869. Although this yield was far below that which immediately preceded the war, the prevailing prices brought to the state an income from cotton that was considerably greater than that of any other year in its history.[29] The Negroes obtained their humble share of this prosperity.

In the years that followed, the general trend of cotton production was upward, but prices fell more rapidly than production rose. The result was that the 1,209,000 bales produced in 1890 brought almost exactly the same gross income as did the 306,000 bales of 1866.[30] The national decline in the prosperity of agriculture produced during this period the great wave of discontent that was reflected in the rise of Populism. The Negroes, who were the mudsill of the agricultural system in Mississippi, were in all of this real, if inarticulate sufferers. The production of more and more cotton did nothing to raise their scale of living. On thousands of scattered plantations, in clothes that seemed ever more ragged, they made the same old trip from their wretched hovels to the neighboring store, to return with the corn meal and "fat back" for which, with good luck, they would pay at the end of the season.

[29] R. H. Moore, *op. cit.*, p. 71, offers an elaborate study of this item.
[30] *Ibid.*, pp. 71-72.

CHAPTER IX

NON-AGRICULTURAL OCCUPATIONS

Of the 300,000 Negroes gainfully employed in Mississippi in 1890, approximately 250,000 were engaged in agriculture. Of the remaining 50,000, fully half were house servants or laundresses, leaving for other lines of endeavor only very small fractions of the population. These small groups were significant, however, since they contained more than their share of the more articulate and enterprising members of the race.

An early opportunity for freedmen to escape from the agricultural system grew out of the need for rebuilding the shattered railroads of the state. Within two months after the close of the war a number of the Negroes who were serving with the Union army were put into this type of work. There were no less than twelve hundred of them on the line between Jackson and Vicksburg alone.[1] Many of them, either for wages or as convicts, continued this work in later years, and supplied the common labor for the greater part of the new railroad construction. Robert Somers, in 1871, found large numbers of Negroes employed on the roadbed of the Alabama & Chattanooga above Meridian at a wage of $1.75 per day without rations.[2] This rate was probably unusually high. A contractor near Vicksburg in the following year paid most of his gang $1.34 per day.[3]

In railroad work, as in agriculture, there was an effort to replace Negroes with Chinese coolies. About 700 of the latter were brought to Meridian in 1871 and set to work on the A. & C. Although they were experienced laborers from the California and Pacific Railway, and although their wages were lower than those of the Negroes, the superintendent reported that their work, measured by the cubic yard, was costing the company about three times as much as that of the usual crews. Disgusted by this, he had them shifted to the Chattanooga end of the line.[4]

The real competition for the Negroes in railroad grading and bridge work seems to have come from Irish laborers. In 1872, Patrick Murphy, Irish railroad contractor in western Mississippi, worked both whites and blacks, and paid them the same wages.[5] By 1885, however, he was em-

[1] Ross H. Moore, "Social and Economic Conditions in Mississippi during Reconstruction," p. 114. Unpublished doctoral dissertation, Duke University, 1938.
[2] Robert Somers, *The Southern States since the War*, p. 163.
[3] "Railroad Time Book," vol. 2, Patrick Murphy Papers.
[4] Robert Somers, *op. cit.*, pp. 163-164.
[5] "Railroad Time Book," vol. 2, Patrick Murphy Papers.

ploying Negroes exclusively.[6] According to a report in 1890, the Irish were doing most of the barrow work, while the Negroes drove the mules. The Negroes were said to be as good at labor by the day as the Irish, but were not inclined to try job work. On the other hand, the Irish were much harder to handle, and were likely to complain and leave the work. There was no reference to the employment of native whites.[7] Negroes were also employed in the railroad shops,[8] and as members of train crews. The Census of 1890 showed the total number employed by railroads in the state as 2,736.

Many Negroes were also absorbed into the growing lumber industry. This was especially true in the Delta region, where Western capitalists purchased a million acres of timber land and brought laborers from the decadent plantations of the hills.[9] A number of the freedmen also set themselves up as independent enterprisers to supply wood to steamboats from yards along the banks of the river.[10] The estimate of 1,397 Negroes engaged in lumbering, presented by the Census of 1890, is probably much too low.

Other Negroes quickly found places for themselves as deck hands on steamboats, largely replacing the whites who had been generally used in such jobs before the war. Wages were high, running up to sixty dollars a month, but the work was terribly strenuous, and many of those from the plantations found themselves unable to endure one complete voyage.[11]

Most of the Negroes who left plantations at the end of the war found employment in the towns, and of these the greater part of the women and some three thousand of the men took places as house servants or laundresses. Those families who were accustomed to the use of house servants made efforts to retain them even in the midst of financial difficulties, and others who had been unable to buy slaves now found themselves able to hire servants by the week or month. This resulted in numerous declarations by the whites that house servants were extremely scarce.[12] Although this scarcity did not bring satisfactory wages, it did permit many Negroes to give slovenly service. The greatest gain by the servants, however, was the ability to carry out a general refusal to stay on the place of the employer.[13] Wages for house servants seem to have maintained a fairly stable level from 1865 to 1890, and indeed were practically the same as those generally paid in the state in 1940. First-class cooks and house-men received fifteen dollars per month and meals, while less desirable workers obtained

[6] "Diary," vol. 16, Patrick Murphy Papers.
[7] Goodspeed Publishing Company, *Memoirs of Mississippi*, II, 75.
[8] *Leading Afro-Americans of Vicksburg, Mississippi*, pp. 13, 33, 35.
[9] *Appleton's Cyclopedia*, 1886, p. 572.
[10] Edward King, *The Great South*, p. 290.
[11] J. T. Trowbridge, *The South*, pp. 388-389.
[12] Hinds County *Gazette*, December 8, 22, 1869, February 9, March 2, 9, 1881.
[13] *Ibid.*, February 8, 1867.

as little as one dollar per week. Leading families paid coachmen from twenty to twenty-five dollars per month and meals.[14]

Free Negroes also found many other occupations open to them in the growing towns. As early as 1864, in those communities under Federal control, they were receiving wages as artisans, hackmen, porters, seamstresses, nurses, and waiters.[15] In the rest of the state, they quickly secured such jobs immediately after the end of the war.[16] On the rivers and bayous of the state, Negroes generally were the ferrymen.[17]

Wages in these various lines of employment seem to have remained almost constant. With the exception of two old men at $15.00, Negro workers for a large firm at Vicksburg received from 1865 to 1871 unvarying wages on a schedule ranging from $30.00 to $60.00 per month.[18] In 1874, the state Commissioner of Immigration listed the following as standard wages:

Hack-drivers	$35.00 to $40.00	per month
Wagoners	30.00 to 40.00	" "
Blacksmiths, shoers, etc.	2.00 to 3.00	per day
Carpenters and builders	2.00 to 3.00	" "
Plasterers	2.50 to 4.00	" "
Brickmasons	2.00 to 4.00	" "[19]

As early as 1865, newspapers of the state called for discrimination against Negro artisans and day laborers in favor of whites.[20] Railroad shops and a foundry established in Water Valley in 1866 barred Negro laborers.[21] It was not until the rise of extreme political animosities in 1874, however, that opposition to Negro workers began to be really effective. In that year, for the first time, merchants in Vicksburg began to hire white porters. The editor of the *Gazette* saw this as a proper move against the Negro voter, and went on to say, "Our wonder is that the sharp-sighted Vicksburgers fed, clothed and pampered him so long."[22] In the same year, the Vicksburg & Meridian Railroad replaced all of its Negro mail agents with whites.[23] During the campaign of the following year, newspapers called on their subscribers to patronize white Democrats,[24] and employers

[14] J. T. Trowbridge, *op. cit.*, p. 295; "Cash and Account Book," 1865-1879, Stephen Duncan Papers.
[15] John Eaton, *Grant, Lincoln, and the Freedmen*, p. 132.
[16] Whitelaw Reid, *After the War*, pp. 289, 390, 391.
[17] A. T. Morgan, *Yazoo*, pp. 33, 58.
[18] Schwartz and Stewart Collection, Louisiana State University, "Ledger," 1865-1870.
[19] Richard Griggs, *Guide to Mississippi*, p. 31.
[20] Meridian *Clarion*, August 10, 1865; Hinds County *Gazette*, October 7, 1865; Ross H. Moore, *op. cit.*, p. 358, quoting the Kosciusko *Chronicle*, November 25, 1865.
[21] Julia C. Brown, "Reconstruction in Yalobusha and Grenada Counties," *P.M.H.S.*, XII, 261.
[22] Hinds County *Gazette*, August 12, 1874.
[23] *Ibid.*, September 9, 1874.
[24] *Ibid.*, August 11, 1875.

128   THE JAMES SPRUNT STUDIES

in Natchez discharged numbers of Negro workers.[25] In general, however, the displacement of Negro artisans, draymen, porters, clerks, and domestics was a slow and incomplete process. In the seventies and eighties few of the native whites were willing to accept menial positions, and even fewer employers were willing to hire those of their own race so long as the more docile Negroes were available at low wages.

From the first months of freedom, a number of the more ambitious Negroes managed to avoid being drawn into the wage system, and set themselves up as independent enterprisers in various mechanical and commercial activities.[26] As artisans of various types, as barbers, bakers, peddlers, hackmen, and draymen, and as keepers of hotels, restaurants, and saloons they enjoyed varying amounts of success.[27] The Natchez *Democrat* carried protests against the excessive activities of Negro restauranteurs and fish-women, who set up tables on the sidewalks, and who frequently fried their fish over fires built in the streets.[28] Negro stores and saloons enjoyed the patronage of many whites until 1890 or later.[29]

A list of the occupations of the leading members of the African Methodist Episcopal Church at Jackson for 1902 is informative:

H. T. Risher, "owner of a large bakery"
J. S. Harvey, "contractor and builder"
George Robinson and two sons, "brick masons and large contractors"
Mrs. Julia Brown, "a business woman and owner of property in Jackson and Yazoo City"
Marcus Brown, "a leading plasterer and a large contractor in his line"
Lafayette Garrette, "skilled painter"
James W. Dennis, "representative of tailoring firms"
John Carson, "restaurant owner"
Mrs. Melvina Scott, "fashionable dressmaker"
Robert Day, Jr., "painter"
Mrs. Josie B. Washington, "teacher"[30]

Those listed for the corresponding church in Natchez included:

Dr. J. B. Banks, "the pioneer colored physician of the city"
Charles Russell, "leading confectioner"
Wm. Kennedy, "painter"
Mrs. A. V. Walker, "seamstress and property owner"
Mrs. Irby Robinson, "trained nurse"
A. C. Montgomery, "a prominent ice dealer"
Mrs. Josephine New, "dressmaker"

[25] *Senate Miscellaneous Documents,* no. 45, 44th Congress, 2d session, p. 137.
[26] John Eaton, *op. cit.,* p. 132.
[27] *Ibid.,* pp. 102, 105; A. T. Morgan, *op. cit.,* pp. 33, 163, 243; Whitelaw Reid, *op. cit.,* p. 289; *Leading Afro-Americans of Vicksburg, Mississippi,* p. 31; *Senate Miscellaneous Documents,* no. 45, 44th Congress, 2d session, p. 137; *ibid.,* no. 166, 50th Congress, 1st session, p. 121; Natchez *Daily Courier,* May 31, September 15, 1866; "Cash and Account Book," 1865-1879, Stephen Duncan Papers.
[28] Natchez *Tri-Weekly Democrat,* January 11, 1868.
[29] A. T. Morgan, *op. cit.,* p. 243; Mississippi *Weekly Pilot,* June 12, 1875, quoting the Vicksburg *Monitor;* statement of E. L. Patton, Jackson, January 15, 1939.
[30] R. A. Adams, *Cyclopedia of African Methodism in Mississippi,* p. 108.

Mrs. Susan Brady, "teacher"
Rueben Sims, "truck farmer"
Mrs. Amanda Russell, "trained nurse"
Lewis Pulley, "plasterer"[31]

Before 1890, very few Negroes had entered upon the practice of the higher professions in the state. The first Negro physician appeared in Vicksburg in 1865,[32] while another, a man with training, intelligence, and some capital, located in Enterprise early in 1866.[33] Another was reported to be practicing in Columbus in 1874.[34] Altogether, however, the entrance of Negroes into this profession was very slow. The Census of 1890 listed only thirty-four in the state who professed to be physicians or surgeons.

Even fewer Negroes found their way into the legal profession, although the system of admissions used until 1880 made such entry fairly easy. In the incomplete list prepared by I. C. Mollison, only four of the ten admitted to the bar of the state before 1878 were of Southern birth, while only two were natives of Mississippi. The other six were from Ohio and Canada. On the other hand, all of the six listed as admitted between 1877 and 1890 were born in the state. According to Mollison, all of the Negro lawyers of the period practiced in the black counties west of the Illinois Central Railroad.[35] It appears, however, that at least one was admitted to the bar in the northeastern portion of the state.[36] Most of these lawyers found it necessary to combine other lines of work with their legal practice. Besides those who engaged in politics, some held appointive public offices, taught school, or entered business. William H. Smallwood, who practiced in Jackson, was recognized as the city's leading expert on leases, deeds, and contracts, an excellent penman, and an able auditor and bookkeeper.[37] In addition to serving as reporter for the *Clarion,* he audited the books of some of the leading firms of the city, including one of the larger banks.[38] L. K. Atwood combined his legal practice with the management of a mercantile establishment.[39] A number of these men also held executive positions in various Negro benevolent societies.[40]

In most of the towns of any size, there was an immediate tendency for the Negro residential and business sections to become distinct from those of the whites. To a certain extent this segregation grew out of the poverty of the Negroes, but the most effective force was the increasing desire of

[31] *Ibid.,* p. 152.   [32] *Leading Afro-Americans of Vicksburg,* Mississippi, p. 5.
[33] Jackson *Clarion,* March 24, 1866, quoting the Meridian *Messenger.*
[34] Ross H. Moore, *op. cit.,* p. 349, quoting the Vicksburg *Daily Times,* July 27, 1874.
[35] I. C. Mollison, "Negro Lawyers in Mississippi," *Journal of Negro History,* XV (1930), 40-41.
[36] Hinds County *Gazette,* August 14, 1872.
[37] Jackson *Weekly Clarion,* April 18, 1883; statement of E. L. Patton, Jackson, January 15, 1939.
[38] Statement of E. L. Patton, Jackson, January 15, 1939.
[39] *Ibid.*   [40] *Ibid.,* Jackson *Weekly Clarion,* April 18, 1883.

the whites to avoid Negro neighbors. As early as 1860, the eastern section of Columbus, known as "Kirkville" was recognized as the part of the town which was to be used especially by Negroes. The white mayor of Columbus even went so far as to appoint Jeff Kirk, a plasterer, as "mayor" of the section. It was reported that he ruled his village with judgment and firmness. During his "administration," only one arrest was necessary, and that for an accidental shooting.[41] "Baptist Town," however, gained a reputation as "the Negro pest hole of Okolona."[42] By 1889, a Negro section was recognized as distinct in Raymond, and white businessmen opened an adjoining subdivision in which the lots were to be used only by Negroes.[43]

The Negroes of Jackson came to be concentrated in a section of land west of the city cemetery. This bore the name of "Boston."[44] Both in Jackson and in other towns of the state, however, the process of segregation was slow and incomplete. Small groups of Negroes continued for many years to live in all parts of the towns. M. M. McLeod and James Hill, prosperous Negro leaders, lived in fine homes on West Capitol Street, not far from the residence of Senator J. Z. George. James Lynch also had a home on Capitol Street.[45]

In general, an even smaller percentage of the urban Negroes became home-owners than those of their race on the farms. Of 51,422 non-farm homes occupied by Negroes in the state in 1890, only 5,177 were entirely owned by their occupants. Two hundred fifty-three others had been purchased, but were still encumbered.[46] In later years, however, the town-dwellers showed much greater progress in this line of development than the rural population. By 1910, Negroes owned partially or entirely 13,783 of their 68,609 non-farm homes.[47]

Statistics offered by the Census of 1890[48] indicate that the Negroes still held a practical monopoly of jobs as house servants and as unclassified common laborers. As merchants and as keepers of shops and boarding-houses they were showing some progress, but as artisans they were losing ground. Fully half of their women were still gainfully employed. More than 1,500 Negroes had become teachers in public schools, but this number did not nearly meet the needs of the population. The increase of physicians and lawyers was encouraging, although the number of each was still almost negligible. The Negroes of Mississippi in 1890, as in 1865, were essentially a race of laborers, and it was upon the elevation of that class, white and black, that their future progress depended.

[41] Natchez *Daily Courier*, June 26, 1866.
[42] Jackson *Weekly Clarion*, September 29, 1881.
[43] Raymond *Gazette*, January 5, 1889.
[44] *Senate Miscellaneous Documents*, no. 166, 50th Congress, 1st session, p. 309.
[45] Statement of E. L. Patton, Jackson, January 15, 1939.
[46] Bureau of the Census, *Negro Population, 1790-1915*, p. 470.
[47] *Ibid.*, p. 486.   [48] *Census of 1890*, vol. I, part II, p. 574.

CHAPTER X

THE LEGAL STATUS OF THE FREEDMEN

The question as to when the Negroes of Mississippi became legally free cannot be settled. The confiscation acts of Congress in August, 1861, and July, 1862, and the Emancipation Proclamation of President Lincoln had no practical application for the mass of the Negroes in the interior of the state. The abolition of slavery was one of the absolute requirements which President Johnson suggested to the state constitutional convention in the summer of 1865.[1] Yet the members of that convention knew that, except for some few Negroes on remote plantations, slavery had actually ceased to exist in the state several months before they met. Most of the members were lawyers, and to their legalistic minds the entire situation was baffling.

In his call for the assembly of the convention, Provisional-Governor William Sharkey had pointed to the fact that the slaves were free—"free by the fortunes of war—free by the proclamation—free by common consent—free practically as well as theoretically. . . ." He felt that it would be a waste of time to dwell on the theories and technicalities of the question.[2] The convention's committee on the state constitution was inclined to take a similar view on the matter. Its recommendation fell into four sections. First, the constitution was to be amended by striking out the three sections and an amendment which related to slaves. Second, there was to be inserted a new article which declared

That neither slavery nor involuntary servitude, otherwise than in the punishment of crimes, whereof the party shall have been duly convicted, shall hereafter exist in this State; and the Legislature at its next session, and thereafter as the public welfare may require, shall provide by law for the protection of the person and property of the freedmen of the State, and guard them and the State against any evils that may arise from their sudden emancipation.

The third recommendation was that the legislature be allowed to dispense with the use of a grand jury in the prosecution of minor crimes, riots, unlawful assembly, or vagrancy; and might provide for the trial of such cases before justices of the peace, or other inferior courts. The final suggestion was that the boards of county police be given the power to make regulations for the control of apprentices and vagrancy.[3]

Sections one and three were received with almost immediate approval,

[1] Mississippi Constitutional Convention of 1865, *Journal*, p. 152.
[2] *Ibid.*, p. 7.
[3] *Ibid.*, pp. 29-30.

and the fourth was quickly eliminated. On the second section the convention spent the greater part of its time. The mere statement that slavery was no longer to exist was too simple. Hugh Barr of Lafayette insisted on the insertion of the declaration that it had been abolished by action of the government of the United States.[4] William Yerger, for the conservative and conciliatory majority, declared that such a statement would have a bad effect. Anyway, he did not believe that slavery had been abolished by the government; it had been abolished by war. Such matters should be left to the historian.[5] Jarnagin of Noxubee agreed that slavery certainly was dead, but he insisted on finding out what power had killed it. He would not allow the world to believe that Mississippi had abolished it by a voluntary act. He believed that abolition had come through the proclamation of the President and the fortunes of war.[6]

The most vigorous opposition came from George L. Potter, who in 1867 was to lead the fight against the acceptance of Negro suffrage. He was not certain that slavery was dead. "Has any authority competent to bind the State of Mississippi by any ordinance or action, abolished it? No, sir! Is it by any action of the people of Mississippi? That cannot be. Who claims, then sir, to have abolished it?"[7] He went on to present his views in a substitute motion which began: ". . . Certain authorities of the United States, do claim, that by force of certain proclamations of the President, and of certain acts of the Congress . . . , all colored persons, heretofore held as slaves, in this State, are, of right free. . . ." The motion declared that abolition was void and, even if it were upheld, obligation of compensation rested upon Congress. In the meantime, "The good people of this State, reserving . . . their rights and claims . . . do now treat said portions of the colored population as if free, and will continue so to regard and treat them until the said alleged acts and proclamations are annulled by the proper tribunals, or are otherwise lawfully vacated."[8] Potter argued that any positive act by the state would shift to it the burden of compensation which could not otherwise be avoided by Congress. Although he probably represented the attitude of a large portion of the white population, Potter could gain few votes from a body of substantial, conservative leaders who were anxious above all to regain for the state its place in the Union. His motion was defeated by a vote of 63-28.[9]

R. S. Hudson of Yazoo was able to get a great deal more support for a proviso which would prevent the section from becoming effective until the representatives of the state were admitted to Congress, and which would reserve all rights of compensation. Hudson could not believe that slavery was legally dead. There was no power to abolish it in the constitution, or even in the laws of war. The Federal government had no

[4] *Ibid.*, p. 44.
[6] *Ibid.*, pp. 45-46.
[8] *Ibid.*, p. 55.

[5] *Ibid.*, pp. 44-45.
[7] *Ibid.*, p. 49.
[9] *Ibid.*, pp. 68-70.

more power to intervene between master and servant than between husband and wife. He might admit that slavery was abolished in fact, but in law it was not. The slaves had not been surrendered with the Confederate army.[10]

Against Hudson, Potter, and their followers, the conservatives now brought out their leading members. The greatest of these were Judges Amos R. Johnston and William Yerger, former Whigs, whose names were known throughout the Lower South. Judge Johnston insisted that a policy of conciliation should be followed above all else. The essential thing was to regain for the state its place in the Union. Once that was done, its representatives could unite with the President and the conservatives in the North to form "a great party, irresistable in its power, and sufficiently efficacious and strong to control the next Presidential election, to defeat the radicals, and to place some conservative Northern man in the Presidential chair of the United States." Johnston believed that abolition was illegal, unwise, and unjust; slave property was guaranteed by the constitution and sanctioned by God himself. But, he went on, "This institution, such as it was, is . . . not only wounded, but dead, dead, *dead* . . . beyond the power of resurrection, except by the miraculous interposition of the Most High." It was now vain to inquire how it was killed, or to hope for compensation.[11] Judge Yerger in a long and able speech upheld Johnston's views. Those who supported the Hudson substitute, he insisted, ignored the events of the past five years. He then pointed out in detail the facts that must replace their theories.[12]

Soon after the conclusion of Judge Yerger's address, the Hudson substitute was tabled. J. T. Harrison of Lowndes then moved to strike out the initial word "that" from the report of the committee, and to insert in its place the words "The institution of slavery having been destroyed in Mississippi." The amendment was accepted and the section was passed by a vote of 87-11.[13] Thus was slavery done to death, by a perfect passive participle.

This participial preamble did not prevent a later decision by Judge James F. Trotter of Panola County which held that all slaves in the state continued legally in that status until the constitutional changes of 1865 went into effect.[14] The Supreme Court of the state, after declaring that slaves had not been emancipated by Lincoln's proclamation, twice refused to settle the question of the exact date of the coming of freedom.[15] Practically, Negroes had been free from chattel slavery from the moment they entered Federal lines during the war, or from that moment after the war

[10] *Ibid.*, pp. 71-82.   [11] *Ibid.*, pp. 89-92.
[12] *Ibid.*, pp. 141-162.   [13] *Ibid.*, pp. 164-165.
[14] John W. Kyle, "Reconstruction in Panola County," *P.M.H.S.*, XIII, 68.
[15] W. W. Magruder, "Legal Status of the Slaves in Mississippi Before the War," *P.M.H.S.*, IV, 137-138.

in which they gained release from a willing or unwilling master. The ratification of the Thirteenth Amendment by the required number of states in December, 1865, placed a seal upon the matter.

The legal extent of that freedom remained to be determined. Attorney-General Edward Bates held in 1863 that free men of color were citizens of the United States,[16] but that term itself was almost entirely undefined. The real points at issue were the rights and privileges to be enjoyed by the freedmen under the laws of the state of Mississippi.

The first problem to receive any great deal of attention was that of the admission of Negro testimony before the courts. On the advice of President Johnson, Provisional-Governor Sharkey in September, 1865, declared that such testimony must be admitted in all cases in which the interests of Negroes were involved.[17] Colonel Thomas, of the Freedmen's Bureau, immediately announced his acceptance of the Sharkey proposition, and by October 31 he had abolished the last of the special courts for the Negroes.[18] There can be no doubt that this abandonment of the Negro to the civil courts was premature. Outside the city of Vicksburg, little attention was given to his testimony, even in those few cases where it was admitted.[19] Many of the Negroes fled across the state line to Memphis in search of protection.[20] The hiring by the Bureau of one Northern lawyer to handle cases of Negroes in the state courts was a useless gesture.[21]

The question of the admission of the Negro's testimony immediately aroused furious discussion throughout the state. Led by the Jackson *News* and the Kosciusko *Chronicle,* the poor white element loudly declared that there could be no compromise on the issue. Other groups, lining up behind the Meridian *Clarion,* the Jackson *Mississippian,* the Vicksburg *Herald,* the Vicksburg *Journal,* the Brandon *Republican,* the Natchez *Courier,* and the Friar's Point *Coahomian,* urged acceptance of Negro testimony as a matter of expediency. The attitude of the editor of the *Coahomian* was typical of this group:

The question of admitting negro testimony in the civil courts of the country is one . . . which should, like Aaron's rod, swallow up all minor considerations. It is repugnant to our feelings we admit, but so was [*sic*] reconstruction and emancipation, which was crammed down our throats by the results of the war. It behooves us, then to accept negro testimony—as qualified by Governor Sharkey—for the present, uncomplainingly. Negro equality in the courts is not as nauseating a dose as negro equality in all political privileges. . . .[22]

Editors of the other papers in this group all agreed that the admission of testimony, disagreeable as that might be, was the very least concession that

[16] Edward Bates, *Opinion of Attorney General Bates on Citizenship.*
[17] Meridian *Clarion,* October 1, 1865.   [18] *Ibid.,* November 5, 1865.
[19] *Senate Executive Documents,* no. 2, 39th Congress, 1st session, p. 78.
[20] J. T. Trowbridge, *The South,* p. 342.
[21] *Senate Executive Documents,* no. 2, 39th Congress, 1st session, p. 37.
[22] Friar's Point *Coahomian,* October 27, 1865.

could be made to prevent worse things from being imposed by the North.

While the battle raged in the press, it was also carried to the stump in the election of congressmen, legislators, and state officials, and was immediately accepted as the basic issue of the campaign. Here again, the most liberal candidates would go no further than S. J. Evans, the prospective congressman, who declared: "We are not willing that the negro should testify in our courts. We all revolt at it, and it is natural that we should do so; but we must allow it as one of the requisites of our admission to our original standing in the Union."[23] Even such candidates, however, were generally unable to secure election. Judge E. S. Fisher, conservative nominee of the constitutional convention, was defeated for the governorship by General B. G. Humphreys, while a majority in the legislature was gained by the party absolutely opposed to Negro testimony.[24] In disgust, the editor of the Brandon *Republican* declared that the people of his county evidently preferred provost-marshal courts to the continuation of their own with Negro testimony.[25]

Gradually, however, increased pressure on the anti-testimony group in the legislature by leading men of the state began to have its effect, and by November 15, a majority of only five stood against admission. On the following day, a remarkable reversal was seen, and modified Negro testimony was written into law by a vote of sixty-three to twenty-seven.[26] The editor of the *News* angrily charged that the change had been forced by pressure from Washington.[27] It seems more probable that those who changed their votes were convinced that the move was necessary for the restoration of the state to the Union, and that their opposition had been maintained only because of pledges to their constituents. The shift of their stand on the following day was a matter of expediency.[28] A few days later they regained some standing with their voters by participating in the rejection of the Thirteenth Amendment.

Thus Negroes continued to testify in those cases in which members of their race were parties. Such testimony had received more and more general admission in the latter part of 1865. By the latter part of 1866, General Wood was able to report that prejudice against the Negro was effective only in the lower courts; in the higher ones he could practically always gain a fair trial.[29] Similar views were expressed by the Federal commanders in 1867 and 1868.[30] It should be noted, however, that prac-

[23] *Senate Executive Documents,* no. 2, 39th Congress, 1st session, p. 64, quoting the Vicksburg *Journal.*

[24] J. W. Garner, *Reconstruction in Mississippi,* p. 94.

[25] Meridian *Clarion,* October 7, 1865, quoting the Brandon *Republican.*

[26] Meridian *Clarion,* November 5, 17, 1865.

[27] *Ibid.,* November 26, 1865.

[28] *Ibid.,* November 26, 1865.

[29] *Senate Executive Documents,* no. 6, 39th Congress, 2d session, p. 97.

[30] *House Executive Documents,* no. 1, 40th Congress, 2d session, p. 682; *ibid.,* no. 1, 40th Congress, 3d session, p. 525.

tically all cases involving Negroes were settled in the local courts. In spite of this fact, Hiram Cassedy, one of the first attorneys in the state to handle cases for the freedmen, believed that in his county nine Negroes in ten were receiving justice.[31]

The first case in Mississippi in which a white man was convicted of homicide on the testimony of Negroes was tried in the Fifth Judicial District Court in September, 1866, and attracted a great deal of attention. J. A. P. Campbell, one of the ablest and most widely known judges of the state, was on the bench. He immediately overruled the objection of the defense that the testimony of the Negroes was incompetent. An appeal to the jury that the testimony be disregarded was also without effect.[32] The verdict was that of manslaughter. The address of Judge Campbell, widely quoted in the press, gives some insight into contemporary attitudes. He pointed out the unusual nature of the case, and expressed his belief in the value and justice of Negro testimony. He then took up the plea of the prosecuting attorney, who had asked for a light penalty on the ground that the conviction alone had been enough to establish the power of the law. Judge Campbell was inclined to agree with this; he felt that all great changes should be made gradually, lest men's sensibilities be shocked and future attempts to apply the law be rendered vain. He continued: "I am admonished of the propriety of this view by a recurrence to the fact that during this trial, I was painfully impressed with the conviction that yourself and family and friends, together with the public, were not suitably impressed with the danger of the situation; and . . . that it was not deemed possible that conviction could be had on the testimony of negroes. . . ." The judge would not be carried away by "the sympathies of an impressible heart"; he would inflict punishment just as if the prisoner had been convicted of killing a white man. "I must obey the dictates of my judgment. . . . I am convinced . . . that you killed the negro Sam in the heat of violent passion . . . and that the act was unjustifiable and unwarranted. . . ." The sentence was twelve months in the county jail and payment of the costs of court.[33]

In line with the repeal of a number of the laws of 1865 which applied especially to the Negro, the legislature in 1867 removed all limitations on the testimony of the freedmen and placed them on the same basis in the courts of the state as that of the whites.[34] Even after the Negro was driven from the ballot box and the jury bench he retained the right to offer as a witness testimony which received such consideration as a white judge and a white jury considered it to be worth.

[31] Hiram Cassedy to William N. Whitehurst, December 16, 1866, Whitehurst Papers, Mississippi State Archives.
[32] *Appleton's Cyclopedia*, 1866, p. 523.
[33] Jackson *Clarion*, September 25, 1866.
[34] *Laws of Mississippi, 1866-1867*, pp. 232-233.

The legislature of 1867, after repealing most of the laws that made up the Black Code, enacted a special proviso which declared that the new privileges of the Negroes did not include that of serving on grand or petit juries.[35] In April, 1869, however, General Adelbert Ames ordered that all persons, regardless of race or color, who possessed the qualifications prescribed by the code of 1857, were to be admitted to jury service.[36] The Reconstruction legislature of 1870 wrote this provision into the laws of the state.[37]

The attitude of many of the whites was later expressed by Franklin Montgomery: "In the fall of that year [1869], at the October term of the court, negroes were for the first time put on juries. I was on the panel for the week, and so great was my disgust that I at once applied for, and easily obtained, a license to practice law, thus escaping what I thought would have been a degradation."[38] This attitude was still prevalent in 1873, although many of the leading whites served willingly with the Negroes and found them generally kind-hearted, just, and honest.[39] In many of the counties where the population was more or less evenly divided between blacks and whites, the custom developed of using an equal number of each of the races on all juries[40] In the counties with a heavy majority of Negroes, their race generally held a majority on the juries. Even here, however, the Negroes in making their decision tended to follow the wishes of the white members.[41]

After 1875, the Negroes appeared in smaller and smaller numbers on the jury panels, but their complete elimination did not occur until after 1890.[42] In the constitution of that year, it was provided that all persons serving on grand or petit juries must be qualified electors, and must also be able to read and write. Thus the elimination of the Negro as a voter served also to remove him from the jury bench, and in a land of white officers, white judges, white lawyers, and white juries, the term "law," in the Negro's mind, came more and more to mean only a big white man with a badge.

[35] Ibid., pp. 232-233.
[36] General Orders, no. 32, Appleton's Cyclopedia, 1869, pp. 455-456; Vicksburg Daily Times, April 30, 1869.
[37] Mississippi Session Laws, 1870, p. 98.
[38] Franklin A. Montgomery, Reminiscences of a Mississippian in Peace and War, p. 273.
[39] Hinds County Gazette, April 9, 1873.
[40] Ibid., April 24, May 24, August 30, 1871; J. W. Kyle, op. cit., XIII, 67.
[41] F. A. Montgomery, op. cit., pp. 277-278.
[42] Jackson Weekly Clarion, May 24, 1882; Hinds County Gazette, February 22, 1882; Senate Miscellaneous Documents, no. 166, 50th Congress, 1st session, p. 398; Raymond Gazette, March 3, 1888.

CHAPTER XI

NEGROES UNDER THE PROVISIONAL GOVERNMENT, 1865-1870

ENTRANCE OF THE NEGRO INTO POLITICS

From the close of the war until June 13, 1865, Mississippi was entirely under the control of a military commander. From that date until March 5, 1869, there was a peculiar division of authority between a civil and a military governor. W. L. Sharkey, appointed civil governor by President Johnson, was an old citizen of the state, a distinguished jurist, and a former Whig. His policy in general was that of the President. B. G. Humphreys, elected governor by the white citizens of the state and recognized by Johnson in November, 1865, had been a Whig before the war, and had more recently served as a brigadier-general in the Confederate army. Serving until July 15, 1868, he was less inclined to consult the wishes of the President than his predecessor had been. Before the expiration of his term of office, he was removed by the military commander of the state and replaced by Adelbert Ames, a Federal general from Maine. On March 5, 1869, Ames also became military commander, and continued to serve in this dual capacity until the installation of the reconstructed government of the state in January, 1870.

In general, the relations of the military commanders and the native civil governors were surprisingly good. Appointed by President Johnson, Generals G. K. Warren, P. J. Osterhaus, H. W. Slocum, T. J. Wood, and A. G. Gillem usually followed his policies and made themselves actually popular with the whites of the state.[1] On the other hand, General E. O. C. Ord, who served as commander during the latter part of 1867, and General Irwin McDowell, who served for one month in 1868, aroused the dislike of the native whites, chiefly through their policy of removing officials whom they believed to be unsympathetic toward the reconstruction policies. None of the commanders named above showed any special tenderness toward, or interest in, the Negroes. Adelbert Ames, who became provisional-governor July 15, 1868, and military commander March 5,

[1] J. S. McNeily, "From Organization to Overthrow of Mississippi's Provisional Government," *P.M.H.S.C.S.*, I, 267; J. S. McNeily, "War and Reconstruction in Mississippi," *P.M.H.S.C.S.*, II, 299, 300, 356; J. W. Garner, *Reconstruction in Mississippi*, pp. 107, 182, 228, 229, 267; Jackson *Clarion*, February 11, 1866; Hinds County *Gazette*, July 10, 1868, March 11, 1869, May 7, 1873; Adelbert Ames to J. W. Garner, January 25, 1900, J. W. Garner Papers, Mississippi State Archives.

1869, was a man of a different stripe. Although he had been rather quiet and inactive as provisional-governor, he was by the middle of 1869 recognized by the Negroes as their friend and zealous advocate. He was to hold their devotion until he left the state in 1876.

If the commanding officers of the Federal forces in Mississippi showed little sympathy for the Negroes, their private soldiers often gave evidence of actual dislike. Many of them were Democrats, and practically all of them were representatives of the poor white group of the North. Their tendency was to share the prejudices of those of their class in the South. J. S. McNeily, the state's leading Democratic historian of the period, wrote as follows:

In the excitement of the elections of 1867 and 1868, the troops were often "a restraint curbing" the turbulence of the negroes—they were never so regarded by the whites. There was some misuse of them while Ames was military Governor. But as a rule, if not invariably, the sentiment of the troops, and especially the non-commissioned officers and privates, was hostile to the negro.[2]

An English traveler in 1868 found this to be true throughout the South.[3] Troops sent to Hillsboro for the election of 1868 talked openly of their desire to "shoot radicals and niggers."[4] Such feelings were not entirely limited to the ordinary soldiers. Major John Powers, at Holly Springs, was in sympathy with the Democrats,[5] while General Pennypacker, second in command in the state, went so far as to warn Klansmen so that they might escape from parties sent to arrest them.[6] From their relations with the representatives of the Federal government, the Negroes of Mississippi had little cause to expect from that source any further advancement of their status. Yet there were at work in the North certain peculiar combinations of forces which soon would make voters of the freedmen, and deliver into their hands the power to control the government of Mississippi.

To Republican politicians, to sincere abolitionists, and to those interested in tariff-protected industries, the national banking system, and the public debt, the possibility of the restoration of Democratic control brought sheer terror. Yet it seemed that this must come upon the return to the Union of Southern states with increased representation growing out of the abolition of slavery. However reluctantly they might accept the fact, most Republican leaders soon agreed that their only hope lay in the enfranchisement of the freedmen. It was their task to sell the idea to the voters and

---

[2] J. S. McNeily, "The Enforcement Act of 1871 and the Ku-Klux Klan in Mississippi," *P.M.H.S.*, IX, 169; see also J. S. McNeily, "From Organization to Overthrow of Mississippi's Provisional Government," *P.M.H.S.C.S.*, I, 321.

[3] Foster B. Zincke, *Last Winter in the United States*, p. 104.

[4] *House Miscellaneous Documents*, no. 52, 40th Congress, 3d session, part 2, pp. 274-287.

[5] Ruth Watkins, "Reconstruction in Marshall County," *P.M.H.S.*, XII, 189.

[6] Julia C. Brown, "Reconstruction in Yalobusha and Grenada Counties," *P.M.H.S.*, XII, 230, 237.

minor politicians of the North, to many of whom it was just as repugnant
as it was to the Southern Democrats.

It was with the hope of blocking this move that President Johnson in
the summer of 1865 suggested to Southern leaders the possibility of admitting to the suffrage a few small, selected groups of Negroes. This
suggestion received little consideration. Before the end of August, Provisional-Governor Sharkey reported to the President that its application
was impossible in Mississippi.[7] Some of the old Whig leaders of the
state, it is true, saw the intelligence and desirability of such a move. In
the same month that Sharkey made his discouraging report, General J. L.
Alcorn was writing that the people of the South must make the Negroes
their friends, or their path would lie "through a way red with blood and
damp with tears." A limited franchise certainly would not imply social
equality, which was not even granted to white voters who were low and
base. But Alcorn, fully understanding the difficulties of the situation,
closed his letter with a pessimistic note. "Will the Southern people secure
the friendship of the negro? I fear they will not!"[8] Even in the North,
those who were closely acquainted with the Southern attitude were convinced that none of the freedmen would receive the franchise as a voluntary grant. General W. T. Sherman was certain that any effort to force
Negro suffrage upon the South would result in a new civil war more bloody
than the last.[9]

In the meantime, a few of the freedmen in the state were showing
some interest in their political possibilities. In June, 1865, before the all-
white election of delegates to the constitutional convention, a number of
them gathered in a mass meeting at Vicksburg and drew up resolutions
condemning the exclusion of "loyal citizens" from the election, and appeal-
ing to Congress to refuse readmission to Mississippi until she voluntarily
enfranchised the freedmen.[10] The fact that the presiding officer of the
meeting was a Northern soldier raises the question as to whether it was
a genuine expression of Negro sentiment. The only evidence of authen-
ticity is the active participation of Henry Mason, a native Negro who was
a political leader of some importance.

The reaction of the majority of the whites to this effort was immediate, and seemed to justify such fears as those expressed by Sherman.
The editor of the Natchez *Courier* referred to the resolutions of the freedmen, and then solemnly warned that history taught that no two dissimilar
races could live together on a basis of equality. "One *must* be superior—

---

[7] W. L. Sharkey to Andrew Johnson, August 28, 1865, Andrew Johnson Papers,
Library of Congress.
[8] "Indian" to "My Dear Amelia," August 26, 1865, J. L. Alcorn Papers, University of North Carolina.
[9] J. S. McNeily, "War and Reconstruction in Mississippi," *P.M.H.S.C.S.*, II, 275-
276.
[10] *Ibid.*, II, 297.

one *must* be dominant. If the negro should be the master, the whites must either abandon the territory, or there would be another civil war in the South—a war of the races—the whites against the black—and the war would be a war of extermination."[11]

His colleague, the editor of the Natchez *Democrat,* was just as certain that the enfranchisement of the freedmen would never be borne. "We have no objection to negroes voting in Massachusetts or Ohio, or carrying out in those States the doctrine of miscegenation to all its practical consequences; but when Mississippi shall be willing to place the whites and blacks upon a social and political level, to escape the degradation we will become a voluntary exile from the home of our birth and seek an asylum in some more congenial clime."[12] The editor of the *Courier* agreed that the imposition of Negro suffrage would be followed by a mass exodus of the Southern whites "to a better land—for to them any land would then be better."[13]

The unhappy experience of Nelson Fitzhugh of Natchez offers an example of the effect upon white sentiment of the expression by a Negro of an active interest in the current situation. Fitzhugh, freed long before the war, and possessed of some education, had gained modest success in the community, having been a slaveholder and manager of a mercantile establishment. Like William Johnson, the barber, and Robert McCary, the Negro meteorologist, he had been considered a good Confederate, and had been held in high esteem by his white neighbors. Then, in 1866, someone discovered in the Philadelphia *Christian Recorder* a letter from Fitzhugh which indicated that he had been selling subscriptions for that journal. The writer went on to say that the Natchez *Courier* was full of lies, and that he hoped the *Recorder* would make some effort to prevent the kidnaping of Negroes for subsequent sale in Cuba. That was all, but it was enough. The editor of the *Courier* immediately leaped to the attack:

This man Nelson Fitzhugh has been wearing a mask. He is full of deceit and hypocrisy. . . . He has been a systematic hypocrite all his life. . . . Cloaked under the garb of religion, sanctimonious as a pilgrim, seemingly honest and honorable, still kept in kindly remembrance for past good offices, be they well meant or hypocrisies, Nelson Fitzhugh is still a part of this community. . . . He is now a Radical agent and a colporteur among us, and disseminates poisons of the literary kind, stirring up bad blood among people kindly disposed towards each other. . . .[14]

A few days later the paper reported that numerous letters, attacking Fitzhugh as a "turn coat" and a "snake in the grass," had been received from white citizens. There was also a letter from the Negro's daughter, in which she prayed that the condemnation of Fitzhugh not be extended to

[11] Natchez *Tri-Weekly Courier,* July 18, 1865.
[12] Natchez *Tri-Weekly Democrat,* January 6, 1866.
[13] Natchez *Daily Courier,* January 27, 1866.
[14] *Ibid.,* November 8, 1866.

other members of his family. "And now, my dear Southern friends, for the sake of a family who are Southern in sentiment and principle, I hope you will look over my father's indiscretion, for he is old and childish. I really do not believe that he meant what he said, for I never heard him utter a word against the South in all my life. I will now close by asking you to give this to your readers, that they may not hold the family responsible for what my father may have said."[15]

When, early in 1867, it became apparent that the enfranchisement of the freedmen could not be avoided, powerful conservative leaders of the state began an immediate and almost frantic campaign to bring the Negro voters under the control of the Southern whites. Such men as A. G. Brown, Ethelbert Barksdale, J. A. P. Campbell, J. W. C. Watson, and William Yerger, many of them old Whigs, gave the matter the greater part of their time. By May, the *Clarion* was able to report that twenty-two of the papers of the state had swung into line.[16] Judge J. W. Robb sent to the press an urgent declaration that the freedom and suffrage of the Negro were facts, and that the native whites must act quickly if at all.

It is unnecessary to dwell upon the humiliation of our position; I can picture nothing more horrible to myself than the scene which would be presented if the administration of the state government passes from the hands of Southern men into the hands of ignorant and vicious masses, led by imported fanatics. . . .

. . . We cannot hope to convince the colored voter by arguments that we are his best friends so long as we propose nothing and advocate nothing to his benefit, so long as we deny him all the privileges of a freeman and leave the education of his children to imported females from Massachusetts. . . .

. . . I know it to be true that his confidence is easily won and secured for I have not yet seen the one who did not perceive and fully appreciate the fact that his future interest was inseperable [sic] from the interest of all other citizens of the State, and he is only made to feel that his interest is diverse by our action in refusing and neglecting all measures for the promotion of his welfare. We have only to deserve his confidence to procure it, and it would gladden his heart to bestow it upon the white men of the South with whom his future lot is cast. I affirm this as a truth which I have found to be so, and which appears as universal as a sentiment can be among a people.[17]

In a pamphlet circulated throughout the state, J. L. Alcorn urged a realistic view, and immediate and positive action.

The Loyal League is upon you. Even a brief experience of the workings of that voting machine would satisfy you, as it has me, that all which our people claim for the influence of the "old master" on the freedmen is neither more nor less than nonsense. The terrible necessities of our position demand blunt speaking. . . . The "old master," gentlemen, has passed from fact to poetry!

. . . .

The colored man comes, as well as the white man, within the scope of my proposed negotiations. . . . All that Congress has given him I accept as *his* with

[15] *Ibid.,* November 10, 1866.   [16] J. W. Garner, *op. cit.,* p. 179.
[17] Jackson *Weekly Clarion,* June 13, 1867.

all my heart and conscience. I propose to vote with him; to discuss political affairs with him; to sit, if need be, in political counsel with him; and from a platform acceptable alike to him, to me, and to you, to pluck our common liberty and our common prosperity out of the jaws of inevitable ruin.[18]

Strenuous efforts were made to carry out these policies. In May, a bi-racial meeting was held in Copiah County. Resolutions were adopted which declared that it was the duty of the whites to protect and advance the interests of the freedmen, to instruct them in the duties of the elective franchise, and to encourage them in their efforts to educate their children.[19] In June, a bi-racial meeting was held in Terry to plan a public dinner for the Fourth of July, "for the whole people without regard to race or condition." Former Governor A. G. Brown presided, with Alfred Johnson, colored, as his vice-president. It was agreed that the whites were to furnish the supplies, and the blacks were to prepare them. All committees were to consist of three whites and three Negroes. A resolution was adopted which declared:

That it is intended by this movement to give mutual assurance of a cordial, good understanding between the white and colored men of this neighborhood; and therefore this committee are instructed to make no distinctions, but in the matter of inviting speakers, and in everything else, to act in concert—giving an equal voice to the colored men with the white men in all that is necessary in carrying out the objects of this meeting.[20]

Later in the same month, a bi-racial meeting in Hinds County was addressed by Judge Robb on the subject of the mutual interests of the whites and blacks, and of the need for friendship and harmony. A similar meeting was planned for the following week.[21] In August, a meeting at Mississippi Springs was attended by 800 to 1,000 Negroes and about 200 whites. Two of the leading white coöperationists and three freedmen addressed the assembly. On the same day, ex-Governor Brown was speaking to a similar meeting in Copiah County.[22]

The whole movement, however, was a hopeless task from the very start. In the words of J. S. McNeily:

The result was failure, utter and universal. Upon reflection this will be seen to have been natural and inevitable. The Southerner's manner of address, his air of authority, conflicted with the new sense of freedom, and contradicted his professions of acceptance of political equality. Suspicion and distrust in the negro was second nature. He saw that there was no real and lasting fulfillment in that quarter, for the aspirations which the law promised him.[23]

[18] J. L. Alcorn, *Views on the Political Situation in Mississippi,* pp. 3-4.
[19] Hinds County *Gazette,* May 31, 1867.
[20] Jackson *Weekly Clarion,* June 13, 1867.
[21] Hinds County *Gazette,* June 21, 1867.
[22] *Ibid.,* August 9, 1867.
[23] J. S. McNeily, "From Organization to Overthrow of Mississippi's Provisional Government," *P.M.H.S.C.S.,* I, 321.

To McNeily's analysis there must be some additions. The leaders of the coöperationists were men of distinction and substance, but they were not the real leaders of the masses of the people, and in this particular case they represented a comparatively small number of the whites. Furthermore, the movement came too late. In too many hundreds of instances in the past two years, most of the coöperationists, along with the white masses, had made entirely too clear their real attitude toward the Negro and his hopes for a rise in status. The desires of a majority of the old citizens had been reflected in the Black Code, and the very mention of that code now served to make Negroes forget the speeches of Robb and Brown. Finally, the more intelligent Negro leaders of the state easily remembered the attacks under which they had suffered a few months before. It is significant that the McCarys and the Fitzhughs, kinsmen of the persecuted patriarch of the Negroes of Natchez, now abandoned their "Southern principles" to become leaders in the new Republican party.

In the meantime, the coöperationists were losing large sections of their white membership. Such planks in their platform as that asking for public education for blacks and whites were subjected to heavy attack, and they themselves were described as men "once considered the first men in the State, who are now so anxious to pick up the crumbs that fall from radical tables, that they are actually traversing the State, making negro speeches, getting up negro meetings, and playing second fiddle to Sambo, condescending to act as Vice-President at such meetings, while Sambo submits to act as President of the same."[24]   The poor white had spoken, and the protest of the *Clarion* that the extension of the franchise did not mean social equality was of no avail.

The additional requirements for reconstruction imposed by Congress in July drove many into the ranks of the irreconcilables.[25]   The final blow came with the overwhelming rejection of Negro suffrage by the state of Ohio. The conviction now developed in Mississippi that the North would go Democratic in 1868, and that all that was necessary was patient waiting, combined with an absolute refusal to compromise.[26]   All over the state, newspapers which had supported coöperation now seceded and joined the ranks of George L. Potter's "Constitutional Union Party."[27]

In the meantime, many of the Neroes had entered enthusiastically into political activity. Members of the race gathered in Vicksburg in July to set up a Negro Republican organization.[28]   Although a number of officers were selected, it appears that the organization performed no important

[24] Hinds County *Gazette*, June 28, 1867, "In Hoc Signo Vinces" to G. W. Harper.
[25] Hinds County *Gazette*, October 25, 1867.
[26] Jackson *Weekly Clarion*, September 5, 25, October 16, 1867; *Senate Reports*, no. 527, 44th Congress, 1st session, p. 534.
[27] Jackson *Weekly Clarion*, October 16, 1867; Hinds County *Gazette*, October 18, 25, 1867.
[28] Hinds County *Gazette*, July 12, 1867.

function. The Negroes were immediately absorbed into the regular Republican party of the state.

That body held its convention in Jackson on September 10 and 11. Although there was some immediate unpleasantness between the Negroes and Northern men with lily-white tendencies, organization was effected and a platform drawn up. Among the planks, the most significant were those calling for universal free education, and declaring that the party would never recognize any distinction of race or color in education, the ballot, or other civil and political rights.[29]

During the course of registration, General Ord ruled that Negroes were eligible to serve as clerks and judges of the election, and as delegates to the convention which was to provide a constitution for the reconstructed state. The editor of the Vicksburg *Herald* expressed the feeling of the majority of the whites toward this move as follows:

We hoped that this shameful humiliation would have been spared our people, at least until the freemen of Mississippi decide whether they will submit to negro equality at the ballot-box or elsewhere. . . . General Ord has heretofore exhibited a wisdom in his administration which has been highly approved by the people, but we doubt not that lovers of peace throughout the country will condemn the order as injudicious, if not insulting to that race whom God has created the superior of the black man, and whom no monarch can make his equal.[30]

To the further disgust of people who held this attitude, General Ord in September announced the appointment of B. T. Montgomery, prosperous Negro planter and former business manager for Joe and Jefferson Davis, as Justice of the Peace at Davis Bend.[31] Montgomery was probably the first member of his race to hold a state office.

During the process of registration, relations of the races became more and more strained, but there seems to have been no actual outbreak.[32] Efforts to prevent the Negroes from registering were general enough to cause Ord to issue a warning,[33] but such efforts seem to have had little effect.

To the registration offices, as later to the polls, the Negroes generally came in large groups. The editor of the *Gazette,* reporting the registration in Raymond, stated: "Our usually quiet village was enlivened on Monday by the presence from adjacent plantations of from three hundred to five hundred of the newly manufactured 'American citizens of African descent.'" Some of the Negroes understood fully the object of their visit; others had the idea that they were to vote, receive free land, or be taxed. The *Gazette* went on to say:

[29] *Appleton's Cyclopedia,* 1867, p. 516.
[30] *Ibid.,* 1867, pp. 515-516, quoting the Vicksburg *Herald.*
[31] Jackson *Weekly Clarion,* September 19, 1867.
[32] J. S. McNeily, "From Organization to Overthrow of Mississippi's Provisional Government," *P.M.H.S.C.S.,* I, 322-323.
[33] *Ibid.,* I, 307.

We must give our newly-made voters the benefit of the remark, that they conducted themselves throughout the day with decorum and propriety, showing good breeding, and a proper respect for "the situation." As a consequence upon their good behavior, the largest liberty was allowed them by the whites, and we are glad to perceive that they seemed to appreciate the kindness everywhere shown them.[34]

Secure in the belief that the freedmen were rapidly dying out, and misled by the state census of 1866, most of the whites were convinced that the Negro voters would be a minority in the state, or that their majority would be so small as to be of little advantage to them.[35] Thus the results of the registration, showing 46,636 whites and 60,167 Negroes eligible to vote,[36] came as a distinct shock to the white citizens, and added to the number of those who were determined to stand to the last against Negro suffrage.

The large Negro majority also solidified the determination of a majority of the whites to allow the election to go by default and to wait for a Democratic victory in the North to bring their redemption. In many of the counties, those opposed to Reconstruction made no nominations.[37] At the polling booth at Vicksburg, only eight whites cast their votes. One of the local papers offered a dollar for the name of each of these "interesting sneaks."[38] The result was a vote of 76,016 in favor of the convention and of only 6,277 against.[39] From the totals, it is evident that at least twenty or twenty-five thousand whites took part in the election, but those who did not vote for the Republican candidates were able to elect only about twenty-nine conservative or Democratic delegates.[40] Of these, very few were men of ability or reputation.[41] Thus it became apparent that Mississippi's new constitution would reflect the attitudes of native and Northern Republicans and Negroes, almost entirely uninfluenced by the interests of the great mass of the native whites.

THE CONSTITUTION OF 1869

The convention which was to frame a constitution for a reconstructed state assembled January 8, 1868. It was composed of one hundred delegates, of whom, according to the best figures available, sixty-seven were native Southerners. Twenty-four were born in the North, and nine in foreign or unknown countries. Sixty-seven were unqualified Republicans, and of these thirty-three were resident whites. Three were "Reconstructionists," and one was "for Grant." Of the remaining twenty-nine,

[34] Hinds County *Gazette*, July 12, 1867.
[35] Jackson *Weekly Clarion*, June 13, August 22, September 19, 1867; J. W. Garner, *op. cit.*, p. 175.
[36] Jackson *Weekly Clarion*, September 19, 1867.
[37] Robert Bowman, "Reconstruction in Yazoo County," *P.M.H.S.*, VII, 120.
[38] J. W. Garner, *op. cit.*, p. 181.   [39] *Appleton's Cyclopedia*, 1867, p. 519.
[40] J. L. Power, "The Black and Tan Convention," *P.M.H.S.*, III, 77.
[41] John R. Lynch, *The Facts of Reconstruction*, p. 18.

THE NEGRO IN MISSISSIPPI, 1865-1890   14

who made up the more conservative faction, two were listed as Democrats, eight "Conservatives," one "Anti-Radical," two "opposed to Radicals of any kind," one "Union," two "Constitutional Union," two "Union Conservatives," one "Constitution and Laws of the United States," two "Henry Clay Whigs," four "Old Whigs," and two "none." Eighty-four of the delegates were white; sixteen were Negroes.[42] Of the group of one hundred, Negroes and "carpet-baggers" together formed a total of less than forty, but these with the thirty-three resident white radicals were easily able to control the convention.

Very little can be learned of the small group of Negroes who were sent to the convention. In line with the policy of regarding the whole affair as illegal and temporary, the newspapers of the state said little even of the convention itself. Since the official journal made no racial distinctions, even the compilation of the names of the Negro members is a difficult task. Of the sixteen, John C. Brinson, Amos Drane, Wesley Lawson, and Cyrus Myers seem to have returned almost immediately to the obscurity from which they came. They played no active or prominent part either in the convention or in the developments which followed it. Emanuel Handy of Copiah and Doctor Stites of Washington continued their careers as undistinguished members of the state legislature. Isham Stewart, a poorly educated but intelligent native Negro, became a powerful leader in the eastern portion of the state, and even survived the revolution of 1875 as member of the senate from Noxubee, Kemper, and Neshoba counties. Albert Johnson, one of the eight Negro preachers in the convention, later served Warren County in the legislature. In spite of evidence of intelligence in his voting, he was of no importance as a leader, and probably became an early victim of the Vicksburg ring.

The most peculiar career was that of William T. Combash, delegate from Washington County. Born in Maryland, he was said to have been "sold south" for theft. During the war, he escaped through the lines to Philadelphia, and there joined a company of Negro infantry from which he later deserted.[43] In the convention, he sometimes voted with the other Negroes, but more often deserted them to stand with their bitterest opponents on important measures. In the election of 1868, the Democrats made him their candidate for the state senate from Washington and Sunflower counties.[44] Defeated, and evidently in bad standing with his sponsors, he was hanged by the Ku-Klux.[45]

Matthew T. Newsom of Claiborne County and Charles W. Fitzhugh of Wilkinson were Methodist Episcopal preachers of some education and ability. Fitzhugh was a member of one of the leading free-Negro families

[42] J. L. Power, op. cit., P.M.H.S., III, 77.
[43] Meridian Chronicle, September 4, 1868, quoting the Frederick (Md.) Examiner.
[44] Meridian Chronicle, September 4, 1868.
[45] J. W. Garner, op. cit., note, p. 188.

of the Natchez region, and his record in the convention is one of moderate and intelligent activity, with indications of independent thought. Newsom also exercised some influence on the formation of the constitution, and later served his county in the legislature.

Henry Mayson, of Hinds County, was a native Negro who held the friendship and confidence of the local whites until he entered politics.[46] He played an active part in the convention, made speeches favoring the adoption of the constitution, and became a representative in the first reconstructed legislature.

Charles Caldwell, Mayson's colleague from Hinds County, also exercised some influence in the convention. A mulatto, he had been a slave blacksmith in Clinton, and had picked up a smattering of education. A Democratic leader declared he was "far above the average negro in intelligence."[47] Although he was no orator, he was a natural leader. Later, as state senator, he helped to guide his party, and, as "the Warwick of the administration," became one of the strongest supporters of Governor Ames.[48] Unlike the great mass of Negroes of the time, in or out of politics, he was absolutely fearless.[49] Although he used his power for the maintenance of peace between the races,[50] in the crisis of 1875 he led a unit of militia through Clinton, and for this he was marked for death. One night about a month after the overthrow, he was literally riddled with bullets on a street in that town.[51]

The three Negroes who exercised the greatest influence in the convention were T. W. Stringer, Henry P. Jacobs, and J. Aaron Moore, preachers respectively in the African Methodist, Baptist, and Methodist Episcopal Churches. Moore, who led in the organization of Methodist churches in the east-central portion of the state, later was an influential state senator, and centered his power in the town of Meridian. After his elimination from politics, he set up a successful blacksmith shop in Jackson, and soon came to be known once more as "a good citizen."[52]

Much more able than Aaron Moore was Henry P. Jacobs, Baptist preacher and organizer from Adams County. Born in Alabama, he learned to read and write from an insane man for whom he was caretaker. Thus prepared for freedom, he wrote his own pass, and in 1856 cleverly arranged an escape to the North for himself, his wife, three children, and a brother-in-law. After spending some time in Canada, he returned to Michigan. During the war, he went to Natchez, Mississippi, and there began the re-

[46] Jackson *Tri-Weekly Clarion,* June 12, 1869.
[47] W. Calvin Wells, "Reconstruction in Hinds County," *P.M.H.S.,* IX, 101.
[48] J. W. Garner Papers, Alexander Warner to J. W. Garner, May 4, 1900; C. H. Brough, "The Clinton Riot," *P.M.H.S.,* VI, 55.
[49] C. H. Brough, *op. cit.,* VI, 55.
[50] W. Calvin Wells, *op. cit.,* IX, 95-96; C. H. Brough, *op. cit.,* pp. 55-58.
[51] Hinds County *Gazette,* January 5, 1876; *Senate Reports,* no. 327, 44th Congress, 1st session, pp. 328, 437-438.
[52] J. L. Power, *op. cit.,* III, 78.

markable work of organizing Baptist Associations throughout the western portion of the state.[53]   Although the membership of his church was generally more radical than that of the other denominations, Jacobs himself, both in the convention and in the legislature, was inclined toward moderation and compromise.

By far the most influential Negro in the convention, and the most powerful political leader of his race in the state until 1869, was T. W. Stringer of Vicksburg.   A former resident of Ohio, he came to Mississippi as general superintendent of missions and presiding elder for the African Methodist Church, of which he had almost complete control for many years.   The man had a genius for organization.   After a distinguished career in religious and fraternal organizations in Ohio, he led in the development of the African Methodist Episcopal Church in Canada before his move to Mississippi.[54]   Wherever he went in the state, churches, lodges, benevolent societies, and political machines sprang up and flourished.   His influence upon the constitution of 1868 was as great as that of any other man in the convention.

Most of the ideas of the Constitution, however, were those of Republicans from the North and West, modified by the influence of native whites who had gone over to that party.   The opposition came from the small group of native anti-radicals, who were divided among themselves.   Most of them were men of little ability or reputation from the pine-hill counties, who looked to George Stovall, W. T. Stricklin, and Dr. W. M. Compton as their leaders.   As a hopeless minority, this group confined its activities in the convention to oratorical, parliamentary, and physical attacks on the majority delegates.   An even smaller group of intelligent, conservative, native whites formed themselves around J. W. C. Watson and William Hemingway, and exerted some influence on the decisions of the convention until the passage of the section on the franchise.   They then joined the Compton-Stricklin element and resigned from the convention.

The small group of Negro delegates, under the leadership of Stringer and Jacobs, generally went along with the native and Northern white Republicans who controlled the convention.   The one exception was the renegade Combash, who at times voted with the Compton-Stricklin group for clauses which would have limited citizenship, suffrage, and jury service to the white race, or which would have set up a property qualification for membership in the state senate.

At times the interests of the Negroes ran counter to those of the white majority.   They gave support to the efforts of Henry Jacobs to secure equal rights for their race on all public conveyances and voted unanimously for an amendment which would have given them the right "to be enter-

[53] P. H. Thompson, *Negro Baptists in Mississippi*, pp. 51, 607-608.
[54] R. A. Adams, *Cyclopedia of African Methodism in Mississippi*, pp. 190-191; *House Miscellaneous Documents*, no. 53, 40th Congress, 3d session, p. 28.

tained in all public places."[55] In the end, they were able to obtain only a statement in the Bill of Rights that "The right of all citizens to travel upon public conveyances shall not be infringed upon, nor in any manner abridged in this State."[56]

The efforts of T. W. Stringer to secure a provision for compulsory school attendance[57] failed to receive the favor of the convention. The Negroes were more successful when, with the exception of Combash, they voted as a group to table motions of Stovall and Compton to write into the constitution a requirement for separate schools for the races. Later, however, after it had been decided to leave the matter to the legislature, they voted as a group against a resolution of their colleague Charles Fitzhugh which would have put the convention on record as being opposed to the setting up of separate schools.[58]

The Negroes were at first unable to make up their minds on the effort of Stovall to put into the constitution a provision for a heavy penalty on intermarriage of the races. Racial pride prompted four of them to vote for the tabling of the motion; the same force caused an equal number of them to vote against it. Later, the Negro Newsom, with the consent of Stovall, added an amendment to place a very heavy penalty on interracial concubinage or other forms of miscegenation. His colleague Stites wished to add a special provision against white men who were cohabiting with Negro females out of wedlock. Finally, the whole matter was rejected, with all the Negroes except Newsom voting for tabling.[59] The suggestion of T. W. Stringer to empower the legislature to recognize as legally married those who had lived together as husband and wife, and to provide for the punishment of adultery and concubinage finally received the approval of the convention.[60] In the absence of any constitutional provision on the subject, the statute against the intermarriage of whites and blacks continued to stand until its repeal in 1870.

After the secession of the white oppositionists, the Negroes joined the majority in adopting an important provision which prevented the pledging of state credit for the benefit of any private association or corporation.[61] They divided evenly on the proposal of their colleague Stites for an increase in the pay of the delegates.[62] Finally, with the exception of Stites, they supported as a unit the clause which disfranchised those citizens above the rank of private who had given aid to the Confederacy.[63]

Altogether, the constitution of 1868, modeled largely on those of the states of the Middle West, made of the state government a much more positive force than it had ever been before. Its greatly expanded powers

[55] Mississippi Constitutional Convention of 1868, *Journal*, pp. 47, 256.
[56] *Ibid.*, p. 722.   [57] *Ibid.*, p. 315.
[58] *Ibid.*, pp. 316, 317-318, 506.   [59] *Ibid.*, pp. 199-200, 211-212.
[60] *Ibid.*, pp. 333, 542, 739.   [61] *Ibid.*, pp. 441, 529, 737.
[62] *Ibid.*, p. 696.   [63] *Ibid.*, p. 519.

and obligations, especially in matters concerning education and the judiciary, placed the centralized machinery of the state in immediate contact with almost every citizen. This was to come as a rude shock to masses of the whites who had trusted their state government little more than they had that of the nation, and who had even been inclined to allow their county governments to become dormant. The apportionment of the legislature on the basis of total population rather than that of the whites tore away from the poor white counties the control which they had won in the apportionments of 1836 and 1846. The plantation counties were once more in power, and in those plantation counties the new Negro citizens held heavy majorities.

Unlike the other constitutions of the state, that of 1868 was submitted to the people for ratification. It immediately became apparent that the Democrats and "Conservatives" would put up a real battle against its adoption. Success in this effort would mean the continuance of military government under the popular General Gillem. Then, according to the hopes of this group, the Democratic party would gain control of the national government in the fall elections, and the whole matter would be solved. For carrying out these purposes, a convention of white men of all political creeds was called to meet in Jackson in January. This convention adopted a platform centering around a plank which declared

That the nefarious design of the republican party in Congress to place the white men of the Southern States under the governmental control of their late slaves, and degrading the Caucasian race as the inferior of the African negro, is a crime against the civilization of the age, which has only to be mentioned to be scorned by all intelligent men, and we therefore call upon the people of Mississippi to vindicate alike the superiority of their race over the negro and their political power, and to maintain constitutional liberty.[64]

During the following month, the regular Democratic party adopted this platform as its own.[65] Thus the Democrats once more took a stand which made later efforts to bring Negro voters into their ranks almost entirely futile. To make their stand completely clear, they nominated Benjamin Humphreys to succeed himself as governor.

If the Democrats openly scorned and attacked the aspirations of the Negroes, the Republicans were willing to do little more than grant them the franchise and solicit their votes. Native and Northern whites dominated the convention of that party, and took for themselves the nominations for all of the state offices. Efforts of the Negroes to obtain nomination to a minor office for the able T. W. Stringer failed completely.[66] Even this disappointment, however, could not keep the great mass of the freed-

[64] *Senate Miscellaneous Documents,* no. 45, 44th Congress, 2d session, p. 220.
[65] Natchez *Tri-Weekly Democrat,* February 25, 1868.
[66] Hinds County *Gazette,* February 14, 1868.

men from seeing where their interests lay. James D. Lynch, who became the leading Negro worker in the campaign, declared:

The colored people are as anxious as any people in our broad land, to see political passions subside. . . . We desire to live in peace with our ex-masters—we recognize the mutual dependence of the one on the other; and to open a breach between the races is repugnant to every feeling of our natures. . . . That we will stand by the Republican party, the only one that is pledged to equal, civil and political rights which is [sic] as dear to us as life; is as certain as the rising of to-morrow's sun. But that we seek supremacy, or to ostracise, or to force ourselves into social companionship with any class of citizens, is as unfounded as is the hope that the public opinion of the nation will ever deprive us of our rights. If local instances indicate a desire on our part to become legislators and administrators of law, it is because universal hostility, among a certain class, to our political equality, leaves us no other alternative.[67]

The answer of the Democratic Executive Committee to Lynch, and to the Loyal Leagues he was organizing, was a solemn warning:

Freedmen of Mississippi, look before you leap. There is an awful gulf now yawning before you. The vote you cast at this election may be decisive of your fate. If you abandon the people with whom you have ever lived and who now invite you to their protection in the future, you cast your destiny with an enemy between whom and us there is eternal war. . . .[68]

This warning set the general tone of the Democratic efforts to gain the votes of the Negroes. The freedmen must either vote to reject the constitution and to elect Democratic officials, or they must accept the eternal enmity of those upon whom they depended for employment.[69] To threats of discharge from jobs or eviction from farms were added others of physical violence or death.[70] These threats were made effective by the appearance at the polls of Democratic workers who ostentatiously took the names of those who voted the distinctive Republican ticket.[71] Troops sent by General Gillem to some of the more important polling places offered little protection. According to the statement of their commander, the majority of the troops, like most of the sheriffs, were opposed to the constitution.[72] Some of them set themselves up as Democratic electioneering committees, and joined in persuading the Negroes that they must vote for that party.[73] In many places, bad feeling was evident at the polls. From

[67] Vicksburg *Weekly Republican*, May 26, 1868.
[68] *Appleton's Cyclopedia*, 1868, p. 513.
[69] Meridian *Chronicle*, June 13, July 10, 1868; *House Miscellaneous Documents*, no. 53, 40th Congress, 3d session, pp. 94, 139, 206-208, 274; A. T. Morgan, *Yazoo*, p. 198, from the Vicksburg *Times;* Julia Kendel, "Reconstruction in Lafayette County," *P.M.H.S.*, XIII, 237.
[70] Mississippi *Weekly Pilot*, March 5, 1870; *House Miscellaneous Documents*, no. 53, 40th Congress, 3d session, pp. 94, 274.
[71] *House Miscellaneous Documents*, no. 53, 40th Congress, 3d session, pp. 139, 173, 206, 208, 274; Hinds County *Gazette*, July 10, 1868.
[72] *House Miscellaneous Documents*, no. 53, 40th Congress, 3d session, p. 61.
[73] *Ibid.*, p. 255; Vicksburg *Weekly Republican*, June 30, 1868.

Monroe County came the report that the excitement there on the day of the election was "as angry as in the year 1860."[74] In an effort to relieve this situation, and to spare the feelings of some of the whites, Gillem ordered the setting up of segregated polling booths for the Negroes in the larger towns.[75]

Widespread intimidation of the Negroes was not the only factor which assured the defeat of the Republicans and the rejection of the constitution. The section which looked toward the disfranchisement of large numbers of the native whites assured the opposition of practically all of the old citizens, and also of many of the Negroes. Then too, the Republican party of the state was not yet fully organized. In many sections there were as yet no Loyal Leagues, and the technique of giving the freedmen self-assurance by taking them to the polls in large groups was not yet fully developed. Local Negro leaders were largely unrecognized and untrained. The result was the rejection of the constitution by 7,629 votes in a total of 120,091, and the election of Democrats to the governorship and to four of the five congressional posts.[76] These elections, of course, were invalidated by the rejection of the constitution.

The assurance of the continuation of military government under General Gillem was received with great satisfaction by most of the whites of the state. There was still the feeling that it was only necessary to hold firm until the November elections should drive the Radicals from Congress. The editor of the Meridian *Mercury* expressed general relief at the result of the election, and called for a continuation of the fight. He said:

With a sigh of relief, thank God, we can announce that it is over, the election, the most disgusting, disgraceful and degrading thing ever devised by the malice of man. Thank God it is over! and pray His holy name to remove the sin creating thing, negro suffrage, the most abominable of all abominations. . . .

The first preparation for the great work before us is, to shape and temper our firm resolves till they be hard as adamant and true as steel. Then, with the skull and cross bones of the "Lost Cause" before us, we will swear that

This is a White Man's Government; and trusting in our firm purpose our good right arms and God of Right, we will maintain it so![77]

The overwhelming triumph of the Radical Republicans in the national elections of 1868 blasted the foundation of the Democratic plan in Mississippi. As the conviction spread that the Congressional terms of reconstruction must be accepted, the irreconcilables found their leadership repudiated.[78] The final blow came on the day after the inauguration of President Grant. General Gillem, Democrat and native Southerner, was

[74] *House Miscellaneous Documents,* no. 53, 40th Congress, 3d session, p. 136.
[75] *Ibid.*, p. 89.
[76] Natchez *Weekly Democrat,* December 23, 1869.
[77] Meridian *Mercury,* July 7, 1868.
[78] *House Miscellaneous Documents,* no. 53, 40th Congress, 3d session, pp. 298-299.

removed. Adelbert Ames, scion of a family of New England abolitionists, assumed the dual role of provisional-governor and military commander. He immediately began the removal of many of the Democratic and conservative local officials, replacing them with men who were in sympathy with the Congressional program. Many of his appointees were Negroes.[79] No longer was military government preferable to Negro suffrage. The policy of the opposition now came to be that of accepting reconstruction on the best terms that could be obtained, and of continuing the fight from a better position after the restoration of the state to the Union.

The Democratic party had made its stand too clear to be effective under the new conditions. The result was the formation of the National Union Republican Party, which drew into its ranks Democrats, Conservatives, and "National Republicans." To head its state ticket, the party chose Louis Dent, a Northern man and the brother-in-law of President Grant. The candidate for the lieutenant-governorship was also a "carpet-bagger." For secretary of state, the party nominated Tom Sinclair, an obscure Negro from Copiah County, the first man of his race ever to be nominated for a major office in Mississippi. For the four minor state offices, two Northern men and two "old citizens" were nominated.[80]

The regular or "radical" Republicans also chose two "old citizens" and two Northern whites for the minor state offices. As their nominee for the governorship, they selected J. L. Alcorn, an able, egotistic, ambitious former Whig who had been opposed to secession and was one of the largest planters in the state. Their choice for lieutenant-governor was R. C. Powers, who had been a Federal officer and was then a planter. The only place on the ticket which went to a Negro was that for the office of secretary of state.

This nominee, James D. Lynch, was the first man of his race to hold a major office in Mississippi, and was probably the most remarkable of the Negroes who rose to prominence during the period. An able and highly educated Pennsylvanian, he came to Mississippi in 1868 to take charge of the activities of the Methodist Episcopal Church in the state. Within three years, he had gained a place in the hearts of the Negroes that no other leader of either race has ever challenged. A contemporary Democratic leader later wrote of him:

He was a great orator; fluent and graceful, he stirred his great audiences as no other man did or could do. He was the idol of the negroes, who would come from every point of the compass and for miles, on foot, to hear him speak. He rarely spoke to less than a thousand, and often [addressed from] two to five thousand. . . . Imagine one or two thousand negroes standing en masse in a semi-circle facing the speaker, whose tones were as clear and resonant as a silver bell; and of a sudden, every throat would be wide open, and a spontaneous

[79] Vicksburg *Daily Times*, April 15, 23, May 5, 1869.
[80] J. W. Garner, *op. cit.*, p. 242.

shout in perfect unison would arise, and swell, and subside as the voice of one man. . . . I could not understand it, but in the light of the discovery of the laws of psychic phenomena, I am now sure that it was done by the hypnotic power or influence of the speaker.[81]

A Democratic paper called him "the most popular carpet-bagger in the State—the best educated man, and the best speaker, and the most effective orator, of that party, in Mississippi; and, withal, as much of a gentleman as he can be with his present white associations."[82]   To John R. Lynch, one of his colleagues, he was "the Henry Ward Beecher of the colored race."[83]   Throughout his brief career of distinguished service to church and state, Lynch maintained the respect of his white opponents.[84]   In 1875, however, as a candidate for the Republican nomination for Congress, he was dragged into court by white Republican rivals on a charge of adultery.   Deprived of the nomination, he died almost immediately.[85]   Negroes say that the cause was a broken heart.   However true that may be, Lynch was the most brilliant representative of his race ever to play a part in the affairs of the state, and his influence on the freedmen between 1869 and 1873 was greater than that of any other man.

The election toward which the parties looked in the fall of 1869 concerned not only the choice of state officers, but also a new vote on the constitution which had been rejected in the earlier referendum in June. As now submitted, with the unpopular disfranchising clauses offered for a separate vote, the constitution received the approval of both parties.   In fact, there was little apparent disagreement on principles.   With the Democrats supporting a "carpet-bagger" for the governorship, and the radical Republicans an old citizen and former slaveholder, the whole matter had an appearance of confusion.   Actually, however, the situation was clear to the masses of the Negroes.   The group led by Alcorn, to use a continental phrase, was a "party of movement," looking to continued advancement of the status of the freedmen.   That led by Dent was one of "resistance." It might concede to the Negro those rights he had already gained, but further concessions it would make grudgingly, if at all.

All this became clear during the campaign.   Tom Sinclair, the Dent candidate for secretary of state, was an ignorant and servile freedman with no standing among his fellows.   James Lynch, the Alcorn candidate for the same position, was the best-known Negro in the state.   The "Union Republican" nominee for the legislature from black Yazoo County was

[81] W. H. Hardy, "Recollections of Reconstruction in East and Southeast Mississippi," *P.M.H.S.*, IV, 126, 127.
[82] Hinds County *Gazette*, September 15, 1869.
[83] John R. Lynch, "Communications," *Journal of Negro History*, XVI (1931), 106.
[84] Vicksburg *Daily Times*, November 23, 1869; Hinds County *Gazette*, September 15, 1869, January 25, 1871, February 17, 1875; John R. Lynch, *The Facts of Reconstruction*, p. 30.
[85] Hinds County *Gazette*, February 17, 1875.

poor old Reuben Pope, who disgusted the Negroes at political meetings by humbly waiting on his campaign manager and former master. His Republican opponent was W. H. Foote, next to Charles Caldwell the most defiant Negro politician in the state. In order to get a Negro orator of any ability to serve their cause, the Dent party had to send to Virginia for the erratic and unscrupulous L. W. W. Mannaway, whose price was known to Democratic organizations throughout the South. This, in general, was the story throughout the state and throughout the period of Reconstruction. For the basic element of the Democratic party, there could be no real compromise on the Negro question. Those freedmen whom they offered as candidates were known to their fellows either as humble relics of slavery, or as men who openly sold the interests of their race for Democratic money or favor.

The results of the campaign were not long in doubt. The Dent ticket, and the inconsistency of its platform with the spirit of the majority of its prompters, had little appeal even for the mass of the whites. Alcorn and his colleagues gained election to the state offices by a majority of about 40,000 in a total vote of about 114,000. The constitution, shorn of its objectionable clauses, was ratified by a vote of 113,735 to 955. Reconstructed at last to the satisfaction of a Congressional majority, with Negro voters and Negro office-holders, Mississippi re-entered the Union.

CHAPTER XII

THE NEGRO AND POLITICS, 1870-1875

NEGRO LEADERS

The Republican party which took control of the politics of the state in 1869 included in its membership at least ninety per cent of the more than one hundred thousand registered Negro voters. It also included at times from fifteen to twenty thousand of the seventy to eighty thousand white voters.[1] In the beginning, these white Republicans were largely a poverty-stricken element who had been Unionists during the war. There was also an element of planters and businessmen which increased rapidly in numbers until 1874. Many of these men had been Whigs before the war, and they regarded the Democratic party as the organ of their enemies, the small farmers.

The Republican leadership in Mississippi contained an unusually large number of prominent white men who were old residents of the state. The names of J. L. Alcorn, H. F. Simrall, J. L. Wofford, J. F. H. Claiborne, Joshua Morris, R. W. Flournoy, Jason Niles, and R. W. Millsaps will serve as examples. The motives which caused these men to enter the party were many and varied. Colonel R. W. Flournoy, who before the war was the largest slaveholder in northeastern Mississippi, was essentially a humanitarian. For him, the protection and elevation of the Negro was a project that sprang out of deep Christian convictions.[2] To a certain extent, this was also true of Major Millsaps, but he represented especially the rising commercial and financial element that saw the Republican party as the promoter of its interests both in the nation and in the state. Judge W. W. Chisholm of Kemper County was an example of a fairly large group who carried personal feuds into politics. The mortal enemies of his clan, the Gullys and the Balls, were Democrats. Where they went, Chisholm and his friends and relatives could not go. Even less respectable were those native whites, a relatively small group, who became Republicans entirely for the sake of personal advantage. The prominent Dr. William M. Compton of Marshall County furnished an excellent example. A leader of the irreconcilable anti-radicals in the convention of 1868, a "nigger-hater" of high degree, and an organizer of Ku-Klux Klans, he later entered

[1] Mississippi *Weekly Pilot*, August 12, 1870; John R. Lynch, *Some Historical Errors of James Ford Rhodes*, p. 91.
[2] M. G. Abney, "Reconstruction in Pontotoc County," *P.M.H.S.*, XI, 234, 235.

the Alcorn faction, and became superintendent of the state insane asylum.[3]
Among the "carpet-baggers" there was the same variety of types. Adelbert Ames, absolutely honest, and to a large extent unselfish, had become more and more impressed with the needs and possibilities of the Negroes. Almost forty years later, as a cynical old man, he said: "My explanation may seem ludicrous now, but then, it seemed to me that I had a mission with a large M."[4]   His constant refusal to sell out the interests of the freedmen made him their idol; one terrified Negro in 1875 addressed him as "Gov. Ames Dar Father of the State."[5]   There were other able and honest Republican leaders from the North who had little sympathy for the Negroes, and regarded their presence in the party as a necessary evil. Among such men were H. R. Pease, R. C. Powers, and George C. McKee. Finally, there were some unscrupulous "carpet-baggers" who sought only personal advantage and profit, and held to no principle.   The white leader of the corrupt Negro-Republican Vicksburg ring, for example, neatly leaped the divide in 1875 and remained a prominent figure in the equally corrupt Democratic machine in that city.

Whatever the motives or character of these white Republicans might be, to the Democratic press and to the growing mass of white-liners, they were all scoundrels, carpet-baggers, and scalawags.   Thus Jason Niles, described by Charles Nordhoff as "a man of singular purity of character, a quiet scholar, and an old resident of the State," was the subject of constant abuse.[6]   Colonel Flournoy was so bitterly attacked that J. W. Garner has spoken of him as "the most extreme and obnoxious radical in the state."   Yet the Democratic historian of his home county, of which he was the wealthiest and most distinguished old citizen, wrote that he was "highly respected and beloved."   He took an active part in church affairs, and gave freely to all charities.   "The ideas he advocated [among them complete equality for Negroes] were the mistakes of his life."[7]   On the other hand, almost no "carpet-bagger" was too vile to shift to the Democratic party and become a "respectable citizen."   Thus C. E. Furlong, a Northern white who took heavy profits from the Vicksburg ring, received high state offices after changing parties, and in 1877 was suggested for the governorship by one of the leading Democratic papers.[8]

Mississippi was extremely fortunate in the character of her more important Negro Republican leaders.   In the words of Alexander K. McClure:

[3] J. S. McNeily, "War and Reconstruction in Mississippi," *P.M.H.S.C.S.*, II, 420; J. L. Power, "The Black and Tan Convention," *P.M.H.S.*, III, 79; Ruth Watkins, "Reconstruction in Marshall County," *P.M.H.S.*, XII, 163.

[4] Adelbert Ames to J. W. Garner, January 17, 1900, J. W. Garner Papers, Mississippi State Archives.

[5] *Senate Reports*, no. 527, 44th Congress, 1st session, "Documentary Evidence," p. 62.

[6] Charles Nordhoff, *The Cotton States*, p. 77.   [7] M. G. Abney, *op. cit.*, XI, 234.

[8] Hinds County *Gazette*, May 2, 1877, July 7, 1883; C. Nordhoff, *op. cit.*, p. 77.

Mississippi is exceptionable also in the reputable character of her most prominent colored leaders. In all the other southern States the negro leaders have
rivaled the white adventurers in reckless and bewildering robbery, but they
have not done so in Mississippi. Three black men have here reached national
fame as leaders of their race, and they are all esteemed as honest men.

.   .   .   .

These three men . . . have maintained the manhood that should be the pride
of every race, and, much as Mississippi has suffered from the carpet-bag and
colored rule, there has not been a tithe of the demoralization and waste here
that has dishonored the reign of the black man in the Carolinas and the Gulf
States. That much of this comparatively good record of a bad domination is
due to Revels, Bruce, and Lynch, who successfully breasted the wave of corruption, is a fact that should be confessed and justly appreciated.[9]

Hiram Rhodes Revels, the least important of the three named by Mc-
Clure, was the first Negro to serve in the United States Senate, in which
body he completed the unexpired term of Jefferson Davis. Born of free
parents in Fayetteville, North Carolina, September 27, 1827, he received his
early education in a school taught by a Negro woman. The desire to continue his studies caused him to leave North Carolina and go to Indiana,
where he attended a Quaker seminary. After further work at a Negro
seminary in Ohio, he completed his training at Knox College, in Galesburg,
Illinois. After his ordination as an African Methodist Episcopal preacher,
Revels taught, lectured, and preached in Indiana, Illinois, Ohio, Missouri,
and Maryland. During the war, after assisting in the organization of
Negro regiments in Maryland and Missouri, he went to Mississippi, where
he organized churches, lectured, and attempted to organize schools. An
interlude of two years in Kansas and Missouri was followed by his return
to Mississippi, where he settled in Natchez as presiding elder of the Methodist Episcopal Church. Immediately, and almost entirely against his will,
he was drawn into politics.[10]

After a term of service on the city council of Natchez, Revels was
persuaded by John R. Lynch to enter the race for the state senate. His
election to that body opened the way for his advancement to a much higher
office. It had been agreed that the short term available in the United
States Senate should go to a Negro. So impressive was the prayer with
which Revels opened the proceedings of the upper house that he immediately became the candidate of the Negro legislators.

In Washington, Revels naturally attracted a great deal of attention.
Tall, portly, dignified, and an excellent speaker, he delighted those who
had worked for the elevation of his race, and to some extent eased the
misgivings of those who had opposed it. His actual accomplishments as

[9] A. K. McClure, The South, pp. 113, 115-116.
[10] Hiram R. Revels, "Autobiography," Carter G. Woodson Papers, Library of
Congress; Samuel D. Smith, The Negro in Congress, pp. 12-14; W. J. Simmons,
Men of Mark, pp. 948-949; Benjamin Brawley, Negro Builders and Heroes, p. 125;
Dictionary of American Biography, XV, 513.

a new man in the short session of the Senate were few. None of the bills introduced by him was passed. He did, however, speak effectively on several occasions, and in his speaking and voting he showed intelligence and moderation. His support of a bill for the general removal of the political disabilities of Southern whites was especially effective. In his work outside the Senate, he succeeded in obtaining the admission of Negro mechanics to work in the United States Navy Yard.[11]

Upon his return to Mississippi, Revels was appointed to the presidency of Alcorn University, the new state college for Negroes. His work there was complicated by unruly elements in the faculty and student body, but in his appearances outside the college he gained the approval of most of the leading whites. After one of his speeches, the editor of a Democratic paper wrote: "As everywhere and on other occasions he impressed those who saw and heard him as a good man, honestly intent upon doing his people real good and quieting so far as he is able the bitterness between the races. In this work he will have the sympathy and encouragement of the white people."[12] So thoroughly did Revels gain the "sympathy and encouragement of the white people" that he soon lost the confidence of the masses of his own race. Essentially a timid man, more of a scholar than a leader, and anxiously desirous of peace, he came more and more to be dominated by white Democrats. After a brief term as acting secretary of state, he returned to the presidency of Alcorn, only to be ousted from the office by Governor Ames. He worked with the Democrats in the election of 1875, and once more received the presidency of the university from Governor J. M. Stone. After his retirement from that office on account of poor health, he continued to be active in church work until his death at a Methodist Episcopal conference in 1901.[13] In spite of his extreme caution and timidity, Revels throughout his career was a credit to his race. Had there been more like him, both white and black, some compromise would have brought peace in Mississippi.

A much more prominent figure than Revels was Blanche Kelso Bruce, the only Negro ever to serve a full term in the United States Senate, and the man described by Benjamin Brawley as "probably the most astute political leader the Negro ever had."[14] A light mulatto, born in Prince Edward County, Virginia, March 1, 1841, of a mother who was the slave of a wealthy planter, Bruce knew few of the burdens of slavery. He received his early education from a private tutor. Nominally a slave, he was carried before the war to Missouri, where he studied the printing trade, and later dealt in books and papers. Soon after the opening of the war, he

[11] H. R. Revels, op. cit.; S. D. Smith, op. cit., pp. 19, 23.
[12] Hinds County Gazette, October 2, 1872.
[13] H. R. Revels, op. cit.; S. D. Smith, op. cit., pp. 23-25; A. A. Taylor, "Negro Congressmen a Generation After," Journal of Negro History, VII (1922), 131-132.
[14] B. Brawley, op. cit., p. 127.

went to Hannibal, Missouri, where he organized the first Negro school in the state. In 1868, after two years at Oberlin College, Bruce moved to Mississippi, and almost immediately began his political career. After brief experience as election commissioner and as sergeant-at-arms of the state senate, he became assessor, and then sheriff and tax collector of the rich Delta county of Bolivar. His experience also included service as county superintendent of schools and as levee commissioner. During this time he was gaining wealth as a planter. By 1874, after a long campaign in his favor by the Floreyville *Star,* Bruce was ready to make his bid for election to the Senate. In this, with the backing of Governor Ames and of the Negro leader James Hill, he obtained an easy victory.[15]

Upon his entrance to the Senate in March, 1875, Bruce immediately made a favorable impression. A man of magnificent physique and handsome countenance, he was described by a contemporary Mississippi Democrat as possessing "almost the manners of a Chesterfield."[16] Through the influence of Roscoe Conkling, he obtained good committee appointments, and after his first session he became active on the floor. His chief interests lay in the improvement of the Mississippi River, the establishment of a more enlightened policy toward the Indians, the development of interracial harmony, and the clearing up of the affairs of the Freedmen's Bank. On the floor of the Senate, he was often surrounded by a circle of friends similar to those which centered around Blaine, Edmunds, Bayard, and Lamar; while in his home, he and his cultured wife entertained a distinguished group which included the wives of Supreme Court justices and other officials. With the Democrats of the Mississippi delegation, Bruce maintained surprisingly pleasant relations, being especially close to his colleague L. Q. C. Lamar.[17]

After the close of his senatorial term, Bruce was suggested for a place in Garfield's cabinet, receiving the unqualified endorsement of such Mississippi Democrats as Senator Lamar and Congressmen Chalmers, Money, Muldrow, and Singleton.[18] Instead, however, he received an appointment as register of the treasury. Under Harrison, he served as recorder of deeds for the District of Columbia, and with the election of McKinley he once more became register of the treasury. While holding this office he died, March 17, 1898. To the end of his distinguished career, Bruce was always the gentleman, graceful, polished, self-assured, and never humble. He scorned the use of the phrase "colored man," often declaring "I am a negro, and proud of my race."[19]

[15] S. D. Smith, *op. cit.,* pp. 25-27; B. Brawley, *op. cit.,* pp. 127-128; Robert R. Moton, *What the Negro Thinks,* p. 160.
[16] Franklin A. Montgomery, *Reminiscences of a Mississippian in Peace and War,* p. 279.
[17] S. D. Smith, *op. cit.,* pp. 27-41.
[18] *Ibid.,* p. 41; Jackson, *Weekly Clarion,* January 27, 1881.
[19] Raymond *Gazette,* May 19, 1883.

Equally remarkable was the career of John R. Lynch. The son of a slave mother and a wealthy white planter, Lynch was born near Vidalia, Louisiana, September 10, 1847. After the death of the father, both mother and son were sold, and were taken to Natchez, where the boy became the favored body-servant of one of the leading citizens. Upon the occupation of the city by Federal troops, Lynch began to attend night school. Later he continued his studies through wide reading and work with tutors. After a brief term as a justice of the peace, he resigned to become, at the age of twenty-two, a member of the state legislature.[20] There he made a remarkable impression. In spite of his youth, and in spite of the fact that there were only thirty-two Negroes in the House, he was elected speaker in 1872. Democrats and Republicans alike praised his ability and impartiality.[21] In November, 1872, he was elected to Congress, and in December, 1873, he entered that body as its youngest member.

On the floor, Lynch showed himself to be perfectly at ease, making his first formal speech within eight days of the opening of the session. Of a distinctly aristocratic appearance, slender and active, with a very light complexion and regular features, he spoke fluently, tersely, and correctly.[22] Franklin A. Montgomery wrote that he had few, if any, superiors as a stump speaker. His effective delivery and ready wit appealed to blacks and whites alike. Montgomery advised Democratic speakers to avoid clashing with him in debate.[23] Serving in the Forty-Third, Forty-Fourth, and Forty-Seventh Congresses, he probably possessed as much influence at the White House as any Negro has ever had, being frequently called for consultation by Grant and Garfield. Throughout his public career, no scandal ever touched him, and by 1880 the Jackson *Clarion* was calling him "the ablest man of his race in the South."[24]

Refusing offers from Lamar and Cleveland of appointments based on his retirement from politics, Lynch remained in the Republican party, serving as the temporary chairman of its national convention in 1884, and as fourth auditor of the treasury under Harrison. After studying and practicing law, he entered the army in 1898, and served until 1911, when he retired with the rank of major.[25] He then opened law offices in Chicago, and became a power in the Republican organization in that city. In the meantime, he wrote three books on Reconstruction and his political experiences. Two of these, along with a number of articles, have been published. Shortly before his death in November, 1939, at the age of

[20] S. D. Smith, *op. cit.*, pp. 85-86; W. J. Simmons, *Men of Mark*, pp. 1042-1043; A. A. Taylor, *op. cit.*, VII, 127.
[21] Jackson *Clarion*, April 24, 1873; John R. Lynch, *The Facts of Reconstruction*, p. 66.
[22] Samuel D. Smith, *op. cit.*, p. 86.   [23] F. A. Montgomery, *op. cit.*, p. 292.
[24] S. D. Smith, *op. cit.*, pp. 109-111; Jackson *Clarion*, March 17, 1881.
[25] S. D. Smith, *op. cit.*, pp. 111-112; J. R. Lynch, *op. cit.*, pp. 235-238, 278; U. S. Army *Register*, 1914, p. 565.

ninety-three, he reported that he was "taking life quite easily."[26]   In view of the few advantages he had in his youth, and of the distinguished career which he achieved in the face of difficulties, he must be judged worthy of the honors and comforts that came to him in his declining years.

To McClure's list of the outstanding Negro leaders in Mississippi one more must be added. James Hill, a light mulatto, was born July 25, 1846, on the plantation of one J. Hill, near Holly Springs. He received his early education from two daughters of his master, and continued it while working as a youth in the railroad shops at Holly Springs. He received no formal training, although he recognized its value and sent his younger brother Frank to Oberlin. For James Hill himself, study and work were serious businesses. He had no time for any diversions.[27]   He possessed none of the brilliance or oratorical ability of Bruce or Lynch, but for the larger part of the period he was probably a more influential factor in the politics of the state than either of his much more famous colleagues.

After a year as sergeant-at-arms of the house of representatives, Hill entered that body as a member in 1871. By the latter part of 1872, he was powerful enough to promise Bruce that he would be elected senator in 1874.[28]   For himself, Hill chose the office of secretary of state, which he filled quietly and efficiently for three years after the overthrow of 1875. Against him there was never any charge of dishonesty.[29]   After the close of his term, he was postmaster at Vicksburg for a time, and then collector of internal revenue. In 1882, he waged a hopeless campaign for a place in Congress. After that year, he centered his attention on business, and acquired a modest fortune as a successful land agent for the Louisville, New Orleans & Texas Railroad. He closed his career as receiver for the Federal Land Office in Jackson, as an active leader in the African Methodist Church, and as sponsor of other projects looking toward the advancement of his race. His career was at times mysterious and hard to explain. He stood very high in the favor of all of the Republican administrations at Washington. With the exception of the brief periods of his apparently useless campaigns for Congress, the white Democrats of the state seem almost never to have attacked him, and indeed to have worked with him as a colleague. He engaged in large business enterprises, and in projects for the aid of Negroes, almost as quietly and obscurely as he aided the family of the white man who had formerly been his master. The Democratic historian of Marshall County wrote, "He was extremely well thought of by the citizens, and is remembered as a good negro."[30]   He was also "extremely well thought of" by the Negroes, who have named their largest public school in Jackson for "Jim Hill."

[26] Personal letter from John R. Lynch, Chicago, January 3, 1939.
[27] Mississippi *Weekly Pilot,* September 25, 1875; R. Watkins, *op. cit.,* XII, 173.
[28] B. Brawley, *op. cit.,* p. 128.   [29] Hinds County *Gazette,* August 9, 1882.
[30] R. Watkins, *op. cit.,* XII, 173.

Mississippi was not so fortunate in the two other Negroes, A. K. Davis and T. W. Cardozo, who held high offices in the state. Both these men were obscure local politicians, and little can be learned of their background. Davis, who served as lieutenant-governor from 1874 until his impeachment in 1875, was weak, treacherous, and apparently dishonest, although he was cleared in a criminal court of the charge of bribery on which he was convicted by the legislature. He had practically no influence outside his home district of Noxubee County.

Cardozo, superintendent of education from 1874 until his resignation under threat of impeachment in 1876, was an educated mulatto from New York. Nominated as a result of pressure from the Vicksburg machine, he was almost unknown outside Warren County before his election. Although both Ames and Lynch testify as to his intellectual and educational qualifications, neither of them defends his character.[31] He was undoubtedly involved in the corruption at Vicksburg, and was shown to have embezzled more than two thousand dollars of the funds of Tougaloo University.[32] After this episode, he returned to the obscurity from which he came.

LOCAL LEADERS AND THE LOYAL LEAGUES

Even more remarkable than the rise of Bruce, Lynch, and others to prominent positions in the state and nation was the amazingly rapid development of efficient local leaders among the Negroes. There is something fascinating about the suddenness with which, all over the state, they emerged from the anonymity of slavery to become directors and counselors for their race. In general, it can be said that they were not Negroes who had held positions of leadership under the old regime; the characteristics which made a man a slave driver or foreman were not those which would allow him to organize a Loyal League. Almost none of them came from the small group who had been free before the war. Such men, as barbers, artisans, or small farmers, had depended too long on the favor of the whites for the maintenance of their existence. Servility had become a part of them. Most of this group became Democrats, although a number of the younger element in the comparatively liberal region around Natchez gained prominence in the Republican organization.

A large portion of the minor Negro leaders were preachers, lawyers, or teachers from the free states or from Canada. Their education and their independent attitude gained for them immediate favor and leadership. Of the natives who became their rivals, the majority had been urban slaves, blacksmiths, carpenters, clerks, or waiters in hotels and boarding houses; a few of them had been favored body-servants of affluent whites. Most of them were more intelligent than the mass of their fellows, and

[31] J. R. Lynch, *op. cit.*, pp. 74-75.
[32] Mississippi *House Journal*, 1878, p. 9.

had picked up some smattering of education, at least to the point of being able to read and write. There was a general tendency for them to combine preaching with their politics; as Sir George Campbell has said, they were rather preachers because they were leaders than leaders because they were preachers. The death rate of these local organizers, both during and immediately after Reconstruction, was alarmingly high.[33]

The organ through which the local leaders worked was the "Loyal League." This body, an outgrowth of a Northern patriotic organization established during the war, continued to maintain a very vague national connection. The state set-up was equally sketchy. The local groups, of which there was at least one in almost every black-belt community, were extremely active, especially during periods immediately preceding elections. Given a start by whites and Negroes from the North, they made an immediate appeal to the freedmen, and quickly came to rival the churches as centers of social activities. With their elaborate rituals, their multiplicity of offices, and their sashes and badges, they performed a function which later was taken over by the Negro lodges. The general practice in Mississippi was for the Leagues to hold a social gathering twice each month. At these meetings, the Negroes danced and played games, and discussed local affairs, their churches, and their schools. As a rule, the gatherings took place in church or school buildings except in times of violence, when the members collected secretly in secluded spots in the woods.[34]

The clubs also had a political significance, which at times of elections became preëminent. The oath taken by the initiate generally included a section similar to that in the ritual of Tarbell Council no. 4, at Morton: "Furthermore, that I will do all in my power to elect true and reliable Union men and supporters to the Government and none others, to all offices of profit or trust, from the lowest to the highest in Ward, Town, County, State and General Government. And should I ever be called to fill any office, I will faithfully carry out the objects and principles of this L. [sic]"[35] Local or visiting speakers urged the Negroes to protect their freedom and their rights by voting for Republican nominees, and in some of the Leagues a majority vote bound all of the members to vote for the

[33] Forrest Cooper, "Reconstruction in Scott County," *P.M.H.S.*, XIII, 164; Ruth Watkins, *op. cit.*, XII, 172; Julia C. Brown, "Reconstruction in Yalobusha and Grenada Counties," *P.M.H.S.*, XII, 242, 260; E. F. Puckett, "Reconstruction in Monroe County," *P.M.H.S.*, XI, 130; C. H. Brough, "The Clinton Riot," *P.M.H.S.*, VI, 62; Fred Z. Browne, "Reconstruction in Oktibbeha County," *P.M.H.S.*, XIII, 278; J. S. McNeily, "The Enforcement Act of 1871 and the Ku-Klux Klan in Mississippi," *P.M.H.S.*, IX, 131; Elizabeth Caldwell, "Reconstruction in Yazoo County," unpublished master's thesis, University of North Carolina, 1931, pp. 35-36; A. T. Morgan, *Yazoo*, pp. 495-496; Hinds County *Gazette*, December 15, 1875; Mississippi *Weekly Pilot*, November 19, 1870; *Senate Reports*, no. 527, 44th Congress, 1st session, pp. 119, 437-438.
[34] Hattie Magee, "Reconstruction in Lawrence and Jeff Davis Counties," *P.M.H.S.*, XI, 190, 192; J. Kendel, *op. cit.*, XIII, 237, 238; Hinds County *Gazette*, July 10, 1868.
[35] Hinds County *Gazette*, July 10, 1868.

candidates chosen.[36] It was also in the Leagues that preparations were
made for gathering the Negroes in large groups early on the morning of
election days. With their courage thus bolstered, they monopolized the
polls during the early hours, and left them to the white Democrats in the
afternoon.[37]

These clubs also provided political banquets and barbecues, and arranged political processions that were most attractive to the freedmen and
annoying to the white Democrats. These activities involved the wearing
of sashes and badges, the building of floats, and the loud beating of drums.
At a night parade in Holly Springs, the Negroes wore red oilcloth caps
with red feathers, red sashes, and enormous red and blue badges. Torches
and transparencies completed the equipment.[38] At a barbecue in Lawrence
County, the members of the League formed into a large procession and
marched in double file around the courthouse and under a cross of blue
cloth, bowing as they passed beneath it.[39]

These activities, and especially the pompous processions, aroused the
wrath of the white Democrats.[40] Conditions in Oktibbeha County were
typical :

In the early seventies the Democratic political organizations made it a point to
intimidate and if necessary to whip the leaders of the negro drum companies
and break up the meetings of these organizations. If possible the drums were
always secured and destroyed and threats made of more drastic treatment if
any further meeting, marching or drumming was attempted. These measures
of expediency were not always carried through without bloodshed.[41]

This development of a symbolic significance for the use of drums by the
Negroes gave an excuse for violent attacks by white Democratic organizations. In 1876, Negroes in De Soto County published an announcement
that in order to avoid further trouble they would entirely abandon the use
of drums and fifes. This move, although largely ineffective, became a
general policy throughout the state.[42]

Democratic efforts to break up the Leagues also involved the use of
white "detectives" and Negro spies to learn the meeting places of the
groups, and especially to identify their leaders.[43] With this information,
"the Ku Klux Klan lost no time in getting rid of the chief offenders and
leaders."[44] After the successful revolution of 1875, the Leagues rapidly
disappeared, and lodges and benevolent societies gradually took their places.

[36] E. F. Puckett, *op. cit.*, XI, 128.
[37] *Senate Reports*, no. 527, 44th Congress, 1st session, pp. 1707-1708.
[38] R. Watkins, *op. cit.*, XII, 185.
[39] H. Magee, *op. cit.*, XI, 186.
[40] John W. Kyle, "Reconstruction in Panola County," *P.M.H.S.*, XIII, 51, 72;
Jackson *Daily Times*, November 1, March 3, 1876.
[41] Fred Z. Browne, *op. cit.*, XIII, 286-287.
[42] Jackson *Daily Times*, August 26, October 31, 1876.
[43] J. C. Brown, *op. cit.*, XII, 234; J. W. Kyle, *op. cit.*, XIII, 74.
[44] J. C. Brown, *op. cit.*, XII, 234.

NEGRO OFFICIALS IN COUNTY AND MUNICIPAL GOVERNMENTS

By a provision of the new constitution of the state, the terms of all local officials expired with the readmission of Mississippi to the Union. Appointments to local offices were then to be made by the Governor with the advice and consent of the senate. Thus there were no municipal or county elections in the state until the fall of 1871. The Governor, J. L. Alcorn, as an old and relatively conservative citizen of the state, made appointments that at least were up to the usual standard for such officials. In some cases, the entire county lists were made up of Democrats or old Whigs.[45] Alcorn's selections for the judiciary were made up almost entirely of leading members of the state bar.[46] Altogether, the total of his appointments included 247 Republicans, 217 Democrats, and seventy-two members of other opposition groups.[47] So far as possible, Alcorn avoided the appointment of Negroes.[48] It appears that no member of that race except Robert H. Wood of Natchez was made mayor of any town.[49] With the possible exception of Coffeeville and Greenville, no town had a Negro majority on its board of aldermen.

Even after the election of 1871, a Negro majority in a municipal government seems to have been unknown.[50] The city of Jackson, with a powerful Republican machine that maintained its control for thirteen years after the overthrow of the party in the state, only once had more than one Negro on its city council of six members. The one exception followed the election of 1874, when two Negroes became aldermen.[51] In Natchez, where the Negroes held an enormous majority, they placed only three members on a council of seven.[52] Efforts of the Negro majority to gain control of the board in Vicksburg in 1874 lost the support of the white members of their party, and with it the election.[53]

The chief complaint against the participation of the freedmen in the government of the towns grew out of their appointment as policemen. The presence of such officials helped to bring on the Meridian riot in 1871,[54] and

---

[45] Fred M. Witty, "Reconstruction in Carroll and Montgomery Counties," *P.M.H.S.*, X, 120.

[46] Mississippi *Weekly Pilot*, October 1, 1870; Hinds County *Gazette*, October 5, November 2, 1870; J. S. McNeily, "War and Reconstruction in Mississippi," *P.M.H.S.C.S.*, II, 393.

[47] Hinds County *Gazette*, September 6, 1871.

[48] Jackson *Clarion-Ledger*, November 27, 1890.

[49] Hiram Revels' statement in his "Autobiography" that John R. Lynch served as mayor of Natchez seems to be an error.

[50] John R. Lynch, *The Facts of Reconstruction*, p. 92.

[51] Goodspeed Publishing Company, *Biographical and Historical Memoirs of Mississippi*, II, 174.

[52] Edward King, *The Great South*, p. 293; Natchez *Tri-Weekly Democrat and Courier*, August 13, 1873.

[53] J. W. Garner, *op. cit.*, pp. 329-330.

[54] *Report on the Condition of Affairs in the Late Insurrectionary States*, "Mississippi," I, 479.

furnished the central theme of the attack on the Republican government in Jackson.[55] The general attitude of the whites, as expressed by Ethelbert Barksdale, was that "negroes ought not to be put in a position to discharge constabulary functions which it is proper for white men to exercise." Law enforcement implied domination, and as Barksdale said, the white race was "not in the habit of being dominated by the colored race."[56]

In general the few towns which had Republican governments as late as 1874 overthrew them before the state government fell in the fall of 1875. The Democrats took Vicksburg in August, 1874, and Columbus in December. Yazoo City was captured in April, 1875, and Okolona in August. The methods generally used in this process, combining persuasion, intimidation, economic pressure, and violence, were similar to those used later in the state campaign. For towns which had Negro majorities, the legislature assured the continuation of Democratic control by excluding from the corporate limits large portions of the Negro residential sections.[57] The one important exception to the overthrow of Republican municipal governments in the years 1874 and 1875 was the city of Jackson, where a peculiar situation and a large number of white votes maintained that party in power until 1888.

Very little information is available as to the participation of the Negroes in the various county governments. More than half of the counties held white majorities, and most of these naturally eliminated in the elections of 1871 the few Negro officials appointed by Alcorn in 1870. In the elections of 1873, the Democrats carried thirty-nine of the seventy-four counties, and in 1875 sixty-two of the seventy-four. Of course, in several of the predominantly white counties, black beats at times elected one or two supervisors or justices of the peace. Yalobusha, Scott, and Lawrence counties, as examples, generally had one Negro supervisor on the board of five.[58] Such Negroes were almost entirely without influence, and generally found it to their advantage to be "very quiet, good negroes," to use the description given of those in Lawrence.[59]

Even in the minority of the counties which had Negro and Republican majorities, the freedmen seldom obtained many of the offices. By 1873, however, they became assertive enough to take control of a number of counties in which the white population was small. In Marshall County, for example, three of the five supervisors were Negroes who could barely read and write.[60] The three on the board in Yazoo County, the three in

[55] Jackson Clarion-Ledger, December 26, 1889.
[56] Senate Miscellaneous Documents, no. 166, 50th Congress, 1st session, p. 276.
[57] J. C. Brown, op. cit., XII, 217, 269; Lee Richardson and Thomas D. Godman, In and Around Vicksburg, p. 97.
[58] J. C. Brown, op. cit., XIII, 270; Forrest Cooper, op. cit., XIII, 164; Hattie Magee, op. cit., XI, 199.
[59] H. Magee, op. cit., XI, 175.
[60] J. W. Garner, op. cit., p. 309.

Warren, four of the five in Madison, and all five in Issaquena were described as "illiterate."[61]   In these counties, there were also varying numbers of Negro justices of the peace, few of whom were capable of carrying out properly even the simple duties of their office.   There were also a small number of Negro chancery and circuit clerks varying in ability from an "illiterate" in Yazoo to the highly cultured L. J. Winston, who remained as circuit clerk in Adams County, under white Democratic control, until his appointment as collector of the port of Vicksburg in 1897.   According to John R. Lynch, "Out of seventy-two counties in the State at that time, electing on an average twenty-eight officers to a county, it is safe to assert that not over five out of one hundred of such officers were colored men."[62] This statement seems to be approximately correct.

The most important office in the counties, both in responsibilities and in financial returns, was that of sheriff.   According to Lynch, not more than twelve Negroes in Mississippi ever held this office.[63]   Available material supplies the names Blanche K. Bruce of Bolivar, J. J. Evans of De Soto, John Brown of Coahoma, Winslow of Washington, Sumner of Holmes, Merrimon Howard of Jefferson, Peter Crosby of Warren, William McCary and Robert H. Wood of Adams, W. H. Harney of Hinds, Scott of Issaquena, and Joe Spencer Watkins of Monroe.   In regard to Sumner and Watkins, there is almost no information.   Of Blanche K. Bruce, it is sufficient to say that his handling of the office of sheriff fully merited the confidence of the white planters who supplied his bond of $120,000.   The offices of Evans and Winslow seem to have been managed very largely by the whites who supplied their bonds.[64]   Charges of embezzlement against Evans,[65] an ex-slave who was described as a good, sound Negro, seem to have been entirely unjustified.[66]   Scott, judged by his testimony before the Boutwell Committee, was a man of intelligence and ability who, although he was elected by the votes of the Negroes, was completely under the control of white Democrats.   Almost exactly the same description applies to Merrimon Howard of Jefferson, although he at times showed a bit more independence than Scott.[67]   John Brown, run out of Coahoma County after a "race riot" during the campaign of 1875, six years later was declared to have embezzled a large sum for which his sureties were liable.[68]   Peter Crosby, whose violent expulsion by white leaguers led to the Vicksburg riots of 1874, was a member of the infamous

[61] *Senate Reports,* no. 527, 44th Congress, 1st session, pp. 1704, 876, 616; J. W. Garner, *op. cit.,* p. 310.   Illiteracy was fairly common among the officials of the hill counties before the war.   E. C. Coleman, "Reconstruction in Attala County," *P.M.H.S.,* X, 149-150.
[62] John R. Lynch, *op. cit.,* p. 93.   [63] *Ibid.,* p. 17.
[64] Irby C. Nichols, "Reconstruction in De Soto County," *P.M.H.S.,* XI, 307; *Senate Reports,* no. 527, 44th Congress, 1st session, p. 1446.
[65] J. W. Garner, *op. cit.,* p. 306.   [66] I. C. Nichols, *op. cit.,* p. 307.
[67] *Senate Miscellaneous Documents,* no. 45, 44th Congress, 2d session, pp. 156-157.
[68] Jackson *Weekly Clarion,* July 21, 1881.

ring of that city. Yet, strangely enough, subsequent examination of his accounts disclosed them to be entirely in order.[69] Nordhoff's statement that he was illiterate is incorrect.[70] W. H. Harney of Hinds County was a Canadian Negro of some education and ability. He was popular with whites and blacks alike until the development of the bitter campaign of 1875. Charges that he was from twelve to twenty-one thousand dollars short in his accounts occupied the courts for five years. Newspaper reports of the settlement are confusing and contradictory.[71] William McCary and Robert Wood were intelligent members of families who had been free and respected residents of Natchez for several generations.[72] Their conduct seems to have given general satisfaction.

In regard to the quality and activity of county governments between 1870 and 1875, a few generalizations may be drawn. As compared with the period before the war, this was one of greatly increased activity. Bridges, roads, and public buildings destroyed or allowed to go to pieces during the war had to be reconstructed. In addition, the greatly increased business of country stores, the rapid growth of small towns, and expanded social and political activities called for the building of new roads. Under the new system of public education, there were schools to be built and a great number of teachers to be employed. The admission of the freedmen to the courts more than doubled their business. Then too, there was a great burst of enthusiasm for the building of railroads. County after county and town after town made contributions for this purpose after overwhelmingly favorable votes by whites and blacks, and Democrats and Republicans alike. All of this implied an enormous increase in county expenditures, and a proportional increase in taxation. Furthermore, the burden of this increase fell directly on the owners of real estate. The large revenue from the head-tax on slaves was no longer available, and the Republican party, made up largely of propertyless Negroes and of business and professional men, quickly lightened the heavy levies that formerly had been made on artisans, professional men, and commercial enterprisers.

Interestingly enough, there seems to be no correlation at all between the rate of taxation and the political or racial character of the counties. In 1874, at the height of Negro-Republican control, the average rate for the thirty-nine Democratic counties was 12 7/13 mills. That for the thirty-four Republican counties was 13 7/17—a difference of less than one mill. The county tax in the Democratic units ranged from 6.2 mills in Pontotoc to 20.3 in Chickasaw. In the Republican counties, the range was from 5.3

[69] Charles Nordhoff, *The Cotton States*, p. 79.
[70] *Senate Reports*, no. 527, 44th Congress, 1st session, "Documentary Evidence," p. 85.
[71] Hinds County *Gazette*, December 29, February 24, 1875, April 5, 1876, July 31, 1878, July 14, 1880, August 3, 1881; Jackson *Weekly Clarion*, July 14, 1881.
[72] Natchez *Daily Courier*, November 8, 1866; John R. Lynch, *Some Historical Errors of James Ford Rhodes*, pp. 17-18.

in De Soto to 23.2 in Colfax. Negro influence was probably greatest in Madison, Issaquena, Amite, Washington, Warren, Yazoo, Wilkinson, and Hinds. As compared with a state average of 13, the rates in these counties were, respectively, 11, 16, 11, 13½, 14, 10, 19, and 11.4 mills.[73]   Warrants in counties with heavy Negro populations were running at from forty to seventy-five cents on the dollar.[74]   On the other hand, those in Lee County, where no Negro or Republican of any kind ever held office, fell to thirty cents.[75]   The conclusion must be drawn that everywhere in the state a large part of the increase in expenditures was unavoidable. Then too, the wave of extravagance which was sweeping the nation did not fail to touch Mississippi. To a certain extent, the situation probably reflects the new feeling of self-importance and the new influence that had come to the poor whites.

The question of how much fraud existed in the various counties is difficult to answer. Charges, in general terms, were frequently made in the Democratic press. The leading Republican paper assembled the available evidence, and attempted to show that a great deal more dishonesty had been uncovered in Democratic than in Republican counties.[76]   With the exception of J. H. Jones, who charges graft in Wilkinson,[77] it is the general conclusion of the few students who have investigated individual counties that while there was some extravagance, there is no evidence of open fraud.[78]   Their conclusions are hard to reconcile with the many charges which were prevalent at the time.

There can be little doubt that there was a rotten situation in Vicksburg, a city which seldom knew an honest government before the war, and has almost never had one since. City expenditures were enormous. Most of them went for improvement of streets and wharves, and other projects which were really necessary for a town that was rapidly becoming a city, but if half of the charges of extravagance and graft were true, the city was getting little for its money. In this exploitation, Democrats and Republicans shared alike. It is also true that the enormous grants to railroads met almost no opposition at the polls.[79]   It is therefore difficult to say just how much of the extravagance and corruption was real, or how much of it should be charged to Negroes and white Republicans.

The Vicksburg ring also controlled the government of Warren County, and there can be little doubt, in spite of the curious fact that Sheriff

[73] Mississippi *Weekly Pilot*, January 1, 23, 1875; J. W. Garner, *op. cit.,* p. 313.
[74] Vicksburg *Times and Republican*, February 2, 1873.
[75] W. H. Braden, "Reconstruction in Lee County," *P.M.H.S.*, X, 136.
[76] Mississippi *Weekly Pilot*, October 23, 1875.
[77] J. H. Jones, "Reconstruction in Wilkinson County," *P.M.H.S.*, VIII, 164.
[78] F. M. Witty, *op. cit.,* X, 119, 120, 122; E. C. Coleman, *op. cit.,* X, 150, 155, 156, 161; W. H. Braden, *op. cit.,* 136; R. Watkins, *op. cit.,* XII, 183, 208; H. Magee, *op. cit.,* XI, 181.
[79] C. Nordhoff, *op. cit.,* p. 76; Hinds County *Gazette*, July 31, 1872.

Crosby's accounts were found to be in order, that several of the county officials, Negroes and whites, were engaged in extensive embezzlement through such methods as the forgery of warrants.[80] Unfortunately, it must be recorded that the thrifty black and white tax-payers who joined the violent white "Modocs" in overthrowing the Republican city government in 1874, and the county government in the following year, saw control pass into the hands of the least desirable element of the whites. The result was that conditions in city and county became worse rather than better.[81]

In conclusion it may be stated that although Negroes formed a majority of the population in thirty counties in Mississippi, they almost never took advantage of their opportunity to place any large number of their race in local offices. Of those who did hold offices, the twelve sheriffs were moderately satisfactory; most of them were at least capable of exercising the functions of their office. No Negro in the state ever held any higher judicial office than that of justice of the peace, and those who held that office seem generally to have been incompetent. Among the small number of chancery and circuit clerks there was a wide range of ability; most of them were not suitable men for their positions. Negroes who gained election to the boards of supervisors of the various counties, even in those cases where they formed a majority, generally were dominated by white Republicans, either natives or Northerners. Although many of the Negro supervisors were ignorant and incompetent, little difference can be discovered in the administration of their counties and that of counties under Democratic control.

NEGROES AND STATE GOVERNMENT

The first legislature under the new constitution assembled in Jackson in January, 1870. Of the 107 men in the house of representatives, twenty-five were Democrats and eighty-two were Republicans. The number of Negro representatives, originally thirty-one, was immediately reduced to thirty by the death of C. A. Yancey of Panola County. Thus, in a state which held a large Negro majority, members of that race made up less than two-sevenths of the total membership of the house, and less than three-eights of the Republican majority. Their representation in the senate was even smaller. In the total membership of thirty-three, and in a Republican group of twenty-eight, only five were Negroes.[82]

Of the thirty Negroes in the house, eight had served in the constitutional convention. A dozen or more of the group, either by education or

[80] J. W. Garner, op. cit., p. 293; Mississippi Weekly Pilot, March 6, 1875.
[81] C. Nordhoff, op. cit., pp. 76, 81-82; Hinds County Gazette, April 21, 1875; Mississippi Weekly Pilot, August 21, 1875; Vicksburg Herald, August 17, 1875; Hinds County Gazette, June 19, 1878, February 3, 1883.
[82] J. S. McNeily, "War and Reconstruction in Mississippi," P.M.H.S.C.S., II, 381; John R. Lynch, The Facts of Reconstruction, pp. 44-45.

unusual native ability, were entirely capable of meeting their obligations as legislators. Among these were H. P. Jacobs, Henry Mayson, J. F. Boulden, M. T. Newsome, Merrimon Howard, John R. Lynch, J. Aaron Moore, H. M. Foley, J. J. Spelman, and J. H. Piles. All of these men made distinguished records in fields other than politics. Almost as capable were Albert Johnson, Nathan McNeese, A. K. Davis, Doctor Stites, Emanuel Handy, Richard Griggs, and W. H. Foote. The other fourteen members were inclined to be self-effacing, and took little part in the formation of policy.

Of the five members of the senate, three, Charles Caldwell, Hiram Revels, and T. W. Stringer, have already been discussed. Robert Gleed, of Columbus, was a man of fair education, good character, and some financial ability, although he had been a slave until the close of the war.[83] An excellent speaker, he was employed by the Democratic administration after the overthrow of the Republican regime to lecture to the Negroes of the state on educational and agricultural matters. The fifth senator, William Gray of Greenville, was a young Baptist preacher of some education and much natural cleverness. A leader in the demands for civil rights for Negroes, he was lacking in tact, and was probably at times guilty of double-dealing both in politics and in religious affairs.

The election of a new house of representatives in 1871, for the term of 1872 and 1873, brought a heavy reduction of the Republican majority. Of the 115 members, the Republicans claimed sixty-six. Actually, however, several of the white members of their group, calling themselves independents, generally voted with the Democrats and against the administion. Negro membership rose to thirty-eight, but R. R. Applewhite of Copiah was completely under Democratic control, and later announced himself a member of that party. The Negroes now had a theoretical control of the Republican caucus in the lower house, but actually any attempt to press their advantage was generally blocked by the desertion of a number of their white colleagues. It was only after Alcorn urged it as a political necessity that John R. Lynch received enough white Republican votes to gain the speakership.

It may therefore be said that during the first four years of Republican control the dominant group in both houses of the legislature was a combination of native and Northern white Republicans, who were influenced by the desires of their Negro constituents, but were also attentive to the large white element in their party, an element whose numbers they earnestly desired to increase. Their leader until late in 1871 was Governor Alcorn, an old Whig with Hamiltonian sentiments and a dream of bringing into the Republican party of the state men in the Democratic and

[83] J. W. Garner Papers, Mississippi State Archives, Alexander Warner to J. W. Garner, May 4, 1900; J. W. Garner, op. cit., p. 295; Senate Reports, no. 527, 44th Congress, 1st session, p. 795.

Conservative groups who shared his beliefs. When Alcorn resigned in November, 1871, to take his place in the United States Senate, he was succeeded by R. C. Powers, a man of the same sentiments.[84] Both of these men wished to carry out a program which they considered to be for the best interests of whites and blacks alike. Both of them, like many of the white Republicans in the legislature, avoided social contacts with the Negroes as much as possible, and were absolutely opposed to any real control of their party by the Negroes.

In this situation, the Negro minority in the legislature generally followed the lead of the white Republicans, with whom, in matters of routine legislation, they were usually naturally in accord. In such routine business, the more able Negroes, including Stringer, Boulden, Jacobs, Spelman, and Lynch, were about as prominent as any of the white leaders. In fact, when the proportion of their numbers is kept in mind, a survey of the *Journals* reveals little difference between the whites and Negroes in attendance, in service on committees, or in activity on the floor. Negro members almost never suggested legislation to obtain special privileges for their race. The more able Negroes either recognized the weakness of their position or had no desire to gain undue advantage. The few who would have gone further received no encouragement or support.

In his inaugural address, in January, 1870, Governor Alcorn outlined clearly the two basic problems faced by the Republicans. "The obligations resting on us under the new order of things," he said, "extend very greatly the breadth of duty of the State Government. The 'patriarchal' groupings of our society in the days of slavery, confined the work of our political organizations, to a very great extent, to the heads of what we called 'families.'" Under the new regime, every individual had become a distinct entity. In addition to the great increase in the number of individuals concerned, a large increase in the *amount* of government was contemplated. The costs of the new administration must be much greater than those of the old. He would therefore urge the legislature to take advantage of every opportunity for economy. In regard to the state's new citizens, he said: "In the face of memories that might have separated them from me as the wronged from the wronger, they have offered me their confidence. . . . In response to that touching reliance, the most profound anxiety with which I enter my office . . . is that of making the colored man the equal, before the law, of any other man. . . ."[85] Thus, in the beginning, Alcorn presented the problems that doomed the Republican regime. There were many whites who were alienated by the extension of the powers of the state, and even more by the increase in costs and taxes. A larger group, including, to a certain extent, Alcorn himself, absolutely refused to accept

[84] J. W. Garner, *op. cit.*, p. 281; Dunbar Rowland, *History of Mississippi*, II, 176; J. S. McNeily, *op. cit.*, II, 426.
[85] Mississippi *House Journal*, 1870, pp. 56-57.

the implications of Negro equality before the law. Such revolutions. unless maintained by overwhelming force, cannot be accomplished in a decade.

With a treasury balance of about fifty dollars in cash and five hundred dollars in negotiable paper, the Republicans entered upon the program that was to reconstruct the state. During the next four years, they set up, organized, and maintained at state expense a bi-racial system of common school education which, although it did not approach the national average in facilities or expense, was an amazing advance beyond anything the state had known before. They gave state support to normal schools at Holly Springs and Tougaloo, and established Alcorn as a Negro counterpart to the state university. They completely reorganized, coordinated, and centralized the state judiciary, and gave to it a new code of laws. Old public buildings were renovated and enlarged and new ones were constructed. State hospitals were set up and supported at Natchez and Vicksburg, and the facilities of the state asylums for the blind, deaf and dumb, and insane were greatly expanded. All racial discrimination was eliminated from the laws of the state. Finally, after much disagreement, the legislature granted to the Negroes in 1873 a civil rights bill, which in theory guaranteed to them equal access to all places of public entertainment.

Although much of this legislation was expensive, and almost all of it was controversial, a partial acceptance of the program and a loss of faith in the Democratic party produced a sweeping victory in 1872, and the election of Republicans to five of the six congressional seats. By the summer of 1873, the Republican party had reached the height of its power in the state. In this very strength, however, there was a great weakness. The breakdown of Democratic opposition, in the state as in the nation, opened the way for a struggle among the discordant elements in the dominant party. Between 1867 and 1872, it had appeared that this struggle, when it came, would involve a choice by the Negroes between Northern and native whites as their leaders.[86] In spite of efforts of the Democrats to aggravate differences on this basis, it had greatly declined in importance by 1873. The great line of division had come to be the question of the extent to which Negroes were to be allowed to hold offices and to dominate the councils of the party.

This became apparent in the state and county conventions in the summer of 1873. The Negroes, after six years of domination of the party by whites, now declared that they must have a larger share of the offices. Although, in general, their demands were not yet proportional to their party membership, the Negroes overestimated their ability to supply suitable candidates. This became evident when, after Bruce's refusal to accept the lieutenant-governorship, that office went to the weak A. K. Davis. Mat-

[86] Hinds County *Gazette*, November 1, 1867, July 5, August 9, 30, 1871.

ters became worse when the Vicksburg ring, threatening violence and secession, secured the post of superintendent of education for Cardozo. This left James Hill, candidate for the office of secretary of state, as the only really acceptable candidate offered by the Negroes for the three state positions which they demanded. Similar weaknesses were to be found in many of the men whom they chose for places in the legislature and in the county governments. The most important point at issue, however, was the fact that it was now clear that actual domination of the party by the mass of its Negro membership would probably come in the near future. By thousands of white members of the party, and by a majority of its white leaders, such a development could not be accepted.

J. L. Alcorn, already repudiated by the Negroes, undertook to lead the opposition, and announced his candidacy for the governorship in opposition to Adelbert Ames. With him went most of the Republican leaders who were native whites, and a number of those from the North. To 'this group, calling itself the "Republican Party of Mississippi," the Democrat-Conservative organization immediately threw its support.[87]

In an election in which the color line was rather sharply drawn, Ames defeated Alcorn by a vote of 69,870 to 50,490. Seventy-seven of the 115 members of the lower house were Republicans of either the Alcorn or the Ames faction. Fifty-five were Negroes, but one or two of these were Democrats. In a senate of thirty-seven members, twenty-five were Republicans, including nine Negroes. All of the seven state officers were regular Ames Republicans, and three of them, the lieutenant-governor, the secretary of state, and the superintendent of education, were Negroes. Furthermore, a Negro from Warren County, I. D. Shadd, soon became the none-too-competent speaker of the house.

In his inaugural address, Governor Ames made a good impression. After pledging himself to work for economy and reform, he turned to the race problem, analyzed the causes of conflict, and called for tolerance and a mutual recognition of rights and interests.[88] Thus, as Alcorn had done four years before, Ames recognized the two great problems which neither of them could solve. The elevation of the Negro involved a rapid expansion of state services which were inconsistent with the old ideas of economy. The readjustment of the relationship between the races was a matter beyond the power of the governor or the legislature.

The heavy increase in the number of Negroes in the government of the state did not greatly decrease its efficiency or change its character. The secretary of state was both competent and honest, and the superintendent of education at least was competent. The Negro legislators, as a group, were fairly capable of handling their duties, and probably repre-

[87] *Appleton's Cyclopedia*, 1873, p. 514.
[88] Mississippi *Senate Journal*, 1874, pp. 24-25.

sented their race more worthily than did the Negroes in any other Southern legislature. Visiting the state in 1874, Edward King wrote:

. . . [Negroes] lounge everywhere, and there are large numbers of smartly dressed mulattoes, or sometimes full blacks, who flit here and there with the conscious air which distinguishes the freedman. I wish here to avow, however, that those of the negroes in office, with whom I came in contact in Mississippi, impressed me much more powerfully as worthy, intelligent, and likely to progress, than many whom I saw elsewhere in the South. There are some who are exceedingly capable, and none of those immediately attached to the government at Jackson are incapable. In the Legislature there are now and then negroes who are ignorant; but of late both branches have been freer of this curse than have those of Louisiana or South Carolina.

A visit to the Capitol showed me that the negroes, who form considerably more than half the population of Mississippi, had certainly secured a fair share of the offices. Colored men act as officials or assistants in the offices of the Auditor, the Secretary of State, the Public Library, the Commissioner of Emigration [sic], and the Superintendent of Public Instruction. The Secretary of State [James Hill], who has some negro blood in his veins, is the natural son of a well-known Mississippian of the old regime, formerly engaged in the politics of his State; and the Speaker of the House of Representatives at the last session was a black man. The blacks who went and came from the Governor's office seemed very intelligent, and some of them entered into general conversation in an interesting manner.[89]

In spite of Ames' evidently sincere interest in economy, he and his legislature found it very difficult to make any substantial reduction in the expenses of the state government. Under the Republican administration, expenses had grown to what the Democrats declared were fantastic proportions. As a matter of fact, when the abnormal years of the war are omitted, the figures of the state auditors do give the impression that the Republican administrations were extravagant:

Year	Democratic Administrations	Year	Republican Administrations
1856 through		1870	$1,061,249.90
1860—average	$ 767,438.78	1871	1,729,046.34
1865	1,410,250.13	1872	1,596,828.64
1866	1,860,809.89	1873	1,450,632.80
1867	625,817.80	1874	1,319,281.60
1868	525,678.80	1875	1,430,192.83
1869	463,219.71		
1876	518,709.03		
1877	697,018.86		
1878	707,022.46		
1879	553,326.81		
1880	803,191.31		

Thus the average yearly cost of the state government under the six years of Republican control was $1,431,205.35, or almost twice the normal

[89] Edward King, *The Great South*, pp. 314-315.

expenditure of the years immediately preceding the war. Even more spectacular, however, had been the increase in taxation of real estate. For many years, real property had been practically exempt from taxation in Mississippi. In 1869, the last year of Democratic control, the rate on this class of property was only one mill, or a tax of only twenty dollars a year on a plantation assessed by its owner at twenty thousand dollars and worth perhaps fifty thousand. The great sources of revenue were a tax of a dollar a bale on cotton, and privilege and license taxes which seem to have been inordinately high. The Republican regime reversed this system; after abolishing the tax on cotton and almost entirely eliminating the privilege taxes, the Republicans placed almost the entire burden of the support of the state on real and personal property. The result was a rate that rose from five mills in 1871 to fourteen in 1874. However pleasing such a system might be to the advocate of the single tax, there can be no doubt that it brought wrath to the landowners in a period of agricultural depression.

So strong had the protest of the landowners become by the spring of 1875 that the legislature could no longer afford to overlook it. Governor Ames insisted that changes were necessary, and the representatives undertook the problem. The reductions for which they provided, like those made later by the Democrats, were more apparent than real. For a centralized government in a state of more than a million people, it was a simple fact that a cost of $1,400,000 per year was not extravagant. To meet the situation, the legislature put back on the counties the cost of jury, witness, and inquest fees that had been assumed by the state. Thus, at one blow, an item of two hundred thousand dollars a year was chopped from the cost of the government of the state, but it was added to that of the counties. In addition, the legislature presented to the people a constitutional amendment to provide for a great reduction in the number of the circuit judges. It also reduced printing costs by cutting down the number of the legislative journals, and by eliminating the publication of departmental reports. Then, against the opposition of about half of the Negro members, it reduced the salaries of the governor and other state officials, and provided for biennial rather than annual sessions of the legislature. Appropriations to the state universities were reduced, and scholarships were abolished. Another amendment to the constitution provided for the distribution of income from state lands, fines, and liquor licenses rather than their incorporation in the permanent school endowment fund. The ratification of this amendment was to allow a heavy reduction in the state school tax. Finally, turning to the system of taxation, the legislature reduced the *ad volerem* levy to nine and one-fourth mills, placed a tax on railroads, and made a partial return to the use of privilege taxes.[90] Ironically enough, the effect

[90] Mississippi *Session Laws*, 1875.

of most of these reforms could not become apparent until the following year, at which time their benefits were easily claimed by the triumphant Democrats. Their adoption went almost unnoticed in the midst of the tumultuous movement toward the revolution of 1875.

Unlike the Republican administrations in most of the other Southern states, those in Mississippi financed their enterprises almost entirely through taxation. When the party assumed control in January, 1871, the state had an empty treasury and a debt of $1,178,175.33.[91] When the Democrats returned to power in January, 1876, they found $524,388.68 in the treasury and a debt of $3,341,162.89.[92] With the deduction in each case of permanent funds which the state owed to itself, and consideration of the treasury balance, the payable debt in 1876, as in 1871, was approximately half a million dollars, a negligible amount.

Furthermore, the Republican state regime left a remarkable record of honesty. The conclusion of J. W. Garner seems to be approximately correct :

So far as the conduct of state officials who were entrusted with the custody of public funds is concerned, it may be said that there were no great embezzlements or other cases of misappropriation during the period of Republican rule. . . . The treasurer of the Natchez hospital seems to have been the only defaulting state official during the administration of Governor Ames. He was a carpet-bagger, and the amount of the shortage was $7,251.81. The colored state librarian during Alcorn's administration was charged with stealing books from the library. The only large case of embezzlement during the post-bellum period was that of the Democratic treasurer in 1866. The amount of the shortage was $61,962.[93]

It may be added that the next embezzlement or any importance was that of the Democratic "redemption" treasurer who was elected in 1875. His shortage was $315,612.19.[94]

Altogether, as governments go, that supplied by the Negro and white Republicans in Mississippi between 1870 and 1876 was not a bad government. Never, in state, counties, or towns, did the Negroes hold office in proportion to their numbers, although their demands in this direction were undeniably increasing. The Negroes who held county offices were often ignorant, but under the control of white Democrats or Republicans they supplied a form of government which differed little from that in counties where they held no offices. The three who represented the state in the national Congress were above reproach. Those in the legislature sought no special advantages for their race, and in one of their very first acts they petitioned Congress to remove all political disabilities from the whites.

[91] Mississippi *Senate Journal*, 1872, *Appendix*, p. 125.
[92] Mississippi Auditor of Public Accounts, *Report*, 1876.
[93] J. W. Garner, *op. cit.*, pp. 322-323.
[94] Hinds County *Gazette*, March 22, 1890; J. Dunbar Rowland, *History of Mississippi*, II, 242-245; J. D. Rowland, *Encyclopedia of Mississippi History*, II, 743-744.

With their white Republican colleagues, they gave to the state a government of greatly expanded functions at a cost that was low in comparison with that of almost any other state. The legislature of 1875 reduced that cost to some extent, and opened the way for further reductions by the passage of constitutional amendments. It also removed some of the apparent injustices in the system of taxation. But one situation it did not alter. The Republican party had come to be branded as a party of Negroes, and it was apparent that the Negroes were more and more determined to assert their right to control that party. It is also true that many of the Negroes, probably a majority, favored a further expansion of the functions of the state, entirely at the expense, according to the whites, of white tax-payers. The way was open for the formation of a "white-line" party.

CHAPTER XIII

THE REVOLUTION OF 1875

From the beginning of Reconstruction, there were in Mississippi a large number of white men who insisted upon the necessity of accepting the results of the war and of complying with the requirements of the national government. This group, made up largely of old Whigs, and generally men of property, desired above all else order, prosperity, and harmonious relations within the Union. Guaranteeing to the Negro those minimum rights set up in the amendments to the Constitution, they would seek to gain his confidence and his vote by convincing him that their leadership was for the best interests of both races. Such distinguished citizens as A. G. Brown, C. C. Shackleford, H. F. Simrall, Amos R. Johnston, J. A. P. Campbell, Joshua Morris, and J. L. Alcorn were by temperament members of this group, although some worked with the Democratic party and some with the Republican. The essence of their failure lay in the fact that almost none of them could bring himself to deal with a Negro, however able or honest that Negro might be, as a political or social equal. In later years, J. L. Alcorn often declared that he had never been a "negro Republican."[1] Exactly the same was true of such Northern leaders as H. R. Pease, George C. McKee, and R. C. Powers. By 1874, men of this class had to recognize either their failure to make Democrats of the Negroes, or the repudiation of their leadership in the Republican party. Given the assurance that the national government would not intervene, most of these conservatives were then ready to join the mass of the white Democrats in any methods they might use to drive the Negroes from power.

The majority of the white citizens, brought up on the belief that the Negro was an inferior creature who must be kept in subjection, found themselves unable from the beginning to endorse the program of the Conservatives. In December, 1869, the editor of the Columbus *Index* made a bid for the leadership of this group with the declaration: "We have given the negro a fair trial. He has voted solidly against us, and we hoist, from this day, the white man's flag, and will never take it down so long as we have a voice in the government of the State."[2] The year 1870 saw the organization of a number of "White Men's Clubs" throughout the state. One at Bellefontaine, with 152 members, pledged its subscribers to a perpetual and uncompromising opposition to social and political equality of the

---

[1] Jackson *Clarion-Ledger*, November 27, 1890.
[2] Hinds County *Gazette*, December 15, 1869, quoting the Columbus *Index*.

white and black races, and to all measures tending thereto. Believing that
Negro suffrage was "wrong in principle and disastrous in effect," they
pledged themselves to labor unceasingly, from year to year, for the restoration of white supremacy in Mississippi and in the United States.[3] A similar club at West Point agreed to follow a policy that would ignore the
Negro as a voter and as an element in politics.[4] The Columbus *Democrat,*
advocating the union of these groups in a revitalized Democratic party,
declared:

. . . Its leading ideas are, that white men shall govern, that niggers are not
rightly entitled to vote, and that when it gets into power, niggers will be placed
upon the same footing with white minors who do not vote or hold office.

There are professed Democrats who do not understand Democratic principles,
that want the party mongrelized, thinking that the less difference between the
two parties will give them a better chance for the spoils. They are willing for
the niggers to vote, but not to hold office. . . .

Nigger voting, holding office and sitting in the jury box, are all wrong, and
against the sentiment of the country. There is nothing more certain to occur
than that these outrages upon justice and good government will soon be removed, and the unprincipled men who are now their advocates will sink lower
in the social scale than the niggers themselves.[5]

Here was sheer racial antagonism. There was no consideration of the
undesirability of the participation of ignorant and poverty-stricken masses
in the government of the state; the line was drawn on the basis of race.

In the face of the decrepitude of the Democratic party, and of the
certainty of Federal intervention in case of a state-wide movement based
on violence, the program was held in check during 1871, 1872, and 1873.
But with the rejection of Alcorn in the election of 1873, and the great
increase in office holding by Negroes after that election, the movement
gained new strength. Native and Northern whites whose leadership had
been rejected by the Negroes now joined in the demand for white supremacy. The great financial depression of 1873 was reflected in the state by
increased unpleasantness in political and social relations, and in the nation
by a decline of interest in affairs of the South. Furthermore this financial
collapse, along with the discovery of scandals in the Federal government,
served greatly to weaken the power of the Republican party in the nation.
There were predictions of a Democratic president in 1876. When these
predictions were strengthened by the great Democratic victories which
gained control of the House of Representatives in 1874, conservative leaders in Mississippi at last agreed to abandon their caution. The word went
out that the time for revolution was at hand, and the efforts of such men
as A. G. Brown and L. Q. C. Lamar to halt the movement were of no avail.

[3] Mississippi *Weekly Pilot,* July 30, August 12, 1870.
[4] *Ibid.,* November 26, 1870.
[5] *Ibid.,* December 24, 1870, quoting the Columbus *Democrat.*

Greater and greater numbers of white Republicans in Mississippi were now deserting the party and joining the opposing conventions. As Charles Nordhoff was told in the spring of 1875, the Democrats were making it "too damned hot for them to stay out."[6] Economic pressure and threats of physical violence were used, but the most powerful force was that of social ostracism. Colonel James A. Lusk, a prominent native Republican, said to a Negro leader: "No white man can live in the South in the future and act with any other than the Democratic party unless he is willing and prepared to live a life of social isolation and remain in political oblivion." In consideration of the future happiness of his sons and daughters, he felt it necessary to announce his renunciation of all Republican connections.[7] The Canton *Mail* published the names of those whites who must no longer be recognized on the streets, and whose attentions must be scorned by "every true woman."[8]

At the same time that white Republicans were abandoning their party, more and more of the conservative Democratic leaders and newspapers were accepting the "white-line" program. The transition could be seen clearly in most cases.   Editors who for several years had written of the Negroes in terms of sympathy, impatience, or friendly ridicule, and who had even praised them at times in an effort to gain their votes, came to speak of them during the summer of 1874 with open dislike, and finally with hatred.[9] By May of 1875, such original color liners as the Vicksburg *Herald,* Columbus *Index,* Handsboro *Democrat,* Yazoo City *Banner,* Vicksburg *Monitor,* and Okolona *Southern States,* had been joined by the conservative Hinds County *Gazette,* Newton *Ledger,* Brandon *Republican,* Forest *Register,* and Jackson *Clarion,* and by the Republican Meridian *Gazette.*

The general charge made by papers and individuals in renouncing their former conservatism was that the color line had already been drawn by the Negro. As evidence, they offered the fact that almost none of the Negroes ever voted with the whites [Democrats],[10] that in some of the counties the Negroes had taken most of the offices,[11] that in the Republican convention of 1873 Negroes had absolutely demanded three of the seven state offices,[12] and that, on such questions as the reduction of the tax for schools, Negroes in the legislature had voted almost as a unit against the whites.[13] In mak-

[6] Charles Nordhoff, *The Cotton States,* p. 77.
[7] John R. Lynch, *The Facts of Reconstruction,* p. 122.
[8] Mississippi *Weekly Pilot,* September 4, 1875 and September 11, 1875, quoting the Canton *Mail.*
[9] This transition is especially noticeable in the Hinds County *Gazette,* and the Jackson *Clarion.*
[10] Vicksburg *Daily Herald,* November 29, 1874; Hinds County *Gazette,* September 23, 1874.
[11] Hinds County *Gazette,* August 26, 1874.
[12] Columbus *Press,* August 7, 1875.
[13] Hinds County *Gazette,* May 5, 1875.

ing these charges, the Democrats ignored the fact that the Negroes had from the beginning welcomed the leadership of almost any white who would serve with them, that in so doing they had taken into their party from ten to twenty thousand white Mississippians and that they could not be expected to join in any numbers a party which had from the beginning opposed all of the rights upon which their hopes were built.

As time went on the attack became more and more bitter. The Forest *Register* carried at its masthead the slogan: "A white man in a white man's place. A black man in a black man's place. Each according to the 'eternal fitness of things.'" The Yazoo City *Banner* declared, *"Mississippi is a white man's country, and by the Eternal God we'll rule it."*[14] The Handsboro *Democrat* called for *"A white man's Government, by white men, for the benefit of white men."*[15] All of these papers justified their stand in editorials describing the depravity and innate bestiality of the Negro. These reached a climax in one published by the Forest *Register*.

A negro preacher is an *error loci*. God Almighty, in farming out his privileges to mankind, drew a line as to qualifications.

He never exacted from a nation or tribe an impossibility. . . . Does any sane man believe the negro capable of comprehending the ten commandments? The miraculous conception and the birth of our Savior? The high moral precepts taught from the temple on the mount?

Every effort to inculcate these great truths but tends to bestialize his nature, and by obfuscating his little brain unfits him for the duties assigned him as a hewer of wood and drawer of water. The effort makes him a demon of wild, fanatical destruction, and consigns him to the fatal shot of the white man.[16]

Declarations by the rapidly dwindling group of conservative Democrats that the votes of the Negroes could be secured by treating them fairly and reasoning with them met the scorn of the white liners. The editor of the Newton *Democrat* declared that he would just as soon try to reason with a shoal of crocodiles or a drove of Kentucky mules.[17] From Colonel McCardle of the Vicksburg *Herald* came the answer: "The way to treat Sambo is not to argue to him or to reason with him. If you do that, it puffs his vanity and it only makes him insolent. Say to him, 'Here, we are going to *carry* this election; you may vote as you like; but we *are* going to carry it. Then we are going to look after ourselves and our friends; you can look after yourself,' and he will vote with you."[18] Furthermore, when Lamar succeeded in inserting in the Democrat-Conservative platform a vague statement recognizing "the civil and political equality of all men," and inviting the Negroes to vote with the party for good govern-

---

[14] Mississippi *Weekly Pilot,* July 31, 1875, quoting Yazoo City *Banner.*
[15] *Ibid.,* April 10, 1875, quoting the Handsboro *Democrat.*
[16] Forest *Register,* September 15, 1875.
[17] James B. Ranck, *Albert Gallatin Brown,* p. 275.
[18] Mississippi *Weekly Pilot,* May 29, 1875, quoting the Vicksburg *Herald.*

ment, the white liners were quick to deny any allegiance.[19] As a Democratic leader declared the following year, ". . . [The] only issue in the
election was whether the whites or the blacks should predominate; there
was no other politics that I could see in it. Men that had been republicans
all their lives just laid aside republicanism and said that they had to go into
the ranks then."[20] In the words of J. S. McNeily, "It was a part of the
creed of a desperate condition, one easily understood, that any white man,
however odious, was preferable . . . to any negro however unobjectionable
individually."[21]

Once the general policy had been adopted that Negro and Republican
control of the state government was to be broken at any cost, a number of
methods were followed for its accomplishment. One of these involved the
intimidation of those whites who still worked with the Republican party.
There was a general understanding that in the case of the outbreak of a
"race war," carpet-baggers would be the first to be killed.[22] As early as
December, 1874, the Hinds County *Gazette* declared that death should be
meted out to those who continued their opposition. "All other means having been exhausted to abate the horrible condition of things, the thieves
and robbers, and scoundrels, white and black, deserve death and ought to
be killed. . . . The thieves and robbers kept in office by Governor Ames
and his robber associates . . . ought to be compelled to leave the State, or
abide the consequences."[23] After the Clinton "riot," Colonel McCardle
of the *Herald* urged that in future cases of violence white Republicans be
killed and the deluded Negroes spared.[24] At the same time, the editor of
the Columbus *Index* announced, "The White League is resolved to kill
hereafter only those white wretches who incite negroes to riot and murder."[25] According to J. S. McNeily, "There is no doubt that this sentiment made for peace, in the campaign."[26] There is also no doubt that as
time went by the Negroes found fewer and fewer white leaders at their
meetings.

Against the Negroes themselves one of the most powerful forces used
was economic pressure. All over the state, Democratic clubs announced
that no Negro who voted Republican could hope for any form of employment the following year. It was also urged that the boycott be extended

[19] Columbus *Democrat*, August 21, 1875; Mississippi *Weekly Pilot*, September 4,
1875, quoting the Columbus *Democrat*.
[20] Testimony of W. A. Montgomery, *Senate Reports*, no. 527, 44th Congress, 1st
session, p. 542.
[21] J. S. McNeily, "War and Reconstruction in Mississippi," *P.M.H.S.C.S.*, II, 417.
[22] J. S. McNeily, "Climax and Collapse of Reconstruction in Mississippi,"
P.M.H.S., XII, 405.
[23] Hinds County *Gazette*, December 30, 1874.
[24] Mississippi *Weekly Pilot*, October 9, 1875, quoting the Vicksburg *Herald*.
[25] Columbus *Index*, October 8, 1875.
[26] J. S. McNeily, "Climax and Collapse of Reconstruction in Mississippi,"
P.M.H.S., XII, 405.

to the wives of Negro Republicans.[27]   In some cases, doctors announced that they would no longer serve Negroes who did not vote the Democratic ticket.[28]   Lists of Negroes who were pledged for or against the party were prepared, and arrangements were made for checkers to be present at the polls.   After the election, the names of Negroes marked for discharge were printed in the various papers, along with the names of those who deserved special consideration for having refrained from voting or for having worked with the Democrats.[29]

At the same time, except in the counties where the Democrats had a safe majority, strenuous efforts were being made to get the Negroes into the various Democratic clubs.   For those Negroes who would take this step, and participate in the processions and other functions of the clubs, there were pledges of protection and of continued employment.   There were also abundant supplies of flags, transparencies, uniforms, and badges. The Democratic badge in Lafayette County not only protected the wearer from physical violence, but also allowed him to "boss" other Negroes. There were numerous barbecues and picnics at which Negro bands and glee clubs furnished entertainment, and at which Negroes either volunteered or were hired to speak.[30]   In some of the counties, no expense was spared.   In Monroe, the candidates for the legislature gave $1,000.00 each, and subscriptions from private citizens ranged up to $500.00.[31]   In Panola, the Democratic committee supplied $5,000.00 in addition to subscriptions from individuals.   According to one of the leaders in that county, "Our purpose was to overawe the negroes and exhibit to them the ocular proof of our power . . . by magnificent torchlight processions at night and in the day by special trains of cars . . . loaded down with white people with flags flying, drums beating, and bands playing, the trains being chartered and free for everybody."[32]

However pleasing these affairs may have been to those who participated, they had little effect on the campaign.   Negro attendance was usually dis-

[27] Mississippi *Weekly Pilot*, January 30, 1875, quoting the Newton *Ledger;* Aberdeen *Examiner,* September 4, November 4, 1875; Hinds County *Gazette,* November 18, 1874, August 25, September 15, October 27, December 1, 1875; Julia Kendel "Reconstruction in Lafayette County," *P.M.H.S.,* XIII, 251; E. F. Puckett, "Reconstruction in Monroe County," *P.M.H.S.,* XI, 145, 146, 153; *Senate Reports,* no. 527 44th Congress, 1st session, p. xiv; Mississippi *Weekly Pilot,* September 11, 1875 quoting the Canton *Mail.*

[28] E. F. Puckett, *op. cit.,* XI, 145.

[29] Hinds County *Gazette,* August 4, 11, November 10, 17, December 1, 1875 Aberdeen *Examiner,* November 11, 1875; Meridian *Mercury,* November 6, 1875 Mississippi *Weekly Pilot,* November 13, 1875.

[30] Hinds County *Gazette,* July 28, August 11, September 1, 15, 1875; R. Watkins "Reconstruction in Marshall County," *P.M.H.S.,* XII, 177, 185, 189; J. Kendel, *op cit.,* XIII, 250, 251; Fred Z. Browne, "Reconstruction in Yalobusha and Grenada Counties," *P.M.H.S.,* XII, 251, 252; Fred Witty, "Reconstruction in Carroll and Montgomery Counties," *P.M.H.S.,* X, 126; John W. Kyle, "Reconstruction in Panola County," *P.M.H.S.,* XIII, 73; E. F. Puckett, *op. cit.,* XI, 144.

[31] E. F. Puckett, *op. cit.,* XI, 144.   [32] J. W. Kyle, *op. cit.,* XIII, 73.

appointingly small. Most of the Negro speakers and entertainers either had to be hired, or were "Uncle Toms" who had no standing with their fellows. At many of the barbecues, the Negroes were placed at separate tables, and at others many of the whites felt that the whole affair was "ridiculous," and refused to enter into the spirit of the occasion.[33] Of the two methods that were used by the more conservative Democrats to persuade the Negroes to vote away their political power, then, only that involving economic pressure had any appreciable success.

Much more successful was the use of threats and actual violence. It is not to be imagined that this campaign of violence involved all who called themselves Democrats. Many members of the party undoubtedly opposed it, and many more probably considered it regrettable but necessary. It did involve directly thousands of young men and boys of all classes, a large part of the poor white element, and many local political leaders of some importance. Furthermore, it must be admitted that the Democratic leaders of the state, while they often denied the existence of violence, or tried to shift the blame for it to the Negroes, never actually repudiated its use, and in some cases encouraged it. In the meantime, the Democratic press adopted the slogan, "Carry the election peaceably if we can, forcibly if we must."[34] Urged on by newspapers and political leaders, young men all over the state formed militia companies, and Democratic clubs provided themselves with the latest style of repeating rifles.[35] By September, 1875, the Hinds County *Gazette* could announce, "The people of this State are now fully armed, equipped, and drilled. . . ."[36] As described later by the Aberdeen *Examiner*, the situation was well under control in Monroe County:

. . the firmest word was "victory"—to be achieved by arms if necessary. When the central power made treaties in Jackson involving the laying down or stacking of arms, the people in this part of the state burnished their arms and bought more cartridges, and each county conducted the campaign upon its own plan . . . each looking to winning its own home fight in its own home way, and each ready and willing to support its neighbors physically and morally whenever the emergency demanded aid, as was not unfrequently the case.

. . here and elsewhere in the dark counties we guaranteed peace by thoroughly organising for war; and . . . at the call of the County Executive Committee it was easy—as demonstrated on several occasions—to put seventeen hundred well-mounted horsemen into line, that could be transposed into a bri-

[33] Hinds County *Gazette*, July 28, August 11, October 27, 1875; R. Watkins, *op. cit.*, XII, 177, 189; F. M. Witty, *op. cit.*, X, 126, 127; J. W. Kyle, *op. cit.*, XIII, 73; Z. Browne, *op. cit.*, XII, 251, 252.

[34] Yazoo City *Democrat*, September 14, 1875; Hinds County *Gazette*, August 4, 1875; Aberdeen *Examiner*, August 2, 1883.

[35] Vicksburg *Times and Republican*, May 28, 29, June 3, 21, 1873; Hinds County *Gazette*, December 16, 1874; Vicksburg *Herald*, February 26, 1875; Mississippi *Weekly Pilot*, December 26, 1874, quoting the Brandon *Republican;* J. W. Kyle, *op. cit.*, XIII, 75.

[36] Hinds County *Gazette*, September 29, 1875.

gade of cavalry at a moment's notice, to say nothing of a thoroughly organized artillery company and a company of Infantry armed with needle guns, purchased by our citizens, for home service.   In addition to this, our eight hundred square miles of territory was so thoroughly connected by courier lines and posts, that we could communicate with every voter within its borders within a few hours.[37]

With this powerful military force at its command, the white Democracy was ready for its campaign against a mass of Negroes who were timorous, unarmed, and largely unorganized.   The program involved extensive processions and drills, and much firing of cannon, at least one of which was owned by every club of any importance.   As the campaign of intimidation went on, Negro Republicans were ostentatiously enrolled in "dead books."[38] Negro political leaders were warned that another speech would mean death.[39]   Republican political meetings were broken up by violent attacks, or prevented by armed force.[40]   Committees of "active young men" waited on Negroes who tried to prevent others of their race from deserting their party.[41]   Negroes were prevented from registering by sham battles and the firing of pistols at registration points, or by armed pickets who met them on the roads.[42]   Democrats adopted a policy of appearing in force at all Republican meetings, demanding the privilege of presenting Democratic speakers, and compelling Republican speakers to "tell the truth or quit the stand."[43]

In the political, economic, and social subjugation of the freedmen, the most effective weapon ever developed was the "riot."   Because this fact was discovered in the Meridian riot of 1871, that incident deserves some attention.   In the spring of 1871, Meridian, a rapidly growing railroad town in the eastern part of the state, was under the control of white Republicans appointed to office by Governor Alcorn, and of Negro leaders including J. Aaron Moore, William Clopton, and Warren Tyler.   The population of this new town could best be described as "tough," and relations between the races were bad.   For the purpose of discussing the situation, the Negroes were brought together in a mass meeting early in March, and were addressed by the three Negro leaders and William Sturgis, the white Republican mayor.   While the meeting was going on, a fire alarm was heard, and it was discovered that a store owned by Sturgis was on fire.   In the resultant excitement, there was further unpleasantness be-

[37] Aberdeen *Examiner,* August 2, 1883.
[38] W. Calvin Wells, "Reconstruction in Hinds County," *P.M.H.S.,* IX, 102.
[39] J. W. Kyle, *op. cit.,* XIII, 71.
[40] F. M. Witty, *op. cit.,* X, 123; Mississippi *Weekly Pilot,* October 2, 1875; *Senate Reports,* no. 527, 44th Congress, 1st session, pp. 196-197.
[41] Hinds County *Gazette,* July 28, August 18, September 23, 1875.
[42] Mississippi *Weekly Pilot,* October 9, 1875; *Senate Reports,* no. 527, 44th Congress, 1st session, p. 1718.
[43] J. W. Kyle, *op. cit.,* XIII, 72; J. Kendel, *op. cit.,* XIII, 244; Hinds County *Gazette,* August 4, 1875.

tween the whites and the blacks. On the following morning, white citizens persuaded a lawyer who had not been present at the Republican meeting to prepare an affidavit to the effect that the speeches of Warren Tyler, Bill Dennis [Clopton], and Aaron Moore had been of an incendiary character.[44] The trial of these men was held the following Sunday afternoon before Judge Bramlette, a native white Republican, in a crowded court room. According to the prosecutor, one of the Negroes, Warren Tyler, interrupted James Brantley, a white witness, to say, "I want three colored men summoned to impeach your testimony." Brantley then seized the city marshal's stick and started toward the Negro. Tyler, moving toward a side door, reached back as though to draw a pistol, and general firing immediately began in the rear of the court room.[45] Although it seems that no one actually saw Tyler fire, and although Negroes stoutly denied that he did so, the available evidence indicates that he probably shot at the advancing Brantley and, missing him, killed Judge Bramlette.[46] W. H. Hardy, a local Democratic leader, later wrote a description of the affair in which he attributed the shot that killed Bramlette to the Negro Bill Dennis. In this he was probably incorrect, but to the rest of his story there is general agreement.

As quick as a flash the white men sitting in the rear drew their pistols and fired upon Dennis. [Tyler had run through the side door and leaped to the ground from a second-floor veranda.] By the time the smoke cleared away the court room had but few people left in it. Judge Bramlette was found dead and Bill Dennis mortally wounded. The riot [sic] was on and white men and negroes were seen running in every direction; the white men to get their arms and the negroes in mortal terror to seek a place of hiding. Every man that could do so got a gun or a pistol and went on the hunt for negroes. The two men left to guard the wounded Bill Dennis in the sheriff's office grew tired of their job and threw him from the balcony into the middle of the street, saying that their services were needed elsewhere, and they could not waste time guarding a wounded negro murderer. Warren Tyler was found concealed in a shack and shot to death. Aaron Moore had escaped from the courthouse in the confusion and lay out in the woods that night, and the next day made his way to Jackson. . . . It was not known how many negroes were killed by the enraged whites, but the number has been estimated at from twenty-five to thirty. . . .

The mayor, Bill Sturgis, was thoroughly overcome with terror at the vengeance of the people and concealed himself in the garret of his boarding house. Being a member of the Odd Fellows' order he opened communication with a member of the lodge, and it resulted in a cartel by which Sturgis was to resign the office of mayor and was to leave the State in twenty-four hours. . . .[47]

[44] J. S. McNeily, "The Enforcement Act of 1871 and the Ku-Klux Klan in Mississippi," *P.M.H.S.*, IX, 128-130; *House Reports*, no. 41, 42d Congress, 1st session, pt. i, pp. 479-480; *ibid.*, pt. ii, pp. 97-98.

[45] *Ibid.*, pt. i, pp. 480-481; pt. ii, pp. 97-99.

[46] *Ibid.*, pt. i, p. 127; pt. ii, pp. 10, 70, 99, 176, 182, 210, 221.

[47] W. H. Hardy, "Recollections of Reconstruction in East and Southeast Mississippi," *P.M.H.S.*, VII, 205-206.

This affair marked the end of Republican control in the area surrounding Meridian. According to Dunbar Rowland, "The Meridian riot marks an epoch in the transition period of reconstruction, and was a forecast of the end of carpetbag rule in Mississippi."[48]   His opinion endorses that of W. H. Hardy:

It [the Meridian riot] demonstrated the cowardice of both the carpetbaggers and the negro, and that in danger, either real or imaginary, they took counsel of their fear. When the white people failed, after every reasonable appeal to argument, to reason, to justice, to a sense of the public weal, they brought into full play the lessons learned in the Meridian riot, and it proved efficient in the campaign of 1875.[49]

The lesson learned was that the Negroes, largely unarmed, economically dependent, and timid and unresourceful after generations of servitude, would offer no effective resistance to violence. Throughout the period, any unpleasant incident was likely to produce such a "riot." During the bad feeling of 1874 and 1875 there were a great number of unpleasant incidents, and after each resulting riot Negro resistance to white domination in the surrounding area completely collapsed.

With the development of the white-line program in the summer of 1874, the newspapers began to carry a constantly increasing number of stories about clashes between the races. Some of these were reports of real incidents growing out of increasing bitterness; others seem to have been the product of exaggerated rumors, or of an effort to arouse feeling against the Negroes. Soon blood began to flow. In Austin, Negroes raised violent objections to the release of a white man who, in shooting at a Negro man, had killed a Negro girl. In the quarrel which followed, six Negroes were killed; no whites were wounded.[50] In Vicksburg, where the white militia had overthrown Republican control in the municipal election, a number of Negroes prepared to come into town in answer to a call from the Negro sheriff. After they had agreed to go back to their homes, firing started. About thirty-five Negroes were killed. Two whites met death, one possibly by accident.[51] This was in December, 1874. Three months later, the Vicksburg *Monitor* announced, *"The same tactics that saved Vicksburg will surely save the State, and no other will."*[52] In the same city, in the following July, the Republicans held a celebration of Independence Day. Trouble developed with white Democrats. Two Negroes were killed; no whites were wounded. Water Valley was disturbed by a rumor that Negroes were going to attack the town. An exploring party found a group of Negroes concealed under a cliff. An unknown number of Negroes were

[48] J. Dunbar Rowland, *History of Mississippi*, II, 172.
[49] W. H. Hardy, *op. cit.*, VII, 206.
[50] Hinds County *Gazette*, August 19, 1874.
[51] *Ibid.*, December 9, 1874; Vicksburg *Herald*, December, 1874; Mississippi *Weekly Pilot*, March 6, 1875.
[52] Mississippi *Weekly Pilot*, March 20, 1875, quoting the Vicksburg *Monitor*.

illed; no whites were wounded.[53]   In August, Negroes at a Republican meeting in Louisville "succeeded in raising a disturbance."   "Result, two negroes wounded, no white men hurt. Will the negro never learn that he is always sure to be the sufferer in these riots?"[54] Late in the same month, a group of whites near Macon, including more than a hundred horsemen from Alabama, were out looking for a Negro political meeting. After they had failed to find one, they were told by a runner that several hundred Negroes had gathered at a church, where they were preparing to carry aid to those of their race in Vicksburg, on the other side of the state. When the church was found, the Alabamians disobeyed the order of the deputy sheriff and fired into the crowd. Twelve or thirteen Negroes were killed; no white was hurt.[55]

A few nights later, the Republicans endeavored to hold a meeting in Yazoo City. Their hall was invaded by a number of Democrats, led by their "rope-bearer," H. M. Dixon. In the confusion which followed, a native white Republican was killed, and several Negroes were wounded. The white sheriff escaped with his life by fleeing to Jackson. White militia then took charge of the county, and systematically lynched the Negro leaders in each supervisor's district.[56] Three days later, Democrats obtained their customary division of time at a large Republican meeting and picnic at Clinton. Trouble developed between a Negro policeman and a young white who was drunk. In the shooting which followed, two young white Democrats and a white Republican were killed. The number of Negroes killed is unknown; estimates varied from ten to thirty. Two thousand Negroes in wild panic rushed to the woods or to Jackson. By nightfall, armed whites, including the Vicksburg "Modocs," had control of the entire area. During the next four days they scoured the surrounding country, killing Negro leaders. Estimates of the number killed varied between ten and fifty.[57] On the day of the Clinton affair, white Democrats captured a Republican meeting at Utica and compelled a thousand Negroes to listen to Democratic speakers for several hours. There seems to have been no bloodshed.[58] A few days later, there was a minor skirmish at Satartia in which one Negro was killed.[59] Early in the following month,

[53] J. C. Brown, op. cit., XII, 257.
[54] Hinds County Gazette, August 25, 1875, quoting the Kosciusko Star.
[55] Senate Reports, no. 527, 44th Congress, 1st session, pp. 1176-1177; Hinds County Gazette, September 1, 1875.
[56] A. T. Morgan, Yazoo, pp. 465-484; Mississippi Weekly Pilot, September 4, 25, October 2, 1875; Jackson Weekly Clarion, August 27, 1879; Yazoo City Herald, October 15, 1875; Elizabeth Caldwell, "Reconstruction in Yazoo County," unpublished master's thesis, University of North Carolina, 1931, pp. 55-56. Dixon's title of "rope-bearer" was gained through his leadership in lynching expeditions.
[57] Senate Reports, no. 527, 44th Congress, 1st session, pp. 321, 368, 501, 544; Mississippi Weekly Pilot, September 11, 25, 1875; Hinds County Gazette, September 15, 1875; C. H. Brough, "The Clinton Riot," P.M.H.S., VI, 62.
[58] C. H. Brough, op. cit., VI, 54.
[59] Hinds County Gazette, September 15, 1875.

the Negro sheriff was run out of Coahoma County after an encounter i
which five Negroes were killed and five wounded. One white was kille
from ambush; another shot himself by accident.[60] The final clash of th
campaign came at Columbus, a large town with a heavy Negro majority
on the night before the election. A crowd of young whites rushed from
drug store to attack a Negro parade, cutting the heads out of the drum
and scattering the marchers. About an hour later, two old sheds in th
Negro section were found to be burning, and the rumor was spread tha
the blacks were trying to burn the town. The Columbus Riflemen and
large number of visiting Alabamians immediately took charge, and Ne
groes began to flee for safety. Those who refused to halt were fired upon
four men were killed, and several men and one woman were woundee
No whites were hurt.[61]

Long before the day of the election, a Democratic victory was assured
In many of the counties, all efforts to hold Republican meetings wer
abandoned. In several of the black counties, the sheriffs had fled or wer
powerless. White military units held the towns, and pickets patrolled th
roads. The Negroes, with many of their leaders either dead or in hiding
faced the proposition of voting with the Democrats or staying away fror
the polls.

Letters to Governor Ames revealed the panic of the Negroes. From
Yazoo City came the plea, "I beg you most fulley to send the United so
diers here; they have hung six more men since the killing of Mr. Fawn
they wont let the republican have no ticket . . . ; fighting comemense ju
I were closuing, 2 two killed . . . help; send troop and arms pleas. . .
Send help, help, troops. . . ."[62] From Noxubee County came the cry:

Last Saturday, the 30th, the democrats was in Macon town in high rage, rarin
around and shooting of their cannons all up and down the street, and shootin
all their pistols also, and which they have already sword to you for peace; an
I don't think they act much in that way last Saturday, for there was Richar
Gray shot down walking on the pavements, shot by the democrats, and he wa
shot five times, four times after he fell, and was said shot because he wa
nominated for treasurer, and forher more, because he made a speech and sai
he never did expect to vote a democrate ticket, and also advised the colore
citizens to do the same.[63]

From Warren County came a letter from 108 Negroes who could not an
would not register and vote, "for we cannot hold a meeting of no descrip
tion without being molested and broken up; and further our lives are no
safe at nor in our cabins, and therefore we deem it unwise to make

    [60] Ibid., October 13, 1875; Senate Reports, no. 527, 44th Congress, 1st session
pp. 69-70.
    [61] Mississippi Weekly Pilot, November 13, 1875; Senate Reports, no. 527, 44t
Congress, 1st session, pp. 805-820.
    [62] Senate Reports, no. 527, 44th Congress, 1st session, "Documentary Evidence,
p. 99.
    [63] Ibid., p. 73.

target of our body to be shot down like dogs and have no protection. . . ."[64] From Vicksburg came the plea, "The rebles turbulent; are aiming themselves here now to-day to go to Sartartia to murder more poor negroes. Gov., aint the no pertiction?"[65]

There was not any protection. In January, the administration had endeavored to secure the passage of a bill to allow the governor to set up special police bodies in towns where they were needed. Passed in the house by a vote of forty to thirty-eight, it was killed on a color-line vote in the senate.[66] In the desperate days of September, Governor Ames made the formal gesture of commanding the private military bands to disperse. From the *Clarion,* there came a scornful answer that was echoed all over the state: " 'Now, therefore, I, A.A., do hereby command all persons belonging to such organizations to disband.' Ha! ha!! ha!!! 'Command.' 'Disband.' That's good."[67]

The Governor then turned to the Federal government, although he knew his request would be unpopular, even in the North. To Attorney-General Edward Pierrepont, he wrote: "Let the odium, in all its magnitude descend on me. I cannot escape. I am conscious in the discharge of my duty toward a class of American citizens whose only offense consists in their color, and which I am powerless to protect."[68] The plea was hopeless. Negro suffrage, or even Negro freedom, had never been really popular with the masses in the North. Negro suffrage had appeared to be necessary, and had been accepted as such. It had been inaugurated to save a party that a majority of the voters in a number of the Northern states now considered hardly worth saving. Its maintenance had proved to be a troublesome problem. Why should the Negro majority in Mississippi be constantly crying for help? The sending of Federal troops into a state simply to prevent white men from ruling Negroes was distasteful to the average Northern voter.[69] In the final moment of his decision, Grant was visited by a delegation of politicians from Ohio, a pivotal state which was to have an election in October. Mississippi, these visitors declared, was already lost to the party; troops would arrive too late to save the state. Even worse, the order that sent troops to Mississippi would mean the loss of Ohio to the party. The Negroes must be sacrificed.[70] Grant's answer to Ames was a statement that aid could not be sent until all local resources had been exhausted. In the midst of the negotiations,

[64] *Ibid.,* p. 88.
[65] *Ibid.,* p. 89.
[66] Mississippi *Senate Journal,* 1875, p. 302. See also Hinds County *Gazette,* March 3, 1875.
[67] Mississippi *Weekly Pilot,* September 11, 1875, quoting the Jackson *Clarion.*
[68] Mississippi *Weekly Pilot,* September 11, 18, 1875.
[69] J. S. McNeily, "Climax and Collapse of Reconstruction in Mississippi," *P.M.H.S.,* XII, 402, quoting the New York *Herald; Senate Reports,* no. 527, 44th Congress, 1st session, p. 377, quoting the Chicago *Tribune.*
[70] John R. Lynch, *The Facts of Reconstruction,* pp. 150-151.

Pierrepont declared, "The whole public are tired of these annual autumnal outbreaks in the South." "This flippant utterance of Attorney-General Edward Pierrepont," wrote Adelbert Ames twenty years later, "was the way the executive branch of the National government announced that it had decided that the reconstruction acts of congress were a failure."[71]

As a last hope, Ames turned to the organization of a state militia, placing at its head Brigadier General William F. Fitzgerald, an ex-Confederate who had become a Republican. It was the Governor's idea to organize equal companies of whites and blacks, and at first many of the Democrats, under the leadership of J. Z. George, proclaimed their willingness to join. It quickly became apparent, however, that the great mass of the party was absolutely opposed to such a move.[72] If the militia was to be formed, it must be made up almost entirely of Negroes. Difficulties rapidly increased. Democrats secured two blanket injunctions against any further use of the funds which the legislature had appropriated.[73] In several places, state arms were seized by the White Leagues.[74] The refugee sheriff of Yazoo County was convinced that an attempt to use the militia there would bring open war, and finally refused to recommend it.[75] A caucus of the Republican legislators found the Negro members almost as a unit opposed to the plan.[76] By October 15, only two companies, one of whites and the other of Negroes, had been organized. Both of these were at the state capital.

In the meantime, it had become apparent both to Governor Ames and to the Democratic leaders that any activity by a Negro militia would bring immediate conflict. Both parties were anxious to avoid this, Ames for the sake of the Negroes, and the Democratic committeemen because they feared it would bring Federal intervention.[77] The result was a conference between the governor on one side and J. Z. George and his colleagues on the other. Out of this conference came an agreement that Ames should immediately abandon all efforts to form a militia. On their side, the Democratic leaders guaranteed a fair and peaceful election.[78]

There are some aspects of this agreement that are difficult to understand. Ames' report to Pierrepont included the lines: "I have full faith in their honor, and implicit confidence that they can accomplish all they undertake. Consequently, I believe that we shall have peace, order, and a

[71] Adelbert Ames to E. Benjamin Andrews, May 24, 1895, J. W. Garner Papers, Mississippi State Archives.
[72] J. S. McNeily, "Climax and Collapse of Reconstruction in Mississippi," *P.M.H.S.*, XII, 396-398; Mississippi *Weekly Pilot*, October 16, 1875; *ibid.*, quoting the Meridian *Mercury*.
[73] Mississippi *Weekly Pilot*, October 16, 1875.
[74] *Ibid.*, September 4, 1875, October 2, 1875.
[75] J. S. McNeily, "Climax and Collapse of Reconstruction in Mississippi," *P.M.H.S.*, XII, 407.
[76] A. T. Morgan, *Yazoo*, pp. 456-457.
[77] Frank Johnston, "The Conference of October 15, 1875," *P.M.H.S.*, VI, 69.
[78] Mississippi *Weekly Pilot*, October 16, 23, 1875.

fair election."[79]   This does not ring entirely true.   It seems more probable that the Governor had fought a hopeless fight as long as he dared, and was ready to seize an opportunity for an honorable surrender.   More genuine was his remark to George K. Chase, as report after report of breaches of the peace agreement continued to come in: "I wish you would go to see them [J. Z. George and Ethelbert Barksdale], and get this thing fixed, and see what it means, and let us have quiet anyhow; no matter if they are going to carry the State, let them carry it, and let us be at peace and have no more killing."[80]

The Democratic guarantee of peace and a fair election is also hard to understand.   There can be little doubt that such men as J. Z. George, Joshua Green, and Frank Johnston were anxious for peace.   They were convinced that intimidation had already been carried far enough to guarantee Democratic control of the legislature.   Any further violence might serve to reverse Grant's decision in regard to the sending of troops.   From telegrams sent by George before and during the election, it appears that he made a real effort to preserve order; although in some cases, notably in that of Yazoo County, he seems to have sought, for political purposes, pledges which he knew would not be carried out.[81]   The essential difficulty lay in the fact that leaders in some of the black counties were determined to gain redemption not only for the state but also for their local governments. They felt that the work must be carried on through the day of the election. As a result, a large section of the Democratic press immediately repudiated the peace agreement,[82] and local White Leagues "burnished up their arms and bought more cartridges."[83]

On the day of the election, a peculiar quiet prevailed in many of the counties.   "It was a very quiet day in Jackson—fearfully quiet."[84]   According to a witness at Yazoo City, "Hardly anybody spoke aloud."[85]   In Columbus, where many of the Negroes were still in the swamps as a result of the riot on the preceding night, the Democratic mayor reported everything as "quiet as a funeral."[86]   Similar reports came from Bolton, Lake, and Boswell.   At Holly Springs, about 250 Negroes voted with the Democrats, offering their open ballots as proof.[87]   At Meridian, the White League seized the polls, while the Negroes, "sullen and morose," gathered in a mass across the street.   Any Negro who approached without a white Democrat at his side was immediately crowded away from the ballot box.[88]

[79] J. W. Garner, op. cit., p. 389.
[80] Senate Reports, no. 527, 44th Congress, 1st session, p. 1807.
[81] Ibid., pp. 380-420.
[82] Mississippi Weekly Pilot, October 23, 1875.
[83] Aberdeen Examiner, August 2, 1883.
[84] Senate Reports, no. 527, 44th Congress, 1st session, p. 539.
[85] Ibid., p. 527.
[86] Ibid., pp. 800, 805.
[87] Vicksburg Herald, November 3, 1875.
[88] W. H. Hardy, op. cit., IV, 129.

In other sections, the day was not so peaceful. In Scott County, Ne
groes who were carrying the Republican tickets for distribution at the
polls were fired on "by accident" by Democratic squirrel hunters. They
fled, abandoning both the tickets and their mules. At Forest, the county
seat, it was arranged for boys with whips to rush suddenly into the crowd
of Negroes. The voters, already frightened and nervous, feared that this
was the beginning of an outbreak, and left in a panic.[89] In Monroe County
on the day before the election, the Negro candidate for chancery clerk
saved himself and several friends by a promise to leave the state and not
to return.[90] At Okolona, the Negroes, with women and children, gathered
at a church in the edge of town, intending to go from there to the polls in
groups. The Democratic army marched up and formed near the church.
When guns went off by accident, the Negroes stampeded, paying no atten
tion to Democratic invitations for them to come back and vote. At Aber
deen, in spite of the fact that the heavy Negro population in the eastern
part of the county was cut off by an open bridge and pickets along the
Tombigbee, a large number gathered at the polls early in the morning
E. O. Sykes, in charge of the Democratic war department, posted the
cavalry he had imported from Alabama, surrounded the Negroes with in
fantry, loaded a cannon with chains and slugs, and then sent a strong-arm
squad into the crowd to beat the Negroes over the head. They broke and
ran, many of them swimming the river in search of safety. The Repub
lican sheriff, an ex-Confederate, locked himself in his own jail. The
Democrats then carried the box "very quietly," turning a Republican
majority of 648 in 1871 into a Democratic majority of 1,175.[91]

At Grenada, trouble developed between a white and a Negro at the
polls. While the Democrat was beating the Negro over the head with an
axe handle, the Democratic captain called for the cannon, and his men ran
for their guns, which they had left at a neighboring store. General E. C
Walthall quieted the crowd, but the Negroes had stampeded, and would
not return.[92] At Port Gibson, there was trouble between a young white
man and a young Negro. General firing began, resulting in the death of
"an old, inoffensive negro man," and the wounding of four or five others
The Negroes scattered, and few of them returned to vote.[93] In general
however, it can be said that the election was quiet, as elections went in
Mississippi, and that the Republicans polled a heavy vote in many sections

The Democrats came very close to sweeping the state. In some place

[89] Forrest Cooper, "Reconstruction in Scott County," *P.M.H.S.*, XIII, 175-176.
[90] Aberdeen *Examiner*, November 11, 1875.
[91] *Senate Reports*, no. 527, 44th Congress, 1st session, pp. 1029-1030, 1103-110!
1107; Aberdeen *Examiner*, November 11, 1875; E. F. Puckett, "Reconstruction i
Monroe County," *P.M.H.S.*, XI, 153-155.
[92] Julia C. Brown, "Reconstruction in Yalobusha and Grenada Counties," *P.M.H.S*
XII, 255-256.
[93] *Senate Reports*, no. 527, 44th Congress, 1st session, pp. 201-202; Vicksbur
Herald, November 3, 1875.

hey used fraud,[94] but this method was generally unnecessary. In Yazoo County, the center of an overwhelming Negro majority, Republican candidates received only seven votes. In Kemper they received four, and in Tishomingo twelve.[95] They received two votes at Utica, in the black county of Hinds, and none at Auburn.[96] Democrats carried the first, third, fourth, and fifth congressional districts. The second went to G. Wiley Wells, renegade Republican who was working with the Democrats. In the sixth, John R. Lynch, with much white support, held his majorities in the black counties of Adams, Jefferson, and Wilkinson to win by a slim margin over Roderick Seal.[97] In the state senate, of which only half the members had been involved in the election, there were now twenty-six Democrats and ten Republicans. Only five, all of them hold-overs, were Negroes. In the new house of representatives, there were twenty Republicans and ninety-five Democrats. Sixteen of the representatives were Negroes; of these, fifteen were Republicans and one was a Democrat.[98] Sixty-two of the seventy-four counties elected Democrats as their local officials.[99] In the only race for a state office, that for state treasurer, the Democrat, W. L. Hemingway, polled 96,596 votes to 66,155 for George M. Buchanan, a popular and widely known ex-Confederate who was his Republican opponent.

When the Democratic legislature met in the following January, it quickly completed the work by impeaching and removing the Lieutenant-Governor, and by securing the resignations of the Governor and the Superintendent of Education. Thus ended the successful revolution of 1875. In its preparation and execution, economic and political motives played a large part. Essentially, however, it was a racial struggle. This was expressed most clearly, twenty years later, by Adelbert Ames:

There was a time when policy made it advisable for the white men of Mississippi to advance "corruption," "negro mobs," anything and everything but the true reason for their conduct. That time has long since passed. There is no good reason why the truth should not be stated in plain terms.

It is this—they are white men, Anglo-Saxons—a dominant race—educated to believe in negro slavery. To perpetuate the then existing order of things they ventured everything and lost. An unjust and tyrannical power (from their standpoint) had filled their state with mourning, beggared them, freed their slaves and as a last insult and injury made the ex-slave a political equal. They resisted by intimidation, violence and murder. Excuses by the way of justifi-

[94] Hinds County *Gazette*, November 10, 17, 1875; W. Calvin Wells, "Reconstruction in Hinds County," *P.M.H.S.*, IX, 104; E. F. Puckett, *op. cit.*, XI, 135.
[95] J. W. Garner, *op. cit.*, p. 395.
[96] Hinds County *Gazette*, November 10, 1875.
[97] *Ibid.*, November 24, December 1, 1875.
[98] *Senate Reports*, no. 527, 44th Congress, 1st session, part IV, pp. 147-148; Mississippi *Senate Journal*, 1876, pp. 690-691; Mississippi *House Journal*, 1876, pp. 678-82.
[99] J. W. Garner, *op. cit.*, p. 395.

cation were given while the powerful hand of the national government was to be feared. Soon the national government and public opinion ceased to be dreaded. They then announced boldly that this is a white man's government and that the negro and ex-slave should, forever, form no part of it.

This determination has been proclaimed time and again and what is more to the purpose has been acted on. With an excess of 60,000 colored people Mississippi became the seat of a white man's government.[100]

Altogether, it is well that the Federal government did not intervene to protect the Negroes in 1875. The entire process would have been repeated a few years later, with increased animosity and violence. Social revolutions are not accomplished by force, unless that force is overwhelming, merciless, and continued over a long period. The Negro, returned to a status intermediate between that of slavery and that of full citizenship, now finds in education and hard work opportunities for slow but certain advancement. On the other hand, the dominant race, dominant through tradition, education, and superior economic and legal advantages, yields more and more to the promptings of humanitarianism and enlightened self-interest. With each generation there is less violence and injustice, and more recognition of interdependence and of common needs and interests. There are retrogressions, but it is easy to believe that a gradual, healthy progress will be maintained.

[100] Adelbert Ames to E. Benjamin Andrews, May 24, 1895, J. W. Garner Papers.

CHAPTER XIV

THE ELIMINATION OF THE NEGRO AS AN ACTIVE FACTOR IN POLITICS

Upon the completion of the revolution of 1875, Democrats declared that the Negroes had never before been so contented and so happy.[1] These declarations, however, were not confirmed by the reports and actions of the Negroes. From Noxubee County, one wrote to Governor Ames: "We are anxious for you to know the condition of our county. Here is about 25,000 raticals of we colored population never got to cast a vote . . . [The Democrats] have been shooting and raring around this two months. . . . Although we colored people wish to have peace; but I do say we cannot live at this rate."[2] From Winona came a similar letter: "I have taken this optunity to say to you that we, the coul people of Motgomry Co., is inn a bad fix, for we have no rights in the co., and we wornt to knouw if there is any way for us to get ourt of the co. & go to sum place where we can get them. . . ."[3] There were frequent reports of Negro interest in emigration to the West or to Africa.[4] In spite of their discontent, however, the great mass of the Negroes remained in the state, and the Negro question remained in politics.

The congressional and presidential election of 1876 was soon at hand. In preparation for this event, the Democratic legislature passed a complicated election law. Under the new system, registration was placed in the hands of local boards appointed by the governor, the president pro-tem of the senate, and the secretary of state. Of the prospective voters, the registrars were to "require each voter to state, under oath, in what election-district of the county he resides . . . , and in what portion of said district; and, if resident in any incorporated city or town, in what ward of said city or town; and his occupation, and where prosecuted, and, if in the employ of any one, whom, where, and the nature of such employment."[5] Whatever the intention of the legislators may have been, a number of the

[1] Hinds County *Gazette*, December 1, 1875, quoting the Vicksburg *Herald;* Hinds County *Gazette*, December 29, 1875.

[2] *Senate Reports*, no. 527, 44th Congress, 1st session, "Documentary Evidence," p. 73.

[3] *Ibid.*, "Documentary Evidence," p. 62.

[4] *Ibid.*, "Documentary Evidence," pp. 63, 74; Hinds County *Gazette*, December 15, 1875, quoting the Meridian *Mercury; ibid.*, January 6, 1875, quoting the Aberdeen *Examiner.*

[5] Mississippi *Session Laws*, 1876, pp. 66-77.

local boards carried the matter to the extreme of demanding that the Negroes know the section, township, and range in which they lived and worked. At the first incorrect answer or confession of ignorance, the prospective registrant was ordered to "stand aside."[6]

The approach of the campaign brought in many sections a return to the methods of 1875. In the black counties, Democrats once more formed Negro Democratic clubs, and supplied barbecues, parades, and orators.[7] Democratic "certificates of loyalty" were especially valuable. It was reported that each Negro clung to his certificate "like a sick cat to a hot rock, regarding it as a life preserver."[8] Republican local conventions were surrounded and terrorized by white Democrats.[9] Attacks on Negro Republican parades caused a general abandonment of their use throughout the state.[10] Republican meetings were broken up by charges of cavalry, firing of cannon, ringing of bells, and prolonged Democratic "applause."[11] There was a general announcement that Republican candidates were to be allowed to speak nothing but the "truth." This command was enforced by the Democratic military organizations.[12] The usual economic pressure was applied.[13] The Democratic campaign was most vigorous in the district where John R. Lynch, the only Negro nominee, was opposing General J. R. Chalmers.

Some fraud was used at the polls,[14] but in general such methods were not considered necessary. When the results were tabulated, it was found that all six of the Democratic candidates for Congress had been elected, and that Tilden had secured the state's electoral votes by a margin of 56,853.[15] There was a striking decline in the Republican vote in some of the black counties:

[6] Jackson *Daily Times,* August 30, September 25, 1876; *Senate Miscellaneous Documents,* no. 45, 44th Congress, 2d session, pp. 117, 195, 196, 285-286.

[7] Franklin A. Montgomery, *Reminiscences of a Mississippian in Peace and War,* p. 291; Julia C. Brown, "Reconstruction in Yalobusha and Grenada Counties," *P.M.H.S.,* XII, 251-252; Hinds County *Gazette,* July 26, August 16, 23, 30, September 13, 27, October 4, 1876.

[8] Jackson *Daily Times,* September 1, 1876.

[9] *Ibid.,* July 31, 1876; Hinds County *Gazette,* August 2, 9, 1876.

[10] Jackson *Daily Times,* August 26, October 31, November 1, 3, 1876.

[11] Hinds County *Gazette,* August 11, October 25, 1876; Jackson Daily *Times,* October 18, November 1, 1876; Fayette *Chronicle,* August 25, 1876; *Senate Miscellaneous Documents,* no. 45, 44th Congress, 2d session, pp. 138, 164-165.

[12] Fayette *Chronicle,* August 25, October 30, 1876; *Senate Miscellaneous Documents,* no. 45, 44th Congress, 2d session, pp. 164, 168.

[13] Hinds County *Gazette,* September 27, 1876.

[14] *Senate Miscellaneous Documents,* no. 45, 44th Congress, 2d session, pp. 118, 672, 673, 675-676, 691, 693.

[15] Hinds County *Gazette,* December 6, 1876.

County	1873	1876
Amite	1,093	73
Lowndes	2,723	13
Madison	2,323	13
Tallahatchie	840	1
Warren	4,709	623
Yazoo	2,433	2[16]

All of the counties in the state returned Democratic majorities except four which bordered on the Missisippi River.

Although the Democratic sweep of the congressional offices was repeated in 1878, the presence of the Negroes, and their determination to vote for Republicans, Independents or Greenbackers, continued to be embarrassing. Coming generally to emphasize fraud rather than violence after 1880, Democrats constantly found themselves faced with indictments under the Federal election laws, or with congressional investigations of their elections. Matters at times became extremely complicated. J. R. Chalmers, unseated by Lynch in 1882 on charges of fraud in the election of 1880, ran in a different district as a Republican in 1882 and filed charges of fraud against Van H. Manning, who had not at the time disposed of similar charges brought by his Republican opponent in 1880. While local Democrats generally avoided expense, inconvenience, and unfavorable publicity by entering immediate pleas of guilty to charges under the election laws,[17] their colleagues in Congress could not take advantage of this method. Over a period of years, the constant effort to maintain a lie in the face of charges and investigations became acutely unpleasant. Then too, such Negroes as John R. Lynch and James Hill were continually appearing as candidates for congressional posts. There was always a probability that if the Republicans gained a working control of the House of Representatives, Mississippi would once more have a Negro congressman. The crowning embarrassment came with the theft and publication of a letter in which Congressman Catchings suggested that it would be helpful if one or two of the Negro witnesses in Hill's contest should "disappear."[18] By 1890, Mississippi's Democratic congressmen were ready to give enthusiastic support to any scheme that would put a legal face on the elimination of the Negro vote.

With the exception of the city of Jackson, and of temporary interludes in a few other communities, Republican control of municipal governments in Mississippi practically disappeared after 1876. In Jackson, a strong and generally satisfactory Republican organization, with a white mayor and five white aldermen in a total of six, held power until early in 1888. Its overthrow in January of that year involved a revival of all of

[16] Jackson *Daily Times,* December 8, 1876.
[17] Jackson *Weekly Clarion,* October 13, 20, 1881, February 14, 1883.
[18] Raymond *Gazette,* March 29, 1890.

the tactics of intimidation that had been used in 1875.[19]   So successful
were these methods that only one Negro in the entire city even attempted
to vote.   According to the *New Mississippian*, "One old negro attempted
to vote in the South ward about half past 9.   He was an old negro and
looked silly, and he was not hurt, but told to hustle out in double-quick
time, and he hustled."[20]   The events of this election both reflected and
stimulated the movement that was going on throughout the state for the
complete elimination of the Negro voter.

In the state legislature and in some of the counties, Negroes continued
to hold a number of offices throughout the period.   After 1876, the number in the legislature remained practically stable:

Year	House	Senate
1876	16	5
1878	6	1
1880	8	0
1882	10	1
1884	9	1
1886	7	1
1888	7	0
1890	6	0

This situation grew out of a peculiar system known as the "fusion principle."   Under this system, the white Democratic executive committee of
a county would agree with the Negro leaders, who were generally Republican, on the number of offices in the county and in the county's legislative
delegation that were to be held by Negroes.   In theory these Negro candidates were chosen by those of their own race; actually their choice was
subject to review and approval or disapproval by the Democratic committee.   The number and type of the offices given to the Negroes varied according to local conditions.   Generally they included a minority on the
board of supervisors, a few other county offices of low pay and little
responsibility, and one membership in the legislature.   In Hinds County, in
1883, for example, the Democrats took for themselves the offices of sheriff,
chancery clerk, circuit clerk, treasurer, surveyor, four supervisors, and
one legislator.   To the Negroes went the offices of assessor, coroner, one
supervisor, three legislators, and one constable and one justice of the peace
in each supervisor's district.[21]   In Issaquena County, where the Negroes
outnumbered the whites almost ten to one, the Democrats reserved for
themselves in 1877 the offices of sheriff, treasurer, surveyor, coroner, three
supervisors, and one justice of the peace and one constable in each district.

[19] Jackson *Clarion-Ledger*, December, 1887, January, 1888; Jackson *New Mississippian*, December, 1887, January, 1888; *Senate Miscellaneous Documents*, no. 166,
50th Congress, 1st session.
[20] Jackson *New Mississippian*, January 3, 1888.
[21] Jackson *Weekly Clarion*, August 8, 1883.   The three offices in the legislature
were regarded as unimportant because of the large Democratic majority.

In Adams County, the general system was for the Negroes to have the offices of half of the legislators, the circuit clerk, and a few minor officials.[22]

In general, the fusion plan was confined to some six or eight counties in which the white population was relatively very small, and almost entirely dependent on Negro labor. Comparing the peaceful relations of the races and the relative contentment of the Negroes in their counties with the terrorism, dissatisfaction, and desertion of the laborers in such counties as "bloody Yazoo," the advocates of fusion hailed it as the solution of the race question in politics.[23] There can be little doubt that in such counties as Washington, Adams, Issaquena, Bolivar, Sharkey, and Coahoma the fusion system did work to the general satisfaction of a majority of both races. In their selection of offices, the whites carefully arranged that they should have almost complete control of the more important functions of the county government. On the other hand, the Negroes continued to vote with much freedom, and together with the local leaders of their race gained valuable political education and experience.

From the beginning, however, there were weaknesses in the plan. From the white point of view, the system was never any better than a slightly disagreeable method of gaining valuable objectives at low cost. To the natural disfavor of minor politicians who were hungry for the small offices involved, there was added the almost unanimous opposition of the poor whites, especially those who had recently moved down from the hill counties.[24] Furthermore, there was strong opposition from those in other sections of the state who felt that the redemption should be complete, and that the holding of offices by Negroes in the river counties encouraged others to have similar ambitions.[25] Oppositionists also pointed out the fact that in cases of disagreement among white members of the boards of supervisors, a Negro sometimes cast the deciding vote.[26] On the other hand, the Negroes themselves gave the plan only provisional support. Lynch made their position perfectly clear at a fusion meeting in Hinds County in 1883. He approved of the fusion, he said, because it was at the moment the best bargain the Negroes could make. He would not have it thought, however, that the Negroes were accepting the control of the Democratic party which had overthrown them. Instead they would vote with the Democrats, or with any other political group that offered concessions, only until it was possible to vote once more as Republicans.[27]

[22] Raymond *Gazette*, July 7, 1883.
[23] Hinds County *Gazette*, July 11, 1877, May 28, 1879, August 24, November 10, 1881; Raymond *Gazette*, June 9, 18, July 7, 14, 1883, January 12, 1884; *Senate Reports*, no. 693, 46th Congress, 2d session, part ii, p. 266, from the Vicksburg *Herald*.
[24] Raymond *Gazette*, June 9, 16, 1883.
[25] Vicksburg *Herald*, November 14, 1878, quoting the Natchez *Democrat;* Jackson *Weekly Clarion*, November 20, 1878, November 12, 1879.
[26] Raymond *Gazette*, July 12, 19, 1884, January 10, 1885.
[27] *Ibid.*, October 13, 1883.

The accuracy of this analysis was demonstrated, to the disgust of the Democrats, in a number of the congressional campaigns.[28]

The most serious obstacle to the complete elimination of the Negro as a political element came with the development of independent political factions in a number of counties, and of the Greenback-Labor element throughout the state. It was natural that these opposition groups should develop almost immediately after the triumph of 1875; they reflected the differences of opinion and clashes of ambition that exist in every community. It was also natural that in an effort to fight the power of the iron-clad Democratic state and county rings these opposition elements should seek the support of the Negroes. The Negroes themselves were quick to recognize their opportunity. On the advice of their leaders,[29] the mass of the Negroes, in the absence of a fusion arrangement, consistently voted for any independent ticket that threatened Democratic solidity.

In an effort to defend their advantage, the entrenched Democratic machines used almost any method that might be effective. Violence was sometimes used. Independent candidates were run out of their counties, beaten, or murdered.[30] In some sections, the old methods of intimidation were once more brought to bear on the Negroes.[31] In general, however, the method usually applied involved fraud at the polls or in the counting of the votes. Ballot boxes were stuffed, fraudulent returns were made, and thousands of opposition votes were thrown out on technicalities.[32] With mock solemnity, newspapers reported that boxes containing anti-Democratic majorities had been eaten by mules or horses.[33] Appointment of the election commissioners by Democratic state officials made all things possible. Only in rare cases did the Democratic organizations find it advisable or necessary to solicit, buy, or bargain for the Negro vote that was so generally sought by opposition groups.

In general, the policy of the Democratic party in the state and in the counties was to brand any effort toward independent political action as a return of Republicanism in disguise and as a threat to white supremacy. This attitude was adopted in the state platform as early as 1877:

Resolved, That unity and harmony are essential to victory; that all independent movements are dangerous to the integrity of the party organization; that all

[28] Vicksburg *Herald*, November 14, 1878, quoting the Natchez *Democrat*; Jackson *Weekly Clarion*, November 20, 1878.
[29] Hinds County *Gazette*, October 10, 1877.
[30] A. T. Morgan, *Yazoo*, pp. 486, 492; Jackson *Weekly Clarion*, August 13, 27, September 3, 1879; Hinds County *Gazette*, October 10, 1877; Raymond *Gazette*, December 8, 1883, January 26, 1884; J. C. Brown, *op. cit.*, XII, 258.
[31] Hinds County *Gazette*, September 28, October 12, 1881; Jackson *Weekly Clarion*, July 2, 1879.
[32] Hinds County *Gazette*, November 23, 1881; Jackson *Weekly Clarion*, October 3, 1883; Raymond *Gazette*, June 2, 1883, May 3, 1884, August 14, 1886, September 13, 1890.
[33] Hinds County *Gazette*, November 23, 1881; Raymond *Gazette*, November 10, 1883.

independent candidates are inspired solely by a lust for office; that they shall be treated as common enemies to the welfare of the people and avowed enemies to the Democratic party of the State of Mississippi.[34]

It had become apparent that any serious division on political issues among the native whites brought an almost immediate appeal for the votes of the Negroes; an appeal that often involved an offer of political offices for their leaders. On the Greenback ticket of 1883, for example, the Negro J. J. Spelman was the candidate for the office of secretary of state. The logical conclusion of the white-line element, a conclusion strenuously encouraged by the state and county machines, was that controversial matters must be kept out of political conventions and campaigns. Again and again Democratic leaders and Democratic editors declared that white sovereignty was the only point at issue; all others must be suppressed as dangerous to the unity of the dominant race.[35] Candidates for election to the United States Senate were urged not to canvass, lest in their rivalry they arouse disagreement and antagonism and break the Democratic front.[36] Newspapers refused to print letters from subscribers who attacked the party, and suppressed news stories of fraud and violence.[37] Papers that printed such material were accused of betraying the South and the party. At all costs the united front must be preserved. In the words of the editor of the Raymond *Gazette:*

As a Democratic organ, this paper will ever be on guard to sound the note of alarm when for any purpose the party machinery may be seized upon and diverted from the use for which it was intended. In a great crisis in our history as a people, when our very civilization was in imminent jeopardy, we devised and used means that could only be justified in the fear of the great danger by which we were confronted. . . . But the Democratic party of the State, (which means the white people of the State) can't afford to have their swords drawn and their guns fired by every little alarmist or crank that comes along with some pet notion. . . ."[38]

The editor of the most powerful paper in the state was in complete agreement. "In other States," he wrote, "it may be different. In this State for some time to come, there is but one issue. All know what it is."[39]

The white people of the state, then, were to receive without criticism the candidates offered to them by the county and state nominating conventions. Those candidates were not to be questioned as to their stand on any controversial issues. Men who tried to bring about discussion of such issues were to be condemned; if they ran as independents, there were ways

[34] *Appleton's Cyclopedia*, 1877, p. 527.
[35] Hinds County *Gazette*, May 23, June 6, 20, 1877, February 2, 1881; Jackson *Weekly Clarion*, April 23, 1879, July 7, 1881, May 31, 1882; Raymond *Gazette*, August 10, 1889; W. A. Cate, *Lucius Q. C. Lamar*, pp. 329, 390, 400.
[36] Jackson *Weekly Clarion*, July 16, 1879.
[37] Raymond *Gazette*, May 24, 1884, April 18, 1891.
[38] *Ibid.*, March 9, 1889.
[39] Jackson *Weekly Clarion*, August 22, 1882.

and means to keep them in private life and to prevent them from returning to any place of importance in the dominant party. By 1889, a majority of the people of the state, of whom smaller and smaller numbers were even taking the trouble to vote in the formal elections, were disgusted with this scheme of things. Yet they could not bring themselves to work against the party that was identified in their minds with white supremacy. Some way must be found to allow controversy and change within the race and within the party. Somehow, the Negro must be eliminated as a political factor. A constitutional convention was a dangerous experiment; in its election and its deliberations controversy might develop. But by 1889, most of the white voters of Mississippi felt that the danger must be faced.

THE CONSTITUTION OF 1890

The Constitution of 1868, resembling those of the Middle West from which it was largely copied, contained few provisions which could be easily attacked. S. S. Calhoon, chairman of the convention of 1890, said of it:

As a matter of fact, however, the instrument . . . was not, as a whole, a bad constitution. It is a stranger fact that the good in it, we owe to the negroes under the conservative influence of their former owners and eminent white citizens, whom they were trained to respect. But, as may be easily imagined, the effrontery of such a collection of irresponsible men undertaking to frame organic law, aroused intense indignation and scorn, which extended beyond the makers to the work and persisted against that constitution as long as it existed. . . . Without this *vis a tergo* it is very questionable whether all the other reasons combined would have accomplished the result.[40]

Although Judge Calhoon was in error in attributing the virtues of the constitution of 1868 almost entirely to the small number of Negroes who took part in its preparation, he was correct in his estimate of its quality. The prejudice against it as a product of the Republican regime furnished an effective talking point for those who felt that a convention was necessary for the solution of the Negro problem. Almost no other attack could be made.

As a member of the convention of 1890, Judge Chrisman declared:

Sir, it is no secret that there has not been a full vote and a fair count in Mississippi since 1875, that we have been preserving the ascendency of the white people by revolutionary methods. In other words we have been stuffing ballot boxes, committing perjury, and here and there in the state carrying the elections by fraud and violence. The public conscience revolted, thoughtful men everywhere foresaw that there was disaster somewhere along the line of such a policy as certainly as there is a righteous judgment for nations as well as men. No man can be in favor of perpetuating the election methods which have prevailed in Mississippi since 1875 who is not a moral idiot.[41]

[40] S. S. Calhoon, "Causes and Events That Led to the Calling of the Constitutional Convention of 1890," *P.M.H.S.*, VI, 105.
[41] Port Gibson *Reveille*, September 19, 1890; see also Jackson *Clarion-Ledger*, September 11, 1890.

Although a portion of the Democratic press denounced the statements of Chrisman and other "overly virtuous Democrats" as intemperate and unwise, there can be no doubt that they represented the feelings of most of the thinking people of the state. There was a general feeling that methods originally used to assure the continuation of white control were now being employed for less desirable purposes, including the maintenance of the power of machine politicians. There was a great deal of concern over the effect of these methods on the new generation of young men who were beginning to take a leading part in the politics of the state. The general belief was that this new generation, not understanding the terrible necessity which caused the introduction of such methods, would consider them a normal form of political action.[42] Even those old leaders who had used fraud and violence against the Negroes did not desire to see their sons have to use similar tactics. As Colonel B. F. Jones wrote to the *Clarion-Ledger,* "The old men of the present generation can't afford to die and leave their children with shot guns in their hands, a lie in their mouths and perjury on their souls, in order to defeat the negroes. The constitution can be made so this will not be necessary."[43]

The demand for a constitutional convention was especially strong in the white counties. Many of the voters in the hills believed that the state was in the grip of an "infamous ring," which cleverly concealed great wrongs perpetrated at the Capitol, and used the powerful *Clarion-Ledger* as its mouthpiece.[44] This ring was kept in office by the power and the fraud of the Democratic cliques in the black counties. The editor of the Chickasaw *Messenger,* the leading paper of the discontented small farmers, cried out against

. . . a class of corrupt office-seekers, who seeing the immense political power conferred upon the negro counties, hypocritically raised the howl of white supremacy while they debauched the ballot boxes and through this infamous means made themselves potent factors in our State and county governments, and thus, under the pretense of maintaining a rule of intelligence they disregarded the rights of the blacks, incurred useless and extravagant expenditures, raised the taxes, plunged the State into debt, and actually dominated the will of the white people through the instrumentality of the stolen negro vote.[45]

The only solution was the elimination of the necessity of fraud and of ring control in the black counties, and the reduction of the strength of those counties in the government of the state.

Additional pressure for calling a convention came from the organized prohibitionists, who were now a very powerful element. In spite of the

[42] J. F. H. Claiborne Papers, University of North Carolina, General S. D. Lee to J. F. H. Claiborne, June 4, November 10, 1879; J. T. Wallace, *History of the Negroes of Mississippi,* p. 154.
[43] Port Gibson *Reveille,* May 23, 1890, quoting the Jackson *Clarion-Ledger.*
[44] Jackson *Clarion-Ledger,* February 14, 1889.
[45] *Ibid.,* March 14, 1889, quoting the Chickasaw *Messenger.*

ban on controversial matters in politics, they had succeeded in carrying local option elections in more than half of the counties, and were determined to extend their activities until the whole state was dry. According to their view, most of the machine politicians of the state and of the black counties were opposed to their efforts, and had used the black vote to thwart them. In an address to the convention, the calling of which they strongly supported, they declared:

There are seventy-five counties in Mississippi, and forty of them are dry. These dry counties are in the white section. The thirty-five wet counties are mostly in the black belt and are kept wet by the negro vote. . . . What are you here for, if not to maintain white supremacy, especially when a majority of the whites stand for a great principle of public morals and public safety? We especially appeal to the delegates from the black counties. Gentlemen, can you in reason expect the white counties to stand by you and uphold white supremacy for you, while you discard the doctrine which has been our common safety, in the interest of the saloon keepers of your counties? How long is it to be expected that white solidarity can be maintained, if the negro is to be brought forward to arbitrate this great question in the interest of a minority of the whites, and they mostly foreign born, and not in sympathy with our institutions?[46]

In the demand for a constitutional convention and the elimination of the Negro voter, the jealousy of the white counties, disgust with machine control and constant fraud, a determination to open the political field to controversial questions, the rising power of the prohibitionists, and prejudice against a "black and tan" constitution all played a part. But there can be little doubt that the most powerful factor in the desire for a legal elimination of the Negro voter was the change that had occurred in Washington. In 1889, for the first time since 1875, the Republicans gained effective control of all the departments of the national government. The immediate conviction developed that the Republicans would use the opportunity to extend Federal control of elections and to restore the Negro vote, and the introduction of the Lodge Force Bill gave substance to the conviction.[47]

Alarmists did not fail to find evidence that the Republican triumph in the nation had once more aroused the Negroes in the state. The Raymond *Gazette* found reports in exchanges from all over the South that ever since the election there had been "discontents and mutterings" among the Negroes.[48] The editor of the Port Gibson *Reveille* had a vision of 2,500 Negroes presenting themselves at the polls in Claiborne instead of the usual twenty.[49] Negro tax-payers in Hinds County entered a formal re-

[46] Mississippi *White Ribboner*, September 15, 1890; see also Mississippi Constitutional Convention of 1890, *Journal*, pp. 94-95.
[47] Jackson *Clarion-Ledger*, January 31, February 7, March 14, October 24, 1889, May 22, 1890.
[48] Raymond *Gazette*, July 13, 1889.
[49] Port Gibson *Reveille*, May 30, 1890.

quest for representation in the distribution of county offices as a matter of right and justice.[50] A later report had it that they would refuse to pay their taxes until the right to vote was restored to them.[51]

The greatest shock came with the approach of the state election of 1889. Negroes from about forty counties gathered in Jackson to ask the Democratic leaders to adopt a fusion ticket for the state campaign.[52] When this effort brought no results, John R. Lynch, the state chairman, called a Republican convention. This body entered a complete ticket for the first time since 1875, with the Negro lawyer, W. E. Mollison, as its candidate for the office of secretary of state.[53] Although immediate Democratic action broke up Republican meetings and finally caused withdrawal of the ticket,[54] the flurry added the last impetus necessary to assure the calling of a constitutional convention. In spite of the opposition of the conservative press, of leaders in the black counties, and of such men as E. C. Walthall, who feared the development of controversy, the state Democratic convention in July, 1889, ordered that the question be made an issue in the campaign. The new legislature which met early in the following year quickly issued a call for the election of delegates.

After the call had been issued, it became apparent that few of those who had supported the move had any definite ideas as to how the Negro voter might be eliminated. All simple methods were barred by the provisions of the Fifteenth Amendment. Some of the plans that filled the columns of the press during the summer were fantastic in their complexity.[55] Gradually, however, the conservative element and most of the leaders of the black counties lined up in support of educational and property qualifications, with the probable addition of a poll-tax requirement. This group expressed much interest in Judge J. A. P. Campbell's plan to give plural votes, up to five, to property owners.[56] Such ideas aroused the immediate and absolute opposition of large groups of the poor whites, who found difficulty in uniting on any plan save that of greatly reducing the representation of the black counties. Before the summer was over, plans ranging from the use of the Australian ballot to the requirement of proof of legitimacy had been presented and considered, but no general agreement had been reached. As a result, practically all of the delegates went to the convention without instructions.

As the time of the election approached, public letters and editorials on

[50] Raymond *Gazette*, July 13, 1889.
[51] *Ibid.*, March 22, 1890.
[52] Jackson *Clarion-Ledger*, July 4, 1889.
[53] Raymond *Gazette*, July 27, October 5, 1889; Jackson *Clarion-Ledger*, September 26, 1889.
[54] Raymond *Gazette*, October 26, 1889; Jackson *Clarion-Ledger*, October 24, 31, 1889.
[55] For a burlesque of such plans, see Raymond *Gazette*, April 19, 1890.
[56] Raymond *Gazette*, April 5, May 22, 1890; Jackson *Clarion-Ledger*, April 3, 10, May 1, 15, 29, 1890.

the race question became more and more frenzied and inflammatory. Here and there a correspondent offered mild disagreement. "Conservative," writing in the Raymond *Gazette,* insisted that charges against the Negro were exaggerated. His observation was that the freedmen were more and more inclined to cooperate with the better class of the whites in the maintenance of order and the support of the best interests of the community. "Emerging from the condition of absolute slavery and abandoned by his whilom friends to endure whatever social conditions might be imposed by the superior race, he has made a record in twenty-five years for improvement, socially, intellectually and morally, not excelled by any other race in the world's history."[57] A much more prevalent attitude was that of W. E. Farr, who felt that "Every political feud, every factional disturbance, and every race riot that has caused to flow from our veins the martyred blood of our Southern manhood and chivalry, can be traced . . . to the ignorant, presuming negro."[58] Furthermore, the Negro could never be expected to achieve the Anglo-Saxon instinct for government and virtue. A correspondent of the *Clarion-Ledger* expressed a general opinion:

I agree with Senator George that literacy (in its legal sense) is no test of fitness to vote. . . . If every negro in Mississippi was a graduate of Harvard, and had been elected as class orator . . . he would not be as well fitted to exercise the right of suffrage as the Anglo-Saxon farm laborer, *adscriptus glebae* of the South and West. Whose cross "X" mark, like the broad arrow of Locksley, means force and intellect, and manhood—*virtus.*[59]

Late in June, a Negro convention gathered in Jackson to consider the situation. In an address to those of their race in the state, the members urged them to organize and to endeavor to elect delegates who would protect their rights. Democrats were not impressed. According to the editor of the *Clarion-Ledger,* "It will do no harm . . . , because the negroes cannot be persuaded to 'fight a cyclone.' It is well understood that the Convention will be composed exclusively of whites."[60] An open letter from five Negro leaders who endorsed the address of their convention brought from the Raymond *Gazette* solemn warning that any attempt on the part of the Negroes would be "worse than folly," and would bring serious trouble.[61]

In only a few counties did the Republicans go through the formality of selecting candidates. Outside of the river counties only one, F. M. B. Cook, attempted an active campaign. After a few days his body was found, riddled with bullets. The journal of the state government gave the following terse account of the occurrence:

[57] Raymond *Gazette,* April 26, 1890.
[58] *Ibid.,* January 18, 1890.
[59] Jackson *Clarion-Ledger,* August 14, 1890.
[60] *Ibid.,* June 26, 1890.
[61] Raymond *Gazette,* June 28, 1890.

At the time of his death he was canvassing Jasper County as a Republican candidate for the Constitutional Convention, and was daily and nightly denouncing the white people in his speeches and caucuses. . . . Then one or more persons decided that Cook must die. The *Clarion-Ledger* regrets the manner of his killing, as assassination cannot be condoned at any time. Yet the people of Jasper are to be congratulated that they will not be further annoyed by Marsh Cook.[62]

The death of Cook offered convincing evidence that the Democrats did not intend for their warnings to be ignored. The few efforts at organized opposition vanished, and the rest of the campaign was uneventful. Early in August, the delegates were chosen in an election that drew fewer votes than any other since the war. The total vote cast for the delegates from the state at large was about 39,000.[63]

When the convention assembled on August 12, it was composed of 134 delegates. Of these, 130 were Democrats, one a Republican, one a "National Republican," one a "Conservative," and one a Greenbacker. The National Republican was the conservative, native-white H. F. Simrall, who had been appointed to the state Supreme Court by Governor Alcorn. Alcorn himself was the "Conservative." Both were opposed to unlimited Negro suffrage, as was the Greenbacker. The one delegate who listed himself simply as a Republican was the lone Negro in the convention, Isaiah T. Montgomery, a wealthy and conservative planter and businessman who had founded the Negro town of Mount Bayou.

Montgomery's retention of his seat in the convention in the face of Democratic declarations that it was to be an all-white group is difficult to explain. With his white Democratic colleague George B. Melchior, he had been elected as a candidate of the fusion organization that had been functioning successfully in Bolivar County for almost twenty years. A contest brought by their regular Democratic opponents was rejected in the convention by a large majority. The explanation of John R. Lynch is that for some reason Montgomery had secretly promised his support to the faction led by Senator J. Z. George.[64] This was the faction which was determined to eliminate the Negro voters without barring the illiterate whites, to reject all property qualifications, and to reduce the representation of the black counties. Its opponents, under Judge Chrisman, supported the general idea of property and educational qualifications applied honestly to blacks and whites alike. The great mass of the Negroes naturally hoped that the Chrisman faction would prevail. Yet it was with Montgomery's vote that George and his group placed S. S. Calhoon in the chair and gained the vital advantage of being able to organize the convention.[65] It is hard to believe that Montgomery, regarded by whites and blacks alike

[62] Jackson *Clarion-Ledger*, July 31, 1890.
[63] *Ibid.*, August 14, 1890.
[64] John R. Lynch, *The Facts of Reconstruction*, pp. 264-265.
[65] Mississippi Constitutional Convention of 1890, *Journal*, p. 9.

as honorable and sincere, deliberately betrayed his race and his county merely to retain his seat in the convention, an empty honor at best. It is possible that he believed that the best move for his people was that of absolute surrender.

Montgomery's speech in support of the report of the committee on the franchise, of which he was a member, is equally difficult to explain. In an address which lasted almost an hour, he presented an able analysis of the problems the committee had faced. It was his conviction that it was essential to the interests of the state and of both races that the Negro vote be reduced to a total well below that of the whites. This could be done by an honest application of the requirements recommended by the committee, which, according to his estimate, would disfranchise 123,000 Negroes and 12,000 whites, leaving a total Negro vote of about 66,000 and a white majority of more than 40,000. With white control further guaranteed by the increased representation of the white counties, relations between the races would improve, and the Negroes, increasing in knowledge and property, would gradually reënter the electorate as intelligent and desirable voters.[66] This speech drew high praise from the Democratic press throughout the state and nation, and even from ex-President Grover Cleveland.[67] It probably did more than anything else to allay suspicion and opposition in the North. Yet, from his service in the convention and in the committee on the franchise, and from the daily declarations of such men as Judge Calhoon, Montgomery is bound to have known that all calculations based on an honest application of the franchise provisions were meaningless. He knew that it was the intention of the Democratic majority to eliminate Negroes with or without education, and to remove no white voter from the rolls. The mystery remains.

In attacking the problem of the limitation or elimination of Negro suffrage, the members of the convention agreed that the provisions of the Fifteenth Amendment, which forbade discrimination based on race or color must not be openly defied. But there was another limitation on the convention's power which must be disregarded if anything at all was to be accomplished. This was a provision in the act of Congress, approved February 23, 1870, by which Mississippi was readmitted to the Union. According to that act, one of the fundamental conditions of readmission was the pledge that the constitution of the state should never be "so amended or changed as to deprive any citizen, or class of citizens of the United States, of the right to vote, who are entitled to vote by the constitution [of 1868] herein recognized, except as a punishment for such crimes as are now felonies at common law. . . ."[68] The convention chose the only

[66] Jackson *Clarion-Ledger*, September 18, 1890; Raymond *Gazette*, September 20, 1890.
[67] Raymond *Gazette*, November 1, 1890.
[68] Mississippi *Revised Code*, 1871, p. 676.

possible way out. From its own judiciary committee it obtained a declaration that the act was an unconstitutional limitation of the power of a sovereign state, and therefore void and of no effect.[69]

The committee on the franchise, made up of thirty-five members, followed the procedure of having each individual in the group present his own ideas in full.[70] They then spent three weeks in analyzing and synthesizing these individual suggestions, and finally, on September 2, emerged with their report. In spite of strenuous opposition from the conservative members and the conservative press, the report was adopted substantially as it was submitted. Set up as Article XII of the Constitution, it provided for the registration of voters by registrars who were officers of the state. Such registration was declared to be an essential and necessary qualification for voting at any election within the state. Furthermore, only those who were qualified electors were eligible to hold public offices. Those accepted by the registrars were to be male inhabitants of the state (except idiots, insane persons, and Indians not taxed), twenty-one years of age and upwards, who had resided in the state two years, and one year in the election district, or in the incorporated city or town, in which they offered to vote; who had never been convicted of certain crimes, and who had paid all taxes required of them, including a poll tax of two dollars, for the two preceding years. Then followed Section 244 of the Constitution, which had been "the infamous section five" of the committee's report, and was the contribution of Senator J. Z. George:

On and after the first day of January, A.D., 1892, every elector shall, in addition to the foregoing qualifications, be able to read any section of the Constitution of this State; or he shall be able to understand the same when read to him, or give a reasonable interpretation thereof. A new registration shall be made before the next ensuing election after January the first, A.D., 1892.

From the moment of its presentation, this section was the subject of a bitter attack both in and outside the convention. From the floor came charges that it was trickery and fraud and beneath the dignity of the state and of the convention.[71] The delegate from Grenada declared that the trail of the serpent was on it. "The mephitic vapour that arises from the section actually stinks in the nostrils of an honest man and makes one feel like stuffing the registration books."[72] The press of the state was filled with editorials and letters which dubbed the provision "odious section five," "a shameless fraud," "a disgraceful absurdity," "the mongrel hotch-

[69] Mississippi Constitutional Convention of 1890, *Journal*, pp. 83-87.
[70] *Proceedings of a Reunion of the Surviving Members of the Constitutional Convention of 1890*, p. 28.
[71] Jackson *Clarion-Ledger*, September 18, 1890.
[72] *Ibid.*, October 9, 1890.

potch suffrage scheme," or "the fly-blown section."[73]   The editor of the
Raymond *Gazette* declared that the fact that Webster impeached Calhoun's
understanding of the United States Constitution, and Calhoun returned the
compliment with interest "would indicate to ordinary minds that there
might be honest differences of opinion between a corn-field nigger and
inspectors of election."[74]   His colleague of the Port Gibson *Reveille* felt
that the state had been shamed.   "Every State suffers more or less from
corrupt practices at elections, but it was reserved for the State of Mississippi to make its very Constitution the instrument and shield of fraud."[75]
Listing thirty-four papers that had lined up in absolute opposition to the
provision, the editor of the *Clarion-Ledger* declared that it was condemned
by every leading paper in the state except the Vicksburg *Herald,* which
had the convention's patronage.[76]   The general conclusion was that the
law was either fantasy or fraud, although the elimination of fraud had
been one of the chief purposes in calling the convention.   It is not sur-
prising that in the face of this outcry the convention on October 22, 1890,
adopted the following report:

> The Judiciary Committee have considered the proposed ordinance of delegate
> Mr. Coffey, for the submission of the Constitution, which may be adopted by
> this Convention, for ratification or rejection, to the people; and instruct me to
> report that, in the judgment of the Committee, such submission is unnecessary
> and inexpedient.[77]

With the final adoption of the Constitution by the convention, open opposition was greatly diminished.   At all costs, the party line must be maintained.   The editor of the *Clarion-Ledger* took the attitude that further
antagonism could do no possible good, while his colleagues of the *Gazette*
declared that it behooved "all good citizens, Democrats especially, to accept,
cheerfully and willingly what is offered them—in good faith, without doubt
—and in a united spirit work to keep Mississippi in line with the march of
progress. . . ."[78]   The whole matter was almost forgotten in the midst of
general rejoicing over the Democratic landslide of 1890.

Altogether, although they could hardly undertake an open defense of
their methods, the delegates had accomplished their purpose in almost the
only possible manner.   They knew that the majority of their white Democratic constituents wanted the Negro voter eliminated in a manner that

---

[73] Raymond *Gazette,* September 20, 1890; Jackson *Clarion-Ledger,* October 2,
1890; *ibid.,* October 9, 1890, quoting the Natchez *Banner, New Mississippian,* Brandon *Republican, New Farmer,* Grenada *Sentinel,* Greenville *Democrat,* Yazoo City
Herald, Vicksburg *Post,* Lexington *Advertiser,* Port Gibson *Reveille,* Scooba *Herald,*
and Aberdeen *Examiner.*
[74] Raymond *Gazette,* September 20, 1890.
[75] Jackson *Clarion-Ledger,* October 10, 1890, quoting the Port Gibson *Reveille.*
[76] Jackson *Clarion-Ledger,* October 30, 1890, January 8, 1891.
[77] Mississippi Constitutional Convention of 1890, *Journal,* pp. 549-550.
[78] Jackson *Clarion-Ledger,* November 6, 1890; Raymond *Gazette,* November 8,
1890.

would meet the requirements of the Constitution of the United States. That same majority was determined that no white voter should be barred. It so happened that no man could devise any test which, fairly and honestly applied, would accomplish that purpose. There was a general understanding that the interpretation of the constitution offered by an illiterate white man would be acceptable to the registrars; that of a Negro would not.[79] The fear that it would be used by political rings for the elimination of white opponents proved to be largely unjustified. As the best method that could be found to achieve their purpose, it was soon accepted by the white people of Mississippi and imitated, in one form or another, by a number of the Southern states. Its formal legality was upheld by the Supreme Court of Mississippi in 1892, in the case of Sproule vs. Fredericks.[80] The Supreme Court of the United States, in the case of Williams vs. Mississippi, added its approval in 1898.

The adoption of the new regulations did not mean the immediate or complete elimination of the Negroes either as voters or as office holders. The new rolls of 1892 showed a registration of 68,127 whites and 8,615 Negroes. Of these, 1,037 whites and 1,085 Negroes were registered under the "understanding" clause.[81] Furthermore, Adams, Bolivar, and Sharkey counties continued their fusion system and sent Negroes to the state legislature in 1892. Bolivar and Sharkey each had a Negro representative in 1894, and Bolivar retained the system to 1899.[82] Here and there, those who were generally known as "good niggers," or who were close to local politicians, continued to vote into the next century. Altogether, however, rebuffed by unfriendly registrars, frowned on by the mass of the white population, and absolutely forbidden to support any candidates save those of a party based on white supremacy, the Negro voters found it, in the words of one of their leaders, "a mighty discouraging proposition." More and more of them, as time went on, simply abandoned the effort.

[79] Jackson *Clarion-Ledger*, October 30, 1890.
[80] *Appleton's Cyclopedia*, 1892, p. 471.
[81] *Ibid.*, 1892, p. 472. There is no statement available as to the number of either race rejected by the registrars.
[82] See *Journals* of the House of Representatives for these years.

CHAPTER XV

RACE RELATIONS

INTERRACIAL VIOLENCE

Under the system of slavery, the place of the Negro was defined by tradition and by law. The great mass of the slaves spent practically all their time on the plantations of their owners, and had few contacts with the mass of the white population. Although the bad feeling between the Negroes and the poor whites already existed, there were few ways in which it could be expressed. It was possible for the poor whites to curse the Negro in abstract and in person, and it was possible for the Negro to answer with the little song that was known from one end of the South to the other:

> My name's Sam, I don't care a damn;
> I'd rather be a nigger than a poor white man.

Beyond this point, matters could seldom go. The Negro was the property of the most influential whites of the community; as such he was given the full protection of the law. The poor white, at times not so well housed or clothed as the slave, still had two great distinctions to cling to and to preserve. He was a white man, and free; the Negro was black, and a slave. With emancipation, only one of these differences remained. The preservation of that difference, with a universal recognition of its importance, was for the poor white one of the chief aims in life after the Negro became free. In every possible walk of life, he would establish a difference between the white man and the black. In recognition of that difference he would set up a code of behavior for the Negro, and for its maintenance he was willing, if necessary, to fight to the death.

It was natural that a great part of the story of the struggle for the establishment of a racial code should be written in blood. Mississippi in 1860 was still very largely a frontier region; the greater part of the state had been opened to settlement after 1830. Towns were few and very small; communication was difficult; the government of the state touched the daily lives of few of its citizens, and the governments of the counties were not much more effective. There was little respect for laws that could not be enforced; personal vengeance, the "fair fight," and the duel still held their place in the minds of the people, if not in the books of law. An English traveler wrote of the "savage practice of walking about with pistols, knives, and poinards," and declared that casual conversations, on trains and at dinner tables, had "a smack of manslaughter about them."[1]

The practical abandonment of civil law during the war, the period of anarchy and guerilla bands which followed it, and the years of unpopular military and Republican government served to make matters worse. Such conditions drove Federal commanders to despair. One of them finally said, "It is not a military matter, and if the people wish to live in such a lawless manner, they ought to be gratified."[2] Travelers who came into the state during the period wrote of its scattered settlements, its sparse population, and the difficulties of travel and the maintenance of law.[3] Out of such conditions grew the almost universal habit of carrying a pistol as an essential article of dress. The state press, reports of travelers, and the speeches and letters of leading citizens were filled with references to the custom.[4] It was not at all uncommon for prisoners to go armed into the court room.[5] In Panola County, with a population of about twenty thousand, there were five homicides within sixty days during 1871, and at least ten during the last seven months of 1872.[6] Almost complete anarchy existed in Pearl County from its establishment in 1872 until its abolition in 1878.[7] Every week the "Mississippi Items" columns of the Jackson *Clarion*, the Natchez *Democrat*, and the Natchez *Courier*, the "Mississippi Matters" column of the Vicksburg *Times*, and that called "Mississippi Brevities" in the *Pilot* carried in two or three lines of fine print stories of violence that today would call for a headline in practically every paper in the state. Such conditions were not confined to rural sections. In 1866, the mayor of Jackson resigned because of his inability to obtain any support in his efforts to preserve order in a city "full of thieves, robbers and law-breakers."[8] In the same year, the editor of the Natchez *Democrat* agreed with a report in the New York *Herald* that Vicksburg, Natchez, Grenada, and Columbus had been the worst spots in the United States for

[1] William Howard Russell, *My Diary, North and South*, p. 301.

[2] *Senate Executive Documents*, no. 27, 39th Congress, 1st session, p. 46.

[3] Robert Somers, *The Southern States*, pp. 239-240; Whitelaw Reid, *After the War*, pp. 396, 416; Charles Nordhoff, *The Cotton States*, pp. 74, 78; Edward King, *The Great South*, pp. 289, 311, 316, 318.

[4] W. Reid, *op. cit.*, pp. 396, 422; Foster B. Zincke, *Last Winter in the United States*, p. 149; C. Nordhoff, *op. cit.*, pp. 74, 78; *House Miscellaneous Documents*, no. 53, 40th Congress, 3d session, p. 144; Hinds County *Gazette*, March 25, 1874; Jackson *Clarion-Ledger*, June 7, 1888, April 4, 1889; Aberdeen *Examiner*, May 29, 1884; Vicksburg *Times and Republican*, April 10, June 17, 1873.

[5] *House Miscellaneous Documents*, no. 53, 40th Congress, 3d session, p. 144; W. H. Hardy, "Recollections of Reconstruction in East and Southeast Mississippi," *P.M.H.S.*, VII, 205-207; Aberdeen *Examiner*, May 29, 1884; Jackson *Weekly Clarion*, March 31, 1886.

[6] Hinds County *Gazette*, March 1, 1871; John W. Kyle, "Reconstruction in Panola County," *P.M.H.S.*, XIII, 80-81.

[7] *Appleton's Cyclopedia*, 1878, p. 571; Mississippi *House Journal*, 1878, pp. 24-26.

[8] Natchez *Tri-Weekly Democrat*, May 3, 1866.

years past.[9] It was in this atmosphere of violence and lawlessness that the relationship of the two races in Mississippi had to be defined.

An additional complicating factor during the period was the existence in the state of thousands of idle young men and boys. Having come up in the disorganized years of the war, often without a father to control them, they now found themselves unable or unwilling to secure employment or attend school.[10] Lounging about the streets, stores, and bars, and longing for some exciting incident to break the monotony of their existence, they were always ready to take any opportunity to start a disturbance, or to dash off in search of trouble.[11] Such young men and boys were the instigators or chief participants in at least two-thirds of the racial conflicts of the period.[12]

With the approach of the first Christmas after the end of the war, the rumor spread all over the state that the Negroes were prepared for a general insurrection. There can be little doubt that much of the alarm expressed by the whites was real, in spite of the fact that nobody had any exact information.[13] The fact that many of the Negroes were refusing to renew their contracts for the coming year, and were wandering about looking for more desirable places, added to the alarm. Governor Benjamin Humphreys, influenced by the general fear, disgusted by the freedmen's determination to bargain for a better wage, and perhaps not unaware of possibilities of the situation for propaganda, ordered the state militia to patrol the roads and to search the cabins of the Negroes for arms. The work was done with vigor and dispatch, and in some cases with extreme brutality.[14] Nowhere did the expected insurrection develop.

Exactly the same kind of excitement developed in December of the following year, and once more Governor Humphreys sought permission to set the militia to work. This time the refusal of the military commander was upheld by President Johnson.[15] As a result, the militia remained in-

[9] Ross H. Moore, "Social and Economic Conditions in Mississippi during Reconstruction," unpublished doctoral dissertation, Duke University, 1938, p. 355.

[10] C. Nordhoff, *op. cit.*, p. 18; Hinds County *Gazette*, November 30, 1870, September 28, 1881; Vicksburg *Daily Times*, April 10, 1869; Natchez *Tri-Weekly Democrat*, July 11, 1867.

[11] Mississippi *Weekly Pilot*, November 13, 1875; Jackson *Clarion-Ledger*, January 1, 1891; Jackson *Weekly Clarion*, November 7, 1883; Raymond *Gazette*, September 1, 1888; *Senate Reports*, no. 527, 44th Congress, 1st session, p. xiv; *Senate Miscellaneous Documents*, no. 166, 50th Congress, 1st session, p. 139.

[12] Jackson *Daily Times*, October 6, 7, 1876; Jackson *Clarion*, September 10, 1874; Natchez *Tri-Weekly Courier*, September 9, 1865; Fred M. Witty, "Reconstruction in Carroll and Montgomery Counties," *P.M.H.S.*, X, 130-131; M. G. Abney, "Reconstruction in Pontotoc County," *P.M.H.S.*, XI, 248; *Senate Miscellaneous Documents*, no. 166, 50th Congress, 1st session, pp. 15, 39, 241, 339, 363, 371; *Senate Reports*, no. 527, 44th Congress, 1st session, pp. xiv, 55, 114, 321, 322, 506, 544, 681, 811, 820, 829-831, 1107, 1176, 1354.

[13] Jackson *Clarion* December 20, 21, 1865.

[14] James W. Garner, *Reconstruction in Mississippi*, p. 104; Jackson *Clarion*, December 20, 1865; Natchez *Weekly Democrat*, December 9, 1865; John T. Trowbridge, *The South*, pp. 374-375.

[15] J. W. Garner, *op. cit.*, pp. 108-109.

active, but in some cases private parties undertook the work, torturing the freedmen in an effort to persuade them to reveal the places where arms were concealed.[16]   Once more the Negroes failed to rise.

The absence of hostile action on the part of the freedmen in 1865 and 1866 did not prevent the Governor and many white citizens from becoming more alarmed than ever in December of 1867.   All over the South the rumor of approaching insurrection continued to grow, and by the time it reached Washington the story ran that the Negroes throughout the South had a thorough understanding, and planned to repeat all the atrocities of Santo Domingo.   It was said that the whites were entirely unarmed and defenseless, and that scarcely a Negro cabin was without arms for five persons.[17]   Governor Humphreys presented to General Ord confidential information received from "gentlemen of high official and social position in different portions of the State," and received from him permission to use military force if the necessity appeared.   In a proclamation issued December 9, the Governor warned the freedmen to preserve the peace, and asked all citizens to make timely and truthful reports of any conspiracies, with the names of persons and places.[18]   No information was forthcoming, and the Christmas season was entirely uneventful.   Later efforts to learn from Governor Humphreys and Generals Ord and Gillem the sources of the information on which they acted were unsuccessful.[19]   This appears to have been the last of the panics over the possibility of a general insurrection on the part of the Negroes, but similar situations were to develop time and again in various communities during the following years.

With the issuance in September, 1867, of an order against the assembly of any public or private militia organization in the state,[20] the use of force against the Negro was driven underground.   The result was the appearance of the Ku Klux Klan and a number of similar organizations.   Those in Mississippi ranged from genuine "dens" organized by General Forrest, or subordinates under his control, to local gangs of thugs without any name or formal organization.   Among the regularly organized groups that operated in limited areas were the Washington Brothers in Leake County, the Robinson Clubs in Pontotoc and Newton, the Knights of the Black Cross in Lawrence, and Heggie's Scouts in Holmes, Carroll, and Montgomery counties.   The only essential difference in these various organizations lay in the fact that many of the early Klansmen, according to contemporary declarations and later tradition, were leading citizens who acted in a disciplined and remedial fashion, while most of the less distinguished groups included terrorists who went to regrettable extremes.   From 1867 until

[16] M. G. Abney, op. cit., XI, 238.
[17] Hinds County Gazette, November 29, 1867, quoting the New York Herald.
[18] New York Times, December 16, 1867.
[19] Mississippi Constitutional Convention of 1868, Journal, pp. 397-398.
[20] Appleton's Cyclopedia, 1867, p. 516; J. W. Garner, op. cit., p. 101.

1871, these bodies rode through the country at night, terrifying, whipping, or murdering whites and Negroes who, for one reason or another, were to them undesirable. Such groups were very active in 1870, killing or driving out teachers and burning schools and Negro churches in a number of the eastern counties.[21]

In general, it can be said that as long as these organizations confined their activities to the intimidation of "insolent" Negroes and of Republican leaders they held the approval and coöperation of a large majority of the white population. Almost immediately, however, the evils inherent in the system began to be apparent. Roving gangs of terrorists murdered respectable Negro preachers, drove off or killed Negro renters of land, rifled stores and took the lives of Jewish merchants; lynched Negro men, women, and children who were accused of vague crimes; and killed or robbed peaceful white citizens.[22] It is impossible to estimate the number of Negroes tortured or killed during the time that these various gangs flourished. There was a general policy of keeping such stories out of the papers, and testimony before courts and committees was contradictory. Stories of old men who were members of the various organizations seem to be filled with exaggeration. A member of Heggie's Scouts claimed that this group killed 116 Negroes on one occasion and threw their bodies into the Tallahatchie River.[23] According to a similar story, the den of the Klan at Grenada found some Negroes drilling in a field and killed seventy-five of them.[24] Five members of the Klan in Lafayette declared that their group drowned from seventeen to thirty Negroes in Yockana Creek.[25] Although such boastful tales of mass slaughter are entirely unreliable, they reflect the attitude which in 1869 and 1870 made life unsafe for any Negro who departed in any way from his routine task as a laborer.

A very stringent state law against the activities of the Klan and similar groups was enacted in July of 1870,[26] but it was found to be almost entirely ineffective. Officers failed to make arrests, and witnesses were afraid to testify. In some cases where convictions were secured, sympathetic judges assessed small fines that were not paid.[27] Public opinion, which had begun to turn against the night riders in the spring of 1870,[28] carried more

[21] *Report on the Condition of Affairs in the Late Insurrectionary States*, pt. 1, pp. 73, 74, 77; Mississippi *Senate Journal, Appendix*, pp. 181-184; S. G. Noble, *Forty Years of the Public Schools in Mississippi*, p. 37.
[22] Mississippi *Weekly Pilot*, November 19, 1870; Vicksburg *Daily Times*, March 19, 1869; M. G. Abney, *op. cit.*, XI, 248; E. C. Coleman, "Reconstruction in Attala County," *P.M.H.S.*, X, 158-159; Julia C. Brown, "Reconstruction in Yalobusha and Grenada Counties," *P.M.H.S.*, XII, 237, 239; W. H. Braden, "Reconstruction in Lee County," *P.M.H.S.*, X, 145.
[23] F. M. Witty, *op. cit.*, X, 130.   [24] J. C. Brown, *op. cit.*, XII, 242.
[25] Julia Kendel, "Reconstruction in Lafayette County," *P.M.H.S.*, XIII, 242.
[26] Mississippi *Session Laws*, 1870, pp. 89-92.
[27] F. M. Witty, *op. cit.*, X, 130.
[28] Vicksburg *Times and Republican*, April 12, 1870, quoting the Iuka *Gazette* and the Meridian *Gazette;* J. W. Garner, *op. cit.*, p. 345.

weight. The Federal Ku Klux Act of 1871, although it was not enforced, carried enough prestige to put an end to the actvities of most of the gangs. By January of 1872, Governor R. C. Powers, in an optimistic message, was able to declare that the marauders had been completely suppressed.[29]

The most spectacular manifestation of the bad feeling between the races was a series of clashes of various kinds which were generally referred to as riots. There were dozens of these in the period between 1865 and 1890, but the majority of them culminated in nothing more than a few days of excitement, with military bands patrolling and picketing the roads, and with the Negroes hiding in the woods or sticking closely to their cabins. They generally ended after a few of the freedmen had been shot or driven out of the county, and others jailed for planning an insurrection.[30] There were many other cases in which rumors that the Negroes were organizing to slaughter the whites brought much excitement and military activity but resulted in no actual conflict.[31] About twenty of these affairs were of a more serious nature, bringing death to more than two hundred Negroes and some seven or eight whites. It is significant that only three clashes of any importance occurred before 1874, and only two after 1876. On the other hand, there were fifteen during the years 1874, 1875, and 1876, taking the lives of about 150 of the Negroes and all of the whites involved in the above totals. These three years of violence covered the period of the overthrow of the Republican government in the state and in most of the counties and towns.

In general, these clashes can be grouped into five classifications. The bloody affair at Vicksburg in 1874 grew out of the fact that large groups of Negroes, some of them undoubtedly armed, were coming into the town from the surrounding country in answer to a call from the imprisoned Republican sheriff. This encounter, the worst of the entire series, cost the lives of more than thirty Negroes and of two or three whites. It is unique in the fact that the Negroes, although they probably were returning to their homes when the firing began, had actually shown an intention of coming into the town.[32] The minor affair at Vicksburg on July 4, 1875, which brought death to two Negroes, simply marked the breaking up of a Republican meeting. Everything was quiet within a few hours. The trouble at Yazoo City in August of 1875, and at Clinton a few days later, also began at Republican political meetings. Most of the deaths of the Negroes

[29] Mississippi *Senate Journal*, 1872, *Appendix*, p. 1.

[30] Hinds County *Gazette*, August 26, September 2, December 9, 1874, August 9, 1882; Jackson *Weekly Clarion*, August 27, September 3, 1879; James M. Wells, *The Chisholm Massacre*, p. 102.

[31] Hinds County *Gazette*, August 9, September 2, 1874, November 1, 1876, September 1, 1888; Jackson *Weekly Pilot*, September 25, 1875, November 7, 1883; Mississippi *Weekly Clarion*, August 21, 1875, September 20, 1882; *Senate Reports*, no. 527, 44th Congress, 1st session, pp. 164-165.

[32] Vicksburg *Herald*, December 1, 1874, to January 6, 1875; Mississippi *Weekly Pilot*, March 6, 1875.

in these affairs, however, came in days immediately following the original disturbance, when armed bands of whites engaged in wholesale lynching in the surrounding countryside.[33] These two episodes cost the lives of three white Democrats, two white Republicans, and perhaps as many as fifty Negroes. The death of about thirty-five Negroes in Tippah County in 1865, and in Meridian in 1871, also resulted from multiple lynchings after incidents of little importance broke a tension that had been increasing for several months.[34]

Into a fourth classification fall the riots near Dry Grove in 1869, Water Valley, New Hope Church, Satartia, Friar's Point, and Rolling Fork in 1875, in Wilkinson County and at Chapel Hill Church in 1876, near Water Valley in 1879, and in Leflore County in 1889. These affairs, which caused the deaths of seventy-five to one hundred Negroes and of one white, displayed a remarkable similarity in practically all phases of their development. In the midst of relations already strained by conditions in the state or by minor local happenings, some incident of violence occurred, involving one or two whites and a few Negroes. Some excitement and rough talk then took place on the streets and in stores. Wildly excited Negroes carried the story into the surrounding country, where it gradually took the form that the whites were killing all the Negroes in the town and were preparing to come out and slaughter those on the plantations. Within a few hours, Negroes by scores gathered up the few guns and pistols they had managed to preserve from constant searches and seizures, and fled deep into the woods, swamps, or cane-brakes. While this phase was in progress, excited young white men dashed into town with the report that the Negroes, by hundreds and thousands, were organizing to come in and burn the town and slaughter the whites "from the cradle to the grave." The whites then gathered their rifles, formed into companies, and set out to find the Negroes. As they approached the wilderness where the freedmen were in hiding, the whites divided into two or three groups. One of these advanced from the front; the others from the side and rear. When the Negroes caught sight of the first of these groups, they sometimes fired a few shots, almost invariably without results. They then stampeded in panic. Some of them were brought down by volleys from the rifles of the whites, and others were captured. Of those captured, a few considered to be leaders were shot or hanged.[35] Within a few days, the excitement died

[33] Elizabeth Caldwell, "Reconstruction in Yazoo County," unpublished master's thesis, University of North Carolina, 1931, pp. 55-56; A. T. Morgan, *Yazoo*, pp. 478-482; Mississippi *Weekly Pilot*, September 25, October 2, 1875; C. H. Brough, "The Clinton Riot," *P.M.H.S.*, VI, 62.

[34] Natchez *Weekly Democrat*, December 9, 1865; W. H. Hardy, *op. cit.*, VII, 205-207.

[35] Susan Dabney Smedes, *Memorials of a Southern Planter*, pp. 248-250; Mississippi *Weekly Pilot*, September 4, 1875; Hinds County *Gazette*, November 10, 17, 1869, September 15, 1875; Yazoo City *Herald*, September 8, 1875; Vicksburg *Herald*, Extra, December 9, 1875; Jackson *Daily Times*, October 4, 1876, quoting the

down, the Negroes returned to work, and the incident became a local legend, to be embellished as the years went by.

The trouble in Carrollton in 1886 resembled, with the possible exception of the Meridian riot of 1871, none of the other affairs of violence of the period. This incident grew out of the trial of a white man who, with a number of his friends, was charged by two Negroes with assault with intent to murder. Although warnings had been issued that Negroes were not to attend, a large number of them were in the courtroom. While the trial was going on, fifty or more white men, armed with shot-guns and rifles, rode into the town, rushed into the room, and began firing. Some of the Negroes saved themselves by leaping from the windows, but ten met immediate death and a large number of others died later from their wounds. Although it was declared that many of the Negroes were armed, and that they intended to start a fight at the end of the trial, no white was injured in any manner.[36]

The Carrollton massacre brought to a head an opposition to violence that had been growing in the state for a number of years. The editor of the Raymond *Gazette* declared that efforts to place the blame on the Negroes would not be "swallowed" by those who had witnessed similar scenes at other times. He even went so far as to demand that the murderers be identified and punished, and declared that such action would receive the support of all honest citizens.[37] This seems to be the first example of such a suggestion in the entire history of the period. The editor of the Natchez *Democrat* called the affair "an undefensible proceeding." The states of the South, he felt, had passed through a revolution, during which such affairs of violence were to be expected. But now that the political revolution had been accomplished all good citizens wanted violence to cease. He joined in the demand for investigation and punishment.[38] The editor of the *Clarion,* the most powerful paper in the state, adopted a more realistic view, but joined in the condemnation:

There can be no adequate punishment for the injury that has been inflicted upon the good people of Mississippi, by the murderous mob at Carrollton. There will be no punishment of any kind. Time spent in an attempt to bring them before the bar of that temple whose sanctity they have so grossly violated would be time thrown away. . . . They may be powerful and influential citizens whose favor it were well to court and whose displeasure it were dangerous

Prairie *News;* J. C. Brown, *op. cit.,* XII, 257; Fred Z. Browne, "Reconstruction in Oktibbeha County," *P.M.H.S.,* XIII, 287; J. H. Jones, "Reconstruction in Wilkinson County," *P.M.H.S.,* VIII, 171-172; J. S. McNeily, "Climax and Collapse of Reconstruction in Mississippi," *P.M.H.S.,* XII, 462-463; *Senate Reports,* no. 527, 44th Congress, 1st session, pp. 69-70, 602, 681-682, 694, 697, 732, 753, 1176-1177, 1535, 1603, 1607, 1611, 1615, 1623, 1633-1635; Mississippi *House Journal* 1890, pp. 594-597.
[36] Raymond *Gazette,* March 27, 1886; Jackson *Weekly Clarion,* March 24, 31, 1886.
[37] Raymond *Gazette,* March 27, 1886.
[38] *Ibid.,* March 27, 1886, quoting the Natchez *Daily Democrat.*

to arouse. To such considerations we can close our eyes and our ears; but we cannot be blind or deaf to the appeals of the weak who claim and deserve our protection, nor can we be unmindful of the indelible blot that has been put upon the reputation of the State.[39]

Such a stand on the part of a paper that for years had insisted that reports of such affairs be suppressed[40] was an indication of remarkable progress. The same paper took an even more advanced position a few years later. On Christmas night in 1890, a group of young men of the leading families, the same element which had received so much praise for its part in the overthrow of the Republican municipal government in 1888, formed a druken mob and killed an inoffensive Negro on the main street of Jackson. "No more mercy," said a *Clarion* editorial, "should be shown the genteel rough than the loud-mouthed hoodlum. Each should be made to understand that he must stop his devilment."[41] Sufficient public indignation was aroused to bring about the resignation of the entire police force.

The ability of a paper to attack in such a fashion young men of its own city for the killing of a Negro reflected the change in public sentiment. After 1890, "riots" and wholesale lynchings were almost unknown and a majority of the white population were ready, except in unusual cases, to exert their influence for interracial peace.

It is impossible to make any estimate of the number of individual Negroes lynched or murdered by whites during the period. Such matters attracted little or no attention in the press. When reported at all, they were generally given a line or two in very small type in the "Mississippi Brevities" or "Miscellaneous Items" columns of the papers. In one such column in 1881, the *Clarion* mentioned in passing the unprovoked murder of two Negroes and the lynching of two others.[42] The *Gazette* managed to get five lynchings into one line of type which was almost too small to be read: "Four negroes were lynched at Grenada last week; also one at Oxford."[43] Although there were numerous reports of the murder of Negroes by whites, for causes ranging from insolence to assault, indictment in such cases was almost unknown. There are a few records of jail or prison sentences for such murders, but there seems to have been no single instance throughout the period in which a white man was hanged for killing a Negro.

The first case after the war involving the lynching of a Negro for the rape of a white woman was probably one in Oktibbeha County in the summer of 1865. Upon the receipt of a payment of two hundred dollars, the captain of a troop of Federal soldiers stationed in the county allowed the

[39] Jackson *Weekly Clarion*, March 24, 1886.
[40] See comment on attitude of the *Clarion* in Summit *Times*, March 15, 1878.
[41] Jackson *Clarion-Ledger*, January 1, 1891.
[42] Jackson *Weekly Clarion*, December 7, 1881.
[43] Raymond *Gazette*, July 18, 1885.

Negro to be run to death by hounds.[44] There seems to have been an almost universal agreement throughout the period that death by lynching was to be the punishment for either rape or attempted rape. There was a fairly uniform number of such occurrences each year, with a distinct increase in the violent years of 1874 and 1875. There also seems to have been a general understanding that a Negro who murdered a white was to be lynched; to this rule there were few, if any, exceptions. The fact that lynching was considered to be preëminently the punishment for rape and murder did not prevent its use in a wide variety of circumstances. There were reports of Negroes lynched for assault, robbery, being in a woman's room at night, insulting a woman, burning gins, burning barns, stealing hogs, renting land, participating in politics, and robbing a grave to obtain material for a "charm bag."[45] In many cases the crime involved was unknown or not reported.

Not all of the extra-legal executions of the period involved the lynching of Negroes by whites. During 1866, a number of white men in the eastern portion of the state were punished in this fashion for stealing horses.[46] The few occurrences of this type in later years involved rape, attempted rape, or murder.[47] There were also a few cases in which Negroes, usually urged on by whites, lynched members of their own race.[48] Such incidents, however, were so rare as to have little significance. Essentially lynching was recognized as one of the methods of control which were to be used by the dominant race in its relations with the Negroes.

During the greater part of the period, there was little open criticism of lynching as an institution. It was defended, and even applauded, by the press.[49] As late as 1889, the editor of the *Gazette* argued that the people would be justified in lynching insane Negroes, who, kept in county jails because there was no place for them at the asylum, proved to be nuisances and noise makers.[50] The public attitude was most clearly revealed in a case in Jefferson County in 1884. A Negro suspected of attempting the rape of a girl three years old was delivered to the sheriff by the girl's father and finally was carried to the jail in Hinds County for safe-keeping. There was an immediate storm of protest, and citizens gathered in a mass meet-

[44] Fred Z. Browne, *op. cit.*, XIII, 274.

[45] Mississippi *Weekly Pilot*, November 19, 1870; Natchez *Daily Courier*, March 15, 1866; Hinds County *Gazette*, January 26, 1876, April 18, July 11, 1877, September 8, 1883, October 27, 1888; J. C. Brown, *op. cit.*, XII, 239, 240; E. F. Puckett, *op. cit.*, XI, 130; Ruth Watkins, "Reconstruction in Newton County," *P.M.H.S.*, XI, 216-217.

[46] Natchez *Daily Courier*, February 21, March 15, July 26, 1866; Aberdeen *Examiner*, July 15, 1866.

[47] Hinds County *Gazette*, April 27, 1870, June 7, 1884; Mississippi *Weekly Pilot*, August 14, 1875; Raymond *Gazette*, October 24, 1885, April 3, 1886.

[48] Hinds County *Gazette*, August 11, 1875, August 24, 1881; Raymond *Gazette*, July 4, August 8, 1885.

[49] Hinds County *Gazette*, January 26, February 9, 1876, July 23, 1879; Jackson *Weekly Clarion*, May 24, 1882.

[50] Raymond *Gazette*, August 17, 1889.

ing near the scene of the supposed crime. The sheriff, thoroughly alarmed, tried to shift the blame to the public. They had been negligent in allowing the Negro to come into his hands. Even after this occurred, he had given them every possible opportunity to take the man away from him. It was only after four or five days in which they took no action that he, with the approval of the judge, had become convinced that the law and his duty required him to take the Negro out of the county. Public opinion turned even more strongly against the girl's father. Both a neighbor and the sheriff felt that it was necessary to defend him at length. His judgment had been swayed, they declared, by the pleas of a pregnant wife who was sick and extremely nervous.[51] The feeling of the citizens that their community and their county had been disgraced, the anxiety of the sheriff about his political office, and the concern of the father and his friends about his social position were all significant.

Althought lynching continued to be upheld by the mass of the white population, some opposition to it was beginning to be heard by the end of the period. Early in 1889, the editor of the *Clarion-Ledger* suggested that the mobs were going too far, and that the legislature ought to consider some means of checking them.[52] The editor of the Greenville *Times* agreed.[53] Early in the following year the strength of these convictions was put to the test. A Negro named Anthony Thomas was arrested in Hinds County for the murder of a white woman in Smith. On the order of Governor J. M. Stone, the sheriff in Hinds refused to deliver Thomas to deputies who came to carry him back to the scene of the crime. It was generally known that the deputies intended to allow him to be lynched. The Raymond *Gazette* defended the action of the Governor as intended to protect the good name of the state, but also took the attitude that the action was illegal.[54] The *Clarion-Ledger* joined in the half-hearted defense of the Governor, but printed in full a bitter attack on him taken from the New Orleans *Picayune*. Throughout the state, those papers friendly to the Governor gave him qualified support, while others generally based their attacks on the claim that he had exceeded his power.[55]

Governor Stone finally sent Thomas to Smith County with a company of militia for his protection. A newspaper account carried the statement, "There is not a man in the crowd but would enjoy helping to hang the negro, but at the same time they have a high sense of honor and duty, and will carry out their instructions to the letter."[56] Thomas was tried on May 2, and sentenced to be hanged on May 28. Immediately after the

[51] Hinds County *Gazette,* June 7, 21, 1884.
[52] Jackson *Clarion-Ledger,* February 28, 1889.
[53] *Ibid.,* March 14, 1889, quoting the Greenville *Times.*
[54] Raymond *Gazette,* March 22, 1890.
[55] Jackson *Clarion-Ledger,* March 6, 13, 1890.
[56] *Ibid.,* April 10, 1890.

passage of the sentence, he was taken by a mob, but, after an appeal by the judge and other influential leaders, he was returned to the jailer. On the following day a meeting of citizens approved this action, and asked that the law be allowed to take its course.[57] It appears that this was done.

The importance of the Thomas case lay in the fact that it revealed the presence of a large number of whites who were opposed to lynching as a matter of principle, and who were willing to make public their attitude in a case where immediate passion had had time to cool. This group continued to grow in numbers and influence, and that growth has resulted in an encouragingly steady decline in the number of cases in which mob law is applied.

MISCEGENATION

Under the ante-bellum plantation system, there was naturally a certain amount of sexual relationship between some of the owners, their sons, and overseers and the female slaves. The situation was seldom openly discussed. With proper discretion, such indulgence apparently did not seriously affect the relations of the white participant with others of his own social group. Among the Negroes, the mistress of the master often occupied a highly respected and coveted position.

In general, the small farmers and poor whites were strongly opposed to the easy-going tolerance displayed by the planting and professional groups toward such relationships. This attitude was another expression of their lack of economic and social security, and of their determination to emphasize the difference between the Negroes and themselves. It was to this feeling that such leaders as A. G. Brown appealed most effectively in their successful efforts to enlist the support of the non-slaveholders in the campaign for secession. Freedom for slaves, they said, would inevitably mean social equality; Negroes would obtain white girls in marriage, and soon all racial distinction would be lost.[58]

These small-farmer and poor-white groups, who held a controlling influence over the legislature of 1865, took heed of their misgivings, and lost no time in writing into law their feelings on the question. A section of the Black Code, adopted in December, 1865, provided:

. . . it shall not be lawful for any freedman, free negro or mulatto to intermarry with any white person, nor for any white person to intermarry with any freedman, free negro or mulatto, and any person who shall so intermarry shall be deemed guilty of felony, and on conviction thereof shall be confined in the State penitentiary for life; and those shall be deemed freedmen, free negroes and mulattoes who are of pure negro blood, and those descended from a negro to the third generation inclusive, though one ancestor in each generation may have been a white person.[59]

[57] Raymond *Gazette*, May 3, 1890; Port Gibson *Reveille*, May 2, 1890.
[58] P. L. Rainwater, *Mississippi, Storm Center of Secession*, pp. 144-149.
[59] Mississippi *Session Laws*, regular session, 1865, p. 82.

Although it appears that a Northern white officer married a Negro woman in Vicksburg in January or February of 1866,[60] the first case under the law did not come up until June of that year. Ben ***, a Negro who had been a soldier in the Federal army, married Mollie ***, a white girl from Simpson County. A raid by county officers in the early hours of the morning of June 13 was followed by a trial of the couple before the circuit court. Found guilty, each was sentenced to serve six months in the county jail, and to pay a fine of five hundred dollars.[61]

Two months later, a Negro man and a young white woman from Leake County endeavored to be married in Vicksburg. The girl, who was the daughter of the former owner of the Negro, declared that she desired to marry him because she loved him. Investigation revealed the fact that they had been having relations in defiance of the law, and the judge ordered that they be held for trial in the ensuing term of the criminal court.[62] It appears that the matter must have been hushed up in some fashion, as there is no further public record of the case. With the exception of the arrest in Vicksburg of a woman from Lauderdale County on the charge of cohabitation with a Negro,[63] there seems to have been no further application of the law.

The repeal by the legislature of 1870 of all laws involving racial discrimination was followed almost immediately by a case that attracted wide attention. A. T. Morgan, a cultured and formerly affluent planter from Ohio, who had been a member of the constitutional convention, was at the time a state senator, and later served as sheriff of Yazoo County, married a young octoroon teacher who had come down from New York. The state followed with interest the difficulties of their honeymoon journey, which included ejection from a bus in Louisville, Kentucky, and the printing of vulgar comments by Northern papers.[64] This marriage, the only one during the period which received wide attention, appears to have been happily maintained for many years after the couple left the state in 1876.

Another case which attracted some attention within the state was the marriage of Haskins Smith, mulatto member of the state legislature, to the daughter of the owner of the hotel in which Smith worked in Port Gibson. Although leading citizens of the community held Smith to be a good man and refused to be aroused over the matter, lower classes among

[60] Natchez *Tri-Weekly Democrat*, February 24, 1866.

[61] Jackson *Clarion and Standard*, June 14, 1866; Hinds County *Gazette*, June 22, 1866. It is impossible to explain this sentence in terms of the penalty provided by the law.

[62] Natchez *Tri-Weekly Democrat*, August 21, 1866, quoting the Vicksburg *Herald*, August 14, 1866.

[63] Jackson *Clarion*, August 26, 1866.

[64] J. S. McNeily, "War and Reconstruction in Mississippi," *P.M.H.S.C.S.*, II, 403; Hinds County *Gazette*, August 17, 1870; Mississippi *Weekly Pilot*, November 26, 1870; A. T. Morgan, *Yazoo*, pp. 345-351.

the whites created a great deal of disturbance.[65]   References to this marriage in a speech by a Negro in Vicksburg helped to bring about the overthrow of the Republican government in that city a little later in the summer.[66]

It is impossible to estimate how many interracial marriages occurred between more obscure people. It seems probable that there were not very many. Evidence that some did occur is offered by such small items as a passage in the diary of a pious Irish contractor in Claiborne County:

Confirmation at Chadenel I was discusted to see *Joe O Brian* as god father for Boys, he who has a lot of *Niger* Bastards & is now married to a ½ *Niger* wife What a scandle to me[67]

The restoration of Democratic control in the state in 1876 was followed by a return of legal prohibition of intermarriage of the races. Such marriages were declared to be "incestuous [sic] and void," and the parties participating were made subject to the penalties for incest. These included a maximum term of ten years in prison. For the purposes of the act, a Negro was any person who had one-fourth or more of Negro blood.[68]

Very few opportunities were found for the application of the law. In 1883, a white man in Rankin County, who had formerly been fined for unlawful cohabitation with a Negro woman, persuaded a Negro preacher to marry them.[69] Although the newspaper report predicted that he would receive a sentence to prison, no further mention of his case is to be found. In 1885, a resident of Hinds County, charged with incest on the grounds of his marriage to a Negro woman, received the maximum sentence of ten years.[70]

The abolition of the possibilities of legal marriage, which in any case would have involved very few individuals, did not do away with concubinage and unlawful cohabitation. The matter received little public attention, but now and then legal complications or violent tragedies revealed its existence.[71] It appears, however, that such relationships became steadily less frequent as time went on. The racial code of the poor white came more and more to be that of the public at large.

[65] *Senate Reports,* no. 527, 44th Congress, 1st session, pp. 159, 191-192.
[66] *Ibid.*, pp. 1312-1313, 1367; J. S. McNeily, "Climax and Collapse of Reconstruction in Mississippi," *P.M.H.S.,* XII, 297.
[67] Patrick Murphy, "Diary," vol. 16, Sunday, April 12, 1885, Patrick Murphy Papers.
[68] Mississippi *Code,* 1880, sections 1145-1147. The constitution of 1890, like the law of 1865, classified as a Negro any person having one-eighth or more of Negro blood.
[69] Jackson *Weekly Clarion,* January 24, 1883.
[70] Raymond *Gazette,* August 1, 1885.
[71] Hinds County *Gazette,* May 27, June 3, 24, September 2, 1874, August 25, 1880; Jackson *Weekly Clarion,* August 9, 1882; A. T. Morgan, *op. cit.,* pp. 494-495.

JIM CROW LAWS

The determination of the mass of the whites to set up legal differences between the races was further demonstrated in the enactment in 1865 of the first "Jim Crow" law in the South. The few Negroes who traveled on public conveyances before the war had generally been directly in the service of their masters. There was little or no objection to their presence.[72] With the coming of freedom, all this was changed. Large numbers of the freedmen now took advantage of the opportunity to move about from place to place, and there can be no doubt that in the crowded cars the low standards of sanitation observed by most of them added greatly to objections based on racial difference. The better railroads immediately adopted the custom of refusing to Negroes admission to the first-class, or "ladies'" cars.[73] On smaller roads, which did not carry the two classes of cars, the freedmen, although they paid full fare, were relegated to old cars, freight cars, or open platforms.[74] The law approved by the Governor of the state in November, 1865, simply gave legality to a practice which the railroads had already adopted. According to its provisions it became unlawful for an employee of any railroad in the state to allow "any freedman, negro, or mulatto, to ride in any first class passenger cars, set apart, or used by, and for white persons. . . ." The law was not to apply to Negroes traveling with their mistresses in the capacity of nurses.[75] It is to be noticed that under this law those whites who were unable to pay first-class fares, or who did not choose to do so, continued to travel with the Negroes. White men also continued to use the second-class car for smoking, drinking, and impolite conversation. These circumstances not only led to racial difficulties, but also brought discomfort to the small number of cultured Negroes, of both sexes, who were forced to travel in such surroundings.[76] Although the law applied only to railroads, the principle which it recognized was followed on passenger boats, in theaters, and in a number of other places of public entertainment.[77]

With the assembly of the legislature of 1870, a number of the Negro members, especially Senators Robert Gleed and William Gray, set to work to prevent by law any discrimination against those of their race on public conveyances. After several disappointments, they succeeded in gaining enough votes from the reluctant white Republicans to secure the passage of such a law in June,[78] and to retain it in the revised code in the following

[72] Jackson *Clarion*, February 18, 1866.
[73] W. Reid, *After the War*, p. 421.
[74] *Ibid.*, note, p. 386.
[75] Mississippi *Session Laws*, 1865, p. 231.
[76] Mississippi *Weekly Pilot*, May 15, 1870, August 31, 1872.
[77] J. T. Trowbridge, *The South*, p. 352; Natchez *Tri-Weekly Democrat*, July 9, 1867.
[78] Mississippi *Weekly Pilot*, May 15, 28, June 4, 1870; Jackson *Semi-Weekly Clarion*, June 10, 1870.

April.[79] The law provided that the right of any citizen to travel on any railroad, steamboat, other water craft, or stage coach was not to be denied or infringed. Any employee who refused that right, or who should "compel, or attempt to compel, any person or persons to occupy any particular seat, or any particular part" of such conveyances on account of race or color was made subject to a fine, a suit for damages by the person injured, and a term in the county jail.[80] In spite of its stringent provisions, the law had almost no effect. The captains of the river boats, the chief means of travel in the black counties, simply disregarded the law. On the trains, practically all of the Negroes, either from choice or economic necessity, continued to ride in the second-class cars.[81] A conductor in 1871 did not hesitate to ask James Lynch, secretary of state, to leave the "ladies' " car. Lynch immediately complied with the request.[82]

The failure of the general railroad act did not prevent efforts of the Negroes to extend its provisions in a civil rights bill in the next session of the legislature. After a great deal of argument, some chicanery, and much discomfort on the part of the white Republicans, this bill finally failed by one vote to gain the approval of the senate.[83] Renewed agitation in the following year finally gained its passage. In essence, it extended the provisions of the railroad act to cover hotels, inns, and theaters and other places of public amusement, and added to the penalties a requirement for the forfeiture of the charter of any corporation that violated the act.[84]

Early in the following year, a decision in a test case in Vicksburg exempted from the provisions of the act all organizations save those which held a public charter.[85] Although a Supreme Court decision a little later in the year upheld the act in its limited sense,[86] it enjoyed little more success than its predecessors. Here and there a few Negroes braved public wrath by refusing to leave sections set apart for the other race,[87] but such cases were rare. Congressman John R. Lynch, requested to leave a white table in a railroad dining room at Holly Springs, retired without protest.[88]

By 1888, this working arrangement was not satisfactory to the white-line element of the hill counties which was rapidly increasing its influence in the state. The first- and second-class arrangement, with a practical white monopoly of the first-class accommodations, did not sufficiently em-

[79] Jackson *Clarion,* April 14, 1871.
[80] Mississippi *Revised Code,* 1871, sections 2731-2732.
[81] J. S. McNeily, "War and Reconstruction in Mississippi," *P.M.H.S.C.S.,* II, 414-415.
[82] Hinds County *Gazette,* January 25, 1871.
[83] J. S. McNeily, "War and Reconstruction in Mississippi," *P.M.H.S.C.S.,* II, 431.
[84] Mississippi *Session Laws,* 1873, pp. 66-69.
[85] Hinds County *Gazette,* March 19, May 7, 1873; Vicksburg *Herald,* May 8, 1873.
[86] Vicksburg *Times and Republican,* May 7, 1873; Gilbert Stephenson, *Race Distinctions in American Law,* p. 134.
[87] Hinds County *Gazette,* February 11, 1874.
[88] *Ibid.,* July 15, 1874.

phasize racial differences. The result was the passage of "an act to pro-
mote the comfort of passengers on railroad trains." This ordered all
railroads carrying passengers in the state to provide "equal but separate
accommodations" for the races.[89] A few days later, a supplementary act
made this regulation applicable to sleeping car companies "so far as prac-
ticable," and authorized the railroad commissioners to designate and provide, if deemed proper, separate waiting rooms for the sexes and the
races.[90]

Since it was the determination of a large mass of the white population
to apply a code of racial distinctions to all possible situations and places
in which the races might be thrown together, it is apparent that the matter
was not entirely a problem of law. The development of a ritual to be
followed by whites and blacks under varying conditions was a slow and
tedious process. In the early part of the period, most of the saloons served
whites and Negroes at the same bar. Many of the restaurants, using
separate tables, served both races in the same room. By 1890, such cases
were practically unknown. On May 21, 1879, the Negroes of Jackson,
after a parade of their fire company, gave a picnic in Hamilton Park. On
the night of May 29, "the ladies of the Episcopal Church" used Hamilton
Park for a *fete*.[91] After their picnic, the Negroes went to Angelo's Hall
for a dance. This same hall was used for white dances and parties, and
was frequently the gathering place of Democratic conventions. By 1890,
both the park and the hall were closed to the Negroes. Throughout the
state common cemeteries, usually in separate portions, held the graves of
both whites and Negroes. In 1890, the city of Jackson, in line with a
policy which was being adopted all over the state, established a new cemetery, and ruled that on and after January 1, 1891, all interments of
Negroes should take place in it.[92]

Sidewalks, depot platforms, and promenades offered a more difficult
problem. The code held that the Negro on a sidewalk must always give
way to the white man, especially if the white was accompanied by a
woman. "Jostling" sometimes led to beatings, shootings, or lynchings.[93]
Negroes were warned to keep their distance and mind their language in
public gathering places, or the citizens would "make a striking example
of somebody."[94] Negroes at Natchez received instructions that of the
promenades along the river, the bluff to the right of Main Street was "for
the use of the whites, for ladies and children and nurses,—the central Bluff
between Main street and State for bachelors and the colored population,

[89] Mississippi *Session Laws*, 1888, p. 48.
[90] *Ibid.*, 1888, pp. 45-48.
[91] Jackson *Weekly Clarion*, May 21, June 4, 1879.
[92] Jackson *Clarion-Ledger*, January 1, 1891.
[93] Vicksburg *Herald*, April 9, 1873; Hinds County *Gazette*, August 18, 1888;
Senate Miscellaneous Documents, no. 166, 50th Congress, 1st session, pp. 88, 99, 170.
[94] Hinds County *Gazette*, August 18, 1888.

and the lower promenade for the whites." There was no law on the subject, but the people would see to it that the warning was heeded.[95] The question as to what streets were to be used by white and Negro children in their play also demanded attention.[96]

The Negro must also learn to be careful in his expression of an opinion, and to avoid unfavorable criticism of white people or white enterprises. In 1886, the Tougaloo *Quarterly* carried an article entitled "Life Incidents of One of Our Boys." Some of these incidents were not flattering to the white people from whose state treasury came money for the school. The president escaped censure by promising careful examination of all future material.[97] A "little popinjay didapper of a half coon who [had] learned to spell 'baker' at the expense of the tax-payers" wrote to a Negro paper in New Orleans letters which contained "several mischievous lies on the good people of Woodville and Wilkinson County." The editor of the *Clarion-Ledger* demanded that he be identified, strapped across a log, soundly whipped, and made to leave the county.[98]

Newspapers had their own peculiar problems. The Natchez *Courier* took Negro advertising;[99] the *Clarion* refused to handle it without a distinguishing label.[100] Some newspapers of the state carried formal notices of Negro weddings, but the editor of the Hinds County *Gazette* would have none of them.[101] The name used for the race varied with circumstances, usually it was "the negroes," or "our laboring population." When a fusion ticket against Greenbackers or Populists was to be promoted, the terms were "the colored population," or "our colored citizens"; in times of bad feelings the expressions "niggers," "coons," 'kullud pussons," and "blacks" were used. In normal times throughout a large part of the period, Negroes of prominence were given the title "Hon." or "Mr." by most of the papers of the state. By 1890, however, this usage had almost entirely disappeared.

Thus, within twenty-five years after the end of the war, a new code had come to replace the slave code of 1857. Few of its provisions could be found in the statute books. Its application was at times capricious and unpredictable. But, in general, members of both races understood and observed its content. In almost any conceivable contact with a white man, there were certain forms of behavior which the black man must observe. The Negro, at last, was "in his place."

[95] Natchez *Daily Courier,* May 29, 1866.
[96] Hinds County *Gazette,* March 8, 1871; Mississippi *Weekly Pilot,* March 23, 1871.
[97] Jackson *Weekly Clarion,* June 16, 1886.
[98] Jackson *Clarion-Ledger,* October 17, 1889.
[99] Natchez *Daily Courier,* May 31, 1866.
[100] Meridian *Clarion,* November 18, 1865.
[101] Hinds County *Gazette,* March 9, 1866.

CHAPTER XVI

CRIME AND THE CONVICT LEASE

THE NEGRO CRIMINAL

The coming of freedom to more than four hundred thousand slaves placed a great strain upon Mississippi's inadequate system of law enforcement. There was little in the Negro's background or surroundings to give him any respect for, or conception of, law in the abstract. Rules of conduct had varied widely from plantation to plantation. On some of them the slaves had enjoyed a great deal of license; on others, infractions of the rules seldom brought more than the loss of a few privileges, or an occasional whipping. Owning not even his clothing or the bed in which he slept, the slave had almost no conception of the sacredness of property rights; petty thievery, especially of food supplies, was often his only source of minor luxuries. No pride of position, or of family name, existed to restrain him. Generally, he had known no incentive for thrift, or for material or social advancement. Even as a freedman, public opinion meant little to him. The controlling thought of the community held him always to be a "nigger," and as such incapable of any virtue. If he lost his "name" in any given locality, he easily moved on to another. Arriving in the midst of a picking or contracting season, he knew that few questions would be asked about his past. This did not mean that the great mass of the Negroes were entirely without self-respect, or were habitual lawbreakers. But it did mean that large numbers of them were.

The immediate burden of maintaining discipline among the freedmen fell upon the officials of the counties and the towns. The destination of a large mass of the rural Negro population each Saturday afternoon was the nearest town or village. Having arrived there, many of them sought diversion with more enthusiasm than wisdom. Public drunkenness, disorderly conduct, fighting, or the use of profane language led the way to the mayor's court, and from there to the city jail. Reports from towns where the numbers of the Negroes and the whites were about equal show that a very large percentage of those dealt with by the local officials were of the former race. In the jail at Natchez in August, 1866, there were two white women, nine white men, and sixty-seven Negroes.[1] Fifty-three freedmen made up the total population of the jail at Columbus in Novem-

[1] Natchez *Daily Courier*, August 21, 1866.

ber of 1874,[2] and there were seventeen freedmen in the group of eighteen held in Grenada in June of the following year.[3] The register of the jail at Vicksburg from March 1, 1886, to February 28, 1887, held the names of 426 Negroes and only twenty whites. During the same period, Negroes made up 992 of the 1,416 who served time in the municipal workhouse.[4] Some reservations must be made before a conclusion can be drawn from such figures. A great many more rural Negroes than rural whites came into these black-belt towns and became subject to local authorities. Then too, it seems probable that the Negro was more likely to be arrested for minor offenses than was the white man. After such arrests, only small numbers of the freedmen were able to avoid a jail sentence by paying a fine. Even after such allowances are made, it remains apparent that the disorderly Negro presented a real problem.

The general method of handling prisoners in the various jails was to place them in the municipal chain gang for work on the streets. Even the Negro women were often included in such groups.[5] In the black-belt towns these chain gangs quickly assumed a racial character. The feeling that no white man should be included in them caused mayors to remit fines or white citizens to collect funds for their payment.[6]

For crimes more serious than the mere breach of a local ordinance, and yet not great enough to carry a sentence of more than a year, the law-breaker was sent to the county jail. A great majority of the Negroes so sentenced were convicted of petit larceny.[7] The fact that few of the counties were equipped to handle the heavy increase in the number of prisoners caused some agitation throughout the state for the substitution of the whipping post as the punishment for minor offenses.[8] As one of its concessions to the demands of the tax-payers in 1875, the last Republican legislature finally passed a law to allow the leasing of county convicts to responsible persons who would promise to maintain them.[9] The first Democratic legislature, in 1876, broadened the law to allow boards of supervisors to work the convicts or to lease them in any manner they saw fit, and at the same time extended these rights to the officials of cities and towns.[10] In 1892, new laws were adopted to apply to those counties which did not make agreements with a contractor to take all of their convicts. Under this legislation, the employer or landlord of a convict received pref-

[2] Hinds County *Gazette*, November 11, 1874.
[3] *Ibid.*, April 14, 1875.
[4] H. S. Fulkerson, *The Negro*, p. 50.
[5] Vicksburg *Times and Republican*, March 3, 1868.
[6] Vicksburg *Herald*, September 28, 1877.
[7] Natchez *Tri-Weekly Democrat*, February 27, 1866.
[8] Natchez *Daily Courier*, September 14, 1866, quoting the Hernando *Press*; Mississippi *Weekly Pilot*, January 2, 1875, quoting the Meridian *Mercury*; Jackson *Weekly Clarion*, January 23, 1878.
[9] Mississippi *Session Laws*, regular session, 1875, p. 96.
[10] *Ibid.*, 1876, pp. 201-203.

erence in hiring him from the sheriff. The consent of the prisoner was not necessary. Convicts who were not removed in this fashion or leased by their own consent before the first Saturday after the conviction were to be hired out by the sheriff at public outcry.[11] This system was followed in the various counties for a number of years after the method had been abolished in relation to prisoners of the state.

Most counties followed the system of leasing all of the prisoners to an individual contractor, who generally had the privilege of sub-leasing them. It appears probable that the treatment of the convicts by the various county lessees was, on the average, even worse than that received by state prisoners.[12] The report of a grand jury after an investigation of one of the better county camps is informative. This camp, in Hinds County, just outside the capital city of the state, was never the subject of any formal complaint:

We examined the cells in which unruly prisoners are kept. They measure 5 x 8 feet, are sufficiently high pitched for a prisoner to stand erect, and are well ventilated. We also examined the rope, and leather thongs attached, that are used for inflicting punishment by tying up by the thumbs. The leathers are remarkably soft and pliant, so that the only pain inflicted by their application is from the attitude the prisoner is forced to maintain.[13]

It appears that all, or practically all, the Negroes legally executed during the period were convicted of murder of other Negroes. Since an execution was a public affair, and that of a white man was practically unknown in the state, these Negro hangings attracted wide attention. Excursion trains brought crowds from distant points.[14] Negroes, who gathered by the thousands, were even more interested in these affairs than were whites.[15] Those in Bolivar County, according to F. A. Montgomery, once set out to attend a hanging in organized societies, with music and banners. Blanche Bruce, who was the sheriff at the time, persuaded them to disband before coming into the town.

All in all, the source of the great majority of the Negro's trouble with the law from 1865 to 1890 was his penchant for petty thievery. Food from the master's pantry, orchard, or barnyard had been considered fair prey by the slave who could get away with it, and this attitude had been encouraged by the laxity of many planters and overseers. The clever thief who added luxurious morsels to the diet of his family and friends often held the admiration and respect of his fellows. With the coming of freedom sheer poverty and hunger gave an added incentive for such forays. The

[11] *Ibid.*, 1892, pp. 287-299.
[12] J. H. Jones, "Penitentiary Reform in Mississippi," *P.M.H.S.*, VI, 122.
[13] Raymond *Gazette*, July 28, 1888.
[14] Hinds County *Gazette*, September 29, 1880.
[15] *Ibid.*, July 5, 1876, October 24, November 21, 1877; Mississippi *Weekly Pilot*, August 7, 1875; Jackson *Weekly Clarion*, March 3, 1881.

Negro found himself surrounded by temptation. Effective fences were rare, and hogs, sheep, turkeys, and cattle wandered untended in the uncultivated stretches of almost every plantation. The theft of such livestock, frequent enough in ordinary times, increased to alarming proportions in years of poor crops. After the disastrous failure of 1867, General Gillem, the Federal commander who sternly refused to issue any rations to the destitute, white or black, reported with dry formality:

. . . On gathering the crop it has in a majority of cases been ascertained that the share of the laborer does not pay his indebtedness for supplies advanced, and instead of receiving a dividend he is in debt. . . .

The crop . . . having been gathered, the freedmen are now idle, and without, in a great majority of instances, means of support. The result is great complaints from every section of the state of depredations being committed on live stock, hogs, sheep and cattle. This is now the condition of affairs in the state of Mississippi.[16]

General Gillem's only contribution to the situation was an order prohibiting the purchase or delivery of country supplies after sunset. In the meantime, the legislature had established heavy penalties for the trapping of hogs or the milking of wandering cows.[17]

To the owners of livestock, matters became more and more exasperating as the years went by. The editor of the Hinds County *Gazette* offered enthusiastic approval of the whipping of thieves or suspects by vigilantes,[18] and his colleague of the Fayette *Chronicle* adopted the slogan, "Stripes for chicken thieves. Halters for horse thieves."[19] The editor of the Forest *Register* was even more indignant: "Our advice to hog-raisers is, if a man is found under very suspicious circumstances in the woods, drop him, and let the buzzards hold an inquest over his remains."[20]

The result of such agitation was the passage by the first Democratic legislature of a bill which declared the theft of any property valued at more than ten dollars, or of any kind of cattle or swine, regardless of value, to be grand larceny, subjecting the thief to a term up to five years in the state penitentiary.[21] This was the famous "pig law," which was largely responsible for an increase in the population of the state prison from 272 in 1874 to 1,072 at the end of 1877.[22] It was this law that made of the convict lease system a big business enterprise, and it was its repeal in 1887 that reduced the number of convicts from 966 to 484 in fourteen

[16] J. S. McNeily, "From Organization to Overthrow of Mississippi's Provisional Government," *P.M.H.S.C.S.*, I, 342-343.

[17] Mississippi *Session Laws*, regular session, 1865, pp. 209, 236.

[18] Hinds County *Gazette*, February 9, 1876, July 4, 1877.

[19] *Ibid.*, September 5, 1877, quoting the Fayette *Chronicle*.

[20] Forest *Register*, September 15, 1875.

[21] Hinds County *Gazette*, February 9, 1876; Mississippi *Code*, 1880, section 2901.

[22] Hinds County *Gazette*, March 18, 1874; Mississippi *Annual Reports*, 1877, p. 115.

238 THE JAMES SPRUNT STUDIES

months and prepared the way for the abolition of that system.[23] While it lasted, the "pig law" made enormously profitable an institution which, in the words of an official who studied it, "left its trail of dishonor and death which could only find a parallel in some of the persecutions of the Middle Ages."[24]

THE CONVICT LEASE

Early in 1866, Governor Humphreys announced that the state penitentiary, which had been partly destroyed during the war, was once more in condition for the reception of convicts.[25] As a matter of fact, however, proper accommodations for any considerable number of prisoners were never available at any time during the period. There were immediate demands that the legislature find some way to relieve the state of the support of the convicts, who would now be numbered "by thousands rather than hundreds."[26] These demands were quickly met by acts which empowered the Governor to lease the prison and its occupants for a term of years, and which allowed the contractor to use the convicts, under certain conditions, outside the walls of the prison.[27]

It appears that the lease made under these provisions was never put into effect. Instead, General Gillem, commanding the Fourth Military District, made a remarkable contract with Edmund Richardson, planter, capitalist, and speculator, under which Richardson received almost absolute control over the prisoners of the state until November, 1871. Richardson not only gained the labor of the convicts without cost, but also received from the state $18,000 yearly for their maintenance and almost $12,000 for their transportation.[28] There is little wonder that he came to be known as the greatest cotton planter in the world, with a crop that in one year reached the amazing total of 11,500 bales.[29]

With the institution of the Republican government in 1870, Governor Alcorn launched an immediate attack on the system, and demanded that facilities be provided for employing the convicts inside the prison.[30] Nothing was accomplished until early in 1872, when the legislature passed an act for the establishment of an elaborate system of prison farms, to be completed by April, 1876, and to be operated by the state. Pending the completion of these arrangements, a new contract might be made for the lease of the convicts, with the provision that those outside the walls could

[23] Jackson *Clarion-Ledger*, February 28, 1889.
[24] J. H. Jones, *op. cit.*, VI, 112.
[25] Jackson *Clarion*, February 2, 1866.
[26] Hinds County *Gazette*, August 24, 1866.
[27] Mississippi *Session Laws*, 1866-1867, pp. 212-213, 736.
[28] Natchez *Daily Courier*, November 21, 1866, quoting the Hinds County *Gazette* of November 10, 1866; Mississippi *House Journal*, 1870, *Appendix*, p. 58; 1873, p. 556; Mississippi *Senate Journal*, 1872, *Appendix*, p. 8.
[29] Jackson *Weekly Clarion*, April 7, 1881, quoting the Atlanta *Constitution*.
[30] Mississippi *House Journal*, 1870, *Appendix*, p. 58.

be used only on public works.[31]   As a result, most of the convicts were still held by contractors when the last Republican legislature in 1875, as a part of its surrender to the tax-payers, gave up the idea of completing the new system, authorized the extension of a new lease to 1880, and removed the limitation on the type of work to be performed outside the walls.[32]

With the assembly of the Democratic legislature in 1876, and the passage of the "pig law," the convict lease became a tremendous enterprise. Between 1871 and 1875, the total number of the convicts ranged from 200 to 250;[33] from 1876 to 1887, it ran from 800 to more than 1,000.[34] The master of these men from June, 1876, to January, 1887, was Jones S. Hamilton, an almost incredible character who dabbled in Republican and Democratic politics, speculated with race tracks, gas works, railroads, and real estate, and made and spent several fortunes with splendid recklessness. Hailed by many as the first citizen of the state, and cursed by others as its evil genius, he was a counterpart in miniature of his great contemporaries, the "robber barons" of the North and West.   After a gun battle in the streets of Jackson in 1887, he found himself charged with the murder of a leading Prohibitionist editor.   Not allowed to furnish bond, he emerged from the succeeding imprisonment and trial unconvicted, but wrecked in health and fortune.[35]

Hamilton and his minor associates seldom employed the convicts in their own enterprises. Instead, they sub-leased them to a varied group of planters, speculators, and railroad and levee contractors. Having completed these subsidiary leases, they appear to have lost all interest in their charges.   Out over the state, in great rolling cages or temporary stockades, on remote plantations or deep in the swamps of the Delta, the convicts were completely at the mercy of the sub-lessees and their guards. This isolation of the convict camps helps to explain the slow development of an audible protest against the abuses of the system.   Other factors were the absence of any effective opposition in politics, and the belief that the arrangement was enabling the state to maintain a low scale of taxation.

Even more effective in the preservation of the system, however, was the fact that it applied almost entirely to Negroes.   The reasons for this are apparent.   Of the few white men who went to the prison at all, a remarkably large percentage were convicted of very grave crimes with

[31] Mississippi *Session Laws,* 1872, pp. 67-86.
[32] *Ibid.,* regular session, 1875, pp. 107-108.
[33] Mississippi *House Journal,* 1873, *Appendix,* p. 113; 1873, p. 562; Hinds County *Gazette,* March 18, 1874.
[34] Superintendent of the Mississippi Penitentiary, *Report,* 1876, 1877, 1878-1879, 1880-1881, 1882-1883, 1884-1885, 1886-1887.
[35] Mississippi *Weekly Pilot,* February 2, 1875; Hinds County *Gazette,* January 30, 1878, September 15, 1883, May 7, 14, December 3, 1887; Jackson *Weekly Clarion,* August 2, 1882, quoting the Grenada *Sentinel.*

sentences of more than ten years. Under the law, they must remain within the walls. The contractors, generally opposed to the mixing of whites and blacks at common labor, had little use for the few white men who were available. Here and there a few of them might be found in the camps, serving usually at clerical tasks or as "straw bosses." In general, the lease system may be viewed as a method of working Negro convicts.

This is apparent from statistics throughout the period. In April, 1869, there were 364 convicts. Of these 235, all Negroes, were on the levees and plantations. Of the 129 retained within the prison, 105 were white.[36] In December, 1871, the total number of convicts was 234. Of these, Richardson left all of the fifty-six white men and twenty-two Negroes within the walls. All the rest of the Negroes, including six women, were on his plantations.[37] In 1872 only six white men were employed outside the prison, and in 1876 only twenty-three.[38] In the face of the racial antagonism which had been aroused in the early seventies there can be little wonder that as late as 1884, Governor Lowry was able to declare that there was no public sentiment to aid in the protection of the convicts against outrages.[39]

An idea of what was going on in the camps in the meantime can be gained from the table of death rates compiled by Frank Johnston for the use of the investigating committee of 1886:

WHITE CONVICT DEATH RATE

Year	Average Number of Convicts	Deaths	Death Rate %
1880	92	4	4.34
1881	92	5	5.43
1882	83	2	2.40
1883	83	5	6.02
1884	88	5	5.69
1885	88	7	7.95

Average white death rate for 6 years............5.30

NEGRO CONVICT DEATH RATE

Year	Average Number of Convicts	Deaths	Death Rate %
1880	843	52	6.17
1881	843	74	8.77
1882	735	126	17.14
1883	735	84	11.42
1884	698	87	12.49
1885	698	69	9.87

Average Negro death date for 6 years...........10.97[40]

[36] Vicksburg *Daily Times,* April 15, 1869.
[37] Mississippi *Senate Journal,* 1872, *Appendix,* p. 113.
[38] Mississippi *House Journal,* 1873, p. 562; Superintendent of the Mississippi Penitentiary, *Report,* 1876, p. 6.
[39] Mississippi *House Journal,* 1884, p. 30.
[40] J. H. Jones, *op. cit.,* VI, 128.

These figures become more significant when they are compared with the percentages of deaths in six prisons of the Middle West in 1884, 1885, and 1886. These ranged from 0.51 to 1.08 per cent.[41]

From time to time stories of the horrors of the camps were printed by local newspapers.[42] In 1884, an incident at Vicksburg attracted wider attention. Eighteen convicts, being returned to the prison as disabled, proved to be in such a terrible condition from punishment and frost-bite that they had to be smuggled through Vicksburg in a covered wagon. The matter was taken up by a newspaper in that town, and a member of the state legislature demanded an investigation. After causing some excitement, the resulting report was either lost or stolen. Public interest subsided, and the powerful lobby of the leasing system was able to prevent any further action.[43]

In 1887, there came another incident to arouse discussion. The grand jury of Hinds County, wandering off its usual beat, inspected the state prison. To many who had given the matter little attention its report came as a shock:

We found [in the hospital section] twenty-six inmates, all of whom have been lately brought there off the farms and railroads, many of them with consumption and other incurable diseases, and all bearing on their persons marks of the most inhuman and brutal treatment. Most of them have their backs cut in great wales, scars and blisters, some with the skin pealing [sic] off in pieces as the result of severe beatings.

Their feet and hands in some instances show signs of frost bite, and all of them with the stamp of manhood almost blotted out of their faces. . . . They are lying there dying, some of them on bare boards, so poor and emaciated that their bones almost come through their skin, many complaining for the want of food.

. . . We actually saw live vermin crawling over their faces, and the little bedding and clothing they have is in tatters and stiff with filth.

.   .   .   .

As a fair sample of this system, on Jan. 6, 1887, 204 convicts were leased to McDonald[44] up to June 6, 1887, and during this six months 20 died, and 19 were discharged and escaped and 23 were returned to the walls disabled and sick, many of whom have since died.[45]

During the same month, members of the state board of control descended on the camps of the Gulf & Ship Island Railroad in Harrison County. This railroad, which had been using a number of convicts since 1884, had taken over the entire leasing system on very favorable terms

[41] Ibid., VI, 127.
[42] Vicksburg Times and Republican, July 18, 1873; Hinds County Gazette, July 3, 1879; Jackson Weekly Clarion, May 23, 1883, quoting the Port Gibson Reveille.
[43] J. H. Jones, op. cit., VI, 114, 115.
[44] This same man was said to have kept as many as 196 prisoners in a room that measured thirty-five or forty by seventy-five feet. J. H. Jones, op. cit., VI, 126.
[45] Jackson Weekly Clarion, July 13, 1887.

early in 1887. General expectations that its control would bring more favorable conditions were dispelled by the report of the board, which found the railroad camps to be little better than those of the sub-lessees.[46] Widespread indignation and another embarrassing investigation in 1888 finally convinced the president of the railroad that the use of the convicts was not worth its cost in "unjust and harmful criticism."[47] As a result, the corporation canceled its lease and returned the convicts to the prison.

The state then began to lease the convicts, at eight dollars a month for Negroes and seven dollars for white men, to individual planters.[48] This method, followed until 1894, was generally regarded as much more humane than its predecessors. One report had it that the death rate, which had reached a new high of sixteen per cent in 1887 and eleven per cent in 1888, dropped to three per cent in 1889.[49] This improvement, however, was not enough to preserve the system. Public indignation aroused by the revelations of 1887 and 1888, the increasing power of the small-farmer element, and a spirited attack by the Prohibitionist forces[50] convinced the constitutional convention of 1890 that the entire arrangement must be abandoned.

As a result, the new constitution forbade the leasing of any convicts after December 31, 1894, and authorized the legislature to establish a prison farm. In addition, convicts might be used on levees, roads, and other public works under state supervision, but not under private contractors.[51] Thus passed the convict lease, described by J. H. Jones as "the product of human rapacity grafted upon conditions that a defunct slavery had left behind it."[52]

[46] Ibid., July 6, 1887.
[47] Jackson Clarion-Ledger, February 23, 1888.
[48] Appleton's Cyclopedia, 1893, p. 498.
[49] Ibid., 1889, p. 564.
[50] Mississippi White Ribboner, March 15, 1890.
[51] Mississippi Constitution of 1890, Article X, sections 223-226.
[52] J. H. Jones, op. cit., VI, 120.

CHAPTER XVII

EDUCATION

MISSIONARY SCHOOLS, 1865-1870

Negro education in the period between the end of the war and the establishment of the reconstructed government in 1870 continued to be almost entirely a system of missionary schools which collected tuition from the students and received some aid from the Freedmen's Bureau. Here and there the Negroes set up little schools at their own expense, generally under a Negro teacher.[1] Although an investigator reported, in 1867, that the number of children attending these volunteer schools was "quite large,"[2] no accurate information can be obtained. It is probable that most of them, served by incompetent teachers and inadequately financed, lasted only a short time.

Efforts by General Thomas J. Wood to interest the white citizens of the state in the establishment of schools for the freedmen with aid from the Bureau appear to have failed almost completely. Although the plan gained the verbal support of a number of native leaders,[3] no reference to its application can be found except in Wilkinson County.[4] In general, the early attitude of the masses of the white population was one of absolute opposition to the education of the freedmen, and of scorn for the idea that they might be expected to contribute to it.[5] This attitude gained expression in the persecution and ostracism of the "yankee schoolmarms."[6] Attacks on native whites who took up such work were, in some counties, more bitter than those on the missionaries.[7]

[1] M. G. Abney, "Reconstruction in Pontotoc County," *P.M.H.S.*, XI, 259; Whitelaw Reid, *After the War*, p. 511; Jackson *Weekly Clarion*, September 19, 1867.
[2] Ross H. Moore, "Social and Economic Conditions in Mississippi during Reconstruction," unpublished doctoral dissertation, Duke University, 1938, p. 208.
[3] Stuart G. Noble, *Forty Years of the Public Schools in Mississippi*, p. 6.
[4] J. S. McNeily, "From Organization to Overthrow of Mississippi's Provisional Government," *P.M.H.S.C.S.*, I, 237.
[5] *House Executive Documents*, no. 2, 39th Congress, 1st session, pp. 25, 82, 99; Whitelaw Reid, *op. cit.*, p. 424.
[6] Julia Kendel, "Reconstruction in Lafayette County," *P.M.H.S.*, XIII, 258; Julia C. Brown, "Reconstruction in Yalobusha and Grenada Counties," *P.M.H.S.*, XII, 264; E. F. Puckett, "Reconstruction in Monroe County," *P.M.H.S.*, XI, 138; Hattie Magee, "Reconstruction in Lawrence County," *P.M.H.S.*, XI, 196; M. G. Abney, *op. cit.*, XI, 258-259; S. G. Noble, *op. cit.*, p. 15; A. T. Morgan, *Yazoo*, pp. 112-113; Jackson *Daily Mississippi Standard*, May 1, 1866; Hinds County *Gazette*, July 13, 1866, September 15, 1869, March 15, May 26, 1871.
[7] M. G. Abney, *op. cit.*, XI, 258; J. Kendel, *op. cit.*, XIII, 258; H. Magee, *op. cit.*, XI, 174, 195-196; R. H. Moore, *op. cit.*, p. 229.

As it gradually became apparent that Negro education, in one form or another, was a permanent result of the war, many of the more conservative leaders of the state turned to the idea that the work should be undertaken by native white Mississippians. From press and pulpit came the call for action.[8] In practically every case, the reasoning was the same. Negro education was inevitable, and the Negro educated by the Yankee would be more dangerous than the Yankee himself. Furthermore, declared the editor of the *Standard,* "A Southern teacher would instill into the young, Southern ideas of the relative social relations, rights and duties of the races."[9] In spite of evident interest, which reached its peak late in 1866, the movement was almost completely without results. The Panola *Star* reported the establishment of "a little nigger school" under the control of a Confederate veteran; a similar institution set up in Yazoo City to gain Negro votes in 1868 lasted only through the election.[10] The idea seems to have been almost entirely abandoned by the end of the spring of 1867.[11]

In the meantime, neither the constitutional convention of 1865 nor the legislature gave the matter any attention beyond the statute of 1867, which required that apprentices be taught to read and write. As before the war, public education was left to the counties. Those which set up and maintained public schools seem to have opened none of their facilities to the Negroes. As a result, Negro education by January of 1870 had fallen below even the poor records of 1868 and 1869. In the entire state there were only seventy-two registered schools for Negroes. These employed ninety teachers, sixty-one of whom were white. The teachers, in poorly equipped cabins and churches, ministered to a total enrollment of 3,475 students, with an average attendance of 2,586.[12] Thus, after five years of freedom, the task of educating half a million freedmen was still practically untouched.

PUBLIC SCHOOLS, 1870-1875

Immediately after the Constitution of 1868 pledged the state to a complete system of public education, most of the attacks of the Democratic press centered upon the fact that there was no provision for the separation of the races.[13] When it became apparent that the controlling elements in the Republican party had no intention of setting up mixed schools, the attack shifted to other grounds. T. S. Gathright, who was to become the

[8] Hinds County *Gazette,* July 13, 1866; Jackson *Daily Mississippi Standard,* March 24, 1866; Jackson *Clarion,* February 9, 16, March 8, April 18, December 16, 1868; Friar's Point *Coahomian,* April 20, May 4, 1866; Edward Mayes, *History of Education in Mississippi,* p. 282.

[9] Jackson *Daily Mississippi Standard,* March 24, 1866.

[10] *Ibid.,* April 8, 1866, quoting the Panola *Star;* A. T. Morgan, *op. cit.,* pp. 219-220.

[11] S. G. Noble, *op. cit.,* p. 9.

[12] *Ibid.,* p. 24.

[13] Jackson *Daily Clarion,* February 21, April 8, 1868.

first Democratic superintendent of education in 1876, denounced the school law of 1870 as "an unmitigated outrage upon the rights and liberties of the white people of the State . . . enacted to demoralize our people and to proselyte our children in the interest of a political party hostile to the dignity, interests and sensibilities of the white people of Mississippi."[14] Charges were made that the teachers from the North were all radical emissaries in disguise, who not only insidiously inculcated the political creed of their party, but also acted as propagandists for its doctrine of social equality.[15] It was also reported that some of the superintendents were forcing the use of Yankee pronunciation.[16] All of this criticism, however, was subordinated to the cry that the new system involved an enormous expenditure, that the greater part of this was for the benefit of the Negroes, and that all of it came from the pockets of the whites.[17]

Among such men as Gathright and the editors of the *Clarion* and the *Gazette,* much of this attack was built on a desire to gain political advantage, and all of it was kept within the verbal sphere. With many men of humbler station, however, to think was to act. In the hill counties of the eastern and northern portions of the state, small farmers, aggrieved by poor crops and rising taxes, rode out at night to destroy the educational system so strongly denounced by their leaders. During the fall and winter of 1870 and the spring of 1871, the counties of Winston, Monroe, Choctaw, Lowndes, Pontotoc, Lee, Noxubee, and Chickasaw experienced a reign of terror. Teachers were tortured and murdered, or, at best, ordered to leave the county. No free school was safe from attack, but the violence centered on the schools of the Negroes. As yet, public funds had supplied very few buildings for the freedmen in these counties. This did not prevent the raiders from burning structures erected by the Negroes themselves, or churches which were being used as schools. By the summer of 1871, in a number of counties, not a school remained in operation.[18] Before the end of the year, however, there came a change which Superintendent H. R. Pease described as "a marvelous revolution in public sentiment."[19] Violence ceased almost entirely, and attacks in the press greatly decreased in volume and intensity. Reasons for this change are difficult to discover. The disappearance of violence was a part of the decline of the Klan and other marauding groups. The gradual decrease of verbal attacks probably resulted from the discovery that the system of public

---

[14] Hinds County *Gazette,* October 12, 1870.
[15] *Ibid.,* March 15, 1871.
[16] *Ibid.,* April 26, 1871.
[17] *Ibid.,* February 21, March 15, April 5, October 18, 1871; Mississippi *House Journal,* 1873, p. 723; R. H. Moore, *op. cit.,* p. 222.
[18] *Report on the Condition of Affairs in the Late Insurrectionary States,* pt. 1, pp. 73, 74, 75, 77; Mississippi *Senate Journal,* 1872, *Appendix,* pp. 182-183; Forrest Cooper, "Reconstruction in Scott County," *P.M.H.S.,* XIII, 129; J. C. Brown, *op. cit.,* XII, 239; R. H. Moore, *op. cit.,* p. 223.
[19] Mississippi *Senate Journal,* 1872, *Appendix,* p. 181.

education was gaining remarkable support from a growing majority of the white population. It soon came to be known that an unqualified attack on the system was bad politics. The feeling grew that even for the Negro, especially if he was to continue to be a voter, a certain amount of education was not a bad thing.

In the meantime, schools were being established, equipped, and supplied with teachers with remarkable rapidity. By the end of 1871, the first year of extensive operations, 230 schoolhouses had been constructed for Negroes, and 252 for whites.[20] The report of the superintendent shows that these new buildings housed only a small portion of the great number of schools that had been established:

	White Schools	Enrollment	Negro Schools	Enrollment
Primary schools	535	18,312	603	26,303
Grammar schools	400	14,432	51	2,641
High schools	78	5,045	4	640
Mixed grade schools	729	24,577	202	12,370[21]

In spite of great obstacles such as sparse population, scarcity of cities and towns, lack of trained teachers, and economic depression, steady progress was maintained throughout the period of Republican control. Of the 176,945 Negro educables, 89,813 were enrolled in the public schools by the end of 1875. They were served by 2,019 teachers, who received an average monthly salary of $53.45.[22]

The fact that even under Republican government they did not receive their proportionate share of teachers or of equipment did not discourage the almost pathetic faith of the masses of the Negroes in education. Both in the percentage of their enrollment, and in average daily attendance, if the report of the superintendent is correct, they exceeded the white population.[23] Their enthusiasm was further demonstrated by the heavy attendance at the public examinations and exhibitions with which their schools closed their sessions.[24] Finally, in the midst of the surrender of 1875, the Negroes in the state senate, to a man, voted against the reduction of the tax levied for the schools.[25] Education, with the ownership of land and the right to vote, was held in the mind of the Negro to be an integral part of the substance of freedom. It was to this faith in education that Negro leaders appealed when they urged those of their race to disregard the general terror and go to the polls in 1875. The loss of the ballot would mean

[20] S. G. Noble, op. cit., p. 34.
[21] Ibid., p. 39.
[22] Ibid., pp. 139, 141.
[23] Ibid., p. 139.
[24] Mississippi Weekly Pilot, August 5, 1870; Hinds County Gazette, July 10, 17, August 7, 1872, April 28, 1875, July 5, 1876; Vicksburg Times and Republican, April 1, 1873.
[25] Hinds County Gazette, May 5, 1875.

the loss of their schools, and would forever doom them to be hewers of wood and drawers of water.[26] At the time of their surrender in Yazoo County, the only concession the Negroes asked of the Democrats was the preservation of their schools.[27] It was therefore with great anxiety that the freedmen awaited the action of the Democratic legislature of 1876.

NEGRO EDUCATION UNDER DEMOCRATIC CONTROL, 1876-1890

In spite of the appearance of some demands that the entire free school system be abolished as a Yankee importation and a monstrous evil,[28] the more prominent Democratic leaders were convinced of the virtues of education for the Negroes and were determined to preserve as far as possible the pledges their party had made in the campaign of 1870.[29] It was their contention, however, that great economy could be achieved without affecting in any way the efficiency of the system. Some even went so far as to declare that the Democrats would give the Negroes better schools and longer terms for less money.[30] They proceeded to write their theories into law in 1876, and to put them to the test in the years immediately following.

The legislature made no effort to change the fundamental principles of the educational system. Their attack on expenditures, however, was immediate and drastic. Salaries of county superintendents were reduced to twenty per cent of the schedule of 1874, and those of teachers to a maximum of forty dollars a month. There was a specific provision that no school funds of the state or the counties were to be used for any other purpose than the payment of the salaries of teachers and superintendents. The absence of extensive or reliable information makes an analysis of the effects of this legislation almost impossible. The conclusion of the writer who has given the education of the period most careful study is as follows :

The school laws, passed by the legislature of 1876, had in view the curtailment of expenses. They certainly did not have in view the wrecking of the public school system and the abandonment of Negro education. Yet, as a result of these laws, the efficiency of the system was greatly reduced.[31]

In this period of deflation, the Negro schools seem to have suffered more heavily than those of the whites. Such statistics as are available indicate a large decline in the number of their teachers, and in enrollment and average daily attendance.[32] This is at first difficult to understand, in view of

[26] Mississippi *Weekly Pilot,* October 2, 1875; Hinds County *Gazette,* January 5, 1876.
[27] *Senate Miscellaneous Documents,* no. 45, 44th Congress, 2d session, p. 211.
[28] Mississippi *Weekly Pilot,* November 13, 1875, quoting the Meridian *Mercury.*
[29] Hinds County *Gazette,* January 5, October 18, 1876; Governor J. M. Stone, *Message,* 1877, p. 11; S. G. Noble, *op. cit.,* p. 49.
[30] Hinds County *Gazette,* January 5, 1876, quoting the Holly Springs *Reporter.*
[31] S. G. Noble, *op. cit.,* p. 49.
[32] *Ibid.,* pp. 51, 139, 141.

the fact that under the law every school in each county had an equal claim upon the funds so long as they lasted. The explanation appears to lie in the fact that the determination of the number and the location of the various schools lay entirely in the hands of the county boards and superintendents. It seems that in the move for economy within the counties more Negro than white schools were closed.[33] In some of the counties all schools, white and black, were ordered closed until the local debts had been paid.[34]

In 1879, the number of teachers in the Negro schools once more reached that of 1875, and there began an increase in enrollment and attendance that generally paralleled that of the whites until 1890. This does not mean, however, that the development could be regarded as satisfactory. In the face of increasing demands upon the teachers and the schools, property values and the resultant revenues continued to decline. This situation, combined with a determination not to increase taxes, was reflected in the reduction of the salaries of teachers, white and black, from an average of more than fifty-five dollars a month in 1875, and thirty dollars in 1880, to twenty-eight dollars and seventy-four cents in 1885.[35] Reports on the physical equipment of the schools reveal a poverty that must have been disheartening to teachers and pupils alike.

It is impossible to learn how the equipment of Negro schools compared with that of the whites. Under the law, no state or county funds could be used for buildings and supplies. In the face of this local responsibility, it is safe to assume that a majority of the Negro schools were located in the log huts and churches that in 1887 supplied more than two-thirds of the buildings used for education in a number of the counties.[36]

It is also impossible to gain any information on the comparative salaries of white and Negro teachers between 1877 and 1886. Under the laws of 1878, teachers were to be ranked by the superintendents as first, second, or third grade, and their salaries were to be adjusted accordingly. Some of the superintendents took advantage of this arrangement to rank all of their white teachers as first-grade, and gave them the maximum of forty dollars a month.[37] It is probable that even an equitable application of the system would have placed most of the Negro teachers in the lower classification, although, in contrast with the whites, the best trained and most ambitious members of their race sought positions in the schools. At any rate, when the reports of the superintendent began to offer separate statistics for the two groups in 1886, it was shown that the average salary for Negro teachers was $27.40 a month, as compared with $31.37 for

[33] Hinds County *Gazette,* August 9, September 20, 1876, June 12, 1878.
[34] *Senate Reports,* no. 527, 44th Congress, 1st session, pp. 1623, 1638.
[35] S. G. Noble, *op. cit.,* p. 141.
[36] *Ibid.,* p. 65.
[37] Hinds County *Gazette,* September 14, 1881.

whites. This disparity continued to increase until the averages, respectively, were $23.20 and $33.37 in 1890, and $21.53 and $33.04 in 1895.[38]

Strangely enough, this relative retrogression of the Negro schools, which became more apparent after 1890, was largely the result of a great increase of interest and faith in education on the part of the mass of the whites. This belief that through education all things were possible greatly resembled that of the Negroes of the early seventies. Under its influence, the lower classes of the white population demanded more and more facilities for their children. They recognized, however, their own poverty and that of the state as a whole. The conviction therefore became stronger and stronger that the additional revenue must come not through an increase in taxation, but through a reduction of the educational opportunities offered to the Negroes. Demands for such action, based on the argument that Negroes paid almost no taxes for the support of the schools, came from all over the state.[39] With the legislative reapportionment under the Constitution of 1890, the white population of the counties in which this attitude had strongest support gained control of the government of the state.

By 1890, then, public education for the Negroes reached a peak from which it declined slowly but steadily for many years. The situation in that year is disclosed by the following table:

	White	Negro
Educable children	191,792	272,682
Enrollment	150,868	183,290
Average daily attendance	96,077	111,627
Number of teachers	4,269	3,097
Average monthly salary	$33.37	$23.20[40]

Of those in school, about 46,000 Negroes and the same number of whites received not more than three months of training each year. There were still 313,572 Negroes over ten years of age who were unable to write, as compared with 45,755 whites in the same category.[41] In the gradual improvement in educational facilities gained by the whites after 1900, the Negroes were not to share. It was the general feeling of the dominant race that, unable to care properly for their own children, they could not be expected to provide from their scanty funds more than a smattering of education for the blacks. For the Negro "in his place" that was enough.

[38] S. G. Noble, op. cit., p. 141.
[39] Hinds County Gazette, December 14, 1881, November 1, 1882, October 11, 1884, May 20, 1889; Jackson Weekly Clarion, September 20, 1882; ibid., February 27, 1882, quoting the Madison Democrat and the Brandon Republican; Jackson Clarion-Ledger, July 4, 1889; Mississippi Superintendent of Education, Biennial Report, 1882-1883, pp. 41, 42; 1884-1885, pp. 51, 62, 64, 81.
[40] S. G. Noble, op. cit., pp. 139, 141. The figure given for the number of educables of each race is for 1889.
[41] U. S. Census, 1890, Vol. II, part ii, pp. 139, 198, 201.

PRIVATE SCHOOLS AND HIGHER EDUCATION

In addition to the public schools, the Negroes had access during the period to a number of private establishments which, as a rule, were under the auspices of some religious organization. Although these schools generally bore the title of institute, college, or university, their curricula were elementary, and in faculty and equipment they seldom ranked far above the better public grammar schools. Depending largely on the fluctuating interest and resources of Northern missionary groups, they were generally in serious financial difficulties, and often collapsed after a few months, or at most a few years, of operation.

Among the more important schools of this type was Shaw University at Holly Springs. Established in 1866 by the Mississippi Conference of the Methodist Episcopal Church, its story throughout the period was one of a devoted faculty and a poverty-stricken student body struggling valiantly to maintain existence. This struggle was complicated for a time by an effort to conduct a commercial institute and a medical school on the campus at Holly Springs, and by the division of available funds with Haven Academy, a "preparatory school" which was established at Meridian in 1868. Although it was overrun with students who were able to contribute little or nothing to its upkeep, and who seldom managed to complete the elementary "classical" course, this institution managed to survive, and gradually to improve its condition. Its name was changed to Rust University in 1890.[42]

Similar efforts on the part of the Negro Baptist Associations of the state, in coöperation with the American Baptist Home Mission Society, involved Natchez Seminary for Freedmen, Natchez College, Jackson College, and several short-lived theological institutes. The Seminary for Freedmen, established at Natchez in 1877, was removed to Jackson in 1883, and reëstablished as Jackson College.[43] Its maintenance was made especially difficult by the independent attitude of the various conventions and associations of the state, and by the desire of each to have its own educational institution. The most important of these semi-independent enterprises was Natchez College, "the Pride of the Race," established at Natchez by the Missionary Baptist Convention in 1885. The story of the efforts of the convention to support this institution was one of heartbreaking sacrifice and continuous misfortune until 1897.[44] In that year the Baptist Home Mission Society was finally able to exert enough pressure to secure the coöperation of the various associations in establishing

[42] Ruth Watkins, "Reconstruction in Marshall County," *P.M.H.S.*, XII, 199-200; Goodspeed Publishing Company, *Biographical and Historical Memoirs of Mississippi*, II, 339; Ulin W. Leavell, *Philanthropy in Negro Education*, p. 41.

[43] Patrick H. Thompson, *Negro Baptists in Mississippi*, pp. 146-148, 400-401, 403.

[44] *Ibid.*, pp. 78, 86, 87, 123, 148, 158, 207, 214, 223, 224, 227, 234, 236, 242, 255, 279.

a board of education which would concentrate its efforts on Jackson College.[45]

Southern Christian Institute, at Edwards, was incorporated by the Christian Church in 1875, as a co-educational institution to give industrial, normal, and ministerial training. After its establishment in 1882, its story was the usual one of a rush of poorly trained, poverty-stricken students that soon carried its enrollment to more than three hundred. The lack of adequate finances caused the abolition of its free-school section in 1887, and resulted in a heavy loss in the number of students. This realistic handling of the sitution, and the possession of eight hundred acres of cotton land, allowed it to survive and gradually to improve its facilities.[46]

Campbell College, established in 1887 with branches at Vicksburg and Friar's Point, was unique in that, as an enterprise of the African Methodist Episcopal Church, it had no connection with any white organization. The two branches of the school maintained a precarious existence until 1898, when they were united in the city of Jackson.[47]

Mount Hermon Female Seminary at Clinton was perhaps the most successful of a number of small institutions established through the efforts of individual enthusiasts. Sarah Dickey, a teacher in the Negro public school at Clinton, conceived in 1873 the idea of establishing for Negro girls of the state a school similar to Mount Holyoke, of which she was a graduate. By soliciting funds from friends in the North and from Negroes in Mississippi, and by giving picnics, suppers, and musical entertainments, Miss Dickey succeeded in raising the necessary funds for establishing her school in 1874. By 1885, she had raised and invested $15,000, and was maintaining the institution in a manner that brought favorable comment from visitors.[48] Running from day to day and month to month without any assured source of income, Mount Hermon managed finally to survive the financial difficulties that wrecked a number of similar enterprises.

None of the schools heretofore mentioned really merited their classification as institutions of higher learning. In fact, throughout the period, there were only three which had any just claims to that distinction. Two of these, the Holly Springs State Normal and Alcorn University, were supported entirely by the state. The third, Tougaloo University, received some aid from public funds until 1891. This assured and continuous revenue, small though it was, gave to these schools a stability which made for progress.

The Normal School at Holly Springs grew out of the assumption of control by the state, in 1870, of the normal department of Shaw University. In return for this control, and for the services rendered, the legis-

[45] *Ibid.*, pp. 346-357.
[46] Goodspeed Publishing Company, *op. cit.*, II, 341, 369.
[47] Revels A. Adams, *Cyclopedia of African Methodism in Mississippi*, p. 42.
[48] Hinds County *Gazette*, April 15, 1874, May 5, 12, 1875; Horace S. Fulkerson, *Rambling Recollections*, p. 135.

lature appropriated to the school $4,000 in 1870 and $5,000 in each of the two following years. In 1873, the school severed its connections with Shaw, and with a special appropriation of $10,000 secured for its use a large brick building and a five-acre campus. By the following year the Normal was in full operation with a creditable supply of books, maps, and scientific apparatus, and an active faculty which stressed literary societies, debating clubs, and musical activities in addition to the regular curriculum. With an annual appropriation of $4,500, a constantly increasing enrollment, and positions open in the public schools for students who had completed as much as one year of the four-year course, a promising and useful future seemed to be assured.[49]

From the beginning, the Normal was run with extreme economy. The annual appropriation of less than five thousand dollars covered the salaries of the teachers, all operating expenses, and student aid, which consisted of an allowance of fifty cents per week to each student who declared his or her intention to teach in a public school. The students paid no tuition, rented their books from the state, and paid board which ranged in cost from $7.50 to $9.00 per month. Beginning with fifty students in 1870, the school had 134 in 1875.[50]

A serious reduction of revenues came with the return of Democratic control. The annual appropriation, reduced to $3,000 in 1877, remained at that level until 1890, when it was lowered to $2,500. Some of the difficulties faced by the Normal are revealed by the report of its principal in 1885, in which year the school had 265 students:

Our annual appropriation is $3,000. This sum is entirely too small to meet our wants. Our school house, which was formerly a *private residence,* has been repaired, and altered from time to time to meet the demands of our growing school. Thus taking all of our surplus funds, and often the salary money to pay for it. The building is now too small and sadly in need of repairs. The outside of the building has not been painted in seventeen years, and is therefore in very bad condition. Our present appropriation has been exhausted some time since on account of taking the salary money for building and repairing purposes. We use the strictest economy in the expenditure of our money, and for that reason it holds out as long as it does. Much of the repairing around the building is done by scholars, thus saving the cost of a carpenter and other mechanics.[51]

This melancholy statement of conditions had no effect upon a legislature in which distaste for the costs of Negro education was a constantly growing force. In the very next year, that body ordered the reorganization of the Normal, reduced its course of study from four years to two, and placed it under the control of a board composed of the state superintendent of education and the superintendent of schools of Marshall County.[52] By 1888 this board had cut expenditures so heavily that the

[49] E. Mayes, *op. cit.,* pp. 266-269; R. Watkins, *op. cit.,* XII, 200.
[50] E. Mayes, *op. cit.,* pp. 268, 270.
[51] Mississippi Superintendent of Education, *Biennial Report,* 1884-1885, p. 93.
[52] Mississippi *Session Laws,* 1886, p. 8.

Governor was able to report that of the appropriation of $3,000, only $2,145 had been used. In 1890, at which time the Normal had 162 students, the formal appropriation was reduced to $2,500. In 1904, with the triumph of James K. Vardaman on an anti-Negro platform, the appropriation was dropped entirely, and the school was closed.

Alcorn University, provided for by the legislature of 1870, was planned as a counterpart of the white university at Oxford. The old plant of Oakland College, in Claiborne County, with good brick buildings and 235 acres of land, was purchased at a cost of $42,500. In February, 1872, with 117 students, Hiram Revels as president, and the assurance of an income of about $55,000 a year from the state, the school began its operations. The large revenue, equal to that of the white university, allowed the awarding of many scholarships in addition to those granted by the legislature, and enabled the institution to supply free food to large numbers of students who had no money. With the addition of an agricultural department in 1872, and a large increase in the enrollment, it appeared that the dream of an outstanding Negro university was approaching fulfillment.[53]

As a matter of fact, however, such a school could not be wished into being, and the bountiful appropriation probably served to add to the confusion. Few of the students had the proper background for advanced work, and disagreement among faculty, president, and trustees prevented the working out of any intelligent program. Although Revels was a man of ability and honor, it is apparent that he was no administrator. In 1875, conditions were such that an investigation was demanded. After the report of its committee, the economizing Republican legislature of 1875 removed Revels, ordered the reorganization of the school and its trustees, abolished all scholarships and the dining hall, and reduced the appropriation to $15,000.[54]

The school was still in a disorganized and unsatisfactory condition when the Democratic legislature took control in 1876. The appropriation was still further reduced to a level of about $5,500 a year, which, with a similar amount from the land-script fund, gave a total annual income of about $11,000. Governor Stone immediately restored Revels, a favorite of the white leaders of the state, to the presidency. Under his administration, the college remained quiet and almost unnoticed, with a student body of about 125, until 1883.[55] Under his successor, John H. Burrus, girls were admitted in 1884. The enrollment grew steadily until 1890, when the school had seven teachers and 245 students.[56]

Throughout the period from 1876 to 1890, certain factors at Alcorn

[53] E. Mayes, op. cit., pp. 270-272, 277; Hinds County Gazette, June 7, 1871, March 10, 1875.
[54] Mississippi Session Laws, regular session, 1875, p. 168; Appleton's Cyclopedia, 1875, p. 513; E. Mayes, op. cit., pp. 273-274; W. H. Furniss to Adelbert Ames, January 27, 1875, Adelbert Ames Papers, Mississippi State Archives.
[55] E. Mayes, op. cit., p. 275; Mississippi Senate Journal, 1882, p. 25; Jackson Weekly Clarion, August 8, 1883, quoting the Port Gibson Gazette.
[56] E. Mayes, op. cit., p. 277; Goodspeed Publishing Company, op. cit., II, 339.

remained constant. The presidents and their teachers were quiet, unobtrusive, and uninspired, content to let things remain much as they found them. In the face of the prevailing attitude of the legislature, such caution was not unwise. After the abolition of the scholarships, few of the students were able to remain for as much as one complete session. The total of the graduates from 1870 to 1890 was forty-six. While the agricultural course was popular, most of the students when they left the school went into teaching. The cash income of twenty dollars or more a month and the higher social status of the profession appealed to them more than drudgery in a declining agriculture. As a normal school, Alcorn continued to perform a useful function, training teachers who, at least, were able to instruct their pupils in reading, writing, and the fundamentals of arithmetic.

A much more encouraging story is that of Tougaloo University, founded by the American Missionary Association, with aid from the Freedmen's Bureau, in 1869. Beginning with a large farm, which included a residence and a number of smaller buildings, the founders immediately erected Washington Hall, with an auditorium, school rooms, and a dormitory for men, and Boarding Hall, which contained the dining room, kitchen, and a dormitory for women. The building program continued with a new dormitory in 1872, and the erection in 1881 of Strieby Hall to replace Washington Hall, which had burned. Other new structures were a blacksmith shop in 1882, carpentry and tin shops in 1883 and 1884, and buildings for the elementary department and the industrial department in 1886 and 1887.[57] In spite of this expansion, and the enlargement of older structures, accommodations were seldom available for all of the students who sought admission.

Throughout the period, the treasury of the Missionary Association bore most of the burden of the upkeep of the school, with the aid of tuition from those students who were able to pay it, and some income from labor performed by the students. With the establishment of the normal department in 1871, an appeal was made for aid from the state. In return for the right to set up a board to control this department, the legislature granted an annual appropriation of $4,000, which became $4,500 in 1874. The Democratic legislature reduced this amount to $3,000 in 1876 and to $2,500 in 1877. After an intermission of two years, an appropriation of from two to three thousand dollars was allowed each year until 1888. Reduced to $1,500 in 1889, it was abolished entirely in 1891, in accordance with a provision of the new state Constitution.[58]

It soon became apparent that the normal department at Tougaloo was

[57] *History of the American Missionary Association*, p. 33; E. Mayes, *op. cit.*, pp. 263-264; Jackson *Weekly Clarion*, January 27, May 26, November 23, 1881.
[58] E. Mayes, *op. cit.*, pp. 259-262; S. G. Noble, *op. cit.*, p. 84; *History of the American Missionary Association*, p. 33.

turning out a superior type of teacher. With entrance requirements that were higher than those at Holly Springs or Alcorn, a remarkably good faculty, and provisions for practice teaching with supervision and criticism, it sent into the public schools a group of young men and women who, throughout the period, received unqualified praise.[59]

By 1890, the college was soundly established, with a student body of about 300, and a capable white faculty of sixteen members. It had about eighty-six acres planted in a variety of crops, and on its three hundred acres of pasture land it kept a large herd of cattle. Its students were subject to a charge of nine dollars a month for board and tuition, but most of them, men and women alike, found an opportunity to discharge a part of this cost by labor at the college and on the farm. Freed from the deadening control of the state legislature, the effects of which were so apparent at Alcorn, the faculty offered effective primary and intermediate training to students who then entered upon the courses which prepared them for teaching or for agricultural and industrial work.

The catalogue for 1888-1889 gives an indication of the wide range of instruction which was offered. The subjects required of those who sought a degree from the normal department were as follows:

Ninth grade.—Arithmetic, grammar, rhetoric, geography, history, physiology, school economy.

Tenth grade.—Algebra, natural philosophy, bookkeeping, American literature, English literature, civil government, methods.

Eleventh grade.—Higher algebra, geometry, general history, geology, botany.

Twelfth grade.—Political economy, mental and moral science, Scripture, history, pedagogics, reviews and methods in common branches, composition.

The industrial course, required of all boys in and above the fifth grade, supplied instruction in carpentry in the first year, blacksmithing and wheelwrighting in the second, and painting, turning, and tinning in the third. In addition to taking the regular courses in agriculture, all boys participated in daily work on the college farm. All girls were instructed in sewing, cooking and housekeeping. Comments on the remarkable qualities of Tougaloo graduates offered proof that the standards outlined by the catalogue were carried into the classrooms. In the absence of proper provision at state expense, Tougaloo University stood as the one institution where the young Negroes of Mississippi might obtain competent training. The value of the work of its students in the Negro public schools, and of their contacts with the mass of the Negro population, is beyond calculation.

[59] Mississippi *Senate Journal*, 1872, *Appendix*, p. 422; E. Mayes, *op. cit.*, p. 261; S. G. Noble, *op. cit.*, p. 57; Mississippi *Weekly Pilot*, June 26, 1875; Jackson *Clarion-Ledger*, May 29, 1890.

CHAPTER XVIII

RELIGION

In the culture of the white man, which he adopted with such remark-able rapidity and willingness, the Negro found nothing more attractive and satisfying than the Christian religion. The appeal of this creed to servile classes, so apparent in the days of the Roman Empire, enabled it to make of the slaves a multitude of devoted converts. Forbidden to hope for any great improvement in their earthly lot, the Negroes grasped eagerly the promises that the haughty were to be overthrown, and the meek and lowly raised up to eternal life in a land of glory. Those promises gave a meaning and a purpose to their lives.

Even before the war, in a few scattered localities, the Negroes had churches of their own. The most prominent example of this sort was Rose Hill Church at Natchez, built through contributions from whites and Negroes, and deeded to a free Negro named Marshall. Many of its members were free, but its preacher, the eloquent Randle Pollard, was a slave. In Vicksburg, the Negroes were given the old Methodist building in 1850 and were served by a white preacher until the structure burned.[2] The Chapel Hill Church at Utica was possibly an independent Negro enterprise after 1857.[3] There were other cases in which the slaves met as separate congregations in some part of the building used by the whites. In Jackson, Negroes began meeting in the basement of the white Baptist Church as early as 1835. Their preacher was a Negro, but several white men attended their services to meet the requirements of the law.[4] Negro Baptists at Columbus met in the basement of the church on Wednesday and Sunday afternoons, but it appears that the regular white minister usually preached to them, as was the case in a similar development at Aberdeen.

These separate Negro congregations were scattered exceptions to the general rule under which the slaves attended the churches of their masters. Occupying seats in the rear or in the balcony, they at times received special attention, when the minister, choosing the apt texts of Saint Paul, urged them to be obedient to their masters, in whose service they glorified God. In the management of the church they had no part, with the ex-

[1] Patrick H. Thompson, *Negro Baptists in Mississippi*, p. 27.
[2] Lee Richardson and T. D. Godman, *In and About Vicksburg*, p. 134.
[3] Mississippi Historical Records Survey, "Church Inventory of Hinds County.
[4] P. H. Thompson, *op. cit.*, pp. 31-33.
[5] *Ibid.*, pp. 25, 29.

ception of a more or less formal participation in the reception or disciplining of other Negro members.[6]

After the coming of emancipation, it appears that most of the white churches were willing or even anxious to have the freedmen retain their membership.[7] To the honest conviction that such a connection was to the best interests of the Negroes, there was added the idea that it would facilitate the continuation of social control by the whites. There also remained the old fear, reflected in the laws of 1865, that in meetings not attended by white men insurrections would be planned.[8] Complicating factors, however, made the retention of the Negroes almost impossible. The situation received careful analysis in a report submitted to the general assembly of the Southern Presbyterian Church in 1866. All Presbyterians, said the author of the report, acknowledged the Scriptural doctrine of the brotherhood of man. In spite of this fact, the white members, although accustomed to using the same building and the same communion table as the Negroes, would not be willing to grant the social and ecclesiastical equality which the Negroes were beginning to desire. Under the circumstances, he felt that the best plan was for the white members to aid the freedmen in the establishment of separate organizations, at the same time making an effort to retain some ecclesiastical connection with them for purposes of control.[9] This same perplexing problem was faced by all the churches. Most of the white members recognized the desirability of retaining the Negroes in their churches, but few were willing to let the former slaves come down out of the gallery or to grant to them any voice in the management of the organization. This attitude was the strongest of several forces which caused the freedmen to move immediately toward the establishment of churches of their own.

When it became apparent that the secession of the Negro members was inevitable, many of the leading white churchmen gave freely of their time and money to aid them in the project. This aid took the form of cash subscriptions, the donation of land and buildings, and assistance in organization.[10] White preachers frequently delivered sermons to the new churches, and in some cases took part in the ordination of the Negro ministers.[11] During 1866 and the first half of 1867, white politicians and professional

[6] Jesse T. Wallace, *History of the Negroes of Mississippi*, p. 101; Forrest Cooper, "Reconstruction in Scott County," *P.M.H.S.*, XIII, 195; A. T. Morgan, *Yazoo*, note, p. 103.

[7] Hinds County *Gazette*, September 8, 1869; J. L. Girardeau, "Our Ecclesiastical Relation to the Freedmen," *Southern Presbyterian Review*, XVIII (1867), pp. 2-6; W. L. Fleming, *Documentary History of Reconstruction*, II, 64.

[8] *Supra*, pp. 85, 87; *House Executive Documents*, no. 2, 39th Congress, 1st session, p. 99.

[9] J. L. Girardeau, *op. cit.*, pp. 2-17.

[10] M. G. Abney, "Reconstruction in Pontotoc County," *P.M.H.S.*, XI, 255; John W. Kyle, "Reconstruction in Panola County," *P.M.H.S.*, XIII, 81; P. H. Thompson, *op. cit.*, p. 39.

[11] P. H. Thompson, *op. cit.*, p. 36; M. G. Abney, *op. cit.*, XI, 254.

men were active in the organization and instruction of Negro Sunday schools.[12] It is unfortunately true that this spirit of coöperation almost entirely disappeared with the rise of political bitterness late in 1867.

Many of the Negro congregations, of course, were unable to gain sufficient resources to supply themselves with buildings. For a number of years, such groups, often numbering several hundred, could be seen gathering under brush arbors or improvised sheds.[13] On one plantation, Whitelaw Reid found a small congregation using one end of a large cabin, while a Negro family still lived in the end opposite the pulpit. On another plantation, the freedmen had fitted up as their church the attic of a stable.[14] Generally, however, such arrangements were regarded as temporary. Disregarding their poverty, the Negroes all over the state undertook the erection of buildings that ranged from a log hut near Toccopola to a $2,800 structure erected on Pine Street in Natchez.[15] Such enterprises involved heavy personal sacrifices, supplemented by the income from concerts, tableaux, and church suppers.[16] Furthermore, the task was never finished. No sooner was a congregation firmly established in a village or town, than sections of it began to break away to establish independent churches in the surrounding countryside. Out of the Pine Grove Church at Aberdeen, for example, grew Bethel, Pleasant Valley, Baptist Grove, New Grove, Ebenezer, Daniel, and Lakeville.[17] Similar divisions and sub-divisions all over the state rapidly carried the independent Negro church into the remotest interior.

The mushroom growth of hundreds of isolated and independent churches occurred most easily and naturally within the Baptist system. Each Baptist Church was a self-sufficient, self-governing body, almost entirely free from any external regulations. Individual congregations followed their own ways of thinking, uniting and dividing as they pleased. As their number grew, the churches easily and naturally formed for themselves voluntary associations, and these associations in turn united to form conventions. In a time of disagreement, an association just as easily withdrew from its convention, or a church from its association. In each case, the Baptist identity was retained. In simplicity, flexibility, and adaptability in a time of rapid growth and change, the system had no equal. The great mass of the Negroes of Mississippi became Baptists as naturally, and often with as little formality, as they became members of family groups.

During the war, the Negro Baptists of Ohio, Illinois, Kentucky, Mis-

[12] Natchez *Daily Courier,* June 21, July 4, 1866; Jackson *Weekly Clarion,* June 13, 1867, quoting the Lexington *Advertiser.*

[13] M. G. Abney, *op. cit.,* XI, 254; P. H. Thompson, *op. cit.,* p. 28; *Leading Afro-Americans of Vicksburg, Mississippi,* p. 63.

[14] Whitelaw Reid, *After the War,* p. 519.

[15] M. G. Abney, *op. cit.,* XI, 255; P. H. Thompson, *op. cit.,* pp. 28, 36-37.

[16] Natchez *Daily Courier,* July 12, 1866; Jackson *Weekly Clarion,* May 28, 1879.

[17] P. H. Thompson, *op. cit.,* p. 37.

souri, Indiana, Michigan, and Connecticut set up the North-Western Baptist Missionary Convention. The purpose of this body was to send missionaries to the South for the organization of churches, associations, and conventions. To Natchez in 1865 came J. F. Boulden, one of the ablest of the missionaries. Finding the work already well begun by Randle Pollard and his Rose Hill Church, Boulden carried on a program of rapid expansion until 1867, when he was called to Columbus, in the northeastern portion of the state.[18]

In the meantime, the work of organization in the central portion of the state was being carried on with remarkable effectiveness by Marion Dunbar, an aged Negro who for many years had been preaching to a congregation in the basement of the white Baptist Church in Jackson. In 1868, Dunbar was ready to crown his achievements by arranging for the establishment of the first permanent Negro Baptist Association in the state. This body, known as the Jackson Baptist Association, included practically all of the churches of the denomination in Hinds, Rankin, Madison, Scott, Claiborne, Holmes, Warren, Smith, Carroll, Yazoo, and Leake counties.[19]

From his church in Columbus, J. F. Boulden was organizing scores of congregations and merging them into associations. In this work he was aided by two other Negro preachers, A. Henderson and L. D. McAllister. By 1872, these men were able to take the next great step, the union of the five associations of the northern and central portions of the state into the General Missionary Baptist Association. At its first meeting, this body brought together the representatives of 226 churches, with more than 21,000 members. By 1890, this membership had grown to 47,200.[20]

The leadership left vacant at Natchez when Boulden went to Columbus was assumed by H. P. Jacobs, more able than his predecessor, and perhaps the most effective organizer the Negro Baptists of the state have ever possessed. Riding through the wilderness, presiding at conventions, abandoning his chair to aid and instruct humbler brethren on the floor, pleading, exhorting, and commanding, Jacobs displayed an energy that at times was nothing less than amazing. Up and down the western section of the state he traveled, leaving behind him churches, associations, and missionary boards without number. In 1869, he gathered a large number of his churches into the Missionary Baptist Convention, which by 1888 included 298 congregations with a total membership of 48,926.[21]

In 1890, the work of organization and coördination so ably begun by Boulden, Dunbar, and Jacobs was completed by the union of the Missionary Baptist Convention and the General Missionary Baptist Associa-

[18] *Ibid.*, pp. 26-28.
[19] *Ibid.*, pp. 439, 442, 445.
[20] *Ibid.*, pp. 361, 364, 437, 445.
[21] *Ibid.*, pp. 41, 42, 46, 51, 55, 255, 445.

tion. This new body, the General Baptist Missionary Convention of Mississippi, brought together 900 churches with a membership of 79,732.[22] Here and there a stubborn local association refused its coöperation, but the existence of the Convention assured the great majority of the members of the denomination the opportunity to work together on a program for the best interests of their church and their race.

For a number of years the policy of the Methodist Episcopal Church, South, toward the freedmen was hesitant and contradictory. The Mississippi Annual Conference of 1865 adopted the general procedure of assigning its white ministers to a definite station "and colored charge."[23] As late as 1869, the Jackson District Conference adopted and ordered distributed a report which included the following declaration:

As a church we have always been faithful to the colored race, ever willing to afford them every advantage at our command, every advantage enjoyed by the white race. As a church we are still willing and ready to receive all into church fellowship who are willing to come and faithfully discharge their duties. . . . And we recommend that our preachers, and official and other members be requested to approach and use every proper means to bring into our churches the people of color.[24]

In the meantime, however, the General Conference of 1866 had recognized the fact that a relatively small portion of the Negro members were willing to retain their inferior status. Of the 207,000 Negro communicants which the denomination had included in 1860, less than 78,000 remained in 1866. The conference therefore suggested that separate annual conferences be formed for the freedmen. These annual conferences were then to be organized into a separate general conference, "bearing the same relation to the General Conference [of the white church] as the annual conferences bear to each other."[25] Since the relationship of the annual conferences seldom went beyond voluntary coöperation, and since there seems to have been no idea of a higher conference to coördinate the work of the white and Negro general conferences, this program was practically one of complete separation. This fact was recognized in the message of the bishops in 1870:

It is our purpose . . . to call a General Conference to be holden next winter for the purpose of organizing them [the Negro members] into an entirely separate Church thus enabling them to become their own guides and governors.[26]

In accordance with the decision of the bishops, a conventional general conference of eight Negro annual conferences met at Jackson, Tennessee, in

[22] Ibid., pp. 264-279.
[23] Hinds County Gazette, November 18, 1865.
[24] Ibid., September 8, 1869.
[25] Charles H. Phillips, History of the Colored Methodist Episcopal Church in America, pp. 23, 25, 26.
[26] Ibid., p. 26.

December, 1870, to form the Colored Methodist Episcopal Church. Bishops Payne and McTyeire of the white church presided, and ordained two Negroes, W. H. Miles of Kentucky and R. H. Vanderhorst of Georgia, as bishops. With the close of this conference, the formal connection between the white and Negro groups was severed.[27]

Among the leaders of this Negro denomination in Mississippi were J. H. Anderson, L. J. Scurlock, R. Polk, and Elias Cottrell, who, after his removal to Tennessee, became a bishop. Although Scurlock's political activity caused him to be hanged by the Klan, most of the leaders and members of this church were inclined to be quiet and conservative. Dominated until 1871 by the Methodist Episcopal Church, South, the Colored Methodist organization was described by Negroes of the independent denominations as "the Rebel Church," "the Democratic Church," or "the Old Slavery Church."[28] This dislike was increased by the fact that the general conference of 1866 had transferred to the trustees of the new Negro annual conferences title to "all property intended for the use and benefit of the people of color."[29] In a number of localities a majority of the members withdrew to establish an independent African Methodist Episcopal Church. In doing so, they insisted on retaining their church buildings. Such instances resulted in quarrels that in some cases lasted for many years.[30] The favor of the white population, however, helped to counterbalance the general disapproval of the majority of the Negroes, and the Colored Methodist Episcopal Church in 1890 claimed a larger membership than either of its Methodist rivals.

The Methodist Episcopal Church of Mississippi, although officially a conference of the great Methodist Episcopal Church of the North, was made up almost entirely of Negro members. Organized as the Mississippi Mission Conference in New Orleans in 1865, it held its first session as a full-fledged conference at Canton in 1869.[31] Its most active organizer in the western portion of the state was N. L. Brakeman, who reported to the conference in 1866 that he had traveled 8,000 miles, preached over 200 sermons, delivered over 100 speeches to various groups, built nine churches and three parsonages, and obtained 363 subscribers to the New Orleans *Advocate*.[32] From 1867 to 1872, the church had as it most distinguished leader James D. Lynch. With the aid of J. Aaron Moore, Lynch extended the influence of the group into the eastern and northern portions of the state.[33] By 1881, it claimed 21,471 members, 309 churches, and 317 Sun-

---

[27] *Ibid.*, pp. 27, 32; James J. Pipkin, *The Story of a Rising Race*, p. 108; *Doctrines and Discipline of the C.M.E. Church in America*, 1883, p. 4.
[28] C. H. Phillips, *op. cit.*, pp. 71, 72, 74.
[29] *Doctrines and Discipline of the C.M.E. Church in America*, 1883, p. 4.
[30] C. H. Phillips, *op. cit.*, pp. 51-52.
[31] Mississippi Mission Conference, *Minutes*, 1865-1866, pp. 1-5; Mississippi Annual Conference, *Journal*, 1881, p. 4.
[32] Mississippi Mission Conference, *Minutes*, 1865-1866, p. 9.
[33] Meridian *Chronicle*, October 22, 1868, quoting the New Orleans *Advocate*.

day Schools.[34]   Continued growth and the difficulty of entertaining large meetings caused a few years later a division of the body into the Mississippi and Upper Mississippi Conferences.

The African Methodist Episcopal Church, established in the North in 1815 by a group of the Negro members of the Methodist Episcopal Church, was represented in Mississippi by the ablest of its organizing missionaries. This man, T. W. Stringer, had been active in the religious and fraternal circles of his race in Ohio, and then had led in the organization of the African Methodist Episcopal Church in Canada.   Coming to Mississippi late in 1865, he directed from his church in Vicksburg the establishment of his denomination throughout the state.   For the duration of his life, he held practical control of all its conferences.   After having received some aid from Hiram R. Revels in the region around Natchez, Stringer reported that his churches were ready for formal recognition.   Bishop James A. Shorter came to Vicksburg and, in October of 1868, presided over the first session of the Mississippi Annual Conference of the African Methodist Episcopal Church.[35]   By the time of its second session, at Greenville in 1870, the conference included 4,982 members, thirty-five churches, and thirty Sunday schools.[36]   Rapid growth resulted in the organization of the North Mississippi Conference, with sixty-two churches and 5,253 members, in 1877.[37]   Further progress and division produced the Central Mississippi Conference in 1893, and the Northeast Mississippi Conference in 1899.[38]

In general, the Negro members of the Presbyterian Church in Mississippi were so small in number that there was almost no effort to set up separate churches for them.   Here and there a few retained their membership in the white churches.[39]   It appears that a temporary organization set up for Negroes in Vicksburg in 1872 was the only one established under the auspices of the white denomination.[40]   The Colored Cumberland Presbyterian Church, organized in Murfreesboro, Tennessee, in 1869, had succeeded in 1890 in organizing in Mississippi only six churches, served by four ministers.[41]

The Mississippi Diocese of the Episcopal Church continued for a number of years to work with its dwindling flock of Negro communicants.   The *Journal* of the Diocese for 1870 gives reports of baptisms, marriages, and

[34] Mississippi Annual Conference, *Journal*, 1881, p. 44.
[35] Revels A. Adams, *Cyclopedia of African Methodism in Mississippi*, pp. 132, 190, 191; *House Miscellaneous Documents*, no. 53, 40th Congress, 3d session, p. 28.
[36] Mississippi Annual Conference, A.M.E. Church, *Minutes*, second session, 1870, pp. 20-21.
[37] R. A. Adams, *op. cit.*, pp. 155, 157.
[38] *Ibid.*, p. 49.
[39] Ruth Watkins, "Reconstruction in Newton County," *P.M.H.S.*, XI, 223.
[40] Hinds County *Gazette*, December 11, 1872.
[41] Goodspeed Publishing Company, *Biographical and Historical Memoirs of Mississippi*, II, 358.

confirmations of Negroes throughout the state. The Jackson Convocation reported in 1873 that it was carrying on active missionary work, and that special services were being held for Negro members at Jackson, Canton, Dry Grove, and Terry. A Sunday school conducted at Terry had seventy-five members.[42] Three years later, in 1876, announcements of the services of the African Episcopal Church were appearing regularly in the Saturday issues of the Jackson *Daily Times*. The rector, D. C. Thompson, was a white man. In 1885, the establishment of churches for the Negroes was still the "pet scheme" of Reverend H. M. Thompson, but the majority of his members offered little support. He succeeded in establishing St. Mary's Episcopal in Vicksburg, which was probably the last church of this type to be organized in the state. Still in existence in 1908, it was served by a Negro rector.[43]

Here and there, minor denominations made efforts to secure Negro members. Dissension among the Baptists near Davis Bend in 1872 allowed the establishment there of three churches of the Campbellite faith.[44] The American Missionary Association organized a Congregational Church in connection with Tougaloo University in 1870, and for a time maintained another in the hall of the Hope Fire Company in Jackson.[45] By 1890, however, it had become apparent that the great mass of the Negroes of Mississippi were to be Baptists or Methodists. Statistics from the census of that year, although they are not much more reliable than the much larger figures offered by the churches themselves, give an indication of the situation:

Denomination	Organizations	Church Edifices	Halls	Communicants
Regular Baptist	1,385	1,333	59	136,647
Colored Methodist Episcopal	293	292		20,107
Methodist Episcopal ...	195	192		14,869
African Methodist Episcopal	42	80		10,270
African Methodist Episcopal Zion	64	50	14	8,519
Cumberland Presbyterian	4	4		278

In their services, most of the Negro churches followed closely the pattern set by the white Baptists and Methodists in the days of the frontier. Each meeting was an intense emotional experience, but these ordinary services were insignificant compared with the protracted meetings, some of

[42] Diocese of Mississippi, *Journal*, 1873, pp. 47-48.
[43] *Leading Afro-Americans of Vicksburg, Mississippi*, p. 65.
[44] P. H. Thompson, *op. cit.*, pp. 97-99.
[45] *History of the American Missionary Association*, p. 40; Jackson *Weekly Clarion*, February 28, 1883.

which ran from three weeks to three months.[46] One of these was described by a Congregational missionary as follows:

Meetings are held in the colored church every night in the week, and continue till twelve o'clock, or even later. The exercises are of the most emotional and demonstrative kind. Women go into a frenzy of excitement and roll on the floor for two or three hours together, screaming and crying, "Lord, take me," "Jesus save me," till, utterly exhausted, they fall asleep, or experience something which they call "coming through," when they jump up in an ecstacy of joy, and shouting "Glory, glory, hallelujah," at the top of their voices till they are hoarse, run all over the house, hugging indiscriminately every man, woman, and child, white or black, that they may come to, and telling them with the most extravagant gesticulations that "Jesus died for me," "Jesus is a precious Savior!" Men walk all round the house on their knees, shouting with the full compass of their voices. . . . And then they sing,—as only they can sing— all joining at the top of their voices, swaying their bodies to the time of the music, and clapping their hands in the most frantic manner.[47]

However much such exhibitions might grieve more highly cultured members of the race, they remained for many years the pattern of behavior for the average Negro church. According to Hugo Munsterberg, "Where religion has been the single intellectual stimulus, it has been an intoxicant for the pining soul; and persons drank until they obtained a sort of hysterical relief from deadly reality."[48] Jerome Dowd, commenting on the confinment of the Negroes in their daily lives to routine and to mental darkness, regarded it as only natural for them "to plunge tumultuously towards the illuminations from above."[49]

In their efforts to preserve their organizations, and to maintain a modicum of progress, the Negro churches faced many problems and difficulties. To many of their members, religion was an escape from the drab monotony of existence; it had no relation to moral behavior. To many of their pastors, the church offered the only available outlet for the instincts of leadership and self-expression; they regarded the church as theirs to use for the gratification of those instincts, and made no effort to set an example of morality or of Christian fellowship for their congregations. Many of those preachers who possessed the deepest piety and sincerity in their work were the victims of ignorance and superstition. Almost all of them found it necessary to gain the greater part of their income in some work outside the church. This problem was often mentioned as a basic one by G. W. Gayles in his messages. To the Mississippi Baptist Convention he said:

When ministers are supported and cared for we will have better churches and congregations. We will then have less laughing in our churches at the repeated blunders of illiterate ministers. . . . How can this be stopped? When you go to call on some of our ministers on church business you will find his

[46] Hinds County *Gazette*, August 12, 1874, October 13, 1880.
[47] *History of the American Missionary Association*, pp. 55-56.
[48] Jerome Dowd, *The Negro in American Life*, p. 180.
[49] *Ibid.*, p. 180.

door closed, and someone who is near will inform you that he is in the field ploughing. Where is his family? The reply is that they are with him. In the city or town the minister is in his shop working for his living. Where is his family? His wife is hired out cooking for Mr. A. . . . Yea, in some instances the minister could not be found to attend a burial or funeral service, all of which should be condemned.[50]

This same leader also cried out time and again against the ordaining of a multitude of preachers who had no churches in which to serve, against the establishment of too many weak churches, against the excesses of the protracted meetings, and against the refusal of ministers and their congregations to recognize the moral requirements of their religion.[51]

The weaknesses and evils that brought sorrow to the hearts of Jacobs, Gayles, and Stringer continued to exist long after their time, but in the meantime the Negro churches showed remarkable powers of survival and gradual improvement. The place of the church in the lives of its communicants can hardly be estimated. It stood as one of the few avenues of expression in which they found themselves relatively free from white control. As an educational institution the early church did not take second place to the schools. The Negroes for generations had had all their decisions made for them; they had been allowed to gain little experience in conscious direction of their activities. In the conduct of their independent churches they found as in no other field training in organization, cooperation, management, finance, and self-government. The lessons learned served them well in the development of the other social and commercial organizations that go to make up community life.

[50] P. H. Thompson, *op. cit.*, p. 180.
[51] *Ibid.*, p. 217.

CHAPTER XIX

THE NEGRO DEFECTIVE

It immediately became apparent at the end of the war that the Negro defectives were to be a serious problem. The responsibility for their care had formerly been borne by their masters. It could not easily be shifted to the Negroes themselves because of their general poverty as a race, and the looseness and informality of their family structure. The Freedmen's Bureau relieved the situation to some extent by maintaining several small hospitals and asylums until 1869.[1]

The Republican state government in 1870 and 1871 set up charity hospitals at Vicksburg and Natchez.[2] Both of these establishments maintained wards for Negroes of the surrounding territory. Their limited facilities, however, only served to emphasize the problem. In some cases, Negroes coming from as much as eighty miles away were turned away to die in the streets.[3] In the main, the freedmen, like the mass of the rural white population, depended for medical care on the services of the "saddlebag" doctor. Those services they were generally able to obtain by having the charges added to their accounts with their employer.[4]

The existence of a multitude of Negro orphans seems not to have presented any very great difficulty. Stories can be found of babies abandoned in the streets or deposited on the steps of officials of the Bureau.[5] In general, however, orphans of any age were absorbed into neighboring families with little delay or formality. This continued to be true in 1939.[6]

The most distressing situation grew around the Negroes who were insane. For them, neither the Bureau nor the state made any provision until late in 1870.[7] An appeal from General Howard to Governor Humphreys brought the reply that the state asylum was so crowded that admission was daily being refused to white citizens. No provision could be made for

[1] *Senate Executive Documents,* no. 27, 39th Congress, 1st session, pp. 40-41; no. 6, 39th Congress, 2d session, pp. 98-99; *House Executive Documents,* no. 1, 40th Congress, 3d session, p. 1024; Natchez *Tri-Weekly Democrat,* February 27, 1866.

[2] Mississippi *Session Laws,* 1870, pp. 616-619; *ibid.,* 1871, pp. 621-622.

[3] Vicksburg *Herald,* February 25, 1875.

[4] Personal letter from R. J. Gossin, St. Louis, Missouri, September 27, 1938; Cash and Account Book, 1866, Stephen Duncan Papers.

[5] Natchez *Daily Courier,* August 22, 1866; Natchez *Tri-Weekly Democrat,* August 3, 1867.

[6] Hortense Powdermaker, *After Freedom,* pp. 59, 199-207.

[7] *Senate Executive Documents,* no. 6, 39th Congress, 2d session, p. 98; *House Executive Documents,* no. 1, 40th Congress, 3d session, p. 1049.

the "imbecile blacks."[8] Those among the freedmen who were regarded as dangerous were locked in the county jails; others were permitted to wander about without attention. The only apparent reaction among the white people seems to have been one of annoyance. The Natchez *Democrat,* for example, reported in 1867: "That crazy negro woman is still permitted to go about the streets, to the annoyance of the public. . . . She is becoming an unbearable nuisance."[9]

The legislature of 1870 quickly made the asylum available to both races, with theoretical equality of services. As a matter of fact, however, all of the available buildings were crowded with white patients. The few Negro patients who were admitted were, therefore, crowded into an abandoned bowling alley, with a low ceiling and very poor ventilation. There were no provisions for cooling it in summer or heating it in winter. The report of the superintendent spoke of "an atmosphere loaded with sickening effluvia, exhaled from filthy bodies. . . ."[10] In the alley the Negroes remained until late in 1872, when the completion of one of the new wings of the hospital allowed them to be moved.

Facilities were still inadequate, and remained so. A majority of the insane Negroes once more found places in the county jails, as had been the case before 1870. The Raymond jail alone held six of them through the greater part of 1889. The editor of the *Gazette* suggested that one of them, who believed himself to be Jesus Christ and was especially noisy and troublesome, should be lynched.[11] A little later, however, in reporting the death of one of the inmates, the same writer took a more merciful tone:

Four others remain in jail, at least two of them being afflicted in a way to warrant the belief that death will ensue shortly. They cannot stand the cold damp iron floor and close confinement in a poorly ventilated prison. Better, a thousand times, if the law would turn the creatures upon the streets, for they are being only smothered to death where they are now.[12]

The wave of protest finally became so great that the legislature, with all its devotion to economy, could no longer disregard it. In 1890, an act was passed "to provide for the care of the insane colored people now in the county jails of this State and to provide for the erection of an additional building on the grounds of the Mississippi Lunatic Asylum at Jackson."[13] An appropriation of $60,000 gave the assurance that at least the most needy cases would henceforth receive some attention.

The legislature of 1870 also took up the problem of care for the deaf

[8] Natchez *Tri-Weekly Democrat,* August 21, 1866.
[9] *Ibid.,* March 19, 1867.
[10] Mississippi *Senate Journal,* 1872, *Appendix,* p. 566.
[11] Raymond *Gazette,* August 17, 1889.
[12] *Ibid.,* October 5, 1889.
[13] Mississippi *Session Laws,* 1890, pp. 58-61.

and dumb. Until that year, a number of the white deaf mutes had been maintained at the expense of the state in the Louisiana Asylum. The Republican legislature continued this arrangement until the completion, late in 1871, of a building to house the unfortunates of both races.[14] Because the reports of the superintendent do not classify the inmates according to race, it is impossible to learn how many Negro children found a place in the institution during the first four years. In 1876, the first year of Democratic control, there were only two Negroes in a student group of forty.[15] In 1880, there were four, as compared with thirty-nine who were white. Careful separation of the races was maintained by keeping the young Negroes in a small house in the yard of the institute.[16] A new superintendent appointed in 1881 encouraged the entrance of Negro children until the house devoted to them was filled. By the end of 1881, he had admitted eighteen, and reported that there were twenty-five on the waiting list.[17] Two years later, on the recommendation of the superintendent, an appropriation of $3,000 was devoted to the establishment of a separate institution for the Negro children. The small sum available was invested in a house, a farm, and farm equipment. By 1885, eighteen students, five of them girls, were crowded into the house, and it was announced that no more could be received.[18]

The laws of 1865 specifically limited admission to the Institute for the Blind to white residents of the state.[19] Provisions were made for Negroes by the legislature of 1870, but the absence of classification by races in the reports of the superintendent prevents any estimate of the number of Negro children who took advantage of the opportunity. There is evidence of an immediate decline in their number with the return of Democratic control in 1876. The superintendent reported in 1879 that for the last three sessions the enrollment of colored students had been very small. In 1878 there were four; in 1879 only one. The superintendent was unable to give a reason for this decline; he declared that demands for admission were always promptly complied with, where the applicants were eligible.[20] In the new institution for the blind which was constructed in 1880, there seems to have been no provision for the admission of Negroes.

Thus by 1890, there was assurance that a large portion of the Negroes who were insane, or who were deaf mutes, would receive some attention from the state. The responsibility assumed in 1870 was never again to be entirely denied. The accommodations offered to them were separate and inferior, but in the steady growth of humanitarian sentiment they received at least a portion of the benefits.

[14] *Appleton's Cyclopedia*, 1870, p. 514.
[15] Board of Trustees, *Report*, 1876, p. 10.
[16] Hinds County *Gazette*, November 17, 1880; Mississippi Institute for the Deaf and Dumb, *Biennial Report*, 1880-1881, p. 7.
[17] *Ibid.*, 1880-1881, p. 8.   [18] *Ibid.*, 1882-1883, p. 10; 1884-1885, p. 9.
[19] Mississippi *Session Laws*, 1865, p. 241.
[20] Superintendent of the Asylum for the Blind, *Biennial Report*, 1878-1879, p. 7.

CHAPTER XX

SOCIAL LIFE

The monotony and the poverty of their daily lives seem to have intensified the delight of the Negroes in social gatherings. They came together by hundreds or even by thousands during the summer season for picnics and barbecues. Until 1876, these gatherings generally had political significance; after that time they continued as purely social functions. For most of the picnics, men, women, and children from miles around began to gather early in the morning. They came on foot, or crowded into borrowed wagons, in families or as organized clubs. Some came with drums and music, carrying banners. All brought food of some kind, to be spread on the common tables. Often there were special refreshment stands, set up by churches or benevolent societies to glean the small coins saved by many for the occasion. At times there were white visitors, for whom special tables were set with the choicest of the food. Mornings generally were given over to gossip and the renewing of acquaintances. For the afternoon, after all the food had been consumed, there were speeches, music from one of a remarkable number of Negro brass bands, ball games, or dancing on a rough platform. At times there were minor brawls among those who had brought cheap whiskey in their baskets, but determined efforts to prevent such incidents seem generally to have been successful. Several hours before darkness fell, various groups began to detach themselves for the trip to the distant plantations, shouting to each other congratulations on the good time that had been had, and promising to meet again, in a week or two, at a similar affair.[1]

Much more spectacular and expensive than the ordinary picnics were the excursions, for which the railroads generally ran special trains at reduced rates. These excursion trips gradually settled into definite patterns. The most popular of all was that of Negroes from the Jackson area to Vicksburg for a trip around the "cutoff" on a river boat. Other popular trips were those from Vicksburg or Natchez to Jackson, from Jackson to Natchez or Canton, and from Canton to Jackson. Negro fire companies, benevolent societies, and religious organizations used the excursion as a means of assembling with similar groups in other towns. At times a group

[1] Hinds County *Gazette*, August 26, 1874, July 12, 1876, May 23, 1877, August 20, 27, September 3, 1879, December 8, 1880, January 3, 1884; Mississippi *Weekly Pilot*, May 29, 1875.

with sufficient resources would sponsor a trip, paying a fixed sum to the railroad, and pocketing the profits or absorbing the loss.[2]

During the eighties, the growing determination of the mass of the white population to place limits on the social behavior of the Negroes was reflected in increased criticism of the excursions. The editor of the *Gazette* suggested that someone test in the courts the right of a railroad "to pour fifteen hundred howling excursionists upon any peaceful community."[3] The growth of this opposition, together with that of Negro preachers, and the increasing intensity of the economic depression served to make the excursion a rare spectacle by 1890.

A more acceptable variation of the excursion idea came with the development of the Colored Fair Association in 1885. The Negro leaders J. J. Spelman and James Hill planned and organized the event. They received remarkable coöperation from state officials, and from the white merchants of Jackson, who subscribed over a thousand dollars in premiums. The fair lasted four days; a wide variety of stock, needle work, and agricultural products was displayed, and speeches were delivered by Governor Lowry, Senators George and Walthall, I. T. Montgomery, and ex-Senator Bruce. The quality of the exhibits and the behavior of the large crowds brought high praise from the press.[4] It seems, however, that the heavy expense involved in the venture made its repetition inadvisable for a number of years.

Much more significant than the informal gatherings of the period was the development by the Negroes of permanent social organizations. These organizations, growing in many cases out of the earlier Loyal Leagues, naturally excited for a number of years the distrust and opposition of a large part of the white population. H. S. Fulkerson still believed in 1885 that they fostered a spirit of antagonism toward the dominant race, and that they offered a means for the revival of political activity on the part of the Negroes.[5] Four years later, the president of the Mount Wade Benevolent Society asked the editor of the *Gazette* to aid him in counteracting reports that his group met secretly to plan opposition to white control. In defense, he declared that white men often visited meetings of the society, and he urged them to continue to do so.[6] Neither white opposition, which gradually subsided, nor the general poverty of the race, prevented a phenomenal growth in the number and membership of these organizations.

Essentially, the various societies and lodges were very much alike. All

[2] Jackson *Weekly Clarion*, June 6, 13, July 4, 1883; Hinds County *Gazette*, July 12, 1876, May 28, June 25, 1879, August 4, 1883; Mississippi *Weekly Pilot*, May 22, 29, June 19, 1875.
[3] Hinds County *Gazette*, September 8, 1880.
[4] Jackson *Weekly Clarion*, August 5, October 28, November 4, 1885; Raymond *Gazette*, September 26, 1885; *Senate Miscellaneous Documents*, no. 166, 50th Congress, 1st session, p. 333.
[5] Horace S. Fulkerson, *The Negro*, pp. 96-97.
[6] Raymond *Gazette*, October 5, 1889.

were secret societies, formed around a ritual that constantly became more elaborate. Practically all of them were local in their origin. Founded in Natchez, Jackson, Vicksburg, or some similar town, they spread rapidly through the surrounding territory. In addition to supplying the social value of meetings, picnics, dances, and parades, they served the very practical purpose of spreading over poverty-stricken groups the costs of medical attention and of funerals. More and more they developed the policy of supplying to the family of a deceased member a small amount of cash in the form of insurance; generally, however, the emphasis was placed on that most satisfying of all thoughts to the dying Negro, a society funeral.

By 1885, one undertaking establishment in Natchez carried on its books the accounts of twenty of these organizations. The credit of a few of them seems to have been very poor, but each could afford a splendid name. They included the Lily of Youth; Daughters of Zion; Hiram R. Revels Lodge; Poor Saints Fund; Good Samaritan Sons and Daughters, City of Natchez; Good Samaritan Sons and Daughters, #1; Good Samaritan Sons and Daughters, #2; Improved Order Sons and Daughters of Jacob of America, Pride of Natchez, #174; Jacobs Benevolent Association; Golden Key Lodge; Universal Brotherhood; Natchez Tabernacle, #4; Mourning Pilgrims Society; D. P. Seaton Degree Lodge; Pride of Natchez Lodge, #1825; Sick and Burial Fund, #7944; Mt. Calvary Lodge, Improved Order of Good Samaritans; Pride of Mississippi Lodge, #3, Improved Order of Good Samaritans; Seven Stars of Consolidation, #159; and the Harvest Field Association.[7] During the next seven years, only three of these societies were dropped from the books. On the other hand, five new ones were added, making a total of twenty-two.[8]

There was practically nothing to distinguish the Negro lodges from the benevolent societies, save the use by the former of names and rituals similar to those already being used by various white fraternal organizations. T. W. Stringer, who had been the first Grand Master of a Negro Masonic order in Ohio, introduced Masonry to the Negroes of Mississippi with the establishment of Stringer Lodge at Vicksburg in 1867.[9] Within the next few years, with the coöperation of James D. Lynch and H. R. Revels, he added chapters at Jackson and at Natchez. From these three centers, the movement grew rapidly enough to justify the organization of the Most Worshipful Stringer Grand Lodge at Vicksburg in July, 1876. This Grand Lodge proceeded to establish the Fraternal Life Insurance Benefit in 1880, which paid to its beneficiaries death claims up to $700. By 1908, this insurance organization had 14,000 members, and owned a

[7] "Ledger," vol. 7, R. H. Stewart Papers, Louisiana State University.

[8] Ibid., vol. 8.

[9] Revels A. Adams, Cyclopedia of African Methodism in Mississippi, p. 192; Leading Afro-Americans of Vicksburg, Mississippi, p. 73; statement of E. L. Patton, Jackson, Mississippi, January 13, 1939.

thousand acres of timber land on the Yazoo and Mississippi Valley Rail-road. In 1907 it paid to its claimants $110,000.[10]

In March, 1875, T. W. Cardozo led in the establishment at Vicksburg of a branch of the Grand United Order of Odd Fellows of America.[11] This order grew rapidly and came to challenge the Masons for leadership in the state. The Negro Knights of Pythias, organized in Vicksburg by T. W. Stringer and T. M. Broadwater, developed much more slowly.[12] It seems that no chapter of the Colored Woodmen of the World was established in the state until 1905.[13]

Perhaps the most exclusive and most expensive groups developed by the Negroes were the volunteer fire companies. Such organizations existed for a number of years at Natchez, Jackson, Brandon, and Canton, and probably in a less elaborate fashion in a number of the other towns. The most prominent company in the state, Hope No. 3 of Jackson, was organized in January, 1870. With its large group of officers, its active and honorary members, and its women's auxiliary, it quickly became the center of the social activities of the Negroes of the town. Its annual parades and public "washings" were matters of elaborate planning and ceremony. Its excursions to Vicksburg, Natchez, and Canton, on which it often cleared several hundred dollars, were among the most popular of the period. It also offered a social program of dances, dinners, picnics, and croquet parties. Owning two engines, for one of which it paid $1,700, the company frequently received praise for its efficiency, and for being first on the scene at fires. During the rise of bad feeling with the overthrow of the Republican government in Jackson in 1887 and 1888, the company announced that it must disband because its members feared to gather in answer to alarms. By 1889, however, it was active once more, and continued to function, as did those in other towns, until the replacement of the volunteer companies, white and black, by professionals.[14]

As a part of their efforts to establish for themselves social organizations separate from, and corresponding to, those of the whites, the Negroes attempted to maintain a number of newspapers for their race. In their attempts they were naturally handicapped by poverty, the lack of advertising, and the absence of a large literate group from which to draw their subscribers. The result was that the average paper established by the Ne-

[10] Jackson *Weekly Clarion*, April 11, 1883; *Leading Afro-Americans of Vicksburg, Mississippi*, p. 73.

[11] Vicksburg *Times and Republican*, March 22, 1875.

[12] *Leading Afro-Americans of Vicksburg, Mississippi*, p. 77.

[13] *Ibid.*, p. 74.

[14] Jackson *Weekly Clarion*, February 26, April 16, May 21, 1879, June 2, 23, 1881, May 16, June 27, 1883; Mississippi *Weekly Pilot*, May 22, 29, 1875; Jackson *Clarion-Ledger*, May 16, 1889; *Senate Miscellaneous Documents*, no. 166, 50th Congress, 1st session, pp. 121, 299, 320, 327; Dave Rattray, *The City of Natchez, Mississippi*, p. 43; Goodspeed Publishing Company, *Biographical and Historical Memoirs of Mississippi*, II, 180.

groes showed a poor quality of materials and workmanship, and generally lasted only a few months. The first newspaper seems to have been the *Colored Citizen,* established in Vicksburg in 1867 by Henry Mason.[15] The same name was used by a paper published by J. J. Spelman and James D. Lynch in Jackson in 1870.[16] It was followed by the *Field Hand,* a monthly, published in Jackson by J. Garrett Johnson, a presiding elder of the Methodist Church. In 1877, J. J. Spelman made another effort with the *People's Journal,* which in later revivals became the *People's Adviser* and the *People's Defender.*[17] In the meantime, the General Missionary Baptist Association maintained its *Reflector* at a heavy loss for about thirteen months in 1873 and 1874.[18] The Missionary Baptist Convention managed with a great deal of difficulty to publish its *Baptist Signal* at irregular intervals from 1880 to 1883.[19] In 1888, J. J. Spelman, apparently undiscouraged by earlier failures, set up in Jackson a short-lived paper called the *Messenger.* It was followed by the *Colored Journal,* a paper of some merit which was controlled by W. H. Rogers and E. L. Patton, and which succeeded for a time in obtaining advertising from both races in Jackson.[20] At the same time, the ubiquitous L. W. W. Mannaway was issuing in Meridian a peculiar personal journal called *Fair Play.*[21] By 1890, however, it had become apparent that the Negroes of the state were unable to support such projects. The absence of a press to coördinate their efforts and to defend their interests continued to be a serious handicap to their development.

[15] Hinds County *Gazette,* May 10, 1867.
[16] William J. Simmons, *Men of Mark,* p. 930.
[17] Hinds County *Gazette,* May 13, July 11, 1874.
[18] Patrick H. Thompson, *Negro Baptists in Mississippi,* pp. 371, 380-381.
[19] *Ibid.,* pp. 173, 189, 190, 191, 204, 222, 243, 256, 298.
[20] Port Gibson *Reveille,* October 31, 1890; statement of E. L. Patton, Jackson, Mississippi, January 13, 1939.
[21] Jackson *Clarion-Ledger,* September 4, 1890.

CONCLUSIONS

Practically all of the 437,000 Negroes in Mississippi in 1860 were slaves. According to prevailing standards, they generally were assured of adequate food, clothing, and housing, and sufficient medical attention to keep them in good condition as laborers. Most of them had absorbed the basic materials of western culture. It was generally understood, however, that they had advanced by 1860 just about as far as they were to be allowed to go. The opinion of the mass of the white population, as expressed in the law, held that definite restrictions on that advancement were essential to the maintenance of the institution of slavery. The Negro slave at the beginning of the war was looked upon as a finished product. He was forbidden to hope that by industry or self-denial he might advance his status or that of his children.

In 1890 the 750,000 Negroes in Mississippi could look back on a quarter of a century of violent flux and change. Since 1865 the members of their race had been legally free, and guarantees of that freedom stood in the constitutions of the state and of the nation. Largely to serve the purposes of a political faction in the North, they had been granted the right to vote and to hold office. For a relatively brief period they had exercised that right, not without making serious mistakes, but in such a fashion as to vindicate the claims made for slavery as an educational institution. Abandoned by their political sponsors, they had been driven from the polls by intimidation, by fraud, by legal complexities, and finally by constitutional trickery. By 1890 they had learned that in Mississippi freedom did not mean the right to political equality.

By 1890 the freedom of the Negro had also been defined in terms of social relationships. The legal code granted to him equal but separate accommodations on public conveyances and in the schools, but the Negro had learned that laws had little effect in such matters. Laws, to a large extent, were instruments in the hands of the white men; the interpretation of those laws depended almost entirely on the attitude of the white men who controlled and enforced them. In all of the daily contacts of life, the Negro had come to recognize and to comply with a code that was stronger than the law, stronger than the Slave Code of 1857 or the Black Code of 1865. Essentially, this new code, gradually evolved through conflict and compromise, established a ritual of behavior for the Negro in his relations with the white man. It marked the completion of the transition from slavery to caste as a method of social control. By 1890 almost all white men in Mississippi agreed that the Negro was in his place, and that, at all costs, he should be kept there. That place, like the place of the slave, was carefully defined, and, theoretically, unalterable.

As a matter of fact, however, many gates had been opened to the Negro that never could be closed again. Through those gates he advanced toward experiences and opportunities that brought changes in his own nature and in his capacities. Those changes in the Negro naturally and inevitably foreshadowed a change in his place in the scheme of things, regardless of the attitude of the white man.

In the first place, the Negro had established the fact that his labor had value outside the system of slavery, and that on the proceeds of that labor he was able to maintain and increase his total number. As a free man, he had, and usually was able to maintain, the right to move about from place to place, and thus to bargain with his employer. His children, although their schools were poor and improved slowly if at all, were able to obtain an education equal to that available to the mass of the white population half a century before. The effects of this elementary education, together with that gained in the churches and the benevolent societies, in stores and on street corners, are only beginning to appear; they must be measured by decades and by generations, rather than from year to year. To the exceptional Negro, the way was now open to a precarious venture into the fields of business or the professions; each man who succeeded made the way easier for those who followed him. Here and there a Negro arose who gained the respect and good will of an influential white editor, businessman, or politician. The eventual effect of such contacts is incalculable. According to one story, James K. Vardaman, who built his political career on rabid attacks on the Negro race, secured a large appropriation for Alcorn College because he had come to know and like the Negro president of the school. "So," Ray Stannard Baker has said, "personal relationships, the solving touch of human nature, play havoc with political theories and generalities. Mankind develops not by rules but by exceptions to rules."[1] The effects on the attitude of the cultured white man produced by contacts with cultured Negroes are apparent and permanent. The opportunities for such contacts, and the number of Negroes able to supply them, increase with each generation. Gradually the exceptional Negro gains for his fellows the right to be considered as individuals rather than as members of a caste. Even in 1890 such forces were at work to undermine the code.

For freedom, then, the Negro sacrified the physical security which he had known as a slave. In its stead, he gained limited rights of movement, self-expression, and self-determination. He generally felt that the trade was to his advantage. In 1860 his position was almost static; in 1890 he

[1] Ray Stannard Baker, *Following the Color Line*, p. 251.

was a changeable element in a nation where change went on interminably. Decade after decade, and generation after generation, in spite of almost insuperable obstacles, he improved his status in ways that were hardly apparent, even to himself. No man could foretell the limits of that improvement. On its continuation depended, to a large extent, the progress of Mississippi and of the South.

BIBLIOGRAPHY

A. Contemporary Sources

I. *Manuscript Material*

Affleck, Thomas, Papers. Louisiana State University Archives, University, Louisiana. This large collection consists of the diaries, business papers, letter books, and miscellaneous correspondence of a planter who moved from Mississippi to Texas in 1857. The material, which covers the years from 1831 to 1868, includes letters from Eli J. Capell, a leading planter of Amite County, Mississippi.

Alcorn, James L., Papers. Southern Historical Collection, University of North Carolina, Chapel Hill. These papers include a brief diary, slave and tax records, and fragments of the correspondence of Alcorn, wealthy planter and former Whig, who became Mississippi's first Republican Governor in 1870.

Ames, Adelbert, Papers. Mississippi Department of Archives and History, Jackson, Mississippi. These are selected materials from the records and correspondence of Ames, who, as military commander, provisional governor, and governor of the state probably worked more effectively for the advancement of the Negroes than any other man.

Auburn Plantation Papers. See Duncan, Stephen.

Bisland, John, Papers. Louisiana State University Archives. This collection of 1,500 items consists chiefly of letters, but also includes plantation records and diaries. Bisland was a planter of the Natchez region. The papers cover the period from 1763 to 1895.

Capell, Eli J., Papers. Louisiana State University Archives. Of the fourteen volumes in this collection, covering the years from 1850 to 1896, only the last two fall within the period of this study. Volume 14, labor records from 1866 to 1886, is especially valuable for 1866, 1867, and 1868. After 1868 it was kept very carelessly. Capell's plantation was in Amite County.

Claiborne, J. F. H., Papers. Southern Historical Collection, University of North Carolina. The 888 items of this collection span the years from 1794 to 1910, and consist chiefly of material assembled by Claiborne for his *History of Mississippi*. Among the letters, there are some of special value from General Stephen D. Lee and Governors James L. Alcorn, John M. Stone, and Adelbert Ames.

Conner, Lemuel P., Papers. Louisiana State University Archives. This is a small but valuable collection of the family papers and plantation records of a planter of the Natchez region. The period covered is from 1867 to 1873.

Duncan, Stephen, Papers. Louisiana State University Archives. Of the six volumes of this collection, two are journals of foreign travel. The other four are journals and account books of Duncan's extensive operations as planter, capitalist, and speculator. Among the 113 unbound items are letters from Wade Hampton in relation to his investments in Mississippi, and also outlines of plans for the importation and use of Chinese labor. The material covers the years from 1856 to 1880.

Farr, Leslie, Papers. Louisiana State University Archives. This small group of ninety-two items, unbound, covers the years between 1862 and 1896. It consists of fragments of the records of the Jenkins and Dunbar families of the Natchez region.

Garner, James W., Papers. Mississippi Department of Archives and History. This material consists of selected letters to the historian of Reconstruction in Mississippi. Of extraordinary value are those from Adelbert Ames, Alexander Warner, and other Republican leaders of the state.

Innisfael Plantation Papers. See Conner, Lemuel P.

Johnson, Andrew, Papers. Manuscripts Division, Library of Congress, Washington, D. C. Included in this extensive collection are a number of letters from leading citizens of Mississippi. Most of them consist of complaints against Federal officials in the state, or of advice on the formation of a policy of Reconstruction.

Koch, C. D., Papers. Louisiana State University Archives. This group of 3,100 items, unbound, covers the years from 1820 to 1890, and deals largely with the Gulf Coast region, for which little other material is available. It includes agricultural, lumbering, and transportation records, and also a large number of letters from the Montana frontier.

Mercer, William, Papers. Louisiana State University Archives. This is the diary, 1848-1873, of a man with planting and commercial interests in the Natchez and New Orleans regions.

Murphy, Patrick, Papers. Louisiana State University Archives. Consisting of 19 time books, 8 ledgers, 12 diaries, and about 300 unbound items, this collection covers the period from 1859 to 1894, and is perhaps the most interesting single source of information for these years on the section from Natchez to Vicksburg. Murphy was an Irish immigrant who became a successful planter and railroad and levee contractor.

Pleasant Hill Plantation Papers. See Capell, Eli. J.

Recard Plantation Papers. See Conner, Lemuel P.

Red Lick Plantation Papers. See Ross, E. B.

Revels, Hiram R., "Autobiography." Carter G. Woodson Papers, Manuscripts Division, Library of Congress. This is a brief sketch in about fifty pages of the life of the first Negro Senator.

Ross, E. B., Papers. Louisiana State University Archives. This small journal and ledger of the Ross Plantation at Red Lick, Mississippi, covers the years from 1885 to 1894.

Schwartz, J. C., Papers. Louisiana State University Archives. These are miscellaneous records of a large mercantile establishment at Natchez. In 1885 Schwartz became a partner of R. H. Stewart, q.v.

Scott, Mrs. Laura, Papers. Louisiana State University Archives. Consisting of 321 items, unbound, this collection covers the period from 1850 to 1936. It includes a number of letters from the region around Port Gibson, Mississippi.

Shields, Joseph D., Papers. Louisiana State University Archives. The 712 items of this collection are especially valuable for information on the efforts of a leading planter to reorganize his labor system and reëstablish his credit arrangements in the period immediately following the war. After the failure of these efforts, Shields practised law at Natchez and Vicksburg.

Stanton, Edwin M., Papers. Manuscripts Division, Library of Congress. Scattered through this well-known collection are a number of letters to or from Mississippians.

Stewart, R. H., Papers. Louisiana State University Archives. Covering the period from 1865 to 1890, this very large collection includes letter books, journals, and account books connected with business enterprises which included planting, undertaking, and general merchandising. In 1885 the business was combined with that of J. C. Schwartz, q.v.

Whitehurst, William N., Papers. Mississippi Department of Archives and History. These papers include a large number of legal documents and correspondence with Democratic and Republican political leaders for the decade between 1865 and 1875.

Woodson, Carter G., Papers. Manuscripts Division, Library of Congress. This rapidly growing collection offers valuable material on the entire history of the Negro in America. Documents dealing especially with Mississippi are rare but useful.

II. *Official Records and Documents*

i. Publications of the United States Government

Bates, Edward, *Opinion of Attorney General Bates on Citizenship.* Washington: Government Printing Office. 1863.

Bureau of the Census, *Negro Population, 1790-1915.* Washington: Government Printing Office. 1918.

————, *Negroes in the United States,* Bulletin 8, 1904. Washington: Government Printing Office. 1904.

————, *Negroes in the United States, 1920-1932.* Washington: Government Printing Office. 1935.

Census, 1860, 1870, 1880, 1890. Washington: Government Printing Office.

Congressional Globe, 1834-1873. Washington: Office of the Congressional Globe, etc.

Congressional Record, 1873-1890. Washington: Government Printing Office.

Department of Agriculture, *Reports,* 1865-1890. Washington: Government Printing Office.

Executive Documents of the House of Representatives, 1865-1890. Washington: Government Printing Office.

Executive Documents of the Senate, 1865-1890. Washington: Government Printing Office.

Miscellaneous Documents of the House of Representatives, 1865-1890. Washington: Government Printing Office.

Miscellaneous Documents of the Senate, 1865-1890. Washington: Government Printing Office.

Official Army Register, 1865-1914. Washington: Government Printing Office.

Official Congressional Directory, 1865-1890. Washington: Government Printing Office.

Reports of the Committees of the House of Representatives, 1865-1890. Washington: Government Printing Office.

Reports of the Committees of the Senate, 1865-1890. Washington: Government Printing Office.

Richardson, James D. (ed.), *A Compilation of the Messages and Papers of the Presidents.* 10 vols. Washington: Government Printing Office.

The War of the Rebellion: A Compilation of the Official Records of the Union and Confederate Armies. 130 vols. Washington: Government Printing Office. 1880-1901.

ii. Publications of the Mississippi State Government

Constitution of the State of Mississippi, as amended with the Ordinances and Resolutions adopted by the Constitutional Convention August, 1865. Jackson, Mississippi: State Printer. 1865.

Constitution and Ordinances of the State of Mississippi, adopted in Convention Assembled in Pursuance of the Reconstruction Acts of Congress . . . in 1868. Jackson, Mississippi: State Printer. 1868.

Constitution of the State of Mississippi, adopted November 1, 1890. Jackson, Mississippi: State Printer. 1891.

Departmental Reports, 1865-1890. Jackson, Mississippi: State Printer. These include the *Messages* of the Governor, and the *Reports* of the Secretary of State, the Attorney General, the Treasurer, the Auditor of Public Accounts, the Superintendent of Public Education, the Board of Education, the County Superintendents of Education, the President of Holly Springs State Normal, the President of Alcorn College, the President of Tougaloo University, the Superintendent of the Blind Institute, the Superintendent of the Institution for the Deaf and Dumb, the Superintendent of the Lunatic Asylum, the Superintendent of the East Mississippi Insane Asylum, the Superintendent of the Penitentiary, the Superintendent of the State Hospital at Natchez, the Superintendent of the State Hospital at Vicksburg, the State Board of Health, the State Architect, the Levee Commissioners, the Swamp Land Commissioners, the Commissioner of Immigration and Agriculture, and the Board of Immigration and Agriculture.

Griggs, Richard (State Commissioner of Immigration), *Guide to Mississippi.* Jackson, Mississippi: State Printer. 1874.

Journal of the House of Representatives, 1865-1890. Jackson, Mississippi: State Printer.

Journal of the Senate, 1865-1890. Jackson, Mississippi: State Printer.

Journal of the Proceedings and Debates in the Constitutional Convention of the State of Mississippi, August, 1865. Jackson, Mississippi: E. M. Yerger. 1865.

Journal of the Proceedings in the Constitutional Convention of the State of Mississippi, 1868. Jackson, Mississippi: E. Stafford. 1871.

Journal of the Proceedings of the Constitutional Convention of the State of Mississippi, begun at the city of Jackson on August 12, 1890, and concluded November 1, 1890. Jackson, Mississippi: E. L. Martin. 1890.

Laws of the State of Mississippi (Session Laws), 1865-1890. Jackson, Mississippi: State Printer.

Mississippi State Board of Immigration and Agriculture, *Handbook of the State of Mississippi.* Jackson, Mississippi: State Printer. 1882.

———, *Handbook of the State of Mississippi.* Jackson, Mississippi: State Printer. 1885.

———, *State of Mississippi.* Jackson, Mississippi: State Printer. 1879.

Revised Code of the Statute Laws of the State of Mississippi. Jackson, Mississippi : State Printer. 1857.

Revised Code of the Statute Laws of the State of Mississippi. Jackson, Mississippi : State Printer. 1871.

Revised Code of the Statute Laws of Mississippi. Jackson, Mississippi : State Printer. 1880.

III. *Newspapers and Periodicals*

Aberdeen *Examiner.*
Aberdeen *Sunny South.*
(Appleton's) *American Annual Cyclopedia,* 1861-1874.
Appleton's Annual Cyclopedia, 1875-1890.
Brandon *Republican.*
Canton *Citizen.*
Canton *Mail.*
Cincinnati (Ohio) *Commercial.*
Columbus *Democrat.*
Columbus *Index.*
DeBow's Review, After the War Series, I-VIII (1866-1870), New Series, I (1879-1880).
Forest *Register.*
Friar's Point *Coahomian.*
Golden Rule Pilot (Steamer "Golden Rule").
Greenville *Times.*
Hinds County *Gazette.*
Holly Springs *Reporter.*
Holly Springs *South.*
Jackson *Clarion.*
Jackson *Clarion and Standard.*
Jackson *Clarion-Ledger.*
Jackson *Mississippian.*
Jackson *New Mississippian.*
Jackson *Mississippi Standard.*
Jackson *News.*
Jackson *Times.*
Lexington *Advertiser.*
Liberty *Southern Herald.*
Macon *Beacon.*
Memphis (Tennessee) *Avalanche.*
Meridian *Chronicle.*
Meridian *Clarion.*
Meridian *Mercury.*
Mississippi *Education Journal.*
Mississippi *Pilot.*
Mississippi *White Ribbon.*
Mississippi *White Ribboner.*
Mobile (Alabama) *Alabama Journal.*
Natchez *Courier.*
Natchez *Courier-Journal.*
Natchez *Democrat.*
Natchez *Democrat and Courier.*
New Orleans (Louisiana) *Crescent.*

New Orleans (Louisiana) *Republican.*
New Orleans (Louisiana) *Times.*
New Orleans (Louisiana) *Times-Democrat.*
Newton *Ledger.*
Okolona *Prairie News.*
Panola *Star.*
Port Gibson *Record.*
Port Gibson *Reveille.*
Port Gibson *Standard.*
Raymond *Gazette.*
Scooba *Herald.*
Stone, Alfred H., *The Negro and Cognate Subjects.* 112 vols. Mississippi
   State Department of Archives and History. Consists chiefly of material
   from periodicals.
Summit *Sentinel.*
Summit *Times.*
Vicksburg *Herald.*
Vicksburg *Commercial.*
Vicksburg *Herald and Mississippian.*
Vicksburg *Journal.*
Vicksburg *Monitor.*
Vicksburg *Republican.*
Vicksburg *Times.*
Vicksburg *Times and Republican.*
Woodville *Republican.*
Yazoo City *Herald.*
Yazoo City *Sentinel.*

   Of these newspapers, the *Clarion,* in its various forms as the Meridian
Clarion, the Jackson *Clarion,* the Jackson *Clarion and Standard,* and the Jackson *Clarion-Ledger,* covers the entire period and is the most valuable single
source for the view of the more conservative elements among the Democrats.
Almost complete coverage can be obtained by combining the use of the files at
the Mississippi Department of Archives and History, the University of Mississippi, and the Library of Congress. The Mississippi *Pilot* offers a remarkable
example of an ably edited Republican journal. Its use is almost indispensable
as a check on the Democratic press. Here again, fairly complete coverage
can be obtained only by combining the resources of the Mississippi Department
of Archives and History, the University of Mississippi, and the Library of
Congress. The only other Republican journal of any importance in the state,
the Vicksburg *Times* (later the Jackson *Times*) shows interesting "lily-white"
tendencies. The Hinds County *Gazette* is especially valuable for the period
between 1865 and 1874 because of the fact that its editor was a former Whig,
and was critical of the methods of both the Republicans and the Democrats.
With the exception of brief interludes, almost complete files, 1865-1890, are
available at the Mississippi Department of Archives and History. This same
institution has broken files and scattered copies of a majority of the other
papers that are listed in this bibliography. The use of these broken files has
been supplemented by that of similar holdings at the Library of Congress. The
most valuable single file at the latter institution, for this study, was that of the
Vicksburg *Commercial,* 1877-1882.

IV. *Travel Accounts, Reports, and Miscellaneous Writings*

Alcorn, James L., *Views of the Hon. J. L. Alcorn on the Political Situation in Mississippi.* Friar's Point, Mississippi: 1867.

Alvord, John W., *Letters from the South Relating to the Freedmen.* Washington: Howard University Press. 1870.

Andrews, Sidney, *The South Since the War.* Boston: Ticknor and Fields. 1866.

Archer, William, *Through Afro-America, an English Reading of the Race Problem.* London: Chapman and Hall. 1910.

Bacon, Edward, *Among the Cotton Thieves.* Detroit: Free Press Steam Book and Job Printing House. 1867.

Baker, Ray Stannard, *Following the Color Line.* New York: Doubleday, Page. 1908.

Biographical and Historical Memoirs of Mississippi. 2 vols. Chicago: Goodspeed. 1891.

Browne, Junius H., *Four Years in Secessia.* Chicago: G. & C. W. Sherwood. 1865.

Campbell, Sir George, *White and Black: The Outcome of a Visit to the United States.* New York: R. Worthington. 1879.

Claiborne, J. F. H., "A Trip to the Piney Woods." *Publications of the Mississippi Historical Society,* IX (1906), 487-538.

Clowes, W. Laird, *Black America: A Study of the Ex-Slave and his Master.* London: Cassell. 1891.

Davenport, F. Garvin (ed.), "Judge Sharkey's Papers." *Mississippi Valley Historical Review,* XX (1933), 75-90.

Dixon, William H., *New America.* 2 vols. London: Hurst and Blackett. 1867.

———, *White Conquest.* London: Chatto and Windus. 1876.

Doctrines and Discipline of the C. M. E. Church in America. Byhalia, Mississippi: E. Cottrell, Agent. 1883.

Documents of the United States Sanitary Commission. 3 vols. New York: 1866-1871.

Evans, Maurice S., *Black and White in the Southern States.* London and New York: Longmans, Green. 1915.

Facts Concerning the Freedmen, their Capacity and their Destiny, Collected and Published by the Emancipation League. Boston: Commercial Printing House. 1863.

Freeman, Edward A., *Some Impressions of the United States.* New York: Henry Holt. 1883.

Fulkerson, Horace S., *The Negro; as he was; as he is; as he will be.* Vicksburg, Mississippi: Commercial Herald Printers. 1887.

Furlong, Charles E., *Origin of the Outrages at Vicksburg.* Vicksburg, Mississippi: Vicksburg Herald Print. 1874.

Girardeau, J. L., "Our Ecclesiastical Relation to the Freedmen," *Southern Presbyterian Review,* XVIII (1867) 1-18.

Glimpses of Vicksburg and Vicinity. New York: Albertype. 1890.

Hilgard, Eugene W., "Cotton Production in the State of Mississippi," U. S. *Census*, 1880, V, 197-358.

History of the American Missionary Association; its Churches and Educational Institutions among the Freedmen, Indians, and Chinese. New York: Green. 1874.

Journal of the Mississippi Annual Conference of the Methodist Episcopal Church. New Orleans: 1881.

Journal of the Mississippi Annual Conference of the Methodist Episcopal Church. Columbus, Mississippi: 1890.

Kennaway, John H., *On Sherman's Track; or The South After the War.* London: Seeley, Jackson, and Halliday. 1867.

King, Edward, *The Great South.* Hartford, Connecticut: American Publishing Company. 1875.

Jannet, Claudio, *Les États-Unis Contemporains; Ou les moeurs, les institutions et les idées depuis la guerre de la sécession.* Paris: E. Pion. 1876.

Knox, Thomas W., *Camp-Fire and Cotton-Field.* New York and Chicago: Blelock. 1865.

McClure, Alexander K., *The South: Its Industrial, Financial, and Political Condition.* Philadelphia: Lippincott. 1886.

Macrae, David, *The Americans At Home; Pen and Ink Sketches of American Men, Manners and Institutions.* 2 vols. Edinburgh: Edmonston and Douglas, 1870.

Marshall, Charles K., *The Exodus: Its Effect upon the People of the South, Colored Labor not Indispensable.* Washington: American Colonizatic ι Society. 1880.

Minutes of the Mississippi Annual Conference of the African Methodist Episcopal Church, second session, 1870. Jackson, Mississippi: 1870.

Minutes of the Mississippi Mission Conference of the Methodist Episcopal Church, 1865 and 1866. New Orleans: 1867.

McKay, James, *The Mastership and its Fruits.* New York: W. C. Bryant. 1864.

Nordhoff, Charles, *The Cotton States in the Spring and Summer of 1875.* New York: D. Appleton. 1876.

Northwestern Freedmen's Aid Commission, *Second Annual Report.* Chicago: James Barnet. 1865.

Origin and Progress of the Vicksburg Troubles, as reported daily in the columns of the Vicksburg Herald. Vicksburg, Mississippi: Vicksburg Herald. 1874.

Proceedings of the Colored National Labor Convention. Washington: Office of the *New Era.* 1870.

Proceedings of the National Conference of Colored Men of the United States. Washington: R. H. Darby. 1879.

Proceedings of the National Convention of Colored Men of America. Washington: Great Republic Press. 1869.

Rattray, Dave, *The City of Natchez, Mississippi.* n.p., n.d.

Reid, Whitelaw, *After the War: A Southern Tour.* Cincinnati, New York and London: Moore, Wilstach and Baldwin. 1866.

Richardson, Lee and Godman, Thomas D., *In and About Vicksburg.* Vicksburg, Mississippi: Gibraltar. 1890.

Riley, Franklin L. (ed.), "The Diary of a Mississippi Planter," *Publications of the Mississippi Historical Society,* X (1909), 305-482.

Rowland, J. Dunbar (ed.), *Jefferson Davis, Constitutionalist: His Letters, Papers, and Speeches.* 10 vols. Jackson, Mississippi: Department of Archives and History. 1923.

Russell, William H., *My Diary, North and South.* Boston: T. O. H. P. Burnham. 1863.

Somers, Robert, *The Southern States since the War, 1870-1871.* London and New York: Macmillan. 1871.

Trowbridge, John T., *The South.* Hartford, Connecticut: L. Stebbins. 1866.

Yeatman, James E., *Report on the Condition of the Freedmen of the Mississippi Valley,* St. Louis: Western Sanitary Commission Rooms. 1864.

———, *Suggestions of a Plan of Organization for Freed Labor and the Leasing of Plantations.* St. Louis: Rooms of the Western Sanitary Commission. 1864.

Zincke, Foster B., *Last Winter in the United States.* London: J. Murray. 1868.

B. Non-Contemporary Sources

I. *Autobiographies, Memoirs, and Reminiscences*

Aughey, John H., *Tupelo.* Lincoln, Nebraska: State Journal. 1888.

Bowman, Robert, "Reconstruction in Yazoo County," *Publications of the Mississippi Historical Society,* VII (1903), 115-130.

———, "Yazoo County in the Civil War," *Publications of the Mississippi Historical Society,* VII (1903), 57-74.

Carter, Theodore G., "The Tupelo Campaign," *Publications of the Mississippi Historical Society,* X (1909), 91-114.

Calhoon, S. S., "Causes and Events That Led to the Calling of the Constitutional Convention of 1890," *Publications of the Mississippi Historical Society,* VI (1902), 105-110.

Davis, Reuben, *Recollections of Mississippi and Mississippians.* Boston: Houghton, Mifflin. 1891.

Deupree, J. G., "The Capture of Holly Springs, December 20, 1862," *Publications of the Mississippi Historical Society,* IX (1901), 49-62.

———, "Reminiscences of Service with the First Mississippi Cavalry," *Publications of the Mississippi Historical Society,* VII (1904), 85-100.

Eaton, John, *Grant, Lincoln, and the Freedmen.* New York: Longmans, Green. 1907.

Fulkerson, Horace S., *Rambling Recollections of Early Days in Mississippi.* Vicksburg, Mississippi: 1885.

Grigsby, Melvin, *The Smoked Yank.* Sioux Falls, South Dakota: Dakota Bell. 1888.

Hardy, William H., "Recollections of Reconstruction in East and Southeast Mississippi," *Publications of the Mississippi Historical Society,* IV, (1901), 104-132; VII (1903), 199-216; VIII (1904), 137-152.

Johnston, Frank A., "The Conference between General George and Governor Ames," *Publications of the Mississippi Historical Society*, VI (1902), 65-78.

————, "Suffrage and Reconstruction in Mississippi," *Publications of the Mississippi Historical Society*, VI (1902), 141-244.

Jones, J. H., "Penitentiary Reform in Mississippi," *Publications of the Mississippi Historical Society*, VI (1902), 111-128.

————, "Reconstruction in Wilkinson County," *Publications of the Mississippi Historical Society*, VIII (1904), 153-176.

Lee, Stephen D., "Sherman's Expedition from Vicksburg to Meridian, Feb. 3rd to March 6th, 1863," *Publications of the Mississippi Historical Society*, IV (1901), 37-47.

————, "The War in Mississippi after the Fall of Vicksburg," *Publications of the Mississippi Historical Society*, X (1909), 47-62.

Lynch, John R., *The Facts of Reconstruction*. New York: Neale. 1913.

————, "Some Historical Errors of James Ford Rhodes," *Journal of Negro History*, II (1917), 345-368.

————, *Some Historical Errors of James Ford Rhodes*. Boston, and New York: Cornhill. [1922.]

Montgomery, Franklin A., *Reminiscences of Mississippians in Peace and War*. Cincinnati: R. Clarke. 1901.

Morgan, Albert T., *Yazoo*. Washington: The Author. 1884.

McNeily, John S., "History of the Measures Submitted to the Committee on Elective Franchise, Apportionment, and Elections in the Constitutional Convention of 1890," *Publications of the Mississippi Historical Society*, VI (1902), 129-140.

Proceedings of a Reunion of the Surviving Members of the Constitutional Convention of 1890. Jackson, Mississippi: Premier. 1927.

Smedes, Susan D., *Memorials of a Southern Planter*. Baltimore: Cushings and Bailey. 1888.

Tarbell, John, "Horace Greeley's Practical Advice, an Incident of Reconstruction in Mississippi," *Magazine of American History*, XVIII (1887), 423-425.

Warren, Henry W., *Reminiscences of a Mississippi Carpet-Bagger*. Holden, Massachusetts: 1914.

Washington, Booker T., *Up From Slavery*. New York: Doubleday, Page. 1901.

Wells, W. Calvin, "Reconstruction and Its Destruction in Hinds County," *Publications of the Mississippi Historical Society*, IX (1906), 85-108.

II. *General Works and Special Studies*

Abney, M. G., "Reconstruction in Pontotoc County," *Publications of the Mississippi Historical Society*, XI (1910), 229-270.

Adams, Revels A., *Cyclopedia of African Methodism in Mississippi*. [Natchez, Mississippi]: 1902.

Alexander, William T., *History of the Colored Race in America*. New Orleans: Palmetto. 1888.

Allen, James S., *The Negro Question in the United States*. New York: International. 1936.

————, *Reconstruction, the Battle for Democracy*. New York: International. 1937.

Bailey, Thomas P., *Race Orthodoxy in the South*. New York: Neale. 1914.

Beale, Howard K., *The Critical Year*. New York: Harcourt, Brace. 1930.

Beckett, Richard C., "Some Effects of Military Reconstruction in Monroe County," *Publications of the Mississippi Historical Society*, VIII (1904), 177-186.

Bettersworth, John K., *Confederate Mississippi*. Baton Rouge: Louisiana State University. 1943.

Bowers, Claude G., *The Tragic Era*. Cambridge: Houghton, Mifflin. 1929.

Boyd, William K., "Educational History in the South Since 1865," *Studies in Southern History and Politics*. New York: Columbia University. 1925.

Braden, W. H., "Reconstruction in Lee County," *Publications of the Mississippi Historical Society*, X (1909), 135-146.

Brandon, Gerard, "Historic Adams County," *Publications of the Mississippi Historical Society*, II (1899), 207-218.

Brawley, Benjamin, *Negro Builders and Heroes*. Chapel Hill: University of North Carolina. 1937.

Brewer, J. Mason, *Negro Legislators of Texas*. Dallas, Texas: Mathis. 1935.

Brough, Charles H., "The Clinton Riot," *Publications of the Mississippi Historical Society*, VI (1902), 53-64.

————, "History of Taxation in Mississippi," *Publications of the Mississippi Historical Society*, II (1899), 113-124.

Brown, Julia C., "Reconstruction in Yalobusha and Grenada Counties," *Publications of the Mississippi Historical Society*, XII (1912), 214-282.

Brown, William W., *The Negro in the American Rebellion*. Boston: Lee & Shepard. 1867.

Browne, Fred Z., "Reconstruction in Oktibbeha County," *Publications 'of the Mississippi Historical Society*, XIII (1913), 273-298.

Cable, George W., *The Silent South*. New York: 1889.

————, *The Silent South, Together with The Freedmen's Case in Equity and The Convict Lease System*. New York: Scribners. 1907.

————, *The Southern Struggle for Pure Government*. Boston: S. Usher. 1890.

Caldwell, Elizabeth, "Reconstruction in Yazoo County." Unpublished master's thesis, University of North Carolina, 1931.

Cate, Wirt A., *Lucius Q. C. Lamar*. Chapel Hill: University of North Carolina. 1935.

Coleman, E. C., Jr., "Reconstruction in Attala County," *Publications of the Mississippi Historical Society*, X (1910), 147-162.

Cooper, Forrest, "Reconstruction in Scott County," *Publications of the Mississippi Historical Society*, XIII (1913), 99-222.

Cromwell, John W., *The Negro in American History*. Washington: American Negro Academy. 1914.

Curry, Jabez L. M., *Difficulties, Complications and Limitations Connected with the Education of the Negro*. Baltimore: Trustees of the Slater Fund. 1895.

———, *Education of the Negro Since 1860*. Baltimore: Trustees of the Slater Fund. 1894.

Davis, Sidney F., *Mississippi Negro Lore*. Jackson, Tennessee: McCowat, Mercer. 1914.

———, "The Negro Law in Mississippi," *Case and Commonwealth*, XX (1920), 329.

Dictionary of American Biography. 20 vols. New York: C. Scribner's Sons. 1928-1936.

Dowd, Jerome, *The Negro in American Life*. New York: Century. 1926.

DuBois, William E. B., *Black Reconstruction*. New York: Harcourt, Brace. 1935.

———, *The Negro American Artisan*. Atlanta, Georgia: Atlanta University. 1912.

———, *The Negro Artisan*. Atlanta, Georgia: Atlanta University. 1902.

———, *The Negro Church*. Atlanta, Georgia: Atlanta University. 1903.

Dunning, William A., *Reconstruction, Political and Economic*. American Nation Series, vol. XXII. New York: Harper. 1906.

Duren, William L., *Charles Betts Galloway*. Emory University, Georgia: Banner. 1932.

Duval, Mary V., "The Chevalier Bayard of Mississippi—Edward Cary Walthall," *Publications of the Mississippi Historical Society*, IV (1901), 404-414.

———, *History of Mississippi and Civil Government*. Louisville, Kentucky: Courier Journal. 1892.

Edwards, T. J., "The Tenant System and Some Changes Since Emancipation," *Annals of the American Academy of Political and Social Science*, XLIX (1913), 38-46.

Evans, Clement A. (ed.), *Confederate Military History*. Atlanta, Georgia: Confederate Publishing Company. 1899.

Fleming, Walter L., "Deportation and Colonization: An Attempted Solution of the Race Problem," *Studies in Southern History and Politics*. New York: Columbia University, 1925.

———, *Documentary History of Reconstruction*. 2 vols. Cleveland, Ohio: A. H. Clark. 1906-1907.

———, *The Freedmen's Savings Bank*. Chapel Hill: University of North Carolina. 1927.

———, *Immigration to the Southern States*. Boston: Ginn. 1905.

———, *Laws Relating to Freedmen*. Morgantown, West Virginia: 1904.

Galloway, Charles B., *The South and the Negro*. New York: Southern Education Board. 1904.

Garner, Alfred W., "The Public Services of E. C. Walthall," *Publications of the Mississippi Historical Society*, IX (1906), 239-254.

Garner, James W., *Reconstruction in Mississippi*. New York: Macmillan. 1901.

———, "Southern Politics Since the Civil War," *Studies in Southern History and Politics*. New York: Columbia University. 1925.

——— (ed.), *Studies in Southern History and Politics*. New York: Columbia University. 1914.

George, James Z., *The Political History of Slavery in the United States.* New York: Neale. 1915.

Greene, Lorenzo J. and Woodson, Carter G., *The Negro Wage Earner.* Washington: Association for the Study of Negro Life and History. 1930.

Hamilton, J. G. de Roulhac, "Southern Legislation in Respect to Freedmen," *Studies in Southern History and Politics.* New York: Columbia University. 1925.

Hawk, Emory Q., *Economic History of the South.* New York: Prentice-Hall. 1934.

Haygood, Atticus G., *Our Brother in Black.* New York: Phillips and Hunt. 1881.

Henderson, Joseph W., *The Colored Man and the Ballot.* Oakland, California: Henderson and Humphrey. 1888.

Herbert, Hilary A. (ed.), *Why the Solid South.* Baltimore: R. H. Woodward. 1890.

Hesseltine, William B., *History of the South.* New York: Prentice-Hall. 1936.

Houston, G. Daniel, "A Negro Senator," *Journal of Negro History.* VII (1922), 243-256.

Jackson, Maurice Elizabeth, "Mound Bayou—a Study in Social Development." Unpublished master's thesis, University of Alabama, 1937.

Johnson, Charles S., *The Negro in American Civilization.* New York: Henry Holt. 1930.

Johnston, Frank A., "The Public Services of General James Z. George," *Publications of the Mississippi Historical Society,* VIII (1904), 201-226.

Kendel, Julia, "Reconstruction in Lafayette County," *Publications of the Mississippi Historical Society,* XIII (1913), 223-272.

Knight, Edgar W., *The Influence of Reconstruction on Education in the South.* New York: Columbia University. 1913.

Kyle, John W., "Reconstruction in Panola County," *Publications of the Mississippi Historical Society,* XIII (1913), 9-98.

Lacey, Nannie, "Reconstruction in Leake County," *Publications of the Mississippi Historical Society,* XI (1910), 271-294.

Leading Afro-Americans of Vicksburg, Mississippi. Vicksburg, Biographia. 1908.

Leavell, Ulin W., *Philanthropy in Negro Education.* Nashville, Tennessee: George Peabody College. 1930.

Leavell, Zachery T. and Bailey, T. J., *A Complete History of Mississippi Baptists.* 2 vols. Jackson, Mississippi: Mississippi Baptist Publishing Company. 1904.

Leftwich, George J., "Reconstruction in Monroe County," *Publications of the Mississippi Historical Society,* IX (1906), 53-84.

Lewinson, Paul, *Race, Class, and Party.* New York: Oxford University. 1932.

Lipscomb, William L., *A History of Columbus, Mississippi, during the 19th Century.* Birmingham, Alabama: 1909.

Mabry, William A., "Disfranchisement of the Negro in Mississippi," *Journal of Southern History,* IV (1938), 318-33.

Maclachlan, John M. "Mississippi: a Regional Social-Economic Analysis." Unpublished doctoral dissertation, University of North Carolina, 1937.

Magee, Hattie, "Reconstruction in Lawrence and Jeff Davis Counties," *Publications of the Mississippi Historical Society,* XI (1910), 163-204.

Magruder, William W., "Legal Status of Slaves in Mississippi Before the War," *Publications of the Mississippi Historical Society,* IV (1901), 133-142.

Mayes, Edward, *History of Education in Mississippi.* Washington: Government Printing Office. 1899.

————, *Lucius Q. C. Lamar: His Life, Times, and Speeches.* Nashville, Tennessee: Publishing House of the Methodist Episcopal Church, South. 1896.

Mississippi Historical Records Survey, "Church Inventory of Hinds County," Jackson, Mississippi: 1937.

Mitchell, Broadus, *The Economic Effects of Slavery.* Baltimore: Johns Hopkins University. 1924.

Mollison, Irvin C., "Negro Lawyers in Mississippi," *Journal of Negro History,* XV (1930), 38-71.

Moore, Ross H., "Social and Economic Conditions in Mississippi during Reconstruction." Unpublished doctoral dissertation, Duke University, 1938.

Moton, Robert R., *What the Negro Thinks.* New York: Doubleday, Doran. 1929.

Murphy, Edgar G., *The Basis of Ascendancy.* New York: Longmans, Green. 1910.

————, *Problems of the Present South.* New York: Macmillan. 1904.

McNeily, John S., "Climax and Collapse of Reconstruction in Mississippi," *Publications of the Mississippi Historical Society,* XII (1912), 283-474.

————, "The Enforcement Act of 1871 and the Ku Klux Klan in Mississippi," *Publications of the Mississippi Historical Society,* IX (1906), 109-172.

————, "From Organization to Overthrow of Mississippi's Provisional Government," *Publications of the Mississippi Historical Society, Centenary Series,* I (1917), 9-403.

————, "War and Reconstruction in Mississippi, 1863-1890," *Publications of the Mississippi Historical Society, Centenary Series,* II (1918), 165-535.

Nichols, Irby C., "Reconstruction in De Soto County," *Publications of the Mississippi Historical Society,* XI (1910), 295-316.

Noble, Stuart G., *Forty Years of the Public Schools in Mississippi.* New York: Columbia University. 1918.

Odum, Howard W., *Social and Mental Traits of the Negro.* New York: Columbia University. 1910.

Payne, Daniel A., *The History of the African Methodist Episcopal Church.* Nashville, Tennessee: Publishing House of the A. M. E. Sunday School Union. 1891.

Peirce, Paul S., *The Freedmen's Bureau.* Iowa City: University of Iowa. 1904.

Phillips, Charles H., *History of the Colored Methodist Episcopal Church in America.* Jackson, Tennessee: Publishing House of the C. M. E. Church. 1925.

Pipkin, James J., *The Story of a Rising Race*. St. Louis: N. D. Thompson. 1902.

Powdermaker, Hortense, *After Freedom*. New York: Viking. 1939.

Power, J. L., "The Black and Tan Convention," *Publications of the Mississippi Historical Society*, III (1900), 73-84.

Puckett, R. P., "Reconstruction in Monroe County," *Publications of the Mississippi Historical Society*, XI (1910), 103-162.

Ranck, James B., *Albert Gallatin Brown*. New York: D. Appleton. 1937.

Rousseve, Charles B., *The Negro in Louisiana*. New Orleans: Xavier University. 1937.

Rowland, J. Dunbar, *A Mississippi View of Race Relations in the South*. Jackson, Mississippi: Harmon. 1903.

———, *Encyclopedia of Mississippi History*. 2 vols. Madison, Wisconsin: S. A. Brant. 1907.

———, *History of Mississippi, the Heart of the South*. 2 vols. Chicago: S. J. Clarke. 1929.

———, "Plantation Life in Mississippi Before the War," *Publications of the Mississippi Historical Society*, III (1900), 85-98.

———, "The Rise and Fall of Negro Rule in Mississippi," *Publications of the Mississippi Historical Society*, II (1899), 189-200.

Simmons, William J., *Men of Mark*. Cleveland, Ohio: G. M. Rewell. 1887.

Smith, Samuel D., *The Negro in Congress, 1870-1901*. Chapel Hill: University of North Carolina. 1943.

Stephenson, Gilbert T., *Race Distinctions in American Law*. New York: D. Appleton. 1910.

Stephenson, W. H., "A Quarter-Century of a Mississippi Plantation: Eli J. Capell of 'Pleasant Hill,'" *Mississippi Valley Historical Review*, XXIII (1936), 335-374.

Stone, Alfred H., *The Early Slave Laws of Mississippi*. [Oxford, Mississippi: 1899.]

———, "The Economic Future of the Negro: The Factor of White Competition," *Publications of the American Economics Association*, third series, VII (1906), 243-294.

———, *Mississippi's Constitution and Statutes in Reference to Freedmen and their Alleged Relation to the Reconstruction Acts and War Amendments*. [Oxford, Mississippi: 1901.]

———, *The Negro in the Yazoo-Mississippi Delta*. [New York, 1902.]

———, *Studies in the American Race Problem*. New York: Doubleday, Page. 1908.

Sydnor, Charles S., "The Free Negro in Mississippi before the Civil War," *American Historical Review*, XXXII (1926-1927), 769-788.

———, "The Life Span of Mississippi Slaves," *American Historical Review*, XXXV (1929-1930), 566-574.

———, *Slavery in Mississippi*. New York: D. Appleton-Century. 1933.

Taylor, Alrutheus A., "Negro Congressmen a Generation After," *Journal of Negro History*, VII (1922), 127-171.

———, *The Negro in South Carolina During the Reconstruction*. Washington: Association for the Study of Negro Life and History. [1924.]

————, *The Negro in the Reconstruction of Virginia*. Washington: Association for the Study of Negro Life and History. [1926.]

Thompson, Patrick H., *The History of the Negro Baptists in Mississippi*. Jackson, Mississippi: R. W. Bailey. 1898.

Thompson, R. H., "Suffrage in Mississippi," *Publications of the Mississippi Historical Society*, I (1898), 25-49.

Timberlake, Elise, "Did Reconstruction Give Mississippi Her Public Schools?" *Publications of the Mississippi Historical Society*, XII (1912), 72-93.

Tucker, J. L., *The Relations of the Church to the Colored Race*. Jackson, Mississippi: Charles Winkley. 1882.

Wallace, Jesse T., *A History of the Negroes of Mississippi from 1865 to 1890*. Clinton, Mississippi: The Author. 1927.

Washington, Booker T., *The Story of the Negro*. New York: Doubleday, Page. 1909.

Watkins, Ruth, "Reconstruction in Marshall County," *Publications of the Mississippi Historical Society*, XII (1912), 155-213.

————, "Reconstruction in Newton County," *Publications of the Mississippi Historical Society*, XI (1910), 205-228.

Weatherford, Willis D., *The Negro from Africa to America*. New York: Doran. 1924.

Wells, James M., *The Chisholm Massacre: a Picture of Home Rule in Mississippi*. Chicago: Chisholm Monumental Fund. 1877.

Wesley, Charles H., *Negro Labor in the United States, 1850-1925*. New York: Vanguard. 1927.

Wiley, Bell I., *Southern Negroes, 1861-1865*. New Haven, Connecticut: Yale University. 1938.

Williams, George W., *History of the Negro Race in America from 1619 to 1880*. New York: Putnam. 1883.

————, *History of the Negro Troops in the War of the Rebellion, 1861-1865*. New York: Harper. 1888.

Wilson, Henry, *History of the Rise and Fall of the Slave Power in America*. 3 vols. Boston and New York: Houghton, Mifflin. 1877.

Witty, Fred M., "Reconstruction in Carroll and Montgomery Counties," *Publications of the Mississippi Historical Society*, X (1909), 115-134.

Woodson, Carter G., *A Century of Negro Migration*. Washington: Association for the Study of Negro Life and History. 1918.

————, *History of the Negro Church*. Washington: Associated Publishers. 1921.

————, *The Negro in Our History*. Washington: Associated Publishers. 1922.

————, *Negro Orators and their Orations*. Washington: Associated Publishers. 1925.

————, *The Negro Professional Man and the Community*. Washington: Association for the Study of Negro Life and History. 1934.

Woofter, Thomas J., Jr., *Landlord and Tenant on the Cotton Plantation*. Washington: Works Progress Administration. 1936.

Work Monroe N., "Some Negro Members of Reconstruction Conventions and Legislatures and of Congress," *Journal of Negro History*, V (1920), 63-125.

INDEX

haRper ✦ ᴄoRchbooks

HUMANITIES AND SOCIAL SCIENCES

American Studies: General

THOMAS C. COCHRAN: The Inner Revolution. *Essays on the Social Sciences in History* TB/1140
EDWARD S. CORWIN: American Constitutional History. *Essays edited by Alpheus T. Mason and Gerald Garvey* ᴬ TB/1136
CARL N. DEGLER, Ed.: Pivotal Interpretations of American History TB/1240, TB/1241
A. HUNTER DUPREE: Science in the Federal Government: *A History of Policies and Activities to 1940* TB/573
A. S. EISENSTADT, Ed.: The Craft of American History: *Recent Essays in American Historical Writing*
Vol. I TB/1255; Vol. II TB/1256
CHARLOTTE P. GILMAN: Women and Economics: *A Study of the Economic Relation between Men and Women as a Factor in Social Evolution.* ‡ *Ed. with an Introduction by Carl N. Degler* TB/3073
OSCAR HANDLIN, Ed.: This Was America: *As Recorded by European Travelers in the Eighteenth, Nineteenth and Twentieth Centuries. Illus.* TB/1119
MARCUS LEE HANSEN: The Atlantic Migration: 1607-1860. *Edited by Arthur M. Schlesinger* TB/1052
MARCUS LEE HANSEN: The Immigrant in American History. TB/1120
JOHN HIGHAM, Ed.: The Reconstruction of American History ᴬ TB/1068
ROBERT H. JACKSON: The Supreme Court in the American System of Government TB/1106
JOHN F. KENNEDY: A Nation of Immigrants. ᴬ *Illus.* TB/1118
LEONARD W. LEVY, Ed.: American Constitutional Law: *Historical Essays* TB/1285
RALPH BARTON PERRY: Puritanism and Democracy TB/1138
ARNOLD ROSE: The Negro in America TB/3048
MAURICE R. STEIN: The Eclipse of Community. *An Interpretation of American Studies* TB/1128
W. LLOYD WARNER and Associates: Democracy in Jonesville: *A Study in Quality and Inequality* ¶ TB/1129
W. LLOYD WARNER: Social Class in America: *The Evaluation of Status* TB/1013

American Studies: Colonial

BERNARD BAILYN, Ed.: Apologia of Robert Keayne: *Self-Portrait of a Puritan Merchant* TB/1201
BERNARD BAILYN: The New England Merchants in the Seventeenth Century TB/1149
JOSEPH CHARLES: The Origins of the American Party System TB/1049

LAWRENCE HENRY GIPSON: The Coming of the Revolution: 1763-1775. † *Illus.* TB/3007
LEONARD W. LEVY: Freedom of Speech and Press in Early American History: *Legacy of Suppression* TB/1109
PERRY MILLER: Errand Into the Wilderness TB/1139
PERRY MILLER & T. H. JOHNSON, Eds.: The Puritans: *A Sourcebook of Their Writings*
Vol. I TB/1093; Vol. II TB/1094
EDMUND S. MORGAN, Ed.: The Diary of Michael Wigglesworth, 1653-1657: *The Conscience of a Puritan* TB/1228
EDMUND S. MORGAN: The Puritan Family: *Religion and Domestic Relations in Seventeenth-Century New England* TB/1227
RICHARD B. MORRIS: Government and Labor in Early America TB/1244
KENNETH B. MURDOCK: Literature and Theology in Colonial New England TB/99
WALLACE NOTESTEIN: The English People on the Eve of Colonization: 1603-1630. † *Illus.* TB/3006
LOUIS B. WRIGHT: The Cultural Life of the American Colonies: 1607-1763. † *Illus.* TB/3005

American Studies: From the Revolution to 1860

JOHN R. ALDEN: The American Revolution: 1775-1783. † *Illus.* TB/3011
MAX BELOFF, Ed.: The Debate on the American Revolution, 1761-1783: *A Sourcebook* ᴬ TB/1225
RAY A. BILLINGTON: The Far Western Frontier: 1830-1860. † *Illus.* TB/3012
W. R. BROCK: An American Crisis: *Congress and Reconstruction, 1865-67* ° ᴬ TB/1283
EDMUND BURKE: On the American Revolution: *Selected Speeches and Letters.* ‡ *Edited by Elliott Robert Barkan* TB/3068
WHITNEY R. CROSS: The Burned-Over District: *The Social and Intellectual History of Enthusiastic Religion in Western New York, 1800-1850* ᴬ TB/1242
GEORGE DANGERFIELD: The Awakening of American Nationalism: 1815-1828. † *Illus.* TB/3061
CLEMENT EATON: The Freedom-of-Thought Struggle in the Old South. *Revised and Enlarged. Illus.* TB/1150
CLEMENT EATON: The Growth of Southern Civilization: 1790-1860. † *Illus.* TB/3040
LOUIS FILLER: The Crusade Against Slavery: 1830-1860. † *Illus.* TB/3029
DIXON RYAN FOX: The Decline of Aristocracy in the Politics of New York: 1801-1840. ‡ *Edited by Robert V. Remini* TB/3064
FELIX GILBERT: The Beginnings of American Foreign Policy: *To the Farewell Address* TB/1200
FRANCIS GRIERSON: The Valley of Shadows: *The Coming of the Civil War in Lincoln's Midwest: A Contemporary Account* TB/1246

---

† The New American Nation Series, edited by Henry Steele Commager and Richard B. Morris.

‡ American Persectives series, edited by Bernard Wishy and William E. Leuchtenburg.

* The Rise of Modern Europe series, edited by William L. Langer.

¶ Researches in the Social, Cultural, and Behavioral Sciences, edited by Benjamin Nelson.

§ The Library of Religion and Culture, edited by Benjamin Nelson.

Σ Harper Modern Science Series, edited by James R. Newman.

° Not for sale in Canada.

ᴬ Not for sale in the U. K.

FRANCIS J. GRUND: Aristocracy in America: *Social Class in the Formative Years of the New Nation* TB/1001

ALEXANDER HAMILTON: The Reports of Alexander Hamilton. ‡ *Edited by Jacob E. Cooke* TB/3060

THOMAS JEFFERSON: Notes on the State of Virginia. ‡ *Edited by Thomas P. Abernethy* TB/3052

JAMES MADISON: The Forging of American Federalism: *Selected Writings of James Madison. Edited by Saul K. Padover* TB/1226

BERNARD MAYO: Myths and Men: *Patrick Henry, George Washington, Thomas Jefferson* TB/1108

JOHN C. MILLER: Alexander Hamilton and the Growth of the New Nation TB/3057

RICHARD B. MORRIS, Ed.: The Era of the American Revolution TB/1180

R. B. NYE: The Cultural Life of the New Nation: 1776-1801. † *Illus.* TB/3026

FRANCIS S. PHILBRICK: The Rise of the West, 1754-1830. † *Illus.* TB/3067

TIMOTHY L. SMITH: Revivalism and Social Reform: *American Protestantism on the Eve of the Civil War* TB/1229

FRANK THISTLETHWAITE: America and the Atlantic Community: *Anglo-American Aspects, 1790-1850* TB/1107

ALBION W. TOURGÉE: A Fool's Errand. ‡ *Ed. by George Fredrickson* TB/3074

A. F. TYLER: Freedom's Ferment: *Phases of American Social History from the Revolution to the Outbreak of the Civil War. 31 illus.* TB/1074

GLYNDON G. VAN DEUSEN: The Jacksonian Era: 1828-1848. † *Illus.* TB/3028

LOUIS B. WRIGHT: Culture on the Moving Frontier TB/1053

American Studies: The Civil War to 1900

THOMAS C. COCHRAN & WILLIAM MILLER: The Age of Enterprise: *A Social History of Industrial America* TB/1054

W. A. DUNNING: Essays on the Civil War and Reconstruction. *Introduction by David Donald* TB/1181

W. A. DUNNING: Reconstruction, Political and Economic: 1865-1877 TB/1073

HAROLD U. FAULKNER: Politics, Reform and Expansion: 1890-1900. † *Illus.* TB/3020

HELEN HUNT JACKSON: A Century of Dishonor: *The Early Crusade for Indian Reform.* ‡ *Edited by Andrew F. Rolle* TB/3063

ALBERT D. KIRWAN: Revolt of the Rednecks: *Mississippi Politics, 1876-1925* TB/1199

ROBERT GREEN MC CLOSKEY: American Conservatism in the Age of Enterprise: 1865-1910 TB/1137

ARTHUR MANN: Yankee Reformers in the Urban Age: *Social Reform in Boston, 1880-1900* TB/1247

WHITELAW REID: After the War: *A Tour of the Southern States, 1865-1866.* ‡ *Edited by C. Vann Woodward* TB/3066

CHARLES H. SHINN: Mining Camps: *A Study in American Frontier Government.* ‡ *Edited by Rodman W. Paul* TB/3062

VERNON LANE WHARTON: The Negro in Mississippi: 1865-1890 TB/1178

American Studies: 1900 to the Present

RAY STANNARD BAKER: Following the Color Line: *American Negro Citizenship in Progressive Era.* ‡ *Illus. Edited by Dewey W. Grantham, Jr.* TB/3053

RANDOLPH S. BOURNE: War and the Intellectuals: *Collected Essays, 1915-1919.* ‡ *Edited by Carl Resek* TB/3043

A. RUSSELL BUCHANAN: The United States and World War II. † *Illus.* Vol. I TB/3044; Vol. II TB/3045

ABRAHAM CAHAN: The Rise of David Levinsky: *a documentary novel of social mobility in early twentieth century America. Intro. by John Higham* TB/1028

THOMAS C. COCHRAN: The American Business System: *A Historical Perspective, 1900-1955* TB/1080

FOSTER RHEA DULLES: America's Rise to World Power: 1898-1954. † *Illus.* TB/3021

JOHN D. HICKS: Republican Ascendancy: 1921-1933. † *Illus.* TB/3041

SIDNEY HOOK: Reason, Social Myths, and Democracy TB/1237

ROBERT HUNTER: Poverty: *Social Conscience in the Progressive Era.* ‡ *Edited by Peter d'A. Jones* TB/3065

WILLIAM L. LANGER & S. EVERETT GLEASON: The Challenge to Isolation: *The World Crisis of 1937-1940 and American Foreign Policy*
Vol. I TB/3054; Vol. II TB/3055

WILLIAM E. LEUCHTENBURG: Franklin D. Roosevelt and the New Deal: 1932-1940. † *Illus.* TB/3025

ARTHUR S. LINK: Woodrow Wilson and the Progressive Era: 1910-1917. † *Illus.* TB/3023

GEORGE E. MOWRY: The Era of Theodore Roosevelt and the Birth of Modern America: 1900-1912. † *Illus.* TB/3022

RUSSEL B. NYE: Midwestern Progressive Politics: *A Historical Study of Its Origins and Development, 1870-1958* TB/1202

WILLIAM PRESTON, JR.: Aliens and Dissenters: *Federal Suppression of Radicals, 1903-1933* TB/1287

WALTER RAUSCHENBUSCH: Christianity and the Social Crisis. ‡ *Edited by Robert D. Cross* TB/3059

JACOB RIIS: The Making of an American. ‡ *Edited by Roy Lubove* TB/3070

PHILIP SELZNICK: TVA and the Grass Roots: *A Study in the Sociology of Formal Organization* TB/1230

IDA M. TARBELL: The History of the Standard Oil Company: *Briefer Version.* ‡ *Edited by David M. Chalmers* TB/3071

GEORGE B. TINDALL, Ed.: A Populist Reader ‡ TB/3069

TWELVE SOUTHERNERS: I'll Take My Stand: *The South and the Agrarian Tradition. Intro. by Louis D. Rubin, Jr., Biographical Essays by Virginia Rock* TB/1072

WALTER E. WEYL: The New Democracy: *An Essay on Certain Political Tendencies in the United States.* ‡ *Edited by Charles B. Forcey* TB/3042

Anthropology

JACQUES BARZUN: Race: *A Study in Superstition. Revised Edition* TB/1172

JOSEPH B. CASAGRANDE, Ed.: In the Company of Man: *Twenty Portraits of Anthropological Informants. Illus.* TB/3047

W. E. LE GROS CLARK: The Antecedents of Man: *Intro. to Evolution of the Primates.* ○ △ *Illus.* TB/559

CORA DU BOIS: The People of Alor. *New Preface by the author. Illus.* Vol. I TB/1042; Vol. II TB/1043

RAYMOND FIRTH, Ed.: Man and Culture: *An Evaluation of the Work of Bronislaw Malinowski* ¶ ○ △ TB/1133

DAVID LANDY: Tropical Childhood: *Cultural Transmission and Learning in a Puerto Rican Village* ¶ TB/1235

L. S. B. LEAKEY: Adam's Ancestors: *The Evolution of Man and His Culture.* △ *Illus.* TB/1019

ROBERT H. LOWIE: Primitive Society. *Introduction by Fred Eggan* TB/1056

EDWARD BURNETT TYLOR: The Origins of Culture. *Part I of "Primitive Culture."* § *Intro. by Paul Radin* TB/33

EDWARD BURNETT TYLOR: Religion in Primitive Culture. *Part II of "Primitive Culture."* § *Intro. by Paul Radin* TB/34

W. LLOYD WARNER: A Black Civilization: *A Study of an Australian Tribe.* ¶ *Illus.* TB/3056

Art and Art History

WALTER LOWRIE: Art in the Early Church. *Revised Edition. 452 illus.* TB/124

EMILE MÂLE: The Gothic Image: *Religious Art in France of the Thirteenth Century.* § △ *190 illus.* TB/44

MILLARD MEISS: Painting in Florence and Siena after the Black Death: *The Arts, Religion and Society in the Mid-Fourteenth Century. 169 illus.* TB/1148
ERICH NEUMANN: The Archetypal World of Henry Moore. △ *107 illus.* TB/2020
DORA & ERWIN PANOFSKY : Pandora's Box: *The Changing Aspects of a Mythical Symbol. Revised Edition. Illus.* TB/2021
ERWIN PANOFSKY: Studies in Iconology: *Humanistic Themes in the Art of the Renaissance.* △ *180 illustrations* TB/1077
ALEXANDRE PIANKOFF: The Shrines of Tut-Ankh-Amon. *Edited by N. Rambova. 117 illus.* TB/2011
JEAN SEZNEC: The Survival of the Pagan Gods: *The Mythological Tradition and Its Place in Renaissance Humanism and Art. 108 illustrations* TB/2004
OTTO VON SIMSON: The Gothic Cathedral: *Origins of Gothic Architecture and the Medieval Concept of Order.* △ *58 illus.* TB/2018
HEINRICH ZIMMER: Myth and Symbols in Indian Art and Civilization. *70 illustrations* TB/2005

Business, Economics & Economic History

REINHARD BENDIX: Work and Authority in Industry: *Ideologies of Management in the Course of Industrialization* TB/3035
GILBERT BURCK & EDITORS OF FORTUNE: The Computer Age: *And Its Potential for Management* TB/1179
THOMAS C. COCHRAN: The American Business System: *A Historical Perspective, 1900-1955* TB/1080
THOMAS C. COCHRAN: The Inner Revolution: *Essays on the Social Sciences in History* △ TB/1140
THOMAS C. COCHRAN & WILLIAM MILLER: The Age of Enterprise: *A Social History of Industrial America* TB/1054
ROBERT DAHL & CHARLES E. LINDBLOM: Politics, Economics, and Welfare: *Planning and Politico-Economic Systems Resolved into Basic Social Processes* TB/3037
PETER F. DRUCKER: The New Society: *The Anatomy of Industrial Order* △ TB/1082
EDITORS OF FORTUNE: America in the Sixties: *The Economy and the Society* TB/1015
ROBERT L. HEILBRONER: The Great Ascent: *The Struggle for Economic Development in Our Time* TB/3030
FRANK H. KNIGHT: The Economic Organization TB/1214
FRANK H. KNIGHT: Risk, Uncertainty and Profit TB/1215
ABBA P. LERNER: Everybody's Business: *Current Assumptions in Economics and Public Policy* TB/3051
ROBERT GREEN MC CLOSKEY: American Conservatism in the Age of Enterprise, 1865-1910 △ TB/1137
PAUL MANTOUX: The Industrial Revolution in the Eighteenth Century: *The Beginnings of the Modern Factory System in England* ° △ TB/1079
WILLIAM MILLER, Ed.: Men in Business: *Essays on the Historical Role of the Entrepreneur* TB/1081
RICHARD B. MORRIS: Government and Labor in Early America △ TB/1244
HERBERT SIMON: The Shape of Automation: *For Men and Management* TB/1245
PERRIN STRYKER: The Character of the Executive: *Eleven Studies in Managerial Qualities* TB/1041
PIERRE URI: Partnership for Progress: *A Program for Transatlantic Action* TB/3036

Contemporary Culture

JACQUES BARZUN: The House of Intellect △ TB/1051
CLARK KERR: The Uses of the University TB/1264
JOHN U. NEF: Cultural Foundations of Industrial Civilization △ TB/1024
NATHAN M. PUSEY: The Age of the Scholar: *Observations on Education in a Troubled Decade* TB/1157
PAUL VALÉRY: The Outlook for Intelligence △ TB/2016
RAYMOND WILLIAMS: Culture and Society, 1780-1950 ° △ TB/1252

RAYMOND WILLIAMS: The Long Revolution.° △ *Revised Edition* TB/1253

Historiography & Philosophy of History

JACOB BURCKHARDT: On History and Historians. △ *Introduction by H. R. Trevor-Roper* TB/1216
WILHELM DILTHEY: Pattern and Meaning in History: *Thoughts on History and Society.* ° △ *Edited with an Introduction by H. P. Rickman* TB/1075
J. H. HEXTER: Reappraisals in History: *New Views on History & Society in Early Modern Europe* △ TB/1100
H. STUART HUGHES: History as Art and as Science: *Twin Vistas on the Past* TB/1207
RAYMOND KLIBANSKY & H. J. PATON, Eds.: Philosophy and History: *The Ernst Cassirer Festschrift. Illus.* TB/1115
ARNOLDO MOMIGLIANO: Studies in Historiography ° △ TB/1288
GEORGE H. NADEL, Ed.: Studies in the Philosophy of History: *Selected Essays from History and Theory* TB/1208
JOSE ORTEGA Y GASSET: The Modern Theme. *Introduction by Jose Ferrater Mora* TB/1038
KARL R. POPPER: The Open Society and Its Enemies △
   Vol. I: *The Spell of Plato* TB/1101
   Vol. II: *The High Tide of Prophecy: Hegel, Marx and the Aftermath* TB/1102
KARL R. POPPER: The Poverty of Historicism ° △ TB/1126
G. J. RENIER: History: Its Purpose and Method △ TB/1209
W. H. WALSH: Philosophy of History: *An Introduction* △ TB/1020

History: General

L. CARRINGTON GOODRICH: A Short History of the Chinese People. △ *Illus.* TB/3015
DAN N. JACOBS & HANS H. BAERWALD: Chinese Communism: *Selected Documents* TB/3031
BERNARD LEWIS: The Arabs in History △ TB/1029
BERNARD LEWIS: The Middle East and the West ° △ TB/1274

History: Ancient

A. ANDREWES: The Greek Tyrants △ TB/1103
ADOLF ERMAN, Ed. The Ancient Egyptians: *A Sourcebook of Their Writings. New material and Introduction by William Kelly Simpson* TB/1233
MICHAEL GRANT: Ancient History ° △ TB/1190
SAMUEL NOAH KRAMER: Sumerian Mythology TB/1055
NAPHTALI LEWIS & MEYER REINHOLD, Eds.: Roman Civilization. *Sourcebook I: The Republic* TB/1231
NAPHTALI LEWIS & MEYER REINHOLD, Eds.: Roman Civilization. *Sourcebook II: The Empire* TB/1232

History: Medieval

P. BOISSONNADE: Life and Work in Medieval Europe: *The Evolution of the Medieval Economy, the 5th to the 15th Century.* ° △ *Preface by Lynn White, Jr.* TB/1141
HELEN CAM: England before Elizabeth △ TB/1026
NORMAN COHN: The Pursuit of the Millennium: *Revolutionary Messianism in Medieval and Reformation Europe* △ TB/1037
G. G. COULTON: Medieval Village, Manor, and Monastery TB/1022
CHRISTOPHER DAWSON, Ed.: Mission to Asia: *Narratives and Letters of the Franciscan Missionaries in Mongolia and China in the 13th and 14 Centuries* △ TB/315
HEINRICH FICHTENAU: The Carolingian Empire: *The Age of Charlemagne* △ TB/1142
F. L. GANSHOF: Feudalism △ TB/1058
DENO GEANAKOPLOS: Byzantine East and Latin West: *Two Worlds of Christendom in the Middle Ages and Renaissance* △ TB/1265
EDWARD GIBBON: The Triumph of Christendom in the Roman Empire *(Chaps. XV-XX of "Decline and Fall," J. B. Bury edition).* § △ *Illus.* TB/46

History: Renaissance & Reformation

History: Modern European

4

E. H. CARR: German-Soviet Relations Between the Two World Wars, 1919-1939   TB/1278

E. H. CARR: International Relations Between the Two World Wars, 1919-1939 ° △   TB/1279

E. H. CARR: The Twenty Years' Crisis, 1919-1939: An Introduction to the Study of International Relations ° △   TB/1122

GORDON A. CRAIG: From Bismarck to Adenauer: Aspects of German Statecraft. Revised Edition   TB/1171

WALTER L. DORN: Competition for Empire, 1740-1763. * Illus.   TB/3032

FRANKLIN L. FORD: Robe and Sword: The Regrouping of the French Aristocracy after Louis XIV   TB/1217

CARL J. FRIEDRICH: The Age of the Baroque, 1610-1660. * Illus.   TB/3004

RENÉ FUELOEP-MILLER: The Mind and Face of Bolshevism: An Examination of Cultural Life in Soviet Russia. New Epilogue by the Author   TB/1188

M. DOROTHY GEORGE: London Life in the Eighteenth Century △   TB/1182

LEO GERSHOY: From Despotism to Revolution, 1763-1789. * Illus.   TB/3017

C. C. GILLISPIE: Genesis and Geology: The Decades before Darwin §   TB/51

ALBERT GOODWIN: The French Revolution △   TB/1064

ALBERT GUÉRARD: France in the Classical Age: The Life and Death of an Ideal △   TB/1183

CARLTON J. H. HAYES: A Generation of Materialism, 1871-1900. * Illus.   TB/3039

J. H. HEXTER: Reappraisals in History: New Views on History and Society in Early Modern Europe △   TB/1100

STANLEY HOFFMANN et al.: In Search of France: The Economy, Society and Political System in the Twentieth Century   TB/1219

A. R. HUMPHREYS: The Augustan World: Society, Thought, & Letters in 18th Century England ° △   TB/1105

DAN N. JACOBS, Ed.: The New Communist Manifesto and Related Documents. Third edition, revised   TB/1078

HANS KOHN: The Mind of Germany: The Education of a Nation △   TB/1204

HANS KOHN, Ed.: The Mind of Modern Russia: Historical and Political Thought of Russia's Great Age   TB/1065

WALTER LAQUEUR & GEORGE L. MOSSE, Eds.: International Fascism, 1920-1945. ° △ Volume I of Journal of Contemporary History   TB/1276

WALTER LAQUEUR & GEORGE L. MOSSE, Eds.: The Left-Wing Intelligentsia between the Two World Wars. ° △ Volume II of Journal of Contemporary History   TB/1286

FRANK E. MANUEL: The Prophets of Paris: Turgot, Condorcet, Saint-Simon, Fourier, and Comte   TB/1218

KINGSLEY MARTIN: French Liberal Thought in the Eighteenth Century: A Study of Political Ideas from Bayle to Condorcet   TB/1114

L. B. NAMIER: Facing East: Essays on Germany, the Balkans, and Russia in the 20th Century △   TB/1280

L. B. NAMIER: Personalities and Powers: Selected Essays △   TB/1186

L. B. NAMIER: Vanished Supremacies: Essays on European History, 1812-1918 °   TB/1088

JOHN U. NEF: Western Civilization Since the Renaissance: Peace, War, Industry, and the Arts   TB/1113

FRANZ NEUMANN: Behemoth: The Structure and Practice of National Socialism, 1933-1944   TB/1289

FREDERICK L. NUSSBAUM: The Triumph of Science and Reason, 1660-1685. * Illus.   TB/3009

DAVID OGG: Europe of the Ancien Régime, 1715-1783 ° △   TB/1271

JOHN PLAMENATZ: German Marxism and Russian Communism. ° △ New Preface by the Author   TB/1189

RAYMOND W. POSTGATE, Ed.: Revolution from 1789 to 1906: Selected Documents   TB/1063

PENFIELD ROBERTS: The Quest for Security, 1715-1740. * Illus.   TB/3016

PRISCILLA ROBERTSON: Revolutions of 1848: A Social History   TB/1025

GEORGE RUDÉ: Revolutionary Europe, 1783-1815 ° △   TB/1272

LOUIS, DUC DE SAINT-SIMON: Versailles, The Court, and Louis XIV. ° △ Introductory Note by Peter Gay   TB/1250

ALBERT SOREL: Europe Under the Old Regime. Translated by Francis H. Herrick   TB/1121

N. N. SUKHANOV: The Russian Revolution, 1917: Eyewitness Account. △ Edited by Joel Carmichael   Vol. I TB/1066; Vol. II TB/1067

A. J. P. TAYLOR: From Napoleon to Lenin: Historical Essays ° △   TB/1268

A. J. P. TAYLOR: The Habsburg Monarchy, 1809-1918: A History of the Austrian Empire and Austria-Hungary ° △   TB/1187

G. M. TREVELYAN: British History in the Nineteenth Century and After: 1782-1919. ° △ Second Edition TB/1251

H. R. TREVOR-ROPER: Historical Essays ° △   TB/1269

ELIZABETH WISKEMANN: Europe of the Dictators, 1919-1945 ° △   TB/1273

JOHN B. WOLF: The Emergence of the Great Powers, 1685-1715. * Illus.   TB/3010

JOHN B. WOLF: France: 1814-1919: The Rise of a Liberal-Democratic Society   TB/3019

Intellectual History & History of Ideas

HERSCHEL BAKER: The Image of Man: A Study of the Idea of Human Dignity in Classical Antiquity, the Middle Ages, and the Renaissance   TB/1047

R. R. BOLGAR: The Classical Heritage and Its Beneficiaries: From the Carolingian Age to the End of the Renaissance ×   TB/1125

RANDOLPH S. BOURNE: War and the Intellectuals: Collected Essays, 1915-1919. △ ‡ Edited by Carl Resek   TB/3043

J. BRONOWSKI & BRUCE MAZLISH: The Western Intellectual Tradition: From Leonardo to Hegel △   TB/3001

ERNST CASSIRER: The Individual and the Cosmos in Renaissance Philosophy. △ Translated with an Introduction by Mario Domandi   TB/1097

NORMAN COHN: The Pursuit of the Millennium: Revolutionary Messianism in Medieval and Reformation Europe △   TB/1037

C. C. GILLISPIE: Genesis and Geology: The Decades before Darwin §   TB/51

G. RACHEL LEVY: Religious Conceptions of the Stone Age and Their Influence upon European Thought. △ Illus. Introduction by Henri Frankfort   TB/106

ARTHUR O. LOVEJOY: The Great Chain of Being: A Study of the History of an Idea   TB/1009

FRANK E. MANUEL: The Prophets of Paris: Turgot, Condorcet, Saint-Simon, Fourier, and Comte △   TB/1218

PERRY MILLER & T. H. JOHNSON, Editors: The Puritans: A Sourcebook of Their Writings   Vol. I TB/1093; Vol. II TB/1094

MILTON C. NAHM: Genius and Creativity: An Essay in the History of Ideas   TB/1196

ROBERT PAYNE: Hubris: A Study of Pride. Foreword by Sir Herbert Read   TB/1031

RALPH BARTON PERRY: The Thought and Character of William James: Briefer Version   TB/1156

GEORG SIMMEL et al.: Essays on Sociology, Philosophy, and Aesthetics. ¶ Edited by Kurt H. Wolff   TB/1234

BRUNO SNELL: The Discovery of the Mind: The Greek Origins of European Thought △   TB/1018

PAGET TOYNBEE: Dante Alighieri: His Life and Works. Edited with Intro. by Charles S. Singleton △   TB/1206

ERNEST LEE TUVESON: Millennium and Utopia: A Study in the Background of the Idea of Progress. ¶ New Preface by the Author   TB/1134

PAUL VALÉRY: The Outlook for Intelligence △   TB/2016

Political Science & Government

Psychology

ERICH NEUMANN: Amor and Psyche: *The Psychic Development of the Feminine* △ ᴛʙ/2012

ERICH NEUMANN: The Archetypal World of Henry Moore. △ *107 illus.* ᴛʙ/2020

ERICH NEUMANN : The Origins and History of Consciousness △ Vol. I *Illus.* ᴛʙ/2007; Vol. II ᴛʙ/2008

C. P. OBERNDORF: A History of Psychoanalysis in America ᴛʙ/1147

RALPH BARTON PERRY: The Thought and Character of William James: *Briefer Version* ᴛʙ/1156

JEAN PIAGET, BÄRBEL INHELDER, & ALINA SZEMINSKA: The Child's Conception of Geometry ° △ ᴛʙ/1146

JOHN H. SCHAAR: Escape from Authority: *The Perspectives of Erich Fromm* ᴛʙ/1155

MUZAFER SHERIF: The Psychology of Social Norms ᴛʙ/3072

Sociology

JACQUES BARZUN: Race: *A Study in Superstition. Revised Edition* ᴛʙ/1172

BERNARD BERELSON, Ed.: The Behavioral Sciences Today
● ᴛʙ/1127

ABRAHAM CAHAN: The Rise of David Levinsky: *A documentary novel of social mobility in early twentieth century America. Intro. by John Higham* ᴛʙ/1028

THOMAS C. COCHRAN: The Inner Revolution: *Essays on the Social Sciences in History* ᴛʙ/1140

ALLISON DAVIS & JOHN DOLLARD: Children of Bondage: *The Personality Development of Negro Youth in the Urban South* ❡ ᴛʙ/3049

ST. CLAIR DRAKE & HORACE R. CAYTON: Black Metropolis: *A Study of Negro Life in a Northern City.* △ *Revised and Enlarged. Intro. by Everett C. Hughes*
Vol. I ᴛʙ/1086; Vol. II ᴛʙ/1087

EMILE DURKHEIM et al.: Essays on Sociology and Philosophy: *With Analyses of Durkheim's Life and Work.* ❡ *Edited by Kurt H. Wolff* ᴛʙ/1151

LEON FESTINGER, HENRY W. RIECKEN & STANLEY SCHACHTER: When Prophecy Fails: *A Social and Psychological Account of a Modern Group that Predicted the Destruction of the World* ❡ ᴛʙ/1132

ALVIN W. GOULDNER: Wildcat Strike: *A Study in Worker-Management Relationships* ❡ ᴛʙ/1176

FRANCIS J. GRUND: Aristocracy in America: *Social Class in the Formative Years of the New Nation* △ ᴛʙ/1001

KURT LEWIN: Field Theory in Social Science: *Selected Theoretical Papers.* ❡ △ *Edited with a Foreword by Dorwin Cartwright* ᴛʙ/1135

R. M. MAC IVER: Social Causation ᴛʙ/1153

ROBERT K. MERTON, LEONARD BROOM, LEONARD S. COTTRELL, JR., Editors: Sociology Today: *Problems and Prospects* ❡ Vol. I ᴛʙ/1173; Vol. II ᴛʙ/1174

ROBERTO MICHELS: First Lectures in Political Sociology. *Edited by Alfred de Grazia* ❡ ° ᴛʙ/1224

BARRINGTON MOORE, JR.: Political Power and Social Theory: *Seven Studies* ❡ ᴛʙ/1221

BARRINGTON MOORE, JR.: Soviet Politics—The Dilemma of Power: *The Role of Ideas in Social Change* ❡ ᴛʙ/1222

TALCOTT PARSONS & EDWARD A. SHILS, Editors: Toward a General Theory of Action: *Theoretical Foundations for the Social Sciences* ᴛʙ/1083

JOHN H. ROHRER & MUNRO S. EDMONDSON, Eds.: The Eighth Generation Grows Up: *Cultures and Personalities of New Orleans Negroes* ❡ ᴛʙ/3050

ARNOLD ROSE: The Negro in America: *The Condensed Version of Gunnar Myrdal's* An American Dilemma ᴛʙ/3048

KURT SAMUELSSON: Religion and Economic Action: *A Critique of Max Weber's* The Protestant Ethic and the Spirit of Capitalism. ❡ ° *Trans. by E. G. French. Ed. with Intro. by D. C. Coleman* ᴛʙ/1131

PHILIP SELZNICK: TVA and the Grass Roots: *A Study in the Sociology of Formal Organization* ᴛʙ/1230

GEORG SIMMEL et al.: Essays on Sociology, Philosophy, and Aesthetics. ❡ *Edited by Kurt H. Wolff* ᴛʙ/1234

HERBERT SIMON: The Shape of Automation: *For Men and Management* △ ᴛʙ/1245

PITIRIM A. SOROKIN: Contemporary Sociological Theories. *Through the First Quarter of the 20th Century* ᴛʙ/3046

MAURICE R. STEIN: The Eclipse of Community: *An Interpretation of American Studies* ᴛʙ/1128

FERDINAND TÖNNIES: Community and Society: *Gemeinschaft und Gesellschaft. Translated and edited by Charles P. Loomis* ᴛʙ/1116

W. LLOYD WARNER & Associates: Democracy in Jonesville: *A Study in Quality and Inequality* ᴛʙ/1129

W. LLOYD WARNER: Social Class in America: *The Evaluation of Status* ᴛʙ/1013

RELIGION

Ancient & Classical

J. H. BREASTED: Development of Religion and Thought in Ancient Egypt. *Intro. by John A. Wilson* ᴛʙ/57

HENRI FRANKFORT: Ancient Egyptian Religion: *An Interpretation* ᴛʙ/77

G. RACHEL LEVY: Religious Conceptions of the Stone Age and their Influence upon European Thought. △ *Illus. Introduction by Henri Frankfort* ᴛʙ/106

MARTIN P. NILSSON: Greek Folk Religion. *Foreword by Arthur Darby Nock* ᴛʙ/78

ALEXANDRE PIANKOFF: The Shrines of Tut-Ankh-Amon. △ *Edited by N. Rambova. 117 illus.* ᴛʙ/2011

ERWIN ROHDE: Psyche: *The Cult of Souls and Belief in Immortality Among the Greeks.* △ *Intro. by W. K. C. Guthrie* Vol. I ᴛʙ/140; Vol. II ᴛʙ/141

H. J. ROSE: Religion in Greece and Rome △ ᴛʙ/55

Biblical Thought & Literature

W. F. ALBRIGHT: The Biblical Period from Abraham to Ezra ᴛʙ/102

C. K. BARRETT, Ed.: The New Testament Background: *Selected Documents* △ ᴛʙ/86

C. H. DODD: The Authority of the Bible △ ᴛʙ/43

M. S. ENSLIN: Christian Beginnings △ ᴛʙ/5

M. S. ENSLIN: The Literature of the Christian Movement △ ᴛʙ/6

JOHN GRAY: Archaeology and the Old Testament World. △ *Illus.* ᴛʙ/127

JAMES MUILENBURG: The Way of Israel: *Biblical Faith and Ethics* △ ᴛʙ/133

H. H. ROWLEY: The Growth of the Old Testament △ ᴛʙ/107

GEORGE ADAM SMITH: The Historical Geography of the Holy Land. ° △ *Revised and reset* ᴛʙ/138

D. WINTON THOMAS, Ed.: Documents from Old Testament Times △ ᴛʙ/85

The Judaic Tradition

LEO BAECK: Judaism and Christianity. *Trans. with Intro. by Walter Kaufmann* ᴊᴘ/23

SALO W. BARON: Modern Nationalism and Religion ᴊᴘ/18

MARTIN BUBER: Eclipse of God: *Studies in the Relation Between Religion and Philosophy* △ ᴛʙ/12

MARTIN BUBER: For the Sake of Heaven ᴛʙ/801

MARTIN BUBER: Hasidism and Modern Man. △ *Ed. and Trans. by Maurice Friedman* ᴛʙ/839

MARTIN BUBER: The Knowledge of Man. △ *Edited with an Introduction by Maurice Friedman. Translated by Maurice Friedman and Ronald Gregor Smith* ᴛʙ/135

MARTIN BUBER: Moses: *The Revelation and the Covenant* △ ᴛʙ/837

MARTIN BUBER: The Origin and Meaning of Hasidism △ ᴛʙ/835

MARTIN BUBER: Pointing the Way. △ *Introduction by Maurice S. Friedman* ᴛʙ/103

MARTIN BUBER: The Prophetic Faith ᴛʙ/73

MARTIN BUBER: Two Types of Faith: *the interpenetration of Judaism and Christianity* ° △ ᴛʙ/75